T0280998

Lecture Notes in Computer Science 14388

The series Lecture Notes in Computer Science (LNCS), including its subseries Lecture Notes in Artificial Intelligence (LNAI) and Lecture Notes in Bioinformatics (LNBI), has established itself as a medium for the publication of new developments in computer science and information technology research, teaching, and education.

LNCS enjoys close cooperation with the computer science R & D community, the series counts many renowned academics among its volume editors and paper authors, and collaborates with prestigious societies. Its mission is to serve this international community by providing an invaluable service, mainly focused on the publication of conference and workshop proceedings and postproceedings. LNCS commenced publication in 1973.

Vladimir Voevodin · Sergey Sobolev ·
Mikhail Yakobovskiy · Rashit Shagaliev
Editors

Supercomputing

9th Russian Supercomputing Days, RuSCDays 2023
Moscow, Russia, September 25–26, 2023
Revised Selected Papers, Part I

Editors
Vladimir Voevodin
Research Computing Center (RCC)
Moscow State University
Moscow, Russia

Sergey Sobolev
Research Computing Center (RCC)
Moscow State University
Moscow, Russia

Mikhail Yakobovskiy
Russian Academy of Sciences (RAS)
Keldysh Institute of Applied Mathematics
Moscow, Russia

Rashit Shagaliev
Russian Federal Nuclear Center
Sarov, Russia

ISSN 0302-9743 ISSN 1611-3349 (electronic)
Lecture Notes in Computer Science
ISBN 978-3-031-49431-4 ISBN 978-3-031-49432-1 (eBook)
https://doi.org/10.1007/978-3-031-49432-1

This Springer imprint is published by the registered company Springer Nature Switzerland AG
The registered company address is: Gewerbestrasse 11, 6330 Cham, Switzerland

Paper in this product is recyclable.

Preface

The 9th Russian Supercomputing Days Conference (RuSCDays 2023) was held during September 25–26, 2023. The conference was organized by the Supercomputing Consortium of Russian Universities, the Russian Academy of Sciences, and the Moscow Center of Fundamental and Applied Mathematics. The conference organization coordinator was the Moscow State University Research Computing Center. The conference was supported by platinum sponsors (Cloud.ru, RSC, AMD Technologies, and E-Flops) and silver sponsors (Norsi-Trans and Forsite).

To make the event as safe as possible, the conference was held in a hybrid way, combining offline and online sessions. Every offline session was also available online for remote attendees. There were also several online-only sessions.

RuSCDays was born in 2015 as a union of several supercomputing event series in Russia and quickly became one of the most notable Russian supercomputing international meetings. The conference caters to the interests of a wide range of representatives from science, industry, business, education, government, and academia – anyone connected to the development or the use of supercomputing technologies. The conference topics cover all aspects of supercomputing technologies: software and hardware design, solving large tasks, application of supercomputing technologies in industry, exaflops-scale computing issues, supercomputing co-design technologies, supercomputing education, and others.

All 104 papers submitted to the conference were reviewed by three referees in the first review round. During single-blind peer reviewing, the papers were evaluated according to their relevance to the conference topics, scientific contribution, presentation, approbation, and related works description. After notification of conditional acceptance, a second review round was arranged which aimed at the final polishing of papers and also at the evaluation of authors' work following revision based on the referees' comments. After the conference, the 45 best papers were carefully selected to be included in this volume.

The proceedings editors would like to thank all the conference committee members, especially the Organizing and Program Committee members as well as the referees and reviewers for their contributions. We also thank Springer for producing these high-quality proceedings of RuSCDays 2023.

October 2023

Vladimir Voevodin
Sergey Sobolev
Rashit Shagaliev
Mikhail Yakobovskiy

Preface

Organization

Steering Committee

Victor A. Sadovnichiy (Chair)	Moscow State University, Russia
Vladimir B. Betelin (Co-chair)	Russian Academy of Sciences, Russia
Alexander V. Tikhonravov (Co-chair)	Moscow State University, Russia
Jack Dongarra (Co-chair)	University of Tennessee, USA
Alexey I. Borovkov	Peter the Great Saint Petersburg Polytechnic University, Russia
Vladimir V. Voevodin	Moscow State University, Russia
Georgy S. Elizarov	NII Kvant, Russia
Elena V. Zagainova	Lobachevsky State University of Nizhni Novgorod, Russia
Alexander K. Kim	MCST, Russia
Elena V. Kudryashova	Northern (Arctic) Federal University, Russia
Alexander A. Moskovskiy	RSC Group, Russia
Gennady I. Savin	Joint Supercomputer Center, Russian Academy of Sciences, Russia
Alexey S. Simonov	NICEVT, Russia
Victor A. Soyfer	Samara University, Russia
Leonid B. Sokolinskiy	South Ural State University, Russia
Igor A. Sokolov	Russian Academy of Sciences, Russia
Roman G. Strongin	Lobachevsky State University of Nizhni Novgorod, Russia
Alexey R. Khokhlov	Russian Academy of Sciences, Russia
Boris N. Chetverushkin	Keldysh Institute of Applied Mathematics, Russian Academy of Sciences, Russia

Program Committee

Vladimir V. Voevodin (Chair)	Moscow State University, Russia
Rashit M. Shagaliev (Co-chair)	Russian Federal Nuclear Center, Russia
Mikhail V. Yakobovskiy (Co-chair)	Keldysh Institute of Applied Mathematics, Russian Academy of Sciences, Russia
Thomas Sterling (Co-chair)	Indiana University, USA
Sergey I. Sobolev (Scientific Secretary)	Moscow State University, Russia

Arutyun I. Avetisyan	Institute for System Programming, Russian Academy of Sciences, Russia
David Bader	Georgia Institute of Technology, USA
Pavan Balaji	Argonne National Laboratory, USA
Alexander V. Bukhanovskiy	ITMO University, Russia
Jesus Carretero	University Carlos III of Madrid, Spain
Yury V. Vasilevskiy	Keldysh Institute of Applied Mathematics, Russian Academy of Sciences, Russia
Vasiliy E. Velikhov	National Research Center "Kurchatov Institute", Russia
Vladimir Yu. Volkonskiy	MCST, Russia
Vadim M. Volokhov	Institute of Problems of Chemical Physics, Russian Academy of Sciences, Russia
Victor M. Goloviznin	Moscow State University, Russia
Irek M. Gubaydullin	Institute of Petrochemistry and Catalysis, Ufa Federal Research Centre, Russian Academy of Sciences, Russia
Vyacheslav A. Ilyin	National Research Center "Kurchatov Institute", Russia
Vladimir P. Ilyin	Institute of Computational Mathematics and Mathematical Geophysics, Siberian Branch of Russian Academy of Sciences, Russia
Sergey I. Kabanikhin	Institute of Computational Mathematics and Mathematical Geophysics, Siberian Branch of Russian Academy of Sciences, Russia
Igor A. Kalyaev	NII MVS, South Federal University, Russia
Hiroaki Kobayashi	Tohoku University, Japan
Vladimir V. Korenkov	Joint Institute for Nuclear Research, Russia
Victor A. Kryukov	Keldysh Institute of Applied Mathematics, Russian Academy of Sciences, Russia
Julian Kunkel	University of Hamburg, Germany
Jesus Labarta	Barcelona Supercomputing Center, Spain
Alexey Lastovetsky	University College Dublin, Ireland
Mikhail P. Lobachev	Krylov State Research Centre, Russia
Yutong Lu	National University of Defense Technology, China
Thomas Ludwig	German Climate Computing Center, Germany
Iosif B. Meerov	Lobachevsky State University of Nizhni Novgorod, Russia
Marek Michalewicz	University of Warsaw, Poland
Leili Mirtaheri	Kharazmi University, Iran
Alexander V. Nemukhin	Moscow State University, Russia

Happy Sithole	Centre for High Performance Computing, South Africa
Alexander V. Smirnov	Moscow State University, Russia
Hiroyuki Takizawa	Tohoku University, Japan
Michela Taufer	University of Delaware, USA
Vadim E. Turlapov	Lobachevsky State University of Nizhni Novgorod, Russia
Eugeny E. Tyrtyshnikov	Institute of Numerical Mathematics, Russian Academy of Sciences, Russia
Vladimir A. Fursov	Samara University, Russia
Thorsten Hoefler	Eidgenössische Technische Hochschule Zürich, Switzerland
Boris M. Shabanov	Joint Supercomputer Center, Russian Academy of Sciences, Russia
Lev N. Shchur	Higher School of Economics, Russia
Roman Wyrzykowski	Czestochowa University of Technology, Poland
Mitsuo Yokokawa	Kobe University, Japan

Industrial Committee

A. A. Aksenov (Co-chair)	Tesis, Russia
V. E. Velikhov (Co-chair)	National Research Center "Kurchatov Institute", Russia
A. V. Murashov (Co-chair)	Russian Foundation for Advanced Research Projects, Russia
Yu. Ya. Boldyrev	Peter the Great Saint Petersburg Polytechnic University, Russia
M. A. Bolshukhin	Afrikantov Experimental Design Bureau for Mechanical Engineering, Russia
R. K. Gazizov	Ufa State Aviation Technical University, Russia
M. P. Lobachev	Krylov State Research Centre, Russia
V. Ya. Modorskiy	Perm National Research Polytechnic University, Russia
A. P. Skibin	Gidropress, Russia
A. B. Shmelev	RSC Group, Russia
S. V. Strizhak	Institute for System Programming, Russian Academy of Sciences, Russia

Educational Committee

Vl. V. Voevodin (Co-chair)	Moscow State University, Russia
L. B. Sokolinskiy (Co-chair)	South Ural State University, Russia
Yu. Ya. Boldyrev	Peter the Great Saint Petersburg Polytechnic University, Russia
K. A. Barkalov	Lobachevsky State University of Nizhni Novgorod, Russia
A. V. Bukhanovskiy	ITMO University, Russia
R. K. Gazizov	Ufa State Aviation Technical University, Russia
I. B. Meerov	Lobachevsky State University of Nizhni Novgorod, Russia
V. Ya. Modorskiy	Perm National Research Polytechnic University, Russia
S. G. Mosin	Kazan Federal University, Russia
N. N. Popova	Moscow State University, Russia
O. A. Yufryakova	Northern (Arctic) Federal University, Russia

Organizing Committee

Vl. V. Voevodin (Chair)	Moscow State University, Russia
B. M. Shabanov (Co-chair)	Joint Supercomputer Center, Russian Academy of Sciences, Russia
S. I. Sobolev (Scientific Secretary)	Moscow State University, Russia
A. A. Aksenov	Tesis, Russia
A. P. Antonova	Moscow State University, Russia
A. S. Antonov	Moscow State University, Russia
K. A. Barkalov	Lobachevsky State University of Nizhni Novgorod, Russia
M. R. Biktimirov	Russian Academy of Sciences, Russia
Vad. V. Voevodin	Moscow State University, Russia
T. A. Gamayunova	Moscow State University, Russia
O. A. Gorbachev	RSC Group, Russia
V. A. Grishagin	Lobachevsky State University of Nizhni Novgorod, Russia
V. V. Korenkov	Joint Institute for Nuclear Research, Russia
I. B. Meerov	Lobachevsky State University of Nizhni Novgorod, Russia
D. A. Nikitenko	Moscow State University, Russia
I. M. Nikolskiy	Moscow State University, Russia
N. N. Popova	Moscow State University, Russia

Contents – Part I

Supercomputer Simulation

Contents – Part II

Supercomputer Simulation

Application of HPC for Simulation of Sealant Influence on the Aircraft Assembly Process

Artem Eliseev(✉), Sergey Lupuleac, Julia Shinder, Tatiana Pogarskaia, and Margarita Petukhova

Peter the Great St. Petersburg Polytechnic University, St. Petersburg, Russia
eliseev0@mail.ru, pogarskaya_ta@spbstu.ru

Abstract. Assembly process of modern aircraft structures consists of multiple operations, and one of them includes application of liquid sealant between the parts to be assembled. The mechanical interaction observed during the assembly between sealant and the assembled parts may be considered as a fluid-structure interaction problem. This problem has several distinctive features, such as presence of contact interaction in structural part and presence of free surface in fluid part. Modeling of assembly process with account to part deviations usually requires the solution of multiple problems with similar input data, which may be implemented effectively using task parallelization. In this paper, we briefly describe an approach developed recently for mathematical modeling of sealant influence on the assembly process. The approach is illustrated using test case, which reproduces real-life assembly operations. Finally, the efficiency of task parallelization is investigated and benefits of HPC application are highlighted.

Keywords: Assembly Process · Sealant · Mathematical Modeling · Fluid-Structure Interaction · High-Performance Computing · Task Parallelization

1 Introduction

Nowadays sealant application is considered as an essential intermediate step during the aircraft assembly. Presence of sealant between parts to be assembled protects the inner space of the joint from damage caused by corrosion, abrasion and other destructive processes [1]. Modern aircraft structures are usually assembled with rivets or bolts, which are subsequently installed in a joint according to the assembly technology. The sealant application is done before installation of fastening elements, when thin layer of sealant is put to the surface of one of the assembled parts. During the fastening operations sealant represents a thick liquid, which flows and spreads between the joined parts trying to fill all possible void space.

The result of the fastening (the described technology is usually called 'wet assembly' [2]) is strongly affected by the mechanical interaction observed between sealant and the assembled parts. The corresponding fluid-structure interaction process may be classified as a 'two-way' interaction [3], when both fluid and structural subproblems affect each other without dominating prevalence of one of them. The observed fluid-structure

V. Voevodin et al. (Eds.): RuSCDays 2023, LNCS 14388, pp. 3–16, 2023.
https://doi.org/10.1007/978-3-031-49432-1_1

interaction also has several features connected with specifics of the assembly process. First of all, structural part of the interaction represents a non-linear contact problem, when one has to find displacements of the assembled parts taking into an account both flexibility of the parts and geometrical non-penetration constraints. Then, since sealant is applied as a thin layer, it does not fill all the gap between the parts during initial steps of the fastening. Thus, presence of free surface has to be taken into account in the corresponding fluid dynamics problem.

The complexity of the fluid-structure interaction process observed between sealant and assembled parts makes it hard to develop a suitable mathematical model of the process. Usually some simplification is used in the related papers [4–6], allowing one to neglect the two-way character of the interaction. For example, in [5] adhesion bonding of aircraft parts is considered and contact interaction of the parts is described through the solution of a specific quadratic programming (QP) problem [7]. The interaction between the adhesive flow and the parts deformation is taken into consideration when the solution of the QP problem is corrected according to the so-called squeeze flow model [8]. Thus, only one side of the fluid-structure interaction is resolved in this approach (fluid-to-structural side, to be clear).

Recently a new approach has been developed [9, 10], when the complete two-way formulation of the fluid-structure interaction problem between sealant and the assembled parts is utilized and it is resolved in so-called partitioned manner. It means that the problem is divided into fluid and structural components and the solution of the problem is found through iterations between them. In practice the result of the assembly is also affected by several non-deterministic factors such as manufacturing defects, inaccuracies in parts positioning and others [11]. This is usually reflected in assembly simulation by performing a series of computations with different input data (for example, initial gap between parts may be varied [12]). High-performance computing (HPC) represents an instrument, which allows one to conduct such simulations efficiently when paradigm of task parallelization is utilized.

In this paper, an approach proposed in [9] for simulation of the sealant influence on the assembly process is briefly described (Sect. 2). Then, the approach is illustrated on a test case, when the assembly of full-scaled aircraft structure is simulated (Sect. 3.1). The efficiency of task parallelization is also investigated (Sect. 3.2). The paper is summed up in the last section (Sect. 4).

2 Mathematical Model

As it was mentioned in the previous section, the basic idea behind the approach used in this paper is to separate the complete fluid-structure interaction problem into fluid and structural subproblems and to organize a specific iterative procedure in order to find the solution. The interaction process may be schematically described as follows. The structural problem provides one a field of displacements u, , which corresponds to the current state of the contact interaction between the assembled parts. These displacements constrain the sealant flow and have to be considered in the fluid dynamics problem, which represents one side of the interaction (structural-to-fluid side). Vice versa, sealant pressure field p, , that is resolved in the fluid problem, has to be included in the structural one as an external force, which gives one the reverse side of the interaction (fluid-to-structural one).

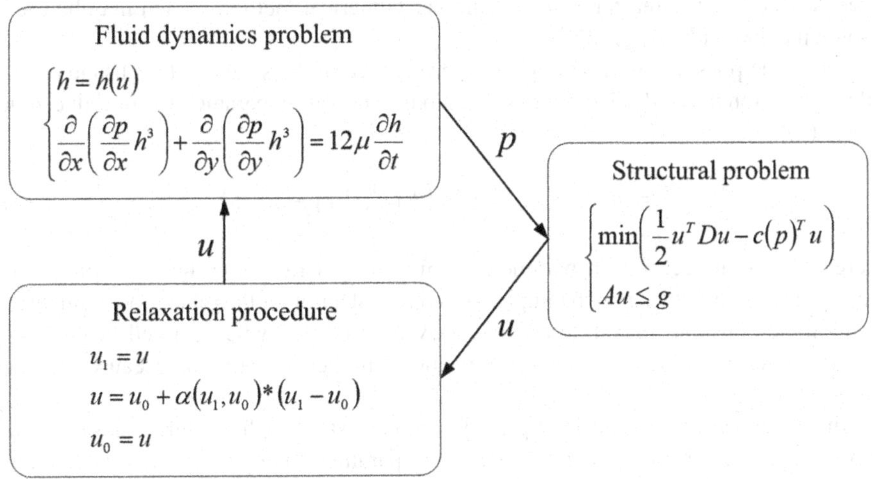

Fig. 1. Basic scheme of the numerical approach

In the present approach numerical solution of the formulated fluid-structure interaction problem consists of iterations between separate modules implementing solution of the structural and fluid dynamics problems respectively. Through these iterations a solution is found, which fulfills two conditions formulated on fluid-structure interface – no-slip condition and normal stress continuity condition. The numerical approach is presented in Fig. 1. It contains two blocks corresponding to the mentioned modules (the inner structure of the modules will be discussed later) and also a block associated with the relaxation procedure, which is used to ensure convergence of the iterations. Details of this procedure are addressed below.

The simplest iterative scheme, that may be used to solve the described fluid-structure interaction problem, may be written as follows:

$$\begin{cases} u^n = S(p^{n-1}) \\ p^n = F(u^n) \end{cases} \tag{1}$$

where n is the number of the present iteration, u^n and p^n denote approximations of the parts displacements field and the sealant pressure field respectively, functions S and F correspond to the numerical procedures required to solve the structural (S) and fluid dynamics (F) problems. We note here that the arguments of the functions S and F are provided in accordance with the peculiarities of the fluid-structure interaction process discussed in the beginning of this section.

From certain point of view, provided iterative scheme may be considered as a fixed-point iteration for a specific problem. Indeed, when the pressure field p^n is excluded from the system (1), one may obtain:

$$u^n = S\left(F\left(u^{n-1}\right)\right) \tag{2}$$

which is basically a fixed-point iteration for the problem $u = S(F(u))$. Unfortunately, for the considered case fixed-point iterations diverge because of the strong two-way character of the fluid-structure interaction. In order to improve the situation, one may try to replace the fixed-point iterations by another numerical method, which may be used to solve the $u = S(F(u))$ problem.

One of the possible ways to improve convergence of the scheme (1) is usage of so-called relaxation methods [13]. In these methods a relaxation parameter is introduced in the Eq. (2):

$$u^n = u^{n-1} + \alpha^{n-1} * \left(S\left(F\left(u^{n-1}\right)\right) - u^{n-1}\right) \tag{3}$$

where α^{n-1} is the relaxation parameter, which in general varies between the iterations. Different strategies may be implemented for selection of the relaxation parameter. Even simple constant relaxation strategy may be used, but when applied to the considered assembly problem it leads to impractical number of iterations because of slow convergence.

Aitken relaxation method [13] provides another strategy for determination of the relaxation parameter. In this method relaxation parameter is updated on each iteration as follows:

$$\alpha^n = -\alpha^{n-1} \frac{\left((S(F(u^n)) - u^n) - \left(S\left(F\left(u^{n-1}\right)\right) - u^{n-1}\right)\right)^T \left(S\left(F\left(u^{n-1}\right)\right) - u^{n-1}\right)}{\left\|(S(F(u^n)) - u^n) - \left(S\left(F\left(u^{n-1}\right)\right) - u^{n-1}\right)\right\|_2^2} \tag{4}$$

where $\| \|_2$ denotes Euclidian norm of the vector. This method may be considered as a generalization of the well-known secant method to the case of multiple equations and it has received wide reception since it has shown good results in different fluid-structure interaction problems [13]. It was suggested in [9] to apply this method in the considered assembly problem and, as numerical results show, it allows one to achieve convergence and resolve the interaction observed between sealant and the assembled parts [10].

Below we briefly describe the fluid and structural models (for details reader is referred to the original work [9]). Let us begin with the structural part of the process. Installation of fasteners during the assembly significantly reduces possible tangential displacements, which allows one to use the node-to-node contact formulation. Then, the variational formulation [14] of the contact problem may be used, when the potential energy of deformation is minimized under the non-penetration constraints. Finally, since fasteners are installed only in relatively small zone, where parts overlap (this zone is usually called 'junction area' [15]), the problem may be considered only in this zone when Guyan reduction [16] is applied. All the mentioned considerations lead to the QP problem, which describes the contact interaction between the assembled parts:

$$\min_{Au \leq g} \left(\frac{1}{2} u^T D u - c^T u \right) \tag{5}$$

where u is the vector of parts displacements, D is the stiffness matrix, c is the force vector, A is the linear operator, which is associated with node-to-node contact formulation, g is the initial gap vector.

It is important to mention, that QP problem (5) is applicable both for stationary and non-stationary contact analysis. In the latter case, the exact formulation for stiffness matrix D and force vector c contains information about the time discretization. Generalized α-method [17] is used for this purpose, as it is suggested in [18, 19]. Note that in the non-stationary case not one but a series of QP problems (5) is considered with one problem at each time-step.

Displacements of assembled parts caused by fasteners installation make sealant to flow, leading to the corresponding fluid dynamics problem. As it was mentioned previously, sealant is applied as a thin layer, which allows one to use lubrication theory for the flow description [20]. Generally speaking, practically used sealants are polymeric liquids, which are known to demonstrate non-Newtonian effects like viscoelasticity and shear-thinning [21]. Corresponding non-Newtonian lubrication models have been developed previously (see [22–24] and papers mentioned there), but application of any such model should be justified by appropriate experimental data confirming strong presence of non-Newtonian effects. In absence of these data, which is common for commercial sealants, one may utilize the classical Reynolds lubrication equation for the Newtonian fluid:

$$\frac{\partial}{\partial x}\left(\frac{\partial p}{\partial x}h^3\right) + \frac{\partial}{\partial y}\left(\frac{\partial p}{\partial y}h^3\right) = 12\mu\frac{\partial h}{\partial t} \tag{6}$$

where x, y represent the longitudinal coordinates in the junction area, p is the sealant pressure, h is the sealant thickness, μ is the sealant viscosity, t is time.

Two subjects have to be discussed here. Firstly, the sealant thickness h taking part in Reynolds Eq. (6) changes with time according to the solution of QP problem (5), which allows one to resolve the one way of the fluid-structure interaction (the structural-to-fluid influence). The other part of the interaction is taken into an account (the fluid-to-structural influence), when force vector c in QP problem (5) is corrected by local distribution of the sealant pressure p obtained from the Reynolds Eq. (6). Note that the mentioned details are reflected in Fig. 1. Secondly, the sealant viscosity μ in Eq. (6) varies in time due to the curing process [10]. This process is a specific chemical reaction, which leads to the sealant solidification at the end of the assembly. In the present study, available experimental data for the particular type of sealant was used to reflect the viscosity change during the curing process.

Resolution of the free surface effects represents a challenging task, since among other things the free surface position should not penetrate through the assembled parts. This condition may be fulfilled when the pseudo-structural method is used [25]. In this method an additional Lagrangian mesh is considered in the QP problem (5), which reflects the free surface movement. Note that in such method the non-penetration conditions between sealant and parts are satisfied naturally in the formulation of the QP problem (5).

3 Numerical Results

Wing-to-fuselage assembly is usually considered as one of the most important steps during the aircraft assembly process. In order to ensure the quality of the assembly presence of multiple supporting parts is provided in the assembly technology, which is pictured in Fig. 2. The wing-to-fuselage joint has two distinctive regions usually called 'upper junction' (parts forming this junction are colored in Fig. 2) and 'lower junction' (it consists of grey colored parts and the wing part). In this paper we consider only the upper junction of the wing-to-fuselage joint and below we provide results of numerical simulations, which illustrate the influence of sealant on the assembly process.

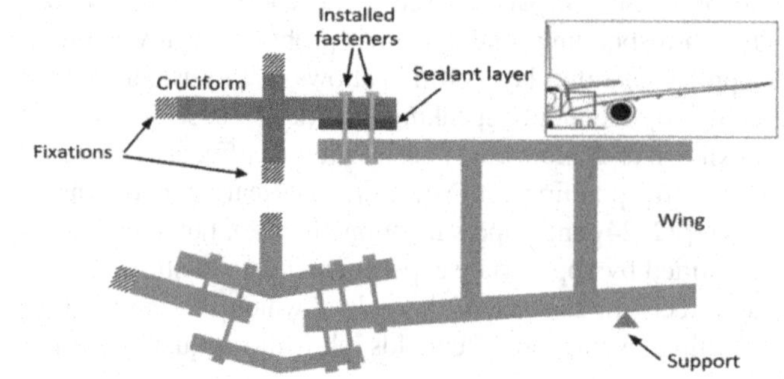

Fig. 2. Wing-to-fuselage upper junction [11]

Fig. 3. Finite element model of the upper junction

Figure 3 demonstrates the finite element model of the upper junction used in the present study. The structural model has 11565 degrees-of-freedom (DOFs) in the junction area, which includes normal displacements both for the assembled cruciform and wing parts and Lagrangian mesh used for the free surface determination. Note that these DOFs are the unknowns in the QP problem (5). During the iterations required in resolution of the fluid-structure interaction each QP problem was solved by Newton projection method [26], which was found to perform well due to application of so-called warm-start technique [27]. Also finite volume method was used for the numerical solution of the Reynolds Eq. (6), having 3855 nodes in the computational mesh.

3.1 Influence of Assembly Parameters on the Assembly Result

The assembly process has a number of variable parameters, that may influence both the intermediate and the final state of the assembly. To name a few, initial gap between parts, initial thickness of sealant layer, fastening mechanical force and order of fasteners installation may be mentioned. All of these parameters vary in quite wide range, which leads to a significant amount of possible assembly configurations (scenarios). Numerical problems of such scale may be solved effectively only when capabilities of high-performance computing (HPC) are utilized. In this section we demonstrate numerical results for several assembly scenarios obtained using HPC facilities located in the Supercomputing Center of Peter the Great St. Petersburg Polytechnic University (SPbPU).

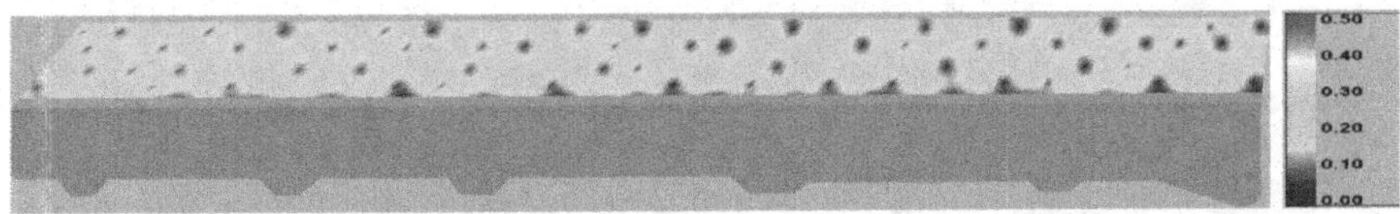

Fig. 4. Intermediate gap between parts for the basic scenario ($t = 100$ s) (Color figure online)

Fig. 5. Intermediate sealant thickness distribution for the basic scenario ($t = 100$ s)

Let's begin with the results for a scenario that will be referred to as a 'basic' one. In this case the uniform initial gap of 5 mm and also uniform initial thickness of sealant layer of 0.15 mm were considered (placement of sealant layer is demonstrated in Fig. 2). Fasteners were installed in preliminary drilled holes by groups of 3 with period of 5 s. Totally 256 holes were considered, thus, having all fasteners installed after about 7 min.

Figure 4 demonstrates the intermediate results for the basic scenario. Here gap between cruciform and wing part is pictured at the moment of $t = 100$ s from the start of the simulation, when almost 25% of fasteners has been installed. Note that this gap is partially filled with sealant. Installation of any fastener applies great mechanical load to the assembly, which is supposed to completely squeeze out the sealant (and, thus, close the gap) in the neighborhood of the fastener. This effect contributes to appearance of dark blue spots in Fig. 4, which correspond to zero gap values located near positions of fastening. Figure 5 also pictures the current distribution of the sealant thickness. The flow of sealant caused by fasteners installation leads to formation of complicated irregular structure, clearly visible in Fig. 5.

When all fasteners are installed (see Fig. 6), the gap is fully filled with sealant. At the same time, the obtained distribution could not be considered as a stationary one, since sealant continues to flow even after the completion of fastening. A characteristic state is achieved after approximately 20 min, which is displayed in Fig. 7. Red spots placed in the center of the junction area correspond to the 'lakes' of sealant, which formed during the fastening and were not squeezed out afterwards. As it turns out, for the majority of

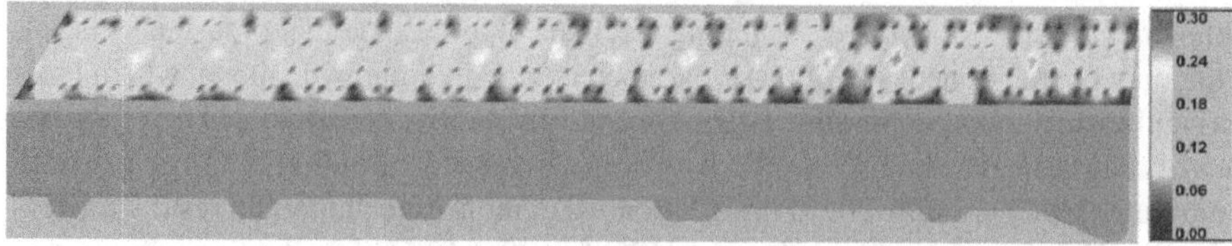

Fig. 6. Intermediate gap between parts for the basic scenario ($t = 427.25$ s)

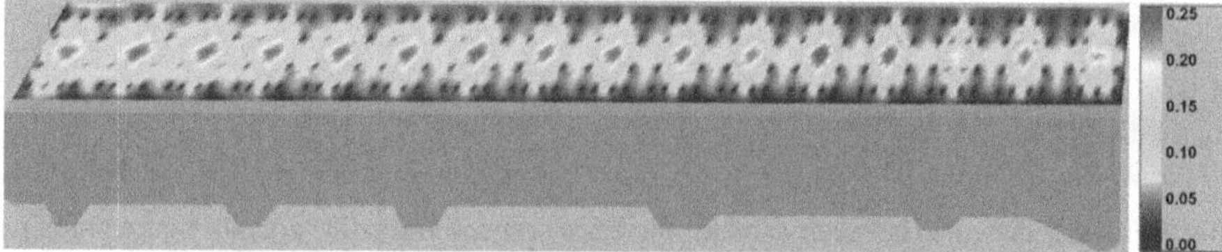

Fig. 7. Final gap between parts for the basic scenario ($t = 1234.75$ s) (Color figure online)

the fasteners placed near these lakes the sealant is not totally squeezed out under them. Such behavior is prohibited by standard assembly requirements [10] and in order to get rid of the lakes one may suggest to increase the fastening force or to reduce the initial amount of sealant, and both of these possibilities are discussed below.

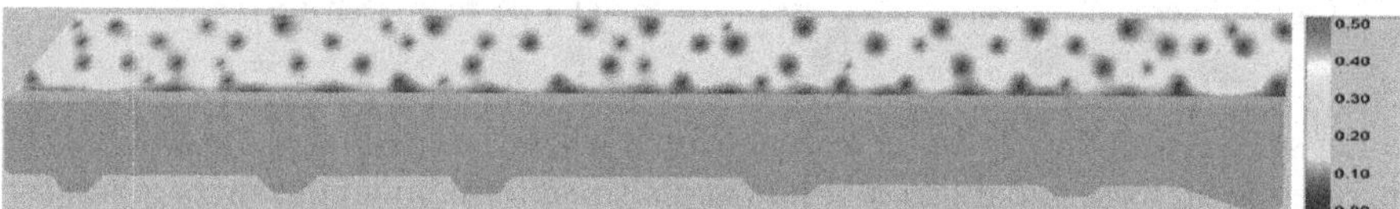

Fig. 8. Intermediate gap between parts for the second scenario ($t = 100$ s)

In the next (second) scenario the initial thickness of sealant layer was reduced from 0.15 mm to 0.1 mm. Note that all other assembly parameters were retained from the basic scenario. As expected, smaller amount of sealant provides less resistance to the mechanical load applied by fastening, which leads to significant decrease of both intermediate (see Fig. 8) and final gap (see Fig. 9). At the same time, lakes of sealant still appear in the center of the junction area and near some of them the gap between parts is still not closed under positions of fasteners, especially in the left half in Fig. 9.

In the third scenario influence of fastening force was considered and 10 times greater values were used as compared to the basic (and second) scenario. Note that the initial sealant thickness value was recovered to the basic one. In Figs. 10, 11 and 12 the evolution of the assembly process for the third scenario is pictured. A different order of fasteners installation also was considered in this scenario, when fasteners were fixed starting from the center of the junction area (see Fig. 10).

The presented results clearly show, that proposed increase in the fastening force leads to the complete squeeze out of sealant under the installed fasteners as it is required by the assembly technology. The obtained results demonstrate that evolution of the assembly

Fig. 9. Final gap between parts for the second scenario ($t = 1234.75$ s)

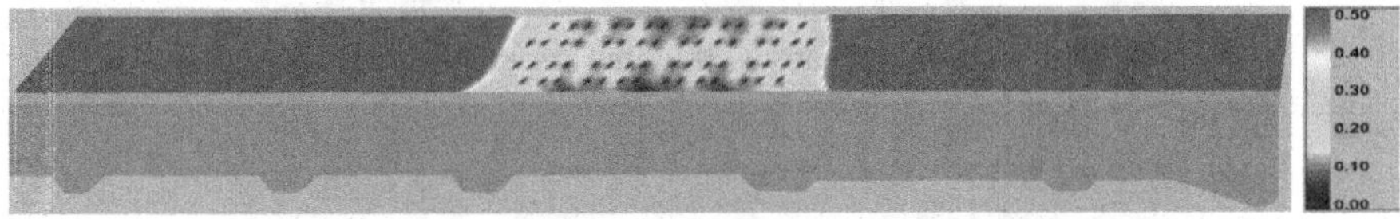

Fig. 10. Intermediate gap between parts for the third scenario ($t = 100$ s)

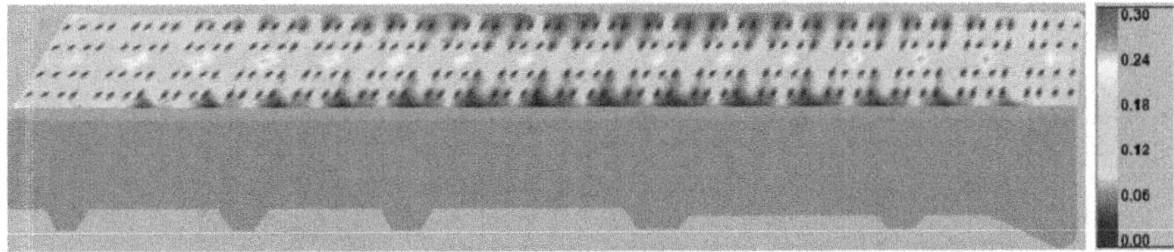

Fig. 11. Intermediate gap between parts for the third scenario ($t = 427.25$ s)

process depends on the selected combination of the assembly parameters and the choice of parameters should be done precisely in order to meet the assembly requirements.

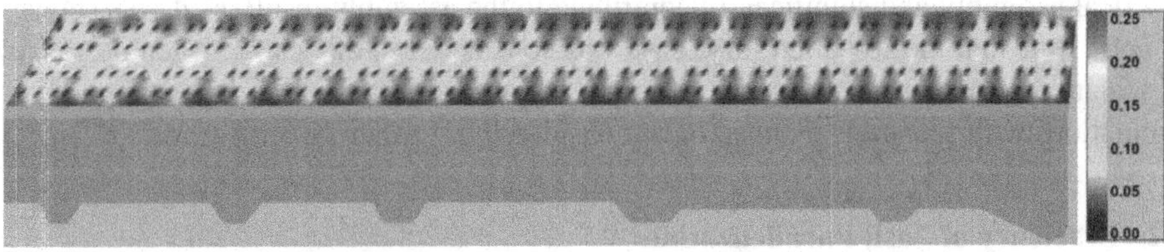

Fig. 12. Final gap between parts for the third scenario ($t = 1234.25$ s)

As it was mentioned in the introduction, assembly simulation is usually done as a series of computations with different input data, which reflects stochastic nature of variance in the assembly parameters. For this purpose, the model from [12] was selected, when different sources of variation are described by the initial gap between the assembled parts. Figure 13 demonstrates a set of generated initial gaps that were used in the computations. Note that in this case all the assembly parameters (except the initial gap) were the same as in the basic scenario.

Despite the significant difference in the initial gaps, the final results of computations almost completely coincide with the basic scenario (see Fig. 14). As it could be noticed,

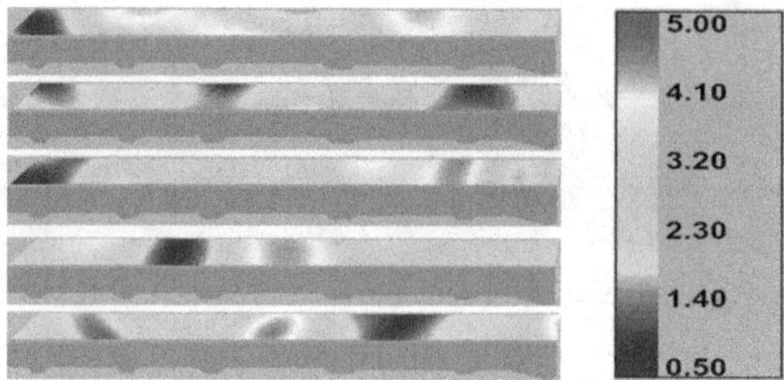

Fig. 13. Set of initial gaps used for the assembly simulation

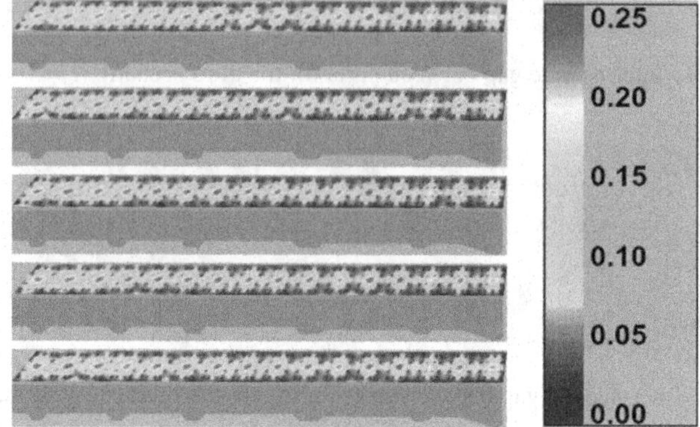

Fig. 14. Final gaps obtained after the assembly simulation

considered initial gaps do not include micro-scaled variations, which are observed in the practical assembly and significantly contribute to the assembly result, as it was shown in [11]. Note that the so-called 'dry' case was considered in this paper, when presence of sealant was neglected. Influence of micro variations in the initial gap as applied to simulations with sealant is planned to be considered in further investigations.

3.2 Efficiency of Task Parallelization

As it was mentioned previously, assembly simulation is done most efficiently when task parallelization is utilized. In order to estimate the efficiency of this mechanism the additional computations were done. In each of these computations a varying number of completely identical tasks was passed to one of the HPC cluster computational nodes for simultaneous execution. We note here that all the computational nodes used in the simulations have 64 GB of RAM and 28 physical cores.

Figure 15 demonstrates corresponding numerical results obtained for the model of wing-to-fuselage upper junction described earlier. In this figure speed up of the computations is pictured against the number of launched tasks. The speed up was calculated as relation between obtained computational time and time of equivalent simulation with all tasks run sequentially. Thus, the maximal theoretical value of speed up for N tasks is

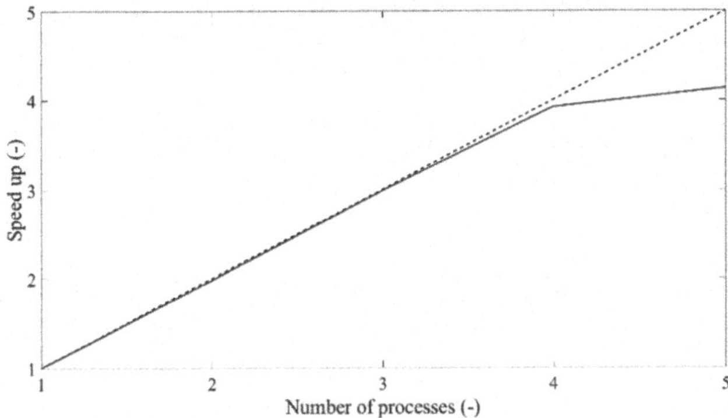

Fig. 15. Speed up of computations for the original model (Color figure online)

equal to N, which corresponds to dashed black line in Fig. 15. The blue curve pictures obtained numerical results, which demonstrate almost ideal acceleration up to the value of $N = 4$ tasks, after which significant decrease is found.

It should be mentioned here, that the assembly model considered in the present study requires significant amount of RAM. For example, matrix D of QP problem (5) is a fully populated matrix [28] because of the Guyan reduction used to cut the problem size (see Sect. 2), which demands significant resources for the considered number of 11565 unknowns. Another reason for RAM allocation is using of the dual formulation [28] of the QP problem (5), which was found to be much more effective in terms of computational time than the original problem statement. For mentioned reasons, only a small number of tasks is possible to run simultaneously on one computational node in case of considered assembly model. In order to improve the situation, one may consider to implement more sophisticated numerical algorithm, which includes single storage of data shared by all tasks, as it was done previously in [29] in context of the assembly simulation. This is supposed to be done in the near future.

For better understanding of the parallelization efficiency a smaller assembly model from [10] was also considered. It has only 3554 DOFs in the structural problem and it allows one to consider the values up to $N = 28$ processes, which is the number of physical cores in each computational node (see Fig. 16). The almost ideal parallelization is found again, which lasts up to the value of $N = 7$ tasks. After that the speed up decreases, but it should be mentioned here that for the biggest number of processes the speed up value was found to be almost 18, which could be considered as significant improvement against serial execution. To sum up, the results provided in this subsection justify that HPC technologies have great potential as applied to aircraft assembly simulation. The usage of state-of-the-art computational resources combined with implementation of effective numerical algorithms may provide a powerful tool for simulation of practically important assembly problems.

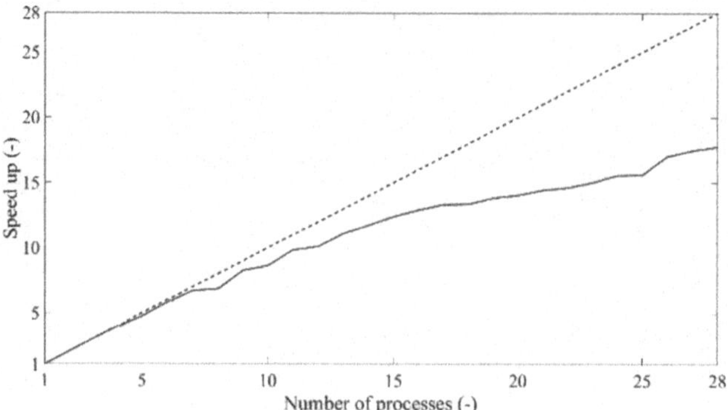

Fig. 16. Speed up of computations for the smaller model

4 Conclusion

This paper presents an example of application of HPC technologies to mathematical modeling of the aircraft assembly process. The sealant influence on the assembly of upper junction of wing-to-fuselage joint was considered. For the first time problem of practical scale was solved by approach suggested in [9], which justifies the capabilities of the approach. Efficiency of task parallelization, which is natural in context of the assembly simulation, was also investigated. The obtained results confirm that development of numerical algorithms based on task parallelization paradigm may be considered as perspective direction of research devoted to aircraft assembly modeling.

The research was supported by Russian Science Foundation (project No. 22-19-00062, https://rscf.ru/en/project/22-19-00062/). The results of the work were obtained using computational resources of Peter the Great Saint-Petersburg Polytechnic University Supercomputing Center (www.spbstu.ru).

References

1. Mardis, C.S.: Form-in-place seals. https://www.gore.com/sites/g/files/ypyipe116/files/2016-09/Form-in-place%20Seals_0.pdf. Accessed 09 Apr 2023
2. da Silva Rodrigues, N.M.: Evaluate the influence of temperature and humidity on the cure process of aeronautic sealants. Master thesis, Lisbon (2016). (in Portuguese)
3. Shvarts, A.G., Yastrebov, V.A.: Fluid flow across a wavy channel brought in contact. Tribol. Int. **126**, 116–126 (2018)
4. Burka, P., Liu, X., Thompson, M.C., Sheridan, J.: Modelling of adhesive bonding for aircraft structures applying the insertion squeeze flow method. Compos. B **50**, 247–252 (2013)
5. Mato, P.C., Webb, P., Xu, Y., Graham, D., Portsmore, A., Preston, E.: Enhanced bondline thickness analysis for non-rigid airframe structural assemblies. Aerosp. Sci. Technol. **91**, 434–441 (2019)
6. Atre, A., Johnson, W.S.: Analysis of the effects of interference and sealant on riveted lap joints. J. Aircr. **44**(2), 353–364 (2007)
7. Lupuleac, S., Petukhova, M., Shinder, Y., Bretagnol, B.: Methodology for solving contact problem during riveting process. SAE Int. J. Aerosp. **4**(2), 952–957 (2011)

8. Smiley, A.J., Chao, M., Gillespie, J.W., Jr.: Influence and control of bondline thickness in fusion bonded joints of thermoplastic composites. Compos. Struct. **2**(3–4), 223–232 (1991)
9. Eliseev, A., Lupuleac, S., Grigor'ev, B., Shinder, J., Bouriquet, J.: Numerical simulation of aircraft assembly process with presence of sealant. In: SAE Technical Papers 2021-01-0001, pp. 1–8 (2021)
10. Eliseev, A., Lupuleac, S., Grigor'ev, B., Shinder, J.: An approach to variation simulation of final aircraft assembly with presence of sealant. ASME J. Comput. Inf. Sci. Eng. **22**(4), 040904-1-040904-6 (2022)
11. Lupuleac, S., et al.: Simulation of the wing-to-fuselage assembly process. ASME J. Manuf. Sci. Eng. **141**(6), 061009-1-061009-9 (2019)
12. Zaitseva, N., Lupuleac, S., Khashba, V., Shinder, J., Bonhomme, E.: Approaches to initial gap modeling in final aircraft assembly simulation. In: Proceedings of the ASME 2020 International Mechanical Engineering Congress and Exposition, vol. 2B, V02BT02A059 (2020)
13. Küttler, U., Wall, W.A.: Fixed-point fluid-structure interaction solvers with dynamic relaxation. Comput. Mech. **43**(1), 61–72 (2008)
14. Hlavacek, I., Haslinger, J., Necas, J., Lovisek, J.: Solution of Variational Inequalities in Mechanics. Springer, New York (1998). https://doi.org/10.1007/978-1-4612-1048-1
15. Lupuleac, S., Kovtun, M., Rodionova, O., Marguet, B.: Assembly simulation of riveting process. SAE Int. J. Aerosp. **2**(1), 193–198 (2010)
16. Guyan, R.J.: Reduction of stiffness and mass matrix. AIAA J. **3**(2), 380 (1965)
17. Chung, J., Hulbert, G.M.: A time integration algorithm for structural dynamics with improved numerical dissipation: the generalized-α method. ASME. J. Appl. Mech. **60**(2), 371–375 (1993)
18. Vasiliev, A., Minevich, O., Lapina, E., Shinder, J., Lupuleac, S., Barboule J.: A novel approach to dynamic contact analysis in the course of aircraft assembly simulation. SAE Technical Papers 2021-01-0004, pp. 1–7 (2021)
19. Vasiliev, A., Lupuleac, S., Shinder, J.: Numerical approach for detecting the resonance effects of drilling during assembly of aircraft structures. Mathematics **9**(22), 2926 (2021)
20. Szeri, A.Z.: Fluid Film Lubrication, 2nd edn. Cambridge University Press, New York (2011)
21. da Silva, L.F.M., Öchsner, A., Adams, R.D.: Handbook of Adhesion Technology, 2nd edn. Springer, Cham (2018). https://doi.org/10.1007/978-3-642-01169-6
22. Tichy, J.A.: Non-Newtonian lubrication with the convected Maxwell model. ASME J. Tribol. **118**(2), 344–348 (1996)
23. Grigor'ev, B., Eliseev, A.: An extended Reynolds equation for non-Newtonian lubrication with the upper convected Maxwell model. ASME J. Tribol. **144**(8), 081805-1–081805-10 (2022)
24. Peiran, Y., Shizhu, W.: A generalized Reynolds equation for non-Newtonian thermal elastohydrodynamic lubrication. ASME J. Tribol. **112**(4), 631–636 (1990)
25. Reddy, J.N., Gartling, D.K.: The Finite Element Method in Heat Transfer and Fluid Dynamics, 3rd edn. CRC Press, Boca Raton (2010)
26. Baklanov, S., Stefanova, M., Lupuleac, S.: Newton projection method as applied to assembly simulation. Optim. Methods Softw. **37**(2), 577–604 (2020)
27. Baklanov, S., Stefanova, M., Lupuleac, S., Shinder, J., Eliseev, A.: Decomposition method for solving the quadratic programming problem in the aircraft assembly modeling. In: Olenev, N., Evtushenko, Y., Jaćimović, M., Khachay, M., Malkova, V., Pospelov, I. (eds.) OPTIMA 2022. LNCS, vol. 13781, pp. 3–17. Springer, Cham (2022). https://doi.org/10.1007/978-3-031-22543-7_1

28. Stefanova, M., et al.: Convex optimization techniques in compliant assembly simulation. Optim. Eng. **21**, 1665–1690 (2020)
29. Zaitseva, N., Pogarskaia, T.: Software package for high-performance computations in airframe assembly modeling. In: Voevodin, V., Sobolev, S., Yakobovskiy, M., Shagaliev, R. (eds.) RuSCDays 2022. LNCS, vol. 13708, pp. 328–341. Springer, Cham (2022). https://doi.org/10.1007/978-3-031-22941-1_24

Block Algebraic Multigrid Method for Saddle-Point Problems of Various Physics

Igor Konshin[1,2,3,4] and Kirill Terekhov[1,3,5](✉)

[1] Marchuk Institute of Numerical Mathematics, RAS, Moscow 119333, Russia
terekhov@inm.ras.ru
[2] Dorodnicyn Computing Centre of FRC CSC, RAS, Moscow 119333, Russia
[3] Moscow Institute of Physics and Technology, Moscow 141701, Russia
[4] Sechenov University, Moscow 119991, Russia
[5] Sirius University of Science and Technology, Sochi 354340, Russia

Abstract. We are investigating a fully coupled solver that utilizes a new block version of the algebraic multigrid method. The use of the AMG method in a block formulation in many cases allows not only to reduce the number of iterations, but also to solve problems that could not be solved earlier by the traditional AMG method. The proposed construction of block algebraic multigrid method is the direct extension of scalar Ruge–Stüben algebraic method for the interpolation and coarse-space construction and uses block Gauss–Seidel method as a smoother. The S^3M framework is used to construct the solver. The method applies to the systems arising from the discretization of coupled problems with the fully-implicit collocated finite-volume method. Current method is limited to the coupled problems with the fixed-sized blocks and uniform physics in the whole domain. The problems of poroelasticity, stationary compressible and incompressible elasticity, multiphase flows in oil & gas problems, the non-stationary Maxwell problem, as well as the Navier–Stokes equations are considered. Most of the problems are of saddle-point nature. Our main goal was not so much to investigate the parallel properties of the proposed method, but to check its robustness on the most complex problems. Therefore, we limited ourselves to parallelization based on OpenMP to speed up problem solving.

Keywords: Saddle-point problem · Sparse linear system · Block multigrid method

1 Introduction

Fedorenko and Bakhvalov investigated the application of the multigrid concept to Poisson problems in their early works [1–4]. Later, Brandt et al. [5] and Hackbusch [6] further developed this idea.

The AMG method has been applied to various systems of equations [7–10], including those arising from multiphase flows in oil & gas problems. In

V. Voevodin et al. (Eds.): RuSCDays 2023, LNCS 14388, pp. 17–34, 2023.
https://doi.org/10.1007/978-3-031-49432-1_2

such systems, an elliptic component is extracted using CPR [11,12] or DRS [13,14] techniques before the algebraic multigrid method is used as part of a multi-stage strategy to rapidly solve the elliptic part of the problem. Although a robust first-stage preconditioner, such as an incomplete LU-factorization [15], is still required, as the remaining part of the system demonstrates an elliptic component due to capillary pressure. In addition, a multigrid reduction technique has been adapted successfully to solve two-phase problems [16,17], while adding rock mechanics introduces an elliptic component that is also addressed with the algebraic multigrid [18,19]. However, in coupled geomechanics problems, saddle-point behavior may occur [20,21].

Several versions of the block algebraic multigrid method was successfully implemented in an open source CFD toolbox OpenFOAM. Selective algebraic multigrid approach was proposed for implicitly coupled block-matrices [22] for pressure–velocity system. There are a computational method that utilizes block coupling for solving 3-D incompressible turbulent flows. The method is based on finite-volume discretization on an unstructured grid and is discussed in [23]. In [24], a computational method that utilizes a fully coupled block algorithm to solve three-dimensional incompressible turbulent flows is explored. The method is designed for use in hydraulic machinery. The study described in [25] applied a methodology for linear elasticity problems on unstructured meshes that uses a coupled cell-centred finite volume approach.

A geometric multigrid for saddle-point systems is well known [26,27]. It is based on inexact Uzawa [28], Braess–Sarazin [29] or Vanka [26] smoothers. A monolithic algebraic multigrid for saddle-point systems was considered in [30,31]. It requires assembly of inexact Schur complement to define the interpolation for the Lagrange multipliers. Moreover, a stabilization ought to be introduced into interpolation operator to maintain good properties of coarse level systems due to inf-sup stability issues [32–34].

In our previous work [35] we developed the Bootstrap Adaptive AMG approach, but in this work we consider the block version of AMG as an alternative approach to increase robustness. The proposed method is based on representing the whole system in a block form, where each matrix element is considered as an square $\mathfrak{b} \times \mathfrak{b}$ matrix with $\mathfrak{b}$ unknowns corresponding to each discretization cell. The Ruge–Stüben method [36] for scalar matrix elements in combination with ideas from [37–39] is generalized to block version using Frobenius matrix norm for each $\mathfrak{b} \times \mathfrak{b}$ matrix block. This approach is implemented with the S^{3}M package [10], where OpenMP parallelization is used at each stage of the block AMG method. We demonstrate the efficiency of our method in parallel computing as well as its reliability in solving systems for various physical problems.

The article is structured as follows. Section 2 discusses the block algebraic multigrid method, including details of the algorithm implementation. Next, Sect. 3 outlines the test cases considered and presents the results of numerical experiments. Finally, the last section offers a summary of the main findings of the study.

2 Block Algebraic Multigrid Method

We consider the block version of AMG method, where the blocksize $\mathfrak{b}$ is the number of unknowns in a discretization cell. Let $Ax = b$ is the system to be solved, where $A = \{a_{ij}\}$ is the original point-wise matrix, $i, j \in \Omega = [1, N\mathfrak{b}]$, where N represents the overall number of cells. In addition, we consider the block matrix $A = \{\mathbf{a}_{ij}\}$, where $i, j \in \Omega = [1, N]$ are the indices of block row and column, respectively. Next, we consider the fixed block test vector $\mathbf{x}$, $\mathbf{x} = \mathbf{1} \otimes \mathbb{I}$, of size $N\mathfrak{b} \times \mathfrak{b}$. By doing so, we ensure that the interpolation is constant-preserving for each unknown component in the block independently. The approximate equality $A\mathbf{x} \approx \mathbf{0}$ for a block row indexed by i is

$$\mathbf{a}_{ii}\mathbf{x}_i \approx -\sum_{i \neq j} \mathbf{a}_{ij}\mathbf{x}_j. \tag{1}$$

Suppose that a coarse-fine splitting $\Omega = \mathcal{C} \cup \mathcal{F}$ exists, where $\mathcal{C}$ and $\mathcal{F}$ contain the coarse and fine cells, respectively. The connections for the i-th row are determined by the set $\mathcal{N}_i = \{j : i \neq j, \mathbf{a}_{ij} \neq \mathbf{0}\}$, which can be further partitioned into strong and weak connections $\mathcal{N}_i = \mathcal{S}_i \cup \mathcal{W}_i$.

Weak connections in $\mathcal{W}_i$ are deemed negligible and are thus included in the diagonal. For each row i, the set of interpolatory connections $\mathcal{I}_i$ is determined by the intersection of $\mathcal{S}_i$ and $\mathcal{C}$, while the set of remaining strong connections $\mathcal{D}_i$ is obtained via the intersection of $\mathcal{S}_i$ and $\mathcal{F}$. To eliminate the strong connections in $\mathcal{D}_i$, the twice-removed interpolation technique is used, which requires that for each $j \in \mathcal{D}_i$, we have $\mathcal{S}_i \cap \mathcal{S}_j \cap \mathcal{C} \neq \varnothing$.

For the sake of versatility, we further partition $\mathcal{D}_i$ into $\mathcal{T}_i$ and $\mathcal{E}_i$. The connections in $\mathcal{T}_i$ permit the use of twice-removed interpolation, while those in $\mathcal{E}_i$ cannot. For any $j \in \mathcal{E}_i$, we have $\mathcal{S}_i \cap \mathcal{S}_j \cap \mathcal{C} = \varnothing$, and the connections in $\mathcal{E}_i$ are absorbed into a coefficient. This partitioning leads to the splitting of the right-hand side in (1):

$$-\sum_{i \neq j} \mathbf{a}_{ij}\mathbf{x}_j = -\sum_{j \in \mathcal{I}_i} \mathbf{a}_{ij}\mathbf{x}_j - \sum_{j \in \mathcal{W}_i} \mathbf{a}_{ij}\mathbf{x}_j - \sum_{k \in \mathcal{T}_i} \mathbf{a}_{ik}\mathbf{x}_k - \sum_{k \in \mathcal{E}_i} \mathbf{a}_{ik}\mathbf{x}_k.$$

Weak connections in $\mathcal{W}_i$ can be approximated using $\mathbf{x}_i$. However, strong non-interpolatory connections require expressions utilizing $\mathbf{x}_j$, where j belongs to $\mathcal{I}_i$. The study in [40] introduced a twice-removed interpolation technique that accounts for the test vector $\mathbf{x}$, while a variant that incorporates absolute values was proposed in [37,38]. This modification permits the elimination of $\mathbf{x}_k$, where k belongs to $\mathcal{T}_i$, by

$$\mathbf{a}_{ik}\mathbf{x}_k = \sum_{j \in \mathcal{S}_i \cap \mathcal{S}_k \cap \mathcal{C}} \frac{\mathbf{a}_{ik}\|\mathbf{a}_{kj}\|}{\sum_{l \in \mathcal{I}_i \cap \mathcal{I}_k} \|\mathbf{a}_{kl}\|}\mathbf{x}_j,$$

and for $k \in \mathcal{E}_i$ we simply average the block among interpolatory connections

$$\mathbf{a}_{ik}\mathbf{x}_k = \sum_{j \in \mathcal{I}_i} |\mathcal{I}_i|^{-1}\mathbf{a}_{ik}\mathbf{x}_j.$$

For this purpose, we employ the sets introduced earlier to rewrite (1) as

$$\left(\mathbf{a}_{ii} + \sum_{j\in\mathcal{W}_i} \mathbf{a}_{ij}\right)\mathbf{x}_i \approx -\sum_{j\in\mathcal{I}_i}\left(\mathbf{a}_{ij} + \sum_{k\in\mathcal{T}_i}\frac{\mathbf{a}_{ik}\|\mathbf{a}_{kj}\|}{\sum_{l\in\mathcal{I}_i\cap\mathcal{I}_k}\|\mathbf{a}_{kl}\|} + \sum_{k\in\mathcal{E}_i}|\mathcal{I}_i|^{-1}\mathbf{a}_{ik}\right)\mathbf{x}_j. \tag{2}$$

By utilizing (2), we can derive an interpolation formula for $\mathbf{x}_i$ that expresses it in terms of $\mathbf{x}_j$ from the set $\mathcal{I}_i$. This formula can be presented as

$$\mathbf{x}_i \approx \sum_{j\in\mathcal{I}_i}\boldsymbol{\omega}_{ij}\mathbf{x}_j,$$

with the following weights

$$\boldsymbol{\omega}_{ij} = \left(\mathbf{a}_{ii} + \sum_{j\in\mathcal{W}_i}\mathbf{a}_{ij}\right)^{-1}\left(\mathbf{a}_{ij} + \sum_{k\in\mathcal{T}_i}\frac{\mathbf{a}_{ik}\|\mathbf{a}_{kj}\|}{\sum_{l\in\mathcal{I}_i\cap\mathcal{I}_k}\|\mathbf{a}_{kl}\|} + \sum_{k\in\mathcal{E}_i}|\mathcal{I}_i|^{-1}\mathbf{a}_{ik}\right). \tag{3}$$

To facilitate this calculation, we introduce a mapping in the coarse set, denoted as $\forall j \in \mathcal{C} : f(j) \in \Omega_{\mathcal{C}}$, where $\Omega_{\mathcal{C}} = [1, N_{\mathcal{C}}]$ and $N_{\mathcal{C}} = |\mathcal{C}|$. Using the block Kronecker delta $\boldsymbol{\delta}_k = \mathbf{e}_k^T \otimes \mathbb{I}$, we can define the respective i-th block row of the prolongator P:

$$P_i = \begin{cases} \sum_{j\in\mathcal{I}_i}\boldsymbol{\omega}_{ij}\boldsymbol{\delta}_{f(j)}, & i\in\mathcal{F}, \\ \boldsymbol{\delta}_{f(i)}, & i\in\mathcal{C}, \end{cases} \tag{4}$$

We define the system for the next level as $B = P^T AP$. In the classical method, the strong connections for the i-th row are identified using

$$\mathcal{S}_i = \{j : \ -\mathbf{a}_{ij} \geqslant \theta \max_{k\in\mathcal{N}_i}(-\mathbf{a}_{ik})\}, \tag{5}$$

which relies on the M-matrix property where off-diagonal elements are negative. It is generally recommended to use a parameter of $\theta = 1/4$.

In the block version we use the absolute block norms

$$\mathcal{S}_i = \{j : \ \|\mathbf{a}_{ij}\| \geqslant \theta \max_{k\in\mathcal{N}_i}(\|\mathbf{a}_{ik}\|)\}, \tag{6}$$

which corresponds to selection of elements with absolute values as in [37–39].

Ruge and Stüben [36] have devised two criteria for splitting data into coarse and fine subsets on the base of the relationships between their strong connections graph $\mathcal{S}$:

- C1: $\forall i \in \mathcal{F} : \forall j \in \mathcal{S}_i \cap \mathcal{F} : \mathcal{S}_i \cap \mathcal{S}_j \cap \mathcal{C} \neq \varnothing$.
- C2: $\mathcal{C}$ is a maximal independent set of graph $\mathcal{S}$.

Implementing rule C1 exactly will result in $\mathcal{E}_i = \varnothing$ for all $i \in \mathcal{F}$. In this work we do not satisfy C1 exactly. To do so, we simply skip the refinement step of coarse space selection of the original Ruge–Stüben algorithm [36].

The *setup stage* of the algorithm is broken down into several steps, including configuring the smoother for the current system, generating the graph of strong connections, selecting an initial coarse space by Algorithm 1, calculating the prolongator using equations (3)–(4), computing the next level system $B = P^T AP$, and continuing to the next level by either solving the smaller system or repeating all previous steps.

The *solution stage* follows the standard V-cycle algorithm, but it is not detailed here to save space.

2.1 Coarse Space Selection

To determine the coarse space for the algorithm, we follow the method of Ruge and Stüben [36] and divide the process into two steps. The first step involves selecting a maximal independent set in the graph $\mathcal{S}$ to satisfy rule C2, while the second step refines the coarse space to satisfy modified rule C1. In the present paper, we do not perform the second step to reduce the size of the coarse system. In [36], the new coarse space node $i \in \mathcal{U} \to i \in \mathcal{C}$ with the highest weight $|\mathcal{S}_i^T \cap \mathcal{U}| + 2|\mathcal{S}_i^T \cap \mathcal{F}|$ is selected sequentially. The set $\mathcal{U} = \Omega \setminus (\mathcal{C} \cup \mathcal{F})$ refers to the candidates that are not already in the fine or coarse spaces.

The Luby's algorithm [41] is employed in our approach to finding a maximal independent set with weights, as shown in Algorithm 1. The weight $|\mathcal{S}_i \cap \mathcal{U}| + 2|\mathcal{S}_i \cap \mathcal{F}|$ used in our algorithm takes into account the number of strong non-interpolatory connections, but does not demand the transpose of graph $\mathcal{S}$. Nodes with more strong non-interpolatory connections and requiring twice-removed interpolation are assigned to the coarse space $\mathcal{C}$. The algorithm can be easily parallelized by synchronizing the update of vector $\mathbf{r}$ and sets $\mathcal{C}$, $\mathcal{F}$, and $\mathcal{U}$. The attribution of a node to a set is achieved through a vector where each entry corresponds to the set index.

Algorithm 1. Coarse-fine space splitting.

```
function CF-SPLITTING(S)                          ▷ S is the strong graph
    Set U = [1, N]                                ▷ Candidate set, N is the system size
    Set C = F = ∅                                 ▷ Coarse and fine sets
    while globally U ≠ ∅ do                       ▷ Check for empty set across processors
        for local i ∈ U do
            r_i = |S_i ∩ U| + 2|S_i ∩ F| + rand   ▷ rand ∈ [0, 1] is a random value
        end for
        Set Ĉ = ∅                                 ▷ New candidates to Ĉ
        for local i ∈ U do
            t = max_{j∈S_i∩U} r_j                 ▷ Check maximum over adjacent candidates
            if r_i > t then Ĉ = Ĉ ∪ {i} end if    ▷ This node attains maximum
        end for
        U = U \ Ĉ, C = C ∪ Ĉ                      ▷ Remove from candidates and add to coarse space
        for local i ∈ U do
            if S_i ∩ C ≠ ∅ then                   ▷ There is a connection to node from C
                U = U \ {i}, F = F ∪ {i}          ▷ Move candidate to set F
            end if
        end for
    end while
    return C, F
end function
```

2.2 Block Gauss–Seidel Smoother

Consider a matrix A that can be represented by the sum of a block lower-triangular L matrix, block upper-triangular transpose U^T matrix, and a block diagonal D matrix. The goal is to use symmetric Gauss–Seidel iteration to solve the system $A\mathbf{x} = \mathbf{b}$, where $\mathbf{x}^n$ is the current estimate to the solution on i-th iteration. This is carried out through the following two steps

$$(L + D)\mathbf{x}^{n+1/2} = \mathbf{b} - U\mathbf{x}^n, \quad (U + D)\mathbf{x}^{n+1} = \mathbf{b} - L\mathbf{x}^{n+1/2},$$

where we need to use forward and backward substitutions with block triangular matrices.

To retrieve parallelism, we apply multicolor ordering to the block matrix. This technique involves computing a maximal independent set in the graph $\mathcal{G}$, which corresponds to the sparse block structure.

2.3 Implementation with S^{3}M Facilities

In order to implement the block AMG method, we utilized the Sparse system solution methods (S^{3}M). This is a header-only C++ library [10] that offers a range of linear solvers and preconditioners that can be used together. The library includes traditional Krylov space acceleration methods, smoothers, as well as more advanced incomplete factorization methods with rescaling and reordering algorithms. When integrated in an algebraic multi-grid fashion, these methods can be used to tackle complex linear systems that arise from various physics problems.

We have used several template classes from S^{3}M library: CSRMatrix, MulticolorBlockGaussSeidel, LU, BICGSTAB as well as especially developed for the current research BlockAMG class. For example, the declaration of the block AMG solver and block Gauss–Seidel solver (will be used for comparison in Sect. 3):

```
BICGSTAB< BlockAMG<MulticolorBlockGaussSeidel,LU> > Solver;
BICGSTAB< MulticolorBlockGaussSeidel > Solver;
```

In this case, the call to the preconditioner construction stage and its iterative application remains the same independently of the solver type:

```
Solver.Setup(A) && Solver.Solve(b, x);
```

To organize the block version of AMG, we have exploited the nested classes of sparse matrices in CSR format. This can be especially important for large blocks, for example, we planned to apply this technology to sparse matrices with a block size of 13 from the blood coagulation problem. In this way, the declaration of original coefficient matrix A and a block version of the same matrix are as follows:

```
CSRMatrix A;
CSRMatrixType<CSRMatrix> bA;
```

It should be noted that converting matrices from one format to another can take a significant amount of time. Moving forward, our intention is to adopt a sparse matrix storage method where the elements are represented as dense blocks. This can significantly increase the performance of both serial and parallel versions of solvers based on the block AMG method.

3 Numerical Experiments

We consider the parallel efficiency of the OpenMP implementation for the block version of AMG method with the Bi-Conjugate Gradient Stabilized (BiCGStab) iterations. The analysis is conducted by evaluating both the overall solution time and the run-time performance of each individual stage, including the setup and iterations. We study the convergence and parallel efficiency of the proposed method for a variety of problems of mathematical physics with different block sizes from 2 to 6.

For almost all parallel tests we have used the cluster of Marchuk Institute of Numerical Mathematics of the Russian Academy of Sciences (INM RAS) [42] with Compute Node Arbyte Alkazar R2Q50 G5, two 20-core processors Intel Xeon Gold 6230@2.10 GHz.

Tables below contain the following parameters: T is the overall solution time in seconds; Ts is the total setup phase time; Tit is the total time for iterations; Nit is the number of iterations; Lvl is the number of levels; S is the actual speedup with respect to the serial run; Ss is the actual speedup for the setup stage; Sit is the actual speedup for the iterative solution stage. The convergence tolerances for the BiCGStab method are $\tau_{\text{abs}} = 10^{-10}$ and $\tau_{\text{rel}} = 10^{-12}$.

3.1 Problems Considered

We have evaluated the performance of our approach by considering several test problems of various physics. For each problem three grids of increasing size is used, subsequently denoted by the digits 1, 2, and 3.

Problem 1 (Ph2-z). *Two-phase oil recovery problem.*
The O-type multi-point flux approximation for non-$\mathbb{K}$-orthogonal polyhedral grids [43] is considered. Fully-implicit cell-centered finite-volume discretization method is described in [44]. Two wells are located in the corners of quarter-five spot problem with heterogeneous anisotropic permeability tensor. The test case is described in [45, Sect. 4.2]. The mesh sizes of quasi two-dimensional grids are $16 \times 16 \times 1$, $32 \times 32 \times 1$, and $64 \times 64 \times 1$, the respective time step sizes are 2.0, 1.0, and 0.5 days. The linear systems from the 13-th time step were considered: Ph2-z1, Ph2-z2, and Ph2-z3. The last number at the linear system name is the number of the mesh.

We consider two-phase dead-oil problem

$$\partial_t(\phi(p)\rho_\alpha(p)S_\alpha) - \operatorname{div}\left(\rho_\alpha(p)k_{r\alpha}(S_\alpha)\mu_\alpha(p)^{-1}\mathbb{K}\nabla p\right) = q_\alpha, \quad \alpha = w, o, \tag{7}$$

where p is the water pressure and S_o is the oil saturation with constraint $S_w + S_o = 1$. The considered linear system has two unknowns (water pressure and oil saturation), the corresponding block size is $\mathfrak{b} = 2$.

Problem 2 (Ph3-injg). *Three-phase black-oil recovery with gas injection.*
Two wells are located in the corners of quarter-five spot problem. Gas is injected

at the well in the bottom-left corner. The same problem with heterogeneous anisotropic permeability tensor is considered. The test case is described in [45, Sect. 4.2] with the black oil properties from [46]. The same grids $16 \times 16 \times 1$, $32 \times 32 \times 1$, and $64 \times 64 \times 1$ are considered, the respective time step sizes are 0.0008, 0.0004, and 0.0002 days. The linear systems from the 8-th time step were considered: Ph3-injg1, Ph3-injg2, and Ph3-injg3.

The system (7) is extended with the equation for gas:

$$\partial_t \left(\phi \rho_g S_g + \phi R_s \rho_{og} S_o\right) - \operatorname{div}\left(\left(\rho_g k_{rg} \mu_g^{-1} + R_s \rho_{og} k_{ro} \mu_o^{-1}\right) \mathbb{K} \nabla p\right) = q_g, \tag{8}$$

see [46] for more details.

The unknowns correspond to oil pressure, water saturation, and either gas saturation or bubble-point pressure, depending on the local physical model state [46]. The block size is $\mathfrak{b} = 3$.

Problem 3 (Ph3-injw). *Three-phase black-oil recovery with water injection.* The test case is similar to Ph3-injg, while water is injected. The same grids $16 \times 16 \times 1$, $32 \times 32 \times 1$, and $64 \times 64 \times 1$ are considered, the respective time step sizes are 0.002, 0.001, and 0.0005 days. The linear systems from the 13-th time step were considered: Ph3-injw1, Ph3-injw2, and Ph3-injw3. The system solved is (7)–(8). The block size is $\mathfrak{b} = 3$.

Problem 4 (Ccfv-sd, Ccfv-sh, Ccfv-st). *Linear elasticity: beam under shear.*
A cell-centered finite-volume (Ccfv) method for the stationary heterogeneous anisotropic linear elasticity problem for compressible materials is considered (see [47, Sect. 9.7]).

We exploit three different types of grids. The first one is the hexahedral grid with regular cubic cells of sizes $4 \times 4 \times 20$, $8 \times 8 \times 40$, $16 \times 16 \times 80$. The second one is the tetrahedral grid (each cube is split into 6 tetra) of sizes $4 \times 4 \times 20 \times 6$, $8 \times 8 \times 40 \times 6$, $16 \times 16 \times 80 \times 6$. The third ones are the corresponding dual to tet grids of sizes 525, 3321, and 23409.

The following set of linear systems were considered: Ccfv-sd, Ccfv-sh, and Ccfv-st. Here "s" means shear, "h", "t", and "d" stand for hexahedral, tetrahedral, and dual grids, respectively.

The following system is solved

$$-\operatorname{\mathbf{div}}(\mathbf{C} : \epsilon) = \mathbf{b}, \quad \epsilon = \frac{\mathbf{u}\nabla^T + \nabla \mathbf{u}^T}{2}, \tag{9}$$

for displacement $\mathbf{u}$, subject to appropriate boundary conditions. The unknowns are the components of displacement vector ($\mathfrak{b} = 3$).

Problem 5 (Ccfv-td, Ccfv-th, Ccfv-tt). *Linear elasticity: beam under torsion.*
A cell-centered finite-volume (Ccfv) method for the stationary heterogeneous anisotropic linear elasticity problem for compressible materials is considered (see

[47, Sect. 9.8]). The system to be solved is (9). The unknowns are the components of displacement vector ($\mathfrak{b} = 3$).

The same three sets of grids are considered. The respective set of linear systems is Ccfv-td, Ccfv-th, and Ccfv-tt. Here the first "t" means torsion, while the last "h", "t", and "d" stand for hex, tet, and dual grids, respectively.

Problem 6 (NS-t). *Navier–Stokes flow in a tube.*
The Poiseuille flow through a cylindrical pipe is considered (see [48,49] and [50, Sects. 3.3, 4.3, A.6]. We use the prismatic mesh for a cylinder with radius 1/2 and length 5.

The following system is solved

$$\partial_t \rho \mathbf{u} + \mathbf{div}\left(\rho \mathbf{u}\mathbf{u}^T - \mu \nabla \mathbf{u} + \mathbb{I}p\right) = \mathbf{0}, \quad \mathrm{div}\,(\mathbf{u}) = 0$$

for velocity $\mathbf{u}$ and pressure p, subject to appropriate boundary conditions.

The unknowns are three velocity components and pressure ($\mathfrak{b} = 4$). Mesh sizes are 820, 5600, and 40720, the respective time step sizes are 1, 0.5, and 0.25 sec.

Problem 7 (Rigid-s). *Stationary incompressible elasticity: beam under shear.*
As the incompressible linear elasticity problem we consider the equation for the elastic body equilibrium [50, Sect. 3.1, 4.1, A.1].

The following system is solved

$$-\,\mathbf{div}\,(\boldsymbol{\sigma} - \mathbb{I}p) = \mathbf{g}, \quad K^{-1}p + \mathrm{div}\,(\mathbf{u}) = 0, \quad \mathbf{S} : \boldsymbol{\sigma} = \frac{\mathbf{u}\nabla^T + \nabla \mathbf{u}^T}{2}, \tag{10}$$

for displacement $\mathbf{u}$ and structural pressure p, closed with the appropriate boundary conditions. The set of unknowns are displacement vector and structural pressure ($\mathfrak{b} = 4$). Mesh sizes are $8 \times 8 \times 20$, $16 \times 16 \times 40$, and $32 \times 32 \times 80$.

Problem 8 (Rigid-t). *Stationary incompressible elasticity: beam under torsion.*
As the incompressible linear elasticity problem we consider the equation for the elastic body equilibrium [50, Sect. 3.1, 4.1, A.2]. System (10) is solved. The unknowns are displacement vector and structural pressure ($\mathfrak{b} = 4$). Mesh sizes are $8 \times 8 \times 20$, $16 \times 16 \times 40$, and $32 \times 32 \times 80$.

Problem 9 (Biot). *Biot poroelasticity problem.*
We study the interaction between a compressible fluid and a compressible porous body in the absence of gravitational forces (see [21] and [50, Sects. 3.2, 4.2, A.3]). Mesh sizes are $22 \times 22 \times 1$, $46 \times 46 \times 1$, $94 \times 94 \times 1$, the respective time step sizes are 4, 2, and 1 sec.

The system of Biot equations is solved

$$-\,\mathbf{div}\,(\mathbf{C} : \epsilon - Bp) = \mathbf{g}, \quad M^{-1}\partial_t p + B : \partial_t \epsilon - \mathrm{div}\left(\mu^{-1}\mathbb{K}\nabla p\right) = q, \tag{11}$$

for displacement $\mathbf{u}$ and fluid pressure p, closed with the appropriate boundary conditions. Here ϵ is defined as in (9). The unknowns are displacement vector and fluid pressure ($\mathfrak{b} = 4$).

Problem 10 (Poromech). *Barry & Mercer poromechanics problem.*
We consider a Barry & Mercer test for Biot system of equations. See description of the problem with pulsating source in [21, Sect. 5.4]. Mesh sizes are $22 \times 22 \times 1$, $46 \times 46 \times 1$, $94 \times 94 \times 1$, the respective time step sizes are 0.04, 0.02, and 0.01 sec. The system is (11) discretized with the method from [21]. The unknowns are displacement vector and fluid pressure ($\mathfrak{b} = 4$). The linear system stored from the first time step.

Problem 11 (Maxwell). *Non-stationary Maxwell problem.*
The system of Maxwell equations describes the interaction of electric and magnetic fields [50, Sects. 3.5, 4.5, A.8]. The bounded square cavity problem with the parameter $k = 1/24$ is considered. The Maxwell system is

$$\partial_t \epsilon \mathbf{E} + \boldsymbol{\sigma} \mathbf{E} = \nabla \times \mathbf{H} - \mathbf{I}, \quad \partial_t \boldsymbol{\mu} \mathbf{H} = -\nabla \times \mathbf{E}, \tag{12}$$

solved for electric field **E** and magnetic field **H** with the appropriate boundary conditions. The primary unknowns are electric and magnetic field vectors ($\mathfrak{b} = 6$). Mesh sizes are $8 \times 8 \times 8$, $16 \times 16 \times 16$, and $32 \times 32 \times 32$, the respective time step sizes are 0.04, 0.02, and 0.01 sec.

3.2 Convergence Results

The structural properties of all the test problems are summarized in Table 1. Here, the problem name ends with the digits 1, 2, and 3 indicating the dimension of the linear system, $\mathfrak{b}$ is the block size, N is the matrix dimension, Nnd is the number of negative diagonal elements, Nnz is the total number of nonzero elements, Nzr = Nnz/N is the average number of nonzero elements per row. One can see the wide range of problem parameters. The block size $\mathfrak{b}$ varies from 2 to 6, matrix dimension are from less than a thousand to more than 600 thousand, the average number of nonzeros per row is from 6 to 164. Most of the systems are the saddle-point ones. The 3-phase problems contain on the main diagonal both positive and negative elements.

Table 2 contain the convergence results for both the block Gauss–Seidel (BGS) method and block AMG (BAMG) method for serial run on INM RAS cluster [42]. The minimal total solution time T is marked in bold. In the present table, we mainly check the reliability of the block AMG method. It can be seen that in most cases, especially for the largest and most complex problems, the BAMG method solves faster. For BGS method, some of the problems fail to converge (Ccfv-st, Ccfv-tt, Rigid-s, and Rigid-t1). In contrast, for the BAMG method all the linear systems are successfully solved, which confirms the high robustness of the proposed method. Both the number of iterations (Nit) and the solution time (T) for BAMG method in most cases are less then that for BGS one. Besides, the number of iterations for BAMG method is almost independent of the problem size (indicated by the last digit in the problem name) as it is by the theoretical considerations.

Table 1. The structural properties of the test problems.

Problem	$\mathfrak{b}$	N	Nnd	Nnz	Nzr	Description
Ph2-z1	2	512	0	3695	7.2	Two-phase oil recovery problem
Ph2-z2	2	2048	0	12576	6.1	
Ph2-z3	2	8192	0	46427	5.6	
Ph3-injg1	3	768	512	10344	13.4	Three-phase black-oil recovery
Ph3-injg2	3	3072	2048	42702	13.9	(gas injection)
Ph3-injg3	3	12288	8192	173454	14.1	
Ph3-injw1	3	768	502	10308	13.4	Three-phase black-oil recovery
Ph3-injw2	3	3072	2032	42652	13.8	(water injection)
Ph3-injw3	3	12288	8162	173330	14.1	
Ccfv-sd1	3	1575	0	55053	34.9	Beam under shear (dual)
Ccfv-sd2	3	9963	0	391473	39.2	
Ccfv-sd3	3	70227	0	2945241	41.9	
Ccfv-sh1	3	960	0	35127	36.5	Beam under shear (hex)
Ccfv-sh2	3	7680	0	291739	37.9	
Ccfv-sh3	3	61440	0	2336498	38.0	
Ccfv-st1	3	5760	0	222144	38.5	Beam under shear (tet)
Ccfv-st2	3	46080	0	1922481	41.7	
Ccfv-st3	3	368640	0	15977699	43.3	
Ccfv-td1	3	1575	0	55053	34.9	Beam under torsion (dual)
Ccfv-td2	3	9963	0	391473	39.2	
Ccfv-td3	3	70227	0	2945241	41.9	
Ccfv-th1	3	960	0	35012	36.4	Beam under torsion (hex)
Ccfv-th2	3	7680	0	291997	38.0	
Ccfv-th3	3	61440	0	2335467	38.0	
Ccfv-tt1	3	5760	0	222145	38.5	Beam under torsion (tet)
Ccfv-tt2	3	46080	0	1922484	41.7	
Ccfv-tt3	3	368640	0	15977695	43.3	
NS-t1	4	11040	0	1709692	154.8	Navier–Stokes flow in a tube
NS-t2	4	80640	0	13248296	164.2	
NS-t3	4	614400	0	97042502	157.9	
Rigid-s1	4	5120	0	190022	37.1	Incompressible elasticity
Rigid-s2	4	40960	0	1319887	32.2	(beam under shear)
Rigid-s3	4	327680	0	9799749	29.9	
Rigid-t1	4	5120	0	190058	37.1	Incompressible elasticity
Rigid-t2	4	40960	0	1319758	32.2	(beam under torsion)
Rigid-t3	4	327680	0	9799179	29.9	
Biot1	4	1936	0	38246	19.7	Biot poroelasticity problem
Biot2	4	8464	0	167070	19.7	
Biot3	4	35344	0	791236	22.3	
Poromech1	4	1936	0	47175	24.3	Barry & Mercer poromechanics
Poromech2	4	8464	0	209244	24.7	
Poromech3	4	35344	0	930623	26.3	
Maxwell1	6	3072	0	59136	19.2	Non-stationary Maxwell problem
Maxwell2	6	24576	0	519168	21.1	
Maxwell3	6	196608	0	4337664	22.0	

Table 2. The convergence of block Gauss–Seidel (BGS) method vs. block AMG method for serial run on INM RAS cluster. †Tolerance not met after 5000 iterations.

	Block Gauss–Seidel				Block AMG				
Problem	T	Ts	Tit	Nit	T	Ts	Tit	Nit	Lvl
Ph2-z1	**0.0057**	0.0031	0.0025	11	0.0066	0.0031	0.0039	11	4
Ph2-z2	0.0433	0.0020	0.0413	138	**0.0352**	0.0196	0.0163	14	5
Ph2-z3	0.2096	0.0079	0.2017	243	**0.1296**	0.0401	0.0907	29	6
Ph3-injg1	**0.0018**	0.0005	0.0013	7	0.0157	0.0114	0.0044	4	4
Ph3-injg2	**0.0078**	0.0010	0.0068	16	0.0397	0.0231	0.0166	9	5
Ph3-injg3	**0.0451**	0.0039	0.0412	22	0.2398	0.0576	0.1825	24	7
Ph3-injw1	**0.0016**	0.0003	0.0013	7	0.0119	0.0084	0.0036	4	4
Ph3-injw2	**0.0077**	0.0012	0.0065	15	0.0254	0.0153	0.0101	6	5
Ph3-injw3	**0.0425**	0.0032	0.0393	21	0.2401	0.0581	0.1821	24	7
Ccfv-sd1	**0.0668**	0.0029	0.0639	124	0.1011	0.0118	0.0943	81	3
Ccfv-sd2	**0.8879**	0.0061	0.8818	283	3.3774	0.1037	3.2912	397	4
Ccfv-sd3	**19.7192**	0.0465	19.6727	576	22.0412	0.7422	21.3195	246	5
Ccfv-sh1	**0.0450**	0.0024	0.0426	112	0.0519	0.0148	0.0393	36	3
Ccfv-sh2	**0.5654**	0.0064	0.5590	245	0.9268	0.1538	0.7778	88	4
Ccfv-sh3	23.0770	0.0501	23.0269	912	**6.4724**	1.1224	5.3551	55	5
Ccfv-st1	0.5357	0.0040	0.5317	308	**0.4421**	0.0672	0.3806	78	4
Ccfv-st2	—	0.0481	—	>5000†	**18.4790**	0.4460	18.0597	331	5
Ccfv-st3	—	0.2646	—	>5000†	**135.8585**	3.7420	132.1320	201	6
Ccfv-td1	**0.0501**	0.0012	0.0489	120	0.0678	0.0130	0.0583	48	3
Ccfv-td2	2.7013	0.0065	2.6947	865	**0.5937**	0.1087	0.4906	58	4
Ccfv-td3	54.8548	0.0468	54.8080	1638	**6.6849**	0.7593	5.9316	66	5
Ccfv-th1	0.0897	0.0009	0.0889	346	**0.0540**	0.0146	0.0424	38	3
Ccfv-th2	0.6018	0.0058	0.5960	260	**0.5158**	0.1311	0.3890	47	4
Ccfv-th3	13.8676	0.0623	13.8053	537	**9.0975**	1.1113	7.9927	83	5
Ccfv-tt1	1.8574	0.0045	1.8528	1076	**0.6177**	0.0686	0.5585	111	4
Ccfv-tt2	—	0.0349	—	>5000†	**6.8887**	0.4479	6.4533	116	5
Ccfv-tt3	—	0.2650	—	>5000†	**65.2358**	3.7711	61.4776	93	6
NS-t1	0.6748	0.4542	0.2206	5	**0.6716**	0.4497	0.2224	5	4
NS-t2	5.4737	3.7791	1.6946	4	**5.3593**	3.6682	1.6915	4	5
NS-t3	52.9388	30.9024	22.0363	6	**52.0222**	30.0262	21.9968	6	6
Rigid-s1	—	0.0133	—	>5000†	**0.4980**	0.1344	0.3672	47	4
Rigid-s2	—	0.0485	—	>5000†	**4.8017**	0.9292	3.8779	50	5
Rigid-s3	—	0.3718	—	>5000†	**105.3866**	8.1746	97.2249	113	6
Rigid-t1	—	0.0168	—	>5000†	**0.4640**	0.1340	0.3341	43	4
Rigid-t2	—	0.0569	—	>5000†	**5.5706**	0.9357	4.6395	59	5
Rigid-t3	—	0.3654	—	>5000†	**127.0479**	8.1730	118.8905	138	6
Biot1	**0.0213**	0.0018	0.0195	53	0.0286	0.0171	0.0123	8	3
Biot2	0.1569	0.0047	0.1522	85	**0.1189**	0.0648	0.0550	9	4
Biot3	1.6261	0.0194	1.6067	183	**0.6088**	0.2695	0.3406	11	5
Poromech1	**0.0304**	0.0022	0.0282	52	0.0444	0.0320	0.0133	8	3
Poromech2	0.1751	0.0047	0.1704	84	**0.1434**	0.0899	0.0545	8	4
Poromech3	1.9545	0.0200	1.9344	201	**0.6932**	0.3040	0.3907	12	5
Maxwell1	**0.0085**	0.0027	0.0057	7	0.0730	0.0599	0.0133	3	3
Maxwell2	**0.0641**	0.0243	0.0399	7	0.8872	0.7182	0.1692	3	4
Maxwell3	**0.6453**	0.0919	0.5534	7	6.6868	5.1525	1.5345	3	6

We shall note, that Ccfv and Rigid problems are steady-state ones, whereas all the rest of the problems are non-stationary. We find that steady-state problems require much more iterations to converge due to problem complexity.

Parallelization of the AMG method is a difficult task, because at the setup stage and the iterative solution stage there is a transition from the upper level with a sufficiently large matrix dimension to the lowest level, at which there can be only a few tens of unknowns. Efficient parallelization is only possible for very large problems, with several ten or hundred thousand unknowns per computational thread. There are MPI and MPI+OpenMP implementations of AMG for quite a large number of computational cores (see [51]), but they use additional information on the grid structure. However, we tried to explore the parallelism of the BAMG method on our set of moderate-dimensional examples without such an information.

The parallel properties of BAMG method are presented in Table 3. It can be seen that in all cases there is a confident speedup in calculations when applying parallelization over OpenMP threads. The numerical experiments were carried out on the INM RAS cluster, utilizing 16 threads. One can see, that speedup 10.58 is achieved for one of the most difficult Rigid-t3 problem.

Table 3. The convergence of block AMG method for parallel run for 16 OpenMP threads on INM RAS cluster for the 3-rd problems of the set.

Problem	T	Ts	Tit	Nit	Lvl	S	Ss	Sit
Ph2-z3	0.1224	0.0323	0.0919	27	6	1.06	1.24	0.99
Ph3-injg3	0.1762	0.0535	0.1231	23	7	1.36	1.08	1.48
Ph3-injw3	0.1809	0.0529	0.1284	24	7	1.33	1.10	1.42
Ccfv-sd3	8.7520	0.3974	8.4062	546	5	2.52	1.87	2.54
Ccfv-sh3	1.8455	0.5675	1.2839	56	5	3.51	1.98	4.17
Ccfv-st3	17.9705	1.7372	16.2523	186	6	7.56	2.15	8.13
Ccfv-td3	1.8186	0.4040	1.4218	70	5	3.68	1.88	4.17
Ccfv-th3	2.6281	0.5804	2.0560	95	5	3.46	1.91	3.89
Ccfv-tt3	9.7643	1.5889	8.1925	93	6	6.68	2.37	7.50
NS-t3	16.3802	13.4383	2.9429	6	6	3.18	2.23	7.47
Rigid-s3	35.4617	3.0153	32.4814	312	6	2.97	2.71	2.99
Rigid-t3	12.0035	3.0038	9.0131	87	6	**10.58**	2.72	13.19
Biot3	0.2299	0.1434	0.0881	11	5	2.65	1.88	3.87
Poromech3	0.2692	0.1747	0.0959	12	5	2.58	1.74	4.07
Maxwell3	2.5852	2.3507	0.2347	3	6	2.59	2.19	6.54

For a more detailed analysis of parallel efficiency, we demonstrate the actual speedup of the block AMG method for Rigid-t3 problem on several clusters (see Fig. 1). For our experiments, we used the mentioned above INM RAS cluster with 2x20-cores processors, as well as Lomonosov-2 supercomputer of Lomonosov

Moscow State University with 14-core Intel Haswell-EP E5-2697v3@2.6 GHz with processors, MVS-10Q cluster of the Joint Supercomputer Center of the Russian Academy of Sciences, equipped with 14-core Intel Xeon E5-2690@2.9 GHz processors, S-HPC cluster of the Sechenov University with 2x26-core Intel Xeon Gold 6230R@2.10 GHz processors, and two clusters of CKP "Informatics" of Federal Research Center "Computer Science and Control" of the Russian Academy of Sciences equipped with 2x16-cores Intel Xeon E5-2683@2.1 GHz processors and Huawei Taishan 200 nodes with 2x64-cores Kunpeng 920@2.6 GHz ARM processors.

The nonmonotonic behavior of speedup for the INM RAS cluster is associated with jumps in the number of iterations. Some results of superlinear speedup for $p = 2, 3, 4$ are not so important and are due to the same reason. The maximum speedup of 10.95 is obtained at $p = 20$. It should be noted that the speedup behavior of both 14-cores MVS-10Q and MSU-L2 clusters with much the same processors are quite similar. The behavior of speedup for MVS-10Q cluster strictly monotonic with a maximal speedup of 5.91, while the speedup behavior of MSU-L2 supercomputer, CKP, S-HPC, and ARM cluster are rather smooth with the maximal speedups of 6.28, 5.44, 8.51, and 7.97, respectively. It should be noted that pinning of thread to a core was not used. Insufficiently high speedup for large number of threads is caused by memory access problems and the presence of stages with the solution of subproblems of small dimension.

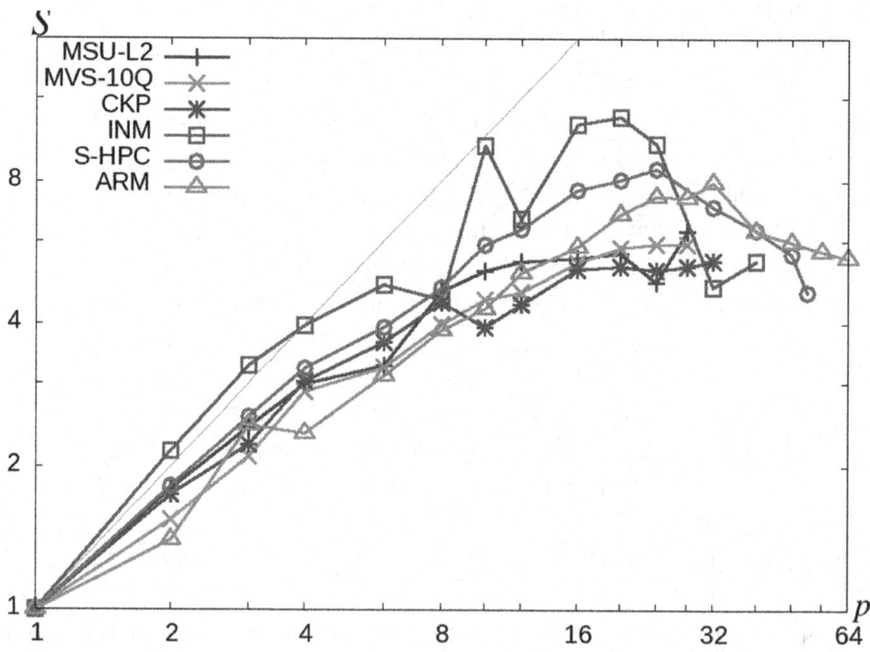

Fig. 1. Actual speedup of block AMG on 14-cores MSU-L2, 14-cores MVS-10Q, 2x16-cores CKP, 2x20-cores INM, 2x26-cores S-HPC, and 2x64-cores ARM clusters for Rigid-t3 problem.

4 Conclusions

This work presents a straightforward extension of scalar algebraic multigrid method into block version. Preliminary tests on a number of complex problems demonstrate very promising and successful results of the method application.

In this work we considered shared-memory parallelism which proves to be difficult, especially for the setup phase. Despite this, the method showed reasonable parallelism on large-sized problems. These results will be used in hybrid distributed-shared version of the method applicable to supercomputers.

We plan to further enhance the method and introduce reduction of unknowns from the coarse space within the blocks, which requires operating with variable-sized blocks. Another promising direction is to apply eigen-decomposition to split each block into weak and strong component and enhance the interpolation formula. At last a block version of adaptive bootstrap algebraic multigrid method may follow. If such computationally intensive efforts will significantly improve the convergence, those could be performed at accelerators.

Acknowledgements. The present work has been supported by the Russian Science Foundation under grant No. 21-71-20024. The research is carried out using the computer facilities of Marchuk Institute of Numerical Mathematics of the Russian Academy of Sciences, CKP "Informatics" of Federal Research Center "Computer Science and Control" of the Russian Academy of Sciences, the Joint Supercomputer Center of the Russian Academy of Sciences, as well as Sechenov University and Lomonosov Moscow State University.

References

1. Fedorenko, R.P.: A relaxation method for solving elliptic difference equations. Zh. Vychisl. Mat. Mat. Fiz. **1**(5), 922–927 (1961). Comput. Math. Math. Phys. **1**(4), 1092–1096 (1962)
2. Fedorenko, R.P.: The speed of convergence of one iterative process. USSR Comput. Math. Math. Phys. **4**(3), 227–235 (1964)
3. Fedorenko, R.P.: Iterative methods for elliptic difference equations. Russ. Math. Surv. **28**, 129–195 (1973)
4. Bakhvalov, N.S.: On the convergence of a relaxation method with natural constraints on the elliptic operator. USSR Comput. Math. Math. Phys. **6**(5), 101–135 (1996)
5. Brandt, A., McCormick, S., Ruge, J.: Algebraic multigrid (AMG) for automatic algorithm design and problem solution. Report, Comput. Studies, Colorado State University, Ft. Collins (1982)
6. Hackbusch, W.: Multi-grid Methods and Applications, vol. 4. Springer, Cham (2013/1985). https://doi.org/10.1007/978-3-662-02427-0
7. Gries, S.: System-AMG approaches for industrial fully and adaptive implicit oil reservoir simulations. Dissertation, Universität zu Köln (2015)
8. Gries, S.: On the convergence of System-AMG in reservoir simulation. SPE J. **23**(2), 589–597 (2018)

9. Shu, S., Liu, M., Xu, X., Yue, X., Li, S.: Algebraic multigrid block triangular preconditioning for multidimensional three-temperature radiation diffusion equations. Adv. Appl. Math. Mech. **13**(5), 0210–1226 (2021)
10. Konshin, I., Terekhov, K.: Sparse system solution methods for complex problems. In: Malyshkin, V. (ed.) PaCT 2021. LNCS, vol. 12942, pp. 53–73. Springer, Cham (2021). https://doi.org/10.1007/978-3-030-86359-3_5
11. Cusini, M., Lukyanov, A., Natvig, J.R., Hajibeygi, H.: A constrained pressure residual multiscale (CPR-MS) compositional solver. In: Proceedings of ECMOR XIV-14th European Conference on the Mathematics of Oil Recovery. Catania, Sicily, Italy (2014)
12. Lacroix, S., Vassilevski, Y.V., Wheeler, M.F.: Decoupling preconditioners in the implicit parallel accurate reservoir simulator (IPARS). Numer. Lin. Alg. with Appl. **8**(8), 537–549 (2001)
13. Gries, S.: System-AMG approaches for industrial fully and adaptive implicit oil reservoir simulations. Ph.D. thesis. Der Universität zu Köln, Köln (2016)
14. Kayum, S., Cancellierei, M., Rogowski, M., Al-Zawawi, A.: Application of algebraic multigrid in fully implicit massive reservoir simulations. In: Proceedings of SPE Europec Featured at 81st EAGE Conference and Exhibition. SPE-195472-MS (2019)
15. Gries, S.: Algebraic wavefront parallelization for ILU(0) smoothing in reservoir simulation. ECMOR XVII **1**, 1–17 (2020)
16. Bui, Q.M., Elman, H.C., Moulton, J.D.: Algebraic multigrid preconditioners for multiphase flow in porous media. SIAM J. Sci. Comput. **39**(5), 5662–5680 (2017)
17. Bui, Q.M., Wang, L., Osei-Kuffuor, D.: Algebraic multigrid preconditioners for two-phase flow in porous media with phase transitions. Adv. Water Resourc. **114**, 19–28 (2018)
18. Gries, S., Metsch, B., Terekhov, K.M., Tomin, P.: System-AMG for fully coupled reservoir simulation with geomechanics. In: SPE Reservoir Simulation Conference (2019)
19. Bui, Q.M., Osei-Kuffuor, D., Castelletto, N., White, J.A.: A scalable multigrid reduction framework for multiphase poromechanics of heterogeneous media. SIAM J. Sci. Comput. **42**(2), 8379–8396 (2020)
20. Terekhov, K.M.: Cell-centered finite-volume method for heterogeneous anisotropic poromechanics problem. J. Comp. Appl. Math. **365**, 112357 (2020)
21. Terekhov, K.M., Vassilevski, Y.V.: Finite volume method for coupled subsurface flow problems, II: poroelasticity. J. Comput. Phys. **462**, 111225 (2022)
22. Uroić, T., Jasak, H.: Block-selective algebraic multigrid for implicitly coupled pressure-velocity system. Comput. Fluids **167**, 100–110 (2018)
23. Mangani, L., Buchmayr, M., Darwish, M.: Development of a novel fully coupled solver in OpenFOAM: steady-state incompressible turbulent flows. Numer. Heat Transfer, Part B: Fundam. **66**(1), 1–20 (2014)
24. Mangani, L., Buchmayr, M., Darwish, M.: A block coupled solver development for hydraulic machinery applications. IOP Conf. Ser. Earth Environ. Sci. **22**(2), 022002 (2014)
25. Cardiff, P., Tuković, Ž., Jasak, H., Ivanković, A.: A block-coupled finite volume methodology for linear elasticity and unstructured meshes. Comput. Struct. **175**, 100–122 (2016)
26. Vanka, S.P.: Block-implicit multigrid solution of Navier–Stokes equations in primitive variables. J. Comput. Phys. **65**(1), 138–158 (1986)
27. Olshanskii, M.: Multigrid analysis for the time dependent Stokes problem. Math. Comput. **81**(277), 57–79 (2012)

28. Elman, H.C., Golub, G.H.: Inexact and preconditioned Uzawa algorithms for saddle point problems. SIAM J. Numer. Anal. **31**(6), 1645–1661 (1994)
29. Braess, D., Sarazin, R.: An efficient smoother for the Stokes problem. Appl. Numer. Math. **23**(1), 3–19 (1997)
30. Metsch, B.: Algebraic multigrid (AMG) for saddle point systems. Dissertation, Universitäts und Landesbibliothek Bonn (2013)
31. Metsch, B., Nick, F., Kuhnert, J.: Algebraic multigrid for the finite pointset method. Comput. Visual. Sci. **23**(1), 1–14 (2020)
32. Webster, R.: Stabilisation of AMG solvers for saddle-point stokes problems. Int. J. Numer. Meth. Fluids **81**(10), 640–653 (2016)
33. Webster, R.: CLC in AMG solvers for saddle-point problems. Numer. Linear Algebra Appl. **25**(2), e2142 (2018)
34. Burstedde, C., Fonseca, J.A., Metsch, B.: An AMG saddle point preconditioner with application to mixed Poisson problems on adaptive quad/cube meshes. arXiv preprint, arXiv:1901.05830 (2019)
35. Konshin, I., Terekhov, K.: Distributed parallel bootstrap adaptive algebraic multigrid method. In: Voevodin, V., Sobolev, S., Yakobovskiy, M., Shagaliev, R. (eds.) RuSCDays 2022. LNCS, vol. 13708, pp. 92–111. Springer, Cham (2022). https://doi.org/10.1007/978-3-031-22941-1_7
36. Ruge, J.W., Stüben, K.: Algebraic multigrid. In: Multigrid Methods, pp. 73–130. SIAM (1987)
37. Chang, Q., Wong, Y.S., Li, Z.: New interpolation formulas of using geometric assumptions in the algebraic multigrid method. Appl. Math. Comput. **50**(2–3), 223–254 (1992)
38. Chang, Q., Wong, Y.S.: A new approach for the algebraic multigrid method. Int. J. Comput. Math. **49**(3–4), 197–206 (1993)
39. Chang, Q., Wong, Y.S., Fu, H.: On the algebraic multigrid method. J. Comput. Phys. **125**(2), 279–292 (1996)
40. Brezina, M., Falgout, R., MacLachlan, S., Manteuffel, T., McCormick, S., Ruge, J.: Adaptive algebraic multigrid. SIAM J. Sci. Comput. **27**(4), 1261–1286 (2006)
41. Luby, M.: A simple parallel algorithm for the maximal independent set problem. SIAM J. Comput. **15**(4), 1036–1053 (1986)
42. INM RAS cluster. http://cluster2.inm.ras.ru/en
43. Aavatsmark, I.: An introduction to multipoint flux approximations for quadrilateral grids. Comput. Geosci. **6**, 405–432 (2002)
44. Terekhov, K., Vassilevski, Yu.: Two-phase water flooding simulations on dynamic adaptive octree grids with two-point nonlinear fluxes. Russ. J. Numer. Anal. Math. Modelling **28**(3), 267–288 (2013)
45. Nikitin, K., Terekhov, K., Vassilevski, Y.: A monotone nonlinear finite volume method for diffusion equations and multiphase flows. Comput. Geosci. **18**(3–4), 311–324 (2014)
46. Konshin, I., Terekhov, K.: Solution of large-scale black oil recovery problem in parallel using INMOST platform. In: Voevodin, V., Sobolev, S. (eds.) RuSCDays 2021. CCIS, vol. 1510, pp. 240–255. Springer, Cham (2021). https://doi.org/10.1007/978-3-030-92864-3_19
47. Terekhov, K.M., Tchelepi, H.A.: Cell-centered finite-volume method for elastic deformation of heterogeneous media with full-tensor properties. J. Comput. Appl. Math. **364**, 112331 (2020)
48. Terekhov, K.M.: Fully-implicit collocated finite-volume method for the unsteady incompressible Navier–Stokes problem. In: Garanzha, V.A., Kamenski, L., Si, H.

(eds.) Numerical Geometry, Grid Generation and Scientific Computing. LNCSE, vol. 143, pp. 361–374. Springer, Cham (2021). https://doi.org/10.1007/978-3-030-76798-3_23

49. Terekhov, K.M.: Presure boundary conditions in the collocated finite-volume method for the steady Navier–Stokes equations. Comput. Math. and Math. Phys. **62**(8), 1345–1355 (2022)
50. Terekhov, K.M.: General finite-volume framework for saddle-point problems of various physics. Russ. J. Numer. Anal. Math. Modelling **36**(6), 359–379 (2021)
51. Baker, A.H., Falgout, R.D., Kolev, T.V., Yang, U.M.: Scaling hypre's multigrid solvers to 100,000 cores. In: High-Performance Scientific Computing: Algorithms and Applications, pp. 261–279 (2012)

Computational Efficiency of Iterative Methods for Solving Inverse Problems

Alexander Goncharsky[1,2], Sergey Romanov[1,2], and Sergey Seryozhnikov[1,2](✉)

[1] Moscow Center of Fundamental and Applied Mathematics, Moscow, Russia
goncharQsrcc.msu.ru
[2] Lomonosov Moscow State University, Moscow, Russia
s2110sjQgmail.com

Abstract. The article is concerned with developing effective methods for solving inverse problems of wave tomography. The underlying mathematical model accounts for such physical effects as ultrasound diffraction, absorption, refraction and multiple scattering of ultrasound waves. Reconstructing a tomographic image using wave tomography involves solving a coefficient inverse problem for the wave equation. The objective is to minimize the residual functional between the measured wave field and the wave field computed for some approximate acoustic parameters of the inspected object. The residual functional may have local minima. To solve such problems, a multistage iterative gradient-based method is proposed. The method uses limited signal spectrum at first stages, ensuring the convergence of approximate solutions obtained at each stage to the sought-for solution. The proposed method is demonstrated on model problems of breast ultrasound tomographic imaging for early-stage cancer diagnosis. The iterative method is computationally expensive. Computational efficiency of the proposed method on multi-core CPU and GPU computing platforms is discussed.

Keywords: Ultrasound tomography · Coefficient inverse problem · Gradient descent method · Computational efficiency

1 Introduction

This study aims to develop efficient methods for solving inverse problems of ultrasound tomography. Important results in this field have been obtained over the recent years [1–5]. In these works, the wave tomography problem is posed as a coefficient inverse problem for a hyperbolic differential equation. The wave equation precisely describes pressure wave propagation, including diffraction, absorption, refraction and multiple scattering of ultrasound waves. Breakthrough results in wave tomography include the possibility of explicit calculation of the gradient of the residual functional, which represents the difference between the wave field registered by the receivers and the wave field which is simulated numerically using some given acoustic parameters of the object [2,6,7]. Given the

V. Voevodin et al. (Eds.): RuSCDays 2023, LNCS 14388, pp. 35–46, 2023.
https://doi.org/10.1007/978-3-031-49432-1_3

representation for the gradient, the residual functional can be minimized using iterative gradient descent methods [8,9]. Such inverse problem features a very large number of unknowns and high computational complexity. The computations can be efficiently parallelized, making it possible to employ modern parallel computing platforms for this task [10,11].

The residual functional in a typical case does not have to be convex and can have local minima, rendering conventional gradient-based algorithms for minimizing functionals ineffective. A number of publications are concerned with the problem of global minimization of functionals [12,13]. In general, such problems are unsolvable. In order to obtain an approximate solution, the proposed multistage iterative method (MSM) uses prior information that is common for a wide range of problems.

The multistage method gradually increases the sounding signal bandwidth from stage to stage. The first stage produces an approximate solution using low-frequency signal. This solution is used as the initial approximation for the gradient descent process at the second stage, and so on. The multistage approach ensures that the gradient descent process converges to the global minimum of the residual functional. The method has been tested on numerous model problems with the parameters chosen close to those used in medical ultrasound tomography, especially for detecting breast cancer at early stages, which is an important field of research in modern medicine.

2 Problem Statement

In this study we consider pressure waves propagating in liquid media and soft tissues. Such waves can be simulated numerically using the scalar wave model, which describes such physical processes as wave diffraction, absorption, refraction, and multiple scattering of waves with high accuracy. Using the equation (1), acoustic pressure $u(\boldsymbol{x}, \boldsymbol{p}, t)$ in the medium can be computed starting from initial conditions (2), assuming that the speed of sound in the medium $v(\boldsymbol{x})$ and the absorption coeffiicent $a(\boldsymbol{x})$ are known.

$$\frac{1}{v^2(\boldsymbol{x})} u_{tt}(\boldsymbol{x}, \boldsymbol{p}, t) + a(\boldsymbol{x}) u_t(\boldsymbol{x}, \boldsymbol{p}, t) - \Delta u(\boldsymbol{x}, \boldsymbol{p}, t) = \delta(\boldsymbol{x} - \boldsymbol{p}) g(t) \tag{1}$$

$$u(\boldsymbol{x}, \boldsymbol{p}, 0) = 0; \; u_t(\boldsymbol{x}, \boldsymbol{p}, 0) = 0. \tag{2}$$

Here, $\boldsymbol{x} \in \mathbb{R}^2$; Δ is the Laplacian operator on $\boldsymbol{x}$; $\boldsymbol{p}$ is the position of a point source of ultrasound waves. The sounding pulse $g(t)$ emitted by the source is represented by Dirac delta function $\delta(\boldsymbol{x} - \boldsymbol{p})$.

Figure 1 shows the scheme of a tomographic experiment. Ultrasound emitters 1 and receivers 2 are placed around the inspected object Q. The medium outside of the object is homogeneous with known parameters $v_0 = const$, $a_0 = 0$. The aim is to determine the acoustic parameters $v(\boldsymbol{x})$, $a(\boldsymbol{x})$ in the object, for $\boldsymbol{x} \in Q$, by measuring the waves scattered by the object on the boundary S. For each emitter located at a point $\boldsymbol{p}_j$, $j = 1, ..., M$, the registered data $U(\boldsymbol{s}, \boldsymbol{p}_j, t)$, $\boldsymbol{s} \in$ S

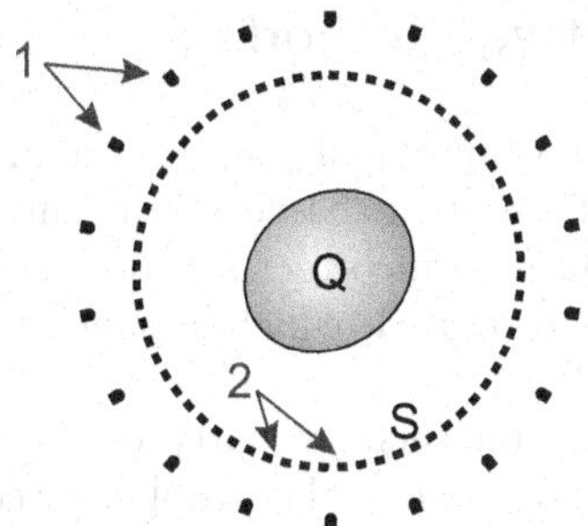

Fig. 1. The tomographic experiment scheme

represent the acoustic pressure registered by a receiver at point $\boldsymbol{s}$ at the time $t \in [0; T]$.

Substituting the parameters of the object $v(\boldsymbol{x})$, $a(\boldsymbol{x})$ into equation (1), the wave field $u(\boldsymbol{s}, \boldsymbol{p}_j, t)$ computed via solving the wave equation should be equal to the measured wave field $U(\boldsymbol{s}, \boldsymbol{p}_j, t)$. Thus, the problem of determining the acoustic parameters inside the object can be posed as a problem of minimizing the discrepancy between $U(\boldsymbol{s}, \boldsymbol{p}_j, t)$ and $u(\boldsymbol{s}, \boldsymbol{p}_j, t)$, which is represented by the residual functional:

$$\Phi(v, a) = \sum_{j=1}^{M} \frac{1}{2} \int_0^T \int_S \left(u(\boldsymbol{s}, \boldsymbol{p}_j, t) - U(\boldsymbol{s}, \boldsymbol{p}_j, t)\right)^2 \, \mathrm{d}\boldsymbol{s} \, \mathrm{d}t. \tag{3}$$

The wave field $u(\boldsymbol{s}, \boldsymbol{p}_j, t)$ computed by solving equations (1)–(2) depends on the coefficients $v(\boldsymbol{x})$ and $a(\boldsymbol{x})$ in the wave equation, so the residual functional also depends on $v(\boldsymbol{x})$ and $a(\boldsymbol{x})$. Coefficients $\{\bar{v}(\boldsymbol{x}), \bar{a}(\boldsymbol{x})\}$ that minimize the residual functional (3) constitute an approximate solution to the inverse problem: $\{\bar{v}(\boldsymbol{x}), \bar{a}(\boldsymbol{x})\} : \min\limits_{v(\boldsymbol{x}), a(\boldsymbol{x})} \Phi(v, a) = \Phi(\bar{v}, \bar{a})$. The gradient Φ' can be computed via solving equations very similar to the presented wave equation. These equations are described in [8,14]. Then the functional can be minimized using gradient descent methods.

The residual functional is summed for all the wave emitters; thus, there are no dependencies between the data gathered from different emitters. This feature of the method makes the computations highly parallelizable.

The wave equations are solved using a finite difference scheme

$$\frac{u_{ij}^{k+1} - 2u_{ij}^{k} + u_{ij}^{k-1}}{v_{ij}^{2} \tau^{2}} + a_{ij} \frac{u_{ij}^{k+1} - u_{ij}^{k-1}}{\tau} - \frac{\boldsymbol{L}_{ij}^{k}}{h^{2}} = 0.$$

This explicit scheme is of a second order of accuracy. Here i, j are discrete spatial coordinates; k is the current time step; h is the grid step and τ is the time step. Discrete Laplacian $\boldsymbol{L}_{ij}^{k}$ is computed using a 5×5-point fourth-order scheme according to [15].

3 Multistage Iterative Method

Local minima of the residual functional pose the main challenge in solving the inverse problem considered. Gradient-based minimization methods may stop at a local minimum and produce an incorrect solution. In this study, a multistage iterative method (MSM) is proposed, which expands the region of convergence of gradient descent methods.

The MSM method relies on such property of the inverse scattering problem that at extremely low frequencies the problem becomes linear. In practice, linear approximations like Born approximation can be successfully used if the wavelength is large enough compared to the object [16]. However, sounding frequencies required to obtain a sufficient spatial resolution for wave tomography are much higher than the frequency range in which linear approximations are applicable.

The proposed multistage method gradually increases the sounding signal bandwidth from stage to stage, starting from low frequencies. Initial stage use only lower frequencies of the signal spectrum, so that the average wavelength is long enough for the gradient descent method to converge. The approximate solution obtained at each stage is used as the initial approximation for the next stage. The multistage approach ensures that the gradient descent process converges to the global minimum of the residual functional.

The method has been tested on numerous model problems with the acoustic parameters close to those used in medical ultrasound tomography, especially for detecting breast cancer at early stages, which is an important field of research in modern medicine.

The following model problem illustrates the operation of the multistage method. The acoustic parameters of the numerical simulation were chosen similar to a breast imaging setup.

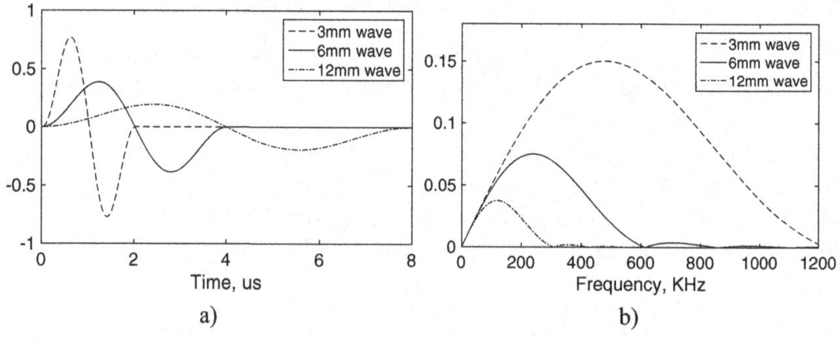

Fig. 2. Sounding signals: waveforms (a), frequency spectra (b)

Figure 2a shows the sounding signal waveforms used for the multistage method. The average wavelengths of the signals are 3 mm, 6 mm and 12 mm. The corresponding frequency spectra of sounding signals are shown in Fig. 2b. The smallest wavelength of 3 mm represents the actual broadband sounding pulse. The spectrum of the 6 mm (250 kHz) wave is a low-frequency part of the broadband spectrum, and the spectrum of the 12 mm (125 kHz) wave represents even smaller part of the broadband spectrum. Low-frequency sounding signals used for initial stages may be obtained via low-pass filtering of the broadband sounding pulse or via using dedicated low-frequency emitters.

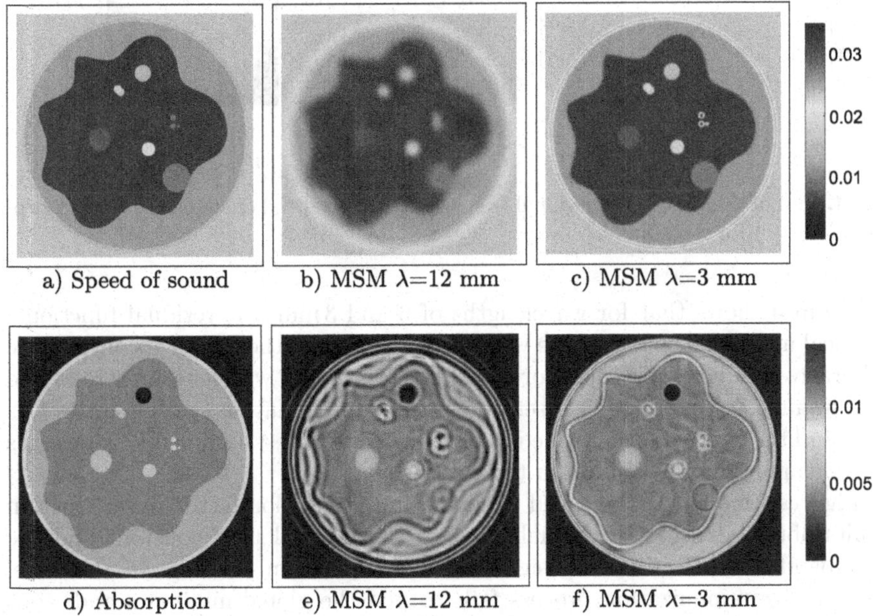

Fig. 3. Exact images (a,d); images reconstructed at the first stage (b,e) and at the last stage (c,f) of the multistage method. Top row (a,b,c) — speed of sound, bottom row (d,e,f) — absorption factor

Figure 3 shows the exact acoustic parameters of the simulated phantom (a,d) and the reconstructed sound speed and absorption images obtained using the MSM method. To ensure the conversence of the gradient descent process, for the the first stage only a frequency band near 125 kHz with a central wavelength λ=12 mm is selected. As the wavelength decreases from stage to stage, the image resolution and precision increases. The first stage (Fig. 3 b,e) produces a coarse approximation, and the last stage (Fig. 3 c,f) produces a high-resolution image. The quality of the absorption factor reconstruction (Fig. 3 e,f) is inferior to that of the sound speed image (Fig. 3 b,c) since the velocity coefficient $v(\boldsymbol{x})$ appears at the second time derivative in the wave equation (1), while the absorption factor $a(\boldsymbol{x})$ appears at the first time derivative of the wave field.

Figure 4a shows a one-dimensional profile of the residual functional $\Phi(\alpha)$ along a line passing through the initial approximation at $\alpha = 0$ and the exact solution at $\alpha = 1$. The acoustic parameters of the simulation for each α are computed as $\{v(\boldsymbol{x}), a(\boldsymbol{x})\} = \{v_0, a_0\} \cdot (1 - \alpha) + \{\bar{v}(\boldsymbol{x}), \bar{a}(\boldsymbol{x})\} \cdot \alpha$. The initial approximation is a constant $\{v_0, a_0\}$. At the exact solution $\{\bar{v}(\boldsymbol{x}), \bar{a}(\boldsymbol{x})\}$ the residual functional equals to zero.

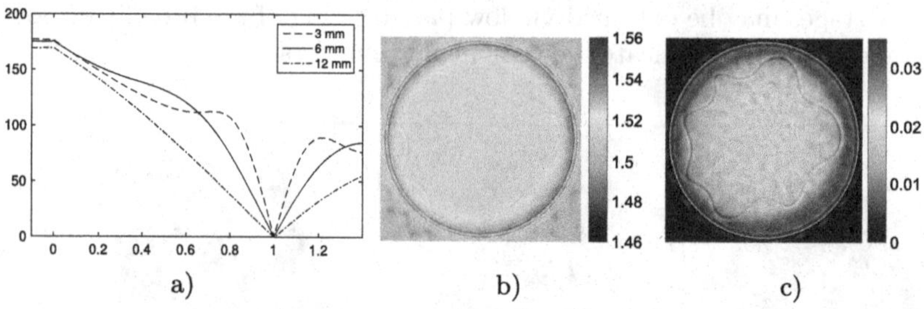

Fig. 4. Plot of the residual functional (a); reconstructed speed of sound (b) and absorption factor (c) for λ=3 mm

Figure 4 shows that for wavelengths of 6 and 3 mm, the residual functional has local minima. The longer the wavelength, the wider the region of convergence of iterative gradient descent algorithms. For the 12 mm wavelength there are no local minima in the range between the initial approximation (a constant in this case) and the exact solution. The gradient descent process successfully converges to some approximate solution in this case.

Figures 4(b,c) show the speed of sound and absorption factor reconstruction results obtained using the initial approximation equal to a constant and the broadband 500 kHz sounding signal with no spectrum limiting. In this case, the iterative minimization process fails to find the global minimum and stops at some local minimum of the functional, producing an incorrect solution. The gradient descent process converges as long as the initial approximation for each stage is sufficiently close to the solution, so that the wave phase difference is sufficiently small.

The presented example demonstrates that in breast ultrasound tomography the residual functional may have local minima, which may stop gradient-based minimizing methods from reaching the solution. The proposed multistage method relies on the fact that as the frequency of sounding signals decreases, the residual functional becomes convex. The convergence of the multistage method is ensured by choosing an appropriate low-frequency signal and small enough difference in wavelength between stages. In this study, the parameters of the method for breast ultrasound tomography in medicine have been determined.

4 Computational Efficiency of the Multistage Method

4.1 Parameters of the Multistage Method

The FDTD method used to solve the wave equations at each iteration is computationally expensive. For each emitter, thousands of time steps of wave simulation must be performed on a megapixel grid, amounting to a number of operations on the order of 10^{13} computed pixels per reconstructed imaging plane, or 10^{15} arithmetic operations. The multistage method was tested on CPU-based computing nodes with Intel Haswell-EP and Intel Xeon Gold 6240R (AVX-512) processors, and GPU-based nodes containing NVidia Tesla P100 and NVidia Tesla V100 GPUs as part of the Lomonosov-2 supercomputer of the Moscow State University [17].

In the presented example, 24 sounding wave sources were located on a circle around the object. The object is 80 mm in diameter. Table 1 summarizes the parameters of the multistage method used in numerical simulations. For the first stage of the MSM method, the initial approximation is set to a constant and the spectrum of the sounding signal is limited to 125 kHz, or a wavelength of 12 mm. The subsequent stages use wavelengths of 6, 4, and 3 mm.

Since the spectrum of the sounding signal is limited at the first stages (Fig. 2), the finite difference grid step may be increased proportionally to the wavelength. The computation time is proportional to the third power of the grid width in pixels, as the wave simulation time step is proportional to the grid step due to the Courant stability condition. Table 1 shows that the total computation time for initial stages 1 – 3 is less than the computation time for the final stage alone.

Table 1. Multistage method parameters. Computation time for NVidia Tesla V100

Stage	Average wavelength	Central frequency	Grid size	Computation time
1	12 mm	125 kHz	480 px	20 s
2	6 mm	250 kHz	800 px	2 min
3	4 mm	375 kHz	1280 px	4.4 min
4	3 mm	500 kHz	1800 px	14 min

The approximate solutions obtained at initial stages of the MSM method are much closer to the exact solution than the constant initial approximation used for the first stage. Consequently, the number of iterations needed to reach the solution at the final stages of the MSM method decreases. This way, the proposed multistage method reduces the computation time, compared to the gradient descent method with fixed parameters.

Table 2 shows the computation time achieved on tested computing platforms using the gradient descent method with a wavelength of 5 mm, using the MSM method with two stages with wavelengths of 12 mm and 5 mm, and using the MSM method with 4 stages and a wavelength of 3 mm in the last stage. The multistage method computation in this example completes almost twice as fast as the gradient descent method with the same wavelength. The target resolution, however, which is determined by the wavelengthat the final stage, has a very high impact on computing time.

Table 2. Gradient descent and MSM computation time

Method	Hi-res iterations	Time, Haswell	Time, 6240R	Time, P100	Time, V100
Single, 5mm wave	70	63 min	24 min	17 min	9 min
MSM up to 5 mm	33	38 min	14 min	10 min	5 min
MSM up to 3 mm	36	178 min	65 min	37 min	20 min

4.2 Multi-core CPU Performance

The algorithm was implemented for multi-core CPUs using AVX2/AVX-512 vector FPU capabilities and OpenMP parallelization. With average grid sizes of 1280×1280 pixels, the 20 – 40 MB cache memory of modern processors can accommodate the data for 1 – 2 ultrasound emitters. As the amount of data used simultaneously becomes larger than the CPU cache size, the performance decreases and eventually becomes limited by the memory access channel.

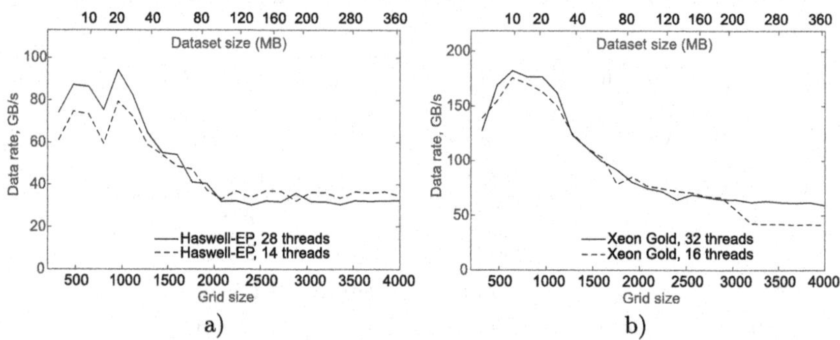

Fig. 5. Performance of Intel Haswell-EP (a) and Intel 6240R (b) CPUs with one and two threads per core launched

Modern Intel-compatible processors feature the HyperThreading mode which uses two threads per CPU core. Figure 5 shows the performance profiles for Intel Haswell-EP (a) and Intel 6240R (b) processors for one and two threads per core launched. The data volume of 30 MB that is efficiently processed in the CPU cache allows for a finite difference grid of 1000×1000 points, which is sufficient for some practical applications. For very small data volumes, the performance slightly decreases due to the thread synchronization overhead. OpenMP synchronization delay did not exceed 3.5 μs, which is negligible for most practical applications.

The algorithm efficiently utilizes multi-core CPU capabilities. Figure 6 plots the CPU performance of Intel Haswell-EP (a) and Intel 6240R (b) depending on the number of threads. Intel Haswell-EP CPU with 14 cores had achieved up to 10-fold acceleration for large data volumes and up to 20-fold acceleration on small data volumes with 28 threads in use, compared to a single thread.

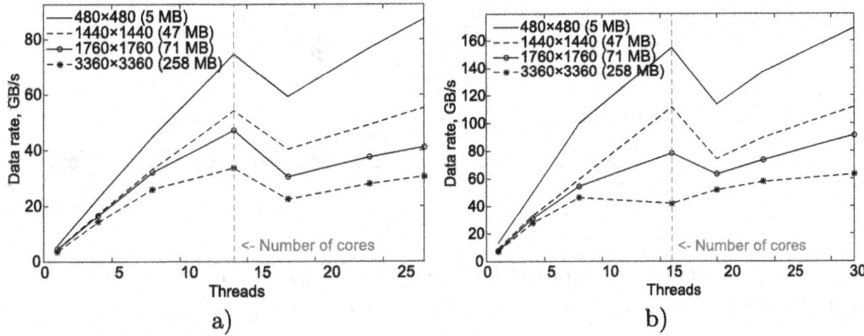

Fig. 6. Intel Haswell-EP (a) and Intel 6240R (b) CPU performance depending on the number of threads launched

Intel 6240R CPU with 16 cores had achieved up to 9-fold acceleration for large data volumes and up to 16-fold acceleration on small data volumes with 32 threads in use. Although the acceleration factor is formally lower than that of Intel Haswell-EP CPU, AVX-512 technology and a larger number of cores result in the overall performance being approximately twice that of Intel Haswell-EP.

Computations can be parallelized on multiple CPUs. Allocating one CPU for each ultrasound emitter is efficient. In this case, data synchronization between CPU nodes is required only once per gradient descent iteration (several seconds to minutes of computing time), making the data synhronization overhead negligible.

4.3 GPU Performance

The multistage method was tested on NVidia Tesla P100, NVidia Tesla V100 and AMD Radeon VII GPU devices. These devices feature HBM2-class on-board memory with throughput rates of 732, 900 and 1000 GB/s, respectively. OpenCL interface was used for GPU computing.

Fig. 7a shows the performance of tested GPU devices in comparison with Intel 6240R depending on the grid size. In this test, the dataset consists of a single ultrasound source with the specified grid size. Fast on-board memory is the main advantage of GPUs in explicit FDTD methods. The test showed the performance reaching 60% of the device memory throughput.

The advantage of GPU devices comparing to CPUs is manifested primarily on large datasets — the GPU performance reaches 4 to 6 times that of Intel 6240R. For small datasets, the noticeable synchronization latency limits the performance of graphics processors due to extremely short task execution times.

In wave tomography applications, the number of emitters is on the order of several dozen and all of these data combined form a GPU dataset. Since the

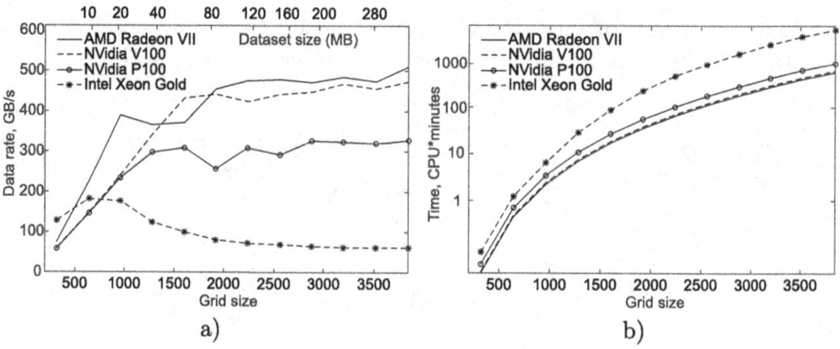

Fig. 7. GPU performance compared to Intel 6240R (a); estimated time to solve a typical inverse problem (b)

computations for all the emitters are identical, the optimal data distribution for a GPU is to process all the data at once. If an optimal amount of data is distributed to the CPU (equal to the CPU cache size) and GPU (all the data at once), the GPU advantage over Intel 6240R amounts to 2 – 3 times.

Figure 7b shows the estimated computation time for a task of reconstructing a single image (a cross-section of the object). The time scale is logarithmic. These estimates assume typical values of parameters used in this study, such as the typical number of emitters and the number of iterations at each stage. The grid size determines the spatial resolution of the reconstructed image.

The tests carried out on various computing platforms have demonstrated that GPU computing has a significant advantage in application to wave tomography image reconstruction, that can be attributed to the presence of fast on-board GPU memory and high data-parallelism of the explicit finite difference method. However, modern CPUs featuring AVX-512 FPU, such as the Intel 6240R, have comparable performance, provided there is enough cache memory to host the data for at least one ultrasound emitter. Thus, the proposed method can be effectively used on modern CPU and GPU computing clusters.

5 Conclusion

The article is concerned with developing effective methods for solving inverse problems of ultrasound tomography. The scalar wave model used in this study describes such processes as diffraction, refraction, absorption and multiple scattering of waves. The image reconstruction problem is posed as a coefficient inverse problem, which is solved via minimizing the residual functional. To address the problem of local minima of the functional, a multistage iterative method is proposed, which ensures the convergence of the gradient-based iterative minimization algorithm to the global minimum.

The choice of the sounding frequency range of 100 to 600 kHz provides high spatial resolution of reconstructed tomographic images — approximately 2 mm.

The presence of low frequencies in the signal ensures that approximate solutions obtained at successive stages of the MSM method converge to the global minimum of the residual functional.

The results showed that the proposed method reconstructs the sound speed image of the object with high resolution and high accuracy. In contrast to X-ray tomography, in which only the absorption factor is determined, wave tomography method can obtain both the speed of sound and the absorption coefficient to aid quantitative tissue characterization in medical imaging.

Supercomputers can be used to implement the proposed algorithms. GPU devices showed the best performance for the problem considered. The efficiency of the multistage method is associated with the possibility of parallelizing the computations and with the grid size varying according to the signal bandwidth used for each stage.

Numerical methods for solving nonlinear inverse problems developed in this study can be applied to reconstructing tomographic images in acoustics, seismics, in problems of non-destructive testing and electromagnetic sounding. To adapt the MSM method for a particular application, the parameters of the method such as the frequency bands and the number of stages can be determined via numerical simulations.

Acknowledgement. The paper was published with the financial support of the Ministry of Education and Science of the Russian Federation as part of the program of the Moscow Center for Fundamental and Applied Mathematics under the agreement No.075-15-2022-284. The research is carried out using the equipment of the shared research facilities of HPC computing resources at Lomonosov Moscow State University.

References

1. F. Natterer, Possibilities and limitations of time domain wave equation imaging, in: AMS Vol. 559: Tomography and Inverse Transport Theory, American Mathematical Society, 2011, pp. 151–162. https://doi.org/10.1090/conm/559.
2. Beilina, L., Klibanov, M.V., Kokurin, M.Y.: Adaptivity with relaxation for ill-posed problems and global convergence for a coefficient inverse problem. J. Math. Sci. **167**(3), 279–325 (2010). https://doi.org/10.1007/s10958-010-9921-1
3. Pratt, R.G.: Seismic waveform inversion in the frequency domain, part 1: theory and verification in a physical scale model. Geophysics **64**(3), 888–901 (1999)
4. Blazek, K.D., Stolk, C., Symes, W.W.: A mathematical framework for inverse wave problems in heterogeneous media. Inverse Prob. **29**(6), 065001 (2013)
5. Goncharsky, A.V., Romanov, S.Y.: Inverse problems of ultrasound tomography in models with attenuation. Phys. Med. Biol. **59**(8), 1979–2004 (2014). https://doi.org/10.1088/0031-9155/59/8/1979
6. Natterer, F., Sielschott, H., Dorn, O., Dierkes, T., Palamodov, V.: Fréchet derivatives for some bilinear inverse problems. SIAM J. Appl. Math. **62**(6), 2092–2113 (2002). https://doi.org/10.1137/s0036139901386375
7. Goncharsky, A.V., Romanov, S.Y.: Iterative methods for solving coefficient inverse problems of wave tomography in models with attenuation. Inverse Probl. **33**(2), 025003 (2017). https://doi.org/10.1088/1361-6420/33/2/025003

8. Goncharsky, A., Romanov, S., Seryozhnikov, S.: Inverse problems of 3D ultrasonic tomography with complete and incomplete range data. Wave Motion **51**(3), 389–404 (2014). https://doi.org/10.1016/j.wavemoti.2013.10.001
9. Goncharsky, A., Romanov, S., Seryozhnikov, S.: A computer simulation study of soft tissue characterization using low-frequency ultrasonic tomography. Ultrasonics **67**, 136–150 (2016). https://doi.org/10.1016/j.ultras.2016.01.008
10. Goncharsky, A.V., Romanov, S.Y., Seryozhnikov, S.Y.: Comparison of the capabilities of GPU clusters and general-purpose supercomputers for solving 3D inverse problems of ultrasound tomography. J. Parallel Distrib. Comput. **133**, 77–92 (2019). https://doi.org/10.1016/j.jpdc.2019.06.008
11. Goncharsky, A.V., Romanov, S.Y., Seryozhnikov, S.Y.: Low-frequency ultrasonic tomography: Mathematical methods and experimental results. Moscow Univ. Phys. **74**, 43–51 (2019). https://doi.org/10.3103/S0027134919010090
12. L. Liberti, N. Maculan, Global Optimization, Springer, US, 2006. https://doi.org/10.1007/0-387-30528-9.
13. A. V. Sulimov, et al.: Tensor train global optimization: Application to docking in the configuration space with a large number of dimensions, in: CCIS, Vol. 793, Springer, Cham, 2017, pp. 151–167. https://doi.org/10.1007/978-3-319-71255-0_1212
14. Goncharsky, A.V., Romanov, S.Y., Seryozhnikov, S.Y.: Low-frequency three-dimensional ultrasonic tomography. Dokl. Phys. **61**(5), 211–214 (2016). https://doi.org/10.1134/s1028335816050086
15. Xia, Hong, Luo, Zhendong: Optimized finite difference iterative scheme based on POD technique for 2D viscoelastic wave equation. Appl. Math. Mech. **38**(12), 1721–1732 (2017). https://doi.org/10.1007/s10483-017-2288-8
16. J. Li, W. Xuesong, T. Wang, On the validity of born approximation, Progress In Electromagnet. Res. 107. https://doi.org/10.2528/PIER10070504.
17. Voevodin, V., et al: Supercomputer Lomonosov-2: Large scale, deep monitoring and fine analytics for the user community, Supercomputing Frontiers and Innovations (2) (2019) 4–11. http://dx.doi.org/10.14529/jsfi190201.

Computer Memory Requirements for Matrix-Forming Approach to Global Stability Analysis of Fluid Flows

Kirill Belyaev(✉), Andrey Garbaruk, and Valentin Golubkov

Peter the Great St. Petersburg Polytechnic University (SPBPU), St. Petersburg, Russia
{kira,agarbaruk}@cfd.spbstu.ru

Abstract. Global Stability Analysis (GSA) is a powerful and efficient tool for studying various forms of instability developing in laminar and turbulent flows. A key element of the GSA is the generalized eigenvalue problem. To solve this problem, the so-called matrix-forming approach is most often used, which implies the explicit formation of the Jacobian matrix of the right-hand sides of the fluid motion equations and the direct solution of corresponding eigenvalue problem. However, this approach requires a lot of computer memory to store elements of the LU-factorized Jacobian matrix. In the present study, based on examples of GSA conducted for a few 2D and 3D flows of various complexity, specific RAM requirements for the matrix-forming approach to GSA and their dependence on the size and type (2D or 3D) of the flows under consideration are defined. This allows an estimate of the maximum size of the GSA problem, which solution is possible on the cluster Tornado of the Supercomputer Center "Politechnichesky" and on other supercomputers with a similar architecture.

Keywords: Global Stability Analysis · Matrix-Forming Approach · Shift-Invert Approach · Implicitly Restarted Arnoldi Method · Tollmien-Schlichting Waves · Transonic Buffet

1 Introduction

Linear stability theory (LST) is a classical approach to studying the stability of various types of flows, which is an efficient alternative to solving complete non-linear unsteady equations of motion. In the 20th century, most LST-based studies were performed using one-dimensional or two-dimensional parabolic equations (the so-called parallel and quasi-parallel approaches, respectively - see, e.g., monographs [1, 2] and review paper [3]). However, by the end of the century, the rapid growth of the computational power made it possible to conduct LST based on the linearized two- and three-dimensional (2D and 3D) full Navier-Stokes (NS) or Reynolds Averaged Navier-Stoke (RANS) equations. Over the past two decades, this approach often referred to Global Stability Analysis (GSA) [4], has been successfully applied to investigate the stability of a wide range of flows, such as boundary layers (development of Tollmien-Schlichting waves) [5], wakes [6], jets [7], turbulent flows around airfoils near stall [8],

V. Voevodin et al. (Eds.): RuSCDays 2023, LNCS 14388, pp. 47–58, 2023.
https://doi.org/10.1007/978-3-031-49432-1_4

the onset of the 2D and 3D transonic buffet [9, 10], and many other flows and has been proven to be a reliable and efficient computational tool. The key element of the GSA is the generalized eigenvalue problem. The most popular approach to solving this problem is the so-called matrix-forming approach, which implies the explicit formation of the Jacobi matrix of the right-hand sides of the fluid motion equations. The advantage of this approach, is its efficiency in terms of required CPU time needed to compute global instability modes, which is achieved by exploiting the sparseness of the Jacobian matrix. However, it requires a lot of computer memory (RAM), which is caused by the need to store elements of LU-factorized Jacobi matrix.

In the present study, based on a set of examples of GSA conducted for a few 2D and 3D flows of different complexity, specific RAM requirements for the matrix-forming approach to GSA are defined and their dependence on the size and type (2D or 3D) of a flow under consideration is established. This allows to estimate the maximum size of the GSA problems, which solution is possible on the cluster Tornado of the Supercomputer Center "Politechnichesky" and on other supercomputers with a similar architecture.

2 Global Stability Analysis Methodology

An objective of GSA is to find out if a steady solution of the NS (for a laminar flow) or RANS (for a turbulent flow) equations is stable or not. The unsteady form of these equations can be written in the following general operator form

$$\frac{\partial q}{\partial t} = -R(q) \tag{1}$$

where q is the vector of the conservative flow variables and R is the nonlinear differential operator of the right-hand side. The dimension of the vector q (the number of variables N_v) as well as the specific variables it includes depend on the considered equations. For example, for the 3D compressible RANS equations with the one-equation Spalart-Allmaras turbulence model [12], $N_v = 6$ and $q = \{\rho, \rho E, \rho u, \rho v, \rho w, \rho v_t\}^T$, whereas for the 2D Navier-Stokes equations, $N_v = 4$ and $q = \{\rho, \rho E, \rho u, \rho v\}^T$, where ρ is the density, E is the specific internal energy, u, v, and w are the components of the velocity vector, and ν_t is the eddy viscosity.

The GST methodology includes two main steps.

The first one is getting a numerical solution, $\overline{q}$, of the steady form of the governing Eq. (1), $R(q) = 0$, which is referred to as the "base flow" or "baseflow solution" for the flow-problem under consideration.

After that, following the conventional procedure of the linear stability analysis, the solution of the unsteady system (1) is presented as the sum of the stationary solution $\overline{q}$ and the small perturbations, q', depending on both space coordinates and time:

$$q(x, y, z, t) = \overline{q}(x, y, z) + q'(x, y, z, t) \tag{2}$$

Substituting (2) to (1) and linearizing obtained system in the vicinity of $\overline{q}$ taking into account that $R(\overline{q}) = 0$, one arrives to the linear system for small perturbations

$$\frac{\partial q'}{\partial t} + J(\overline{q})q' = 0, \tag{3}$$

where $J(\overline{q}) \equiv \frac{\partial R}{\partial q}(\overline{q})$ is the Jacobian of the differential operator in the right-hand side of the governing unsteady Eq. (1).

Due to the linearity of the system (3), its general solution can be represented as a sum of elementary solutions ("modes")

$$q\prime(x, y, z, t) = \hat{q}(x, y, z)\exp(\omega t), \tag{4}$$

where $\hat{q}(x, y, z)$ is the complex vector of the amplitudes of disturbances and $\omega = \omega_r + i\omega_i$ is the complex number, the real part of which is the growth/decay rate of disturbances and the imaginary part is their frequency (only the real part of relation (4) has a physical meaning).

Substituting (4) into (3) leads to the eigenvalue problem for the Jacobian matrix:

$$J\hat{q} = \omega\hat{q}. \tag{5}$$

Its discrete form reads as:

$$M_{kl}\hat{\alpha}_l = \omega\hat{\alpha}_k, \tag{6}$$

where the vector $\hat{\alpha}_l$ is the discrete analogue of the amplitude of the disturbance $\hat{q}$ and the matrix M_{kl} is the discrete analogue of the Jacobian J (indices k and l in the Eq. (6) take values from 1 to $N_m = N_p \times N_v$, where N_p is the number of grid nodes).

The matrix M is sparse, and the number of non-zero elements in its lines depends on the type of a problem in question (2D/3D and laminar/turbulent) and on the stencil of the numerical scheme used for the Jacobian discretization. For instance, for the schemes with the 5-point stencil (3rd order upwind or 4th order central-differences) used in the present study the lines have a maximum of 28 and 69 non-zero elements for 2D laminar flows and for 3D turbulent flows, respectively. So, the density of the Matrix M for the 3D problems is more than two times higher than that for the 2D ones.

At the boundary points of the computational domain, a linearized form of the specified steady boundary conditions to the Eq. (1) is used. Hence, at these points the Eq. (4) takes the following form:

$$M_{kl}\hat{\alpha}_l = 0. \tag{7}$$

Combining (6) and (7), we obtain the following final formulation of the discrete eigenvalue problem, which must be solved in order to find out whether the underlying flow is stable or not:

$$M_{kl}\hat{\alpha}_l = \omega T_{km}\hat{\alpha}_m, \tag{8}$$

where T_{km} is the diagonal matrix with $T_{ii} = 0$ for the boundary grid points, and $T_{ii} = 1$ for the internal points.

Note that to answer the above question, it is only necessary to find the eigenvalue with the largest real part that corresponds to the perturbations with the highest growth rate ("the least stable eigenvalue"). If this largest real part is positive, then the amplitude of disturbances increases with time, and the base-flow is unstable. Otherwise, if it is negative, the base flow is stable.

3 Solution of the Generalized Eigenvalue Problem

For the numerical solution of the eigenvalue problem (8), the Krylov-Schur (K-S) method was used, which is designed to solve eigenvalue problems with large sparse non-Hermitian matrices (the matrix M is of exactly this type). This method is a modification of the implicitly restarted Arnoldi method, which belongs to the class of Rayleigh-Ritz methods based on projection onto the Krylov subspace (see, for example, [13]). The K-S method delivers a number of eigenvalues with the largest absolute values. However, in the context of the GSA, we need to calculate the least-stable eigenvalue. In order to resolve this issue, the original matrix must be preliminarily transformed in such a way that the eigenvalues of the transformed matrix with the largest absolute values would correspond to the eigenvalues of the original matrix with the largest real parts. This transformation called "shift-invert" approach, reduces the problem (8) to a new eigenvalue problem:

$$(M_{kl} - \sigma T_{kl})^{-1} T_{lp} \hat{\alpha}_p = \theta \hat{\alpha}_k. \tag{9}$$

The relation between the eigenvalues of the original and the new problems, ω and θ, has the form and the free complex shift-parameter σ in (9), (10) is responsible for the correspondence of the eigenvalue of the new problem (9) with the largest absolute values to the eigenvalues of the original problem (8) with the largest real parts.

$$\omega = \sigma + 1/\theta, \tag{10}$$

In order to compute the elements of the inverse matrix $(M_{\text{kl}} - \sigma T_{\text{kl}})^{-1}$ in (7) at each Arnoldi iteration, one needs to solve the linear algebraic system. Two types of methods can be used for this purpose, namely iterative and direct ones.

The iterative methods require much less RAM than the direct methods, but the iterations converge only if the matrix has strong diagonal dominance. In the framework of the shift-invert approach, this can be achieved by choosing the shift-parameter σ with a large real part. However, in this case, the eigenvalues of the eigenvalue problem (9), which correspond to the least-stable eigenvalues of the original eigenvalue problem (8), have small absolute values and so cannot be found with the use of the K-S method. Preliminary calculations carried out in the present study have shown that for the GSA problems, finding a compromise value of the shift-parameter, that is a value ensuring both convergence of the iterations and finding the least-stable eigenvalues of the problem (8) is possible only in a very limited number of stability problems.

This problem does not arise in the direct methods, but they require storing not only the elements of the matrix M itself but also the elements of the matrices obtained by its LU-decomposition, that is, are much more RAM-demanding than the iterative methods. Nonetheless, given their universality, the direct methods are preferable for the GSA and were used in the present work.

For solving the linear algebra problems outlined above we used the open library SPEPc/PETSc [14, 15]. This choice was made for two reasons. First, this library has been constantly developed, extensively used, and extensively tested on a large number of various problems for more than 20 years now. Second, it allows straightforward employing various external solvers by selecting corresponding arguments in the command line with no changing the program itself. In particular, in the present work, one such external solvers, MUMPS [16], was used, which implements the massively parallel LU-decomposition and solution of systems of linear equations based on it.

Numerical solution of the steady compressible Navier-Stokes and RANS equations needed for computing the base-flow characteristics, we used an in-house CFD code "Numerical Turbulence Simulation" (NTS) [17], which has been thoroughly validated by comparisons with solutions of a wide range of aerodynamic and stability problems and experimental data available in the literature. Finally, one more in-house code (CompMatr) employing the same spatial discretization as that used in the NTS code, was used for computing the elements of the matrix M.

Note in conclusion that the results of the GSA obtained in the present study were verified by their comparison with the numerical solutions of the original unsteady governing Eq. (1) with the use of the time-accurate branch of the NTS code.

4 Considered Stability Problems

For evaluating RAM requirements for performing GSA of various flows, a set of numerical experiments was conducted.

Corresponding calculations were carried out on the cluster Tornado of the Supercomputer Center "Politechnichesky" of the Peter the Great St. Petersburg Polytechnic University. For the GSA, the main CPU nodes of this cluster were used, each of which has two processors Intel Xeon E5-2697v3 and 64 GB RAM. Tornado has 625 such nodes, but the maximum number of nodes used in the course of the present work for GSA was 140.

In the following subsections, we briefly outline the considered problems and present computational grids and corresponding sizes of the matrices M. Note that in all the considered problems, the computational grids used for computing the base-flows were the same as those employed for the GSA. In principle, this is superfluous, since sufficient base-flow resolution typically is reached on much coarser grid than those needed for accurate resolution of the eigenvectors in GSA. However, the use of different grids for the base-flow and for the GSA leads to necessity of interpolation of coarse grid base-flow solutions on finer grids used in the GSA, which inevitably results in a noticeable inaccuracy.

4.1 GSA-Based Prediction of Forming and Evolution of Tollmien-Schlichting Waves in Laminar Flow Over a Flat Plate with Rectangular Cavity

The first example of GSA application is assessment of the effect of surface irregularities on the development of Tollmien-Schlichting waves in the laminar flow past the flat plate with a rectangular cavity. The values of the Mach number and the Reynolds number based on the plate length were equal to 0.05 and $6{\cdot}10^6$, respectively. The cavities if different length and depth are located at $\mathrm{Re}_x = 1.5{\cdot}10^6$.

The problem is two-dimensional and a size of the computational (x, y)-grid used in the computation is about $2.0{\cdot}10^6$ cells total. The grid is gradually refined in the y-direction near the plate and cavity walls and in the x-direction near the leading edge of the plate and the vertical walls of the cavity. The grid steps are sufficient for resolving Tollmien-Schlichting waves in the entire range of frequencies of practical interest.

The matrix M has about $N_m \approx 7.5{\cdot}10^6$ lines and contains about $N_{nz} \approx 2.1{\cdot}10^7$ non-zero elements.

For extracting characteristics of the Tollmien-Schlichting waves from the "raw" results of the GSA, including streamwise distribution of their amplification factor (N-factor), a special post-processing of the GSA results was developed (see [5] for details).

4.2 GSA-Based Prediction of Onset of Transonic Buffet in Turbulent Flow Past Infinite Swept Wing

The second example of the GSA application considered in the present work is predicting the transonic buffet onset in the turbulent flow past the infinite swept wing with the supercritical airfoil OAT15A at different angles of attack α (see [9, 18] for more details).

Two different GSA versions were used for this flow.

The first one, referred to as quasi-3D (q-3D) approach [18], the spanwise homogeneity of the base-flow, and decomposes the disturbances into Fourier modes in spanwise (periodic) direction z. Each Fourier mode is characterized by a spanwise wavelength λ_z, defined by the wave number β ($\lambda_z/c = 2\pi/|\beta|$, c is the length of the airfoil chord), which is a free parameter of the q-3D stability problem. Considering that the q-3D eigenmodes are two-dimensional, this version of GSA sometimes referred to as "biglobal" [3]. The second GSA version ("triglobal" stability analysis [3]) is the fully-3D GSA of the flow past a section of the wing with the length L_z.

Specific computations performed in the present work are carried out at different angles of attack α varying in the range from 2.75° up to 3° and fixed values of the wing sweep angle $\Lambda = 30°$ at the Reynolds and Mach numbers based on the free-stream velocity component normal to the wing leading-edge $\mathrm{Re}_n = 3{\cdot}10^6$ and $M_n = 0.73$, respectively. The flow is assumed to be fully turbulent and is modeled in the framework of the RANS equations with the use of the Spalart-Allmaras turbulence model [12] with the Compressibility Correction [19] (SA CC model).

The computational domain and the grid in the XY-plane used in the computations are shown in Fig. 1. The domain has a radius of about 30c (c – airfoil chord), which, along with the use of the characteristic non-reflecting characteristic boundary conditions with the Riemann invariants defined by the free-stream parameters, ensure an adequate representation of the transonic flow past the wing. The structured computational grid has two overlapping blocks, shown in Fig. 1 by blue and green grid lines. The total cell number of the grid in (x, y) plane is about 85,000. Over a wide area encompassing the shock location, the grid-step in the streamwise direction Δx reduces by a factor of ten. The step in the wall-normal direction decreases toward the wing surface so that the size of the first near-wall cell in the coordinates of the law of the wall $\Delta^+_{y,1}$ is less than 1.0.

For the q-3D GSA problem the matrix M has about $5.0{\cdot}10^5$ lines and contains about $1.4{\cdot}10^6$ non-zero elements.

The fully-3D stability analysis was performed on grids with different number of cells in the spanwise direction of N_z. With the available RAM, the maximum affordable grid size for these computation was about 2 million cells. With the (x, y) grid of 85000 cells,

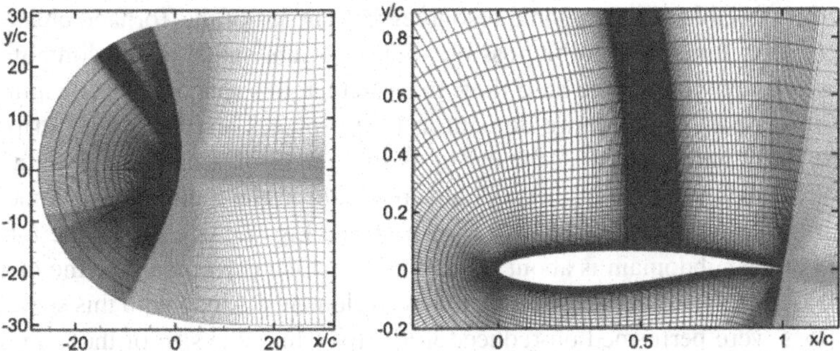

Fig. 1. Computational domain and two-block grid in *XY* plane: entire domain (left) and zoomed in view in the vicinity of the wing (right)

this allows a maximum number of cells in the spanwise direction $N_z = 22$. Corresponding matrix M has about $N_m \approx 11.2 \cdot 10^6$ lines and contains about $N_{nz} \approx 7.7 \cdot 10^8$ non-zero elements.

4.3 GSA-Based Prediction of Onset of Transonic Buffet in Turbulent Flow Past Simplified NASA Common Research Model (CRM) of Airplane

The flow past the CRM [20] is essentially 3D and, therefore, the GSA of the steady RANS solutions for this flow should be fully 3D as well. Taking into account the symmetry of the flow with respect to the plane $z = 0$, the computations were performed for the half of the simplified (without the nacelle and tail rudder and stabilizers) CRM geometry at the Reynolds numbers based on the reference chord, $\text{Re} = 1.5 \cdot 10^6$, the Mach number $M = 0.85$, and the angle of attack α with the range from 3.5^0 up to 3.9^0.

A multi-block grid with a total number of cells of about 62 Million (left frame in Fig. 2) was built taking into account the specific features of the flow and, in particular, the presence of a shock on the suction side of the wing (in its neighborhood, the grid is strongly refined in the streamwise direction – see the right frame in Fig. 2).

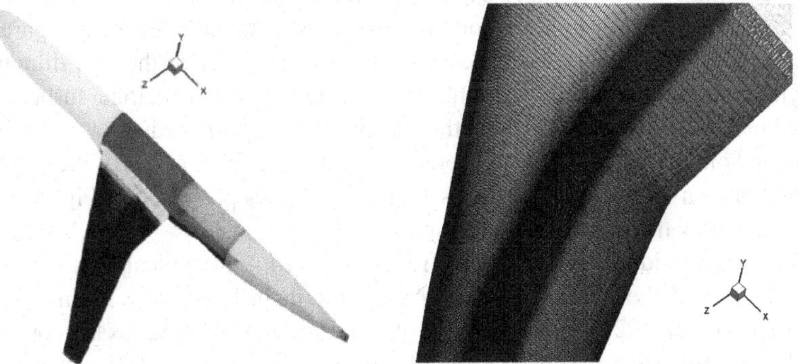

Fig. 2. Structured multi-block surface grid used for steady RANS computations of the CRM flow (left) and its zoomed in view (right) (Colour figure online)

With the available computational resources (140 nodes of the Tornado cluster), the GSA of the flow turned out to be possible only in a subdomain of the computational domain used for computing the base-flow. In particular, this subdomain shown in Fig. 3 includes only a part of the entire domain in (x, y) -planes and the wing "strip" with $z_{min}/L_z = 0.402$ and $z_{max}/L_z = 0.898$ (L_z is the length of a half of CRM in the z-direction). Besides, the grid in this, GSA, subdomain in the z-direction includes only every fourth z-grid surface of the grid shown on the Fig. 2. As a result, the total size of the grid in the subdomain is about $2.5 \cdot 10^6$ cells, which corresponds to the matrix M with $N_m \approx 1.5 \cdot 10^7$ lines and $N_{nz} \approx 10^9$ non-zero elements. Along with this some of the computations were performed on reduced grids, for which the size of the matrix M is about $3.7 \cdot 10^6$.

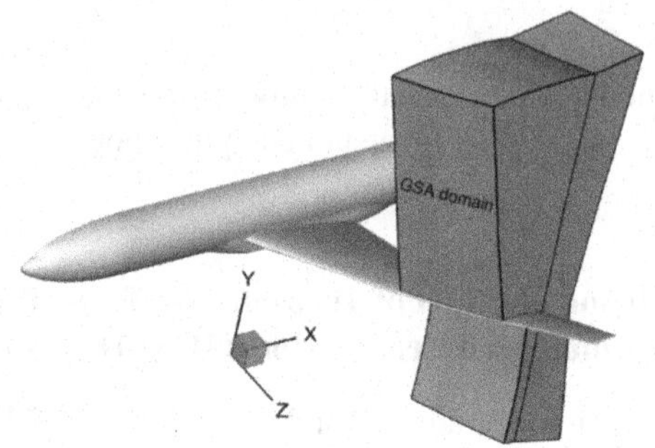

Fig. 3. Subdomain in which 3D GSA was performed

5 Estimates of RAM Requirements

As already mentioned, the major RAM expenses for the GSA performed in the framework of the matrix-forming approach are associated with storing elements of the LU decomposition of the Jacobian matrix. In the massively parallel computations, these expenses are known to be strongly dependent on the number of parallel MPI processes (N_{MPI}) used for the LU decomposition [18]. To investigate the effect of this parameter, two series of calculations were carried out, one for the GSA of the two-dimensional laminar flow outlined in Sect. 4.1 and the other for the three-dimensional turbulent flow described in Sect. 4.3. In the first case, the size of the matrix M is equal to $\approx 7.5 \cdot 10^6$ and in the second one $\approx 3.7 \cdot 10^6$. The first series is carried out on 12 nodes of the cluster and the second one on 20 nodes. The results of the both series presented in Fig. 4, Table 1, and Table 2, allow the following conclusions.

In the both considered problems, the required RAM monotonically and almost linearly increases with the increase of N_{MPI}. As a result, in the both cases, 14 times increase of N_{MPI} leads to about 2 times increase of the required RAM. As far as the corresponding wall-clock time is concerned, it rapidly drops with increase of N_{MPI} up to about 100–150 and after that changes very slowly. Therefore, this number is nearly optimal for the considered GSA problems, and its further reduction makes sense only if the RAM

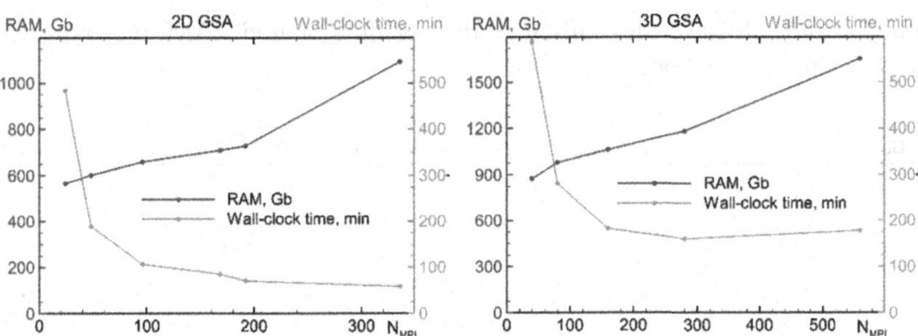

Fig. 4. Required RAM and wall-clock time as the functions of number of MPI processes, N_{MPI}, for the considered 2D (left) and 3D (right) GSA problems

Table 1. Dependence of required RAM and wall-clock time for GSA on number of MPI processes, N_{MPI}, for 2D laminar flow (Sect. 4.1)

N_{MPI}	Required RAM, Gb	Wall-clock time, min
24	567	483
48	601	189
96	660	107
168	709	86
192	728	71
336	1092	59

Table 2. Dependence of required RAM and wall-clock time for GSA on number of MPI processes, N_{MPI}, for 3D turbulent CRM flow (Sect. 4.3)

N_{MPI}	Required RAM, Gb	Wall-clock time, min
40	874	588
80	980	281
160	1064	183
280	1182	160
560	1656	178

deficit is not severe and this open a possibility to solve the problem. Similarly, in order to slightly speed up the solution process, it is possible to increase N_{MPI} compared to its optimal value by 2–3 times staying within the available RAM.

Figure 5 presents plots of the required RAM as the functions of the size of the matrix N_{m} (left frame in the figure) and on the number of its nonzero elements N_{nz} (right frame) for all the 2D and 3D GSA problems presented in Sect. 4 (note that for some of these problems, in order to save the wall-clock time or the required RAM, the N_{MPI} value differed from the optimal one).

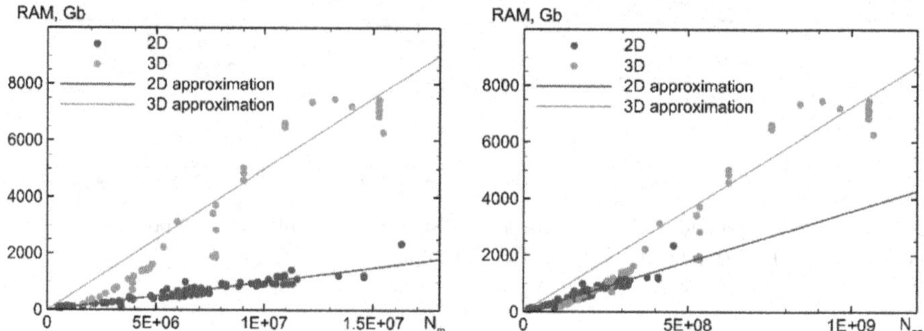

Fig. 5. Required RAM as the function of the matrix size (left) and the number of its non-zero elements (right) based on results of all the considered GSA problems

One can see that the RAM required for GSA is approximately equal to $10^{-4}\cdot N_m$ Gb for the 2D and $5.0\cdot 10^{-4}\cdot N_m$ Gb for the 3D problems, respectively. This corresponds to approximately $3.6\cdot 10^{-6}\cdot N_{nz}$ Gb for the 2D problems and $7.2\cdot 10^{-6}\cdot N_{nz}$ Gb for 3D ones. This difference is explained by the fact that the number of elements of the LU decomposition grows non-linearly with the increase of the density of the matrix M (recall that 3D matrix is more than 2 times denser than 2D one). These relations allow estimating the maximum size of the GSA problems depending on the available RAM, which is of significant practical interest. For example, for the 3D flows, the Tornado cluster (625 nodes with 64 Gb RAM each) allows solving GSA problems with N_m up to $\approx 7.2\cdot 10^7$, which corresponds to a computational grid of approximately $12\cdot 10^6$ sells. Such grids are sufficient for some rather complex flows but are not sufficient for most industrially relevant problems. For instance, the GSA of the flow past the entire CRM geometry (Sect. 4.3) demands RAM of about 200 Tb. Currently, only 2 clusters in Russia have this amount of memory [21]: "Chervonenkis" which is the first in the top50 list and "Christofari Neo" which occupies the fourth place in this list. At the same time, the growth in computer power allows us to hope that the possibility of performing 3D GSA of complex three-dimensional flows will appear in the near future.

6 Conclusions

Based on analysis of results of 2D and 3D GSA of laminar and turbulent 2D and 3D flows of various complexity conducted on "Tornado" cluster of the Supercomputer Center "Politechnichesky", the following conclusions can be drawn.

- An optimal number of MPI processes N_{MPI} used for such problems is nearly proportional to the size of the matrix of the eigenvalue problem associated with GSA and can be estimated as $10^{-5}\cdot N_m$ for the 2D and $5\cdot 10^{-5}\cdot N_m$ for the 3D GSA, respectively. This approximately corresponds to $2.8\cdot 10^6$ non-zero elements of the matrix (N_{nz}) per one MPI process for the 2D case and $1.4\cdot 10^6$ non-zero elements for the 3D cases.

- The amount of RAM required for GSA is approximately equal to $10^{-4}{\cdot}N_{\mathrm{m}}$ Gb for the 2D and $5{\cdot}10^{-4}{\cdot}N_{\mathrm{m}}$ for the 3D GSA, respectively. This approximately corresponds to $3.6{\cdot}10^{-6}{\cdot}N_{\mathrm{nz}}$ for the 2D cases and $7.2{\cdot}10^{-6}{\cdot}N_{\mathrm{nz}}$ for the 3D cases.

These estimates are applicable to other clusters with the architecture similar to that of the "Tornado".

The RAM available on the "Tornado" is sufficient for solving virtually arbitrary 2D GSA problems. However, for 3D problems, the grid size is limited by $\approx$10 Million of cells, which is far from sufficient for conducting GSA of the most industrial flow-problems.

Acknowledgements. The study is conducted with financial support of Russian Scientific Foundation, Grant No. 22–11-00041. The computations were performed on the HP computing facilities of the Peter the Great Saint-Petersburg Polytechnic University (http://www.spbstu.ru).

References

1. Boiko, A.V., Dovgal, A.V., Grek, G.R., Kozlov, V.V.: Physics of Transitional Shear Flows: Instability and Laminar-Turbulent Transition in Incompressible Near-Wall Shear Layers. Springer, Heidelberg (2012). https://doi.org/10.1007/978-94-007-2498-3
2. Schmid, P.J., Henningson, D.S.: Stability and Transition in Shear Flows. Springer, New York (2001). https://doi.org/10.1007/978-1-4613-0185-1
3. Theofilis, V.: Global linear instability. Annu. Rev. Fluid Mech. **43**, 319–352 (2011)
4. Theofilis, V.: Advances in global linear instability analysis of nonparallel and three-dimensional flows. Prog. Aerosp. Sci. **39**(4), 249–315 (2003)
5. Belyaev, K.V., Garbaruk, A.V., Golubkov, V.D., Strelets, M.Kh.: Application of global stability analysis to predicting characteristics of Tollmien-Schlichting waves. St. Petersburg State Polytechnical University Journal. Phys. Math. **16**(1.1), 4–10 (2023)
6. Meliga, P., Sipp, D., Chomaz, J.M.: Effect of compressibility on the global stability of axisymmetric wake flows. J. Fluid Mech. **660**, 499–526 (2010)
7. Nichols, J.W., Lele, S.K.: Global modes and transient response of a cold supersonic jet. J. Fluid Mech. **669**, 225–241 (2011)
8. Busquet, D., Marquet, O., Richez, F., Juniper, M. P., Sipp, D.: Global stability analysis of turbulent flows around an airfoil near stall. Eurogen2017, Madrid (2017)
9. Crouch, J.D., Garbaruk, A., Strelets, M.: Global instability in the onset of transonic-wing buffet. J. Fluid Mech. **881**, 3–22 (2019)
10. Timme, S.: Global instability of wing shock-buffet onset. J. Fluid Mech. **885**, 1–32 (2020)
11. Ohmichi, Y., Yamada, K.: Matrix-free TriGlobal adjoint stability analysis of compressible Navier-Stokes equations. J. Comput. Phys. **437**, 110332 (2021)
12. Spalart, P.R., Allmaras, S.R.: A One-equation Turbulence Model for Aerodynamic Flows. AIAA Paper 1992–0439 (1992)
13. Stewart, G.W.: A Krylov-Schur algorithm for large eigen problems. SIAM J. Matrix Anal. Appl. **23**(3), 601–614 (2001)
14. Balay, S. et al.: PETSc/TAO User's Manual Revision 3.19. Argonne Technical Memorandum ANL-21/39 (2023)
15. Hernandez, V., Roman, J.E., Vidal, V.: SLEPc: a scalable and flexible toolkit for the solution of eigenvalue problems. ACM Trans. Math. Software **31**(3), 351–362 (2005)

16. Amestoy, P.R., Duff, I.S., Koster, J., L'Excellent, J.Y.: A fully asynchronous multifrontal solver using distributed dynamic scheduling. SIAM J. Matrix Anal. Appl. **23**(1), 15–41 (2001)
17. Shur, M., Strelets, M., Travin, A.: High-order Implicit Multi-block Navier-Stokes Code: Ten-year Experience of Application to RANS/DES/LES/DNS of Turbulent Flows. In: 7th Symposium on Overset Composite Grids & Solution Technology, Huntington Beach, CA, USA (2004). https://cfd.spbstu.ru//agarbaruk/doc/NTS_code.pdf. Accessed 10 Apr 2023
18. Belyaev, K.V., Garbaruk, A.V., Kravchenko, S.V., Strelets, M.K.: A comparison of different approaches for predicting transonic buffet onset on infinite swept wings. Supercomputing Front. Innovations **9**(4), 4–17 (2022)
19. Spalart, P.R.: Trends in Turbulence Treatments. AIAA Paper 2000–2306 (2000)
20. Vassberg, J.C., DeHann, M.A., Rivers, S.M., Wahls, R.A.: Development of a Common Research Model for Applied CFD Validation Studies. AIAA Paper–2008–6919 (2008)
21. Supercomputers Top 50 Homepage. http://top50.supercomputers.ru/list. Accessed 10 Apr 2023

CubicEoS.jl: Extensible, Open-Source Isothermal Phase Equilibrium Calculations for Fluids

Stepan Zakharov[1,2(✉)] and Vasily Pisarev[1,2]

[1] Joint Institute for High Temperatures of the Russian Academy of Sciences, Moscow, Russian Federation
stepanzh@gmail.com

[2] Moscow Institute of Physics and Technology (National Research University), Dolgoprudny, Moscow Region, Russian Federation

Abstract. We present open-source software for isochoric isothermal phase equilibrium calculation of fluids extensible on custom equations of state. We demonstrate robustness of the solvers by calculation of binodals and equilibrium parameters for a number of mixtures modelled by a cubic and a SAFT-family equations of state. Additionally, we consider multi-threaded computation of a phase diagram. The solvers are based on quasi-Newton minimization of Helmholtz free energy. The software is written in Julia language, and we discuss language features making it favorable for computational thermophysics problems.

Keywords: Phase equilibrium · Isochoric · Helmholtz free energy · Quasi-Newton optimization · Open-source · Multi-threaded

1 Introduction

Finding phase equilibrium at constant volume, temperature and moles (VT) naturally arises in control-volume hydrodynamic simulations of multiphase flows, particularly, in compositional reservoir modelling [4,22], and in density-based transport coefficients models for fluids [6,8]. In these cases, VT phase equilibrium suits better than conventional isothermal-isobaric (PT) phase equilibrium solvers because of relationships between primary variables of a problem.

A robust VT flash is based on minimization of Helmholtz free energy [11]. Usually, the flash tests thermodynamic stability of a single-phase state, and if the state is unstable, performs a phase split. Performance of a VT flash solver depends on minimization algorithm and choice of primary variables. Nichita compared different variable choices for phase stability [15].

Considering optimization algorithms, the family of quasi-Newton optimizers is attractive for computationally cheap Hessian-free iterations at the cost of slower convergence rate. In practice, an initial guess may lie far from solution, and one has to ensure positive-definiteness of Hessian or its approximation. While

V. Voevodin et al. (Eds.): RuSCDays 2023, LNCS 14388, pp. 59–73, 2023.
https://doi.org/10.1007/978-3-031-49432-1_5

Newton method has to maintain the property each iteration at high cost (e.g. by modified Cholesky decomposition), popular quasi-Newton solvers require the decomposition (or similar procedure) once.

As far as we know, the mentioned researchers did not publish software they used or implemented, whereas software for PT flash is widely known.

We present written in Julia language [2] open-source CubicEoS.jl [19] package which ships VT flash solver for two-phase fluid-fluid equilibrium based on quasi-Newton minimization of Helmholtz free energy. The package is extensible for equations of states (EoS). We show underlying thermodynamics and numerical methods. We present results of VT phase equilibrium calculations for a number of mixtures modelled by a general cubic [3] and CP-PC-SAFT [21] EoS.

2 Problem Statement

Suppose a mixture consisting of n components with mole numbers $\mathbf{N}$ occupying volume V at temperature T. The dimensionless Helmholtz free energy of the mixture in a single-phase state a^I is given by

$$a^I = a(\mathbf{N}, V, T) = -\frac{PV}{RT} + \frac{1}{RT}\sum_{i=1}^{n} N_i\mu_i, \tag{1}$$

where $\mathbf{N} = [N_1, \ldots, N_n]^\top$ is mole numbers of the components, $P = P(\mathbf{N}, V, T)$ is pressure, R is universal gas constant and $\mu_i = \mu_i(\mathbf{N}, V, T)$ is chemical potential of ith component. The chemical potential is defined (up to a temperature-dependant constant) as [13]

$$\frac{1}{RT}\mu_i(\mathbf{N}, V, T) = \ln N_i - \ln V + \ln \gamma_i, \tag{2}$$

where γ_i is inverse to "volume function coefficient" defined in [13].

For a two-phase state, the dimensionless Helmholtz free energy a^{II} is the sum of the energies over phases

$$a^{II} = a(\mathbf{N}', V', T) + a(\mathbf{N}'', V'', T), \tag{3}$$

where $'$ and $''$ are superscripts of the phases. The mole numbers $\mathbf{N}'$, $\mathbf{N}''$ and volumes V', V'' must be non-negative and follow physical (balance) constraints

$$\mathbf{N}' + \mathbf{N}'' = \mathbf{N}, \quad V' + V'' = V. \tag{4}$$

An equation of state may introduce another set of constraints.

Considering balance constraints (4) we obtain difference of the energies of two- and single-phase states $\Delta a = a^{II} - a^I$ at constant temperature

$$\Delta a(\mathbf{N}', V') = a(\mathbf{N}', V', T) + a(\mathbf{N} - \mathbf{N}', V - V', T) - a(\mathbf{N}, V, T). \tag{5}$$

2.1 Phase Stability

Details of the phase stability can be found in [25]. Here we outline that the problem is posed as constrained minimization of the tangent plane distance function $D(\boldsymbol{\eta}') = \lim_{V' \to 0} \Delta a / V'$

$$\min D(\boldsymbol{\eta}'), \quad \text{where } \boldsymbol{\eta}' \text{ are feasible.} \tag{6}$$

where $\boldsymbol{\eta}'$ is concentration of components in test phase. The feasible set of the concentrations is formed by physical constraints $\eta_i' > 0$ and model constraints from EoS. A negative global minimum of D corresponds to an unstable single-phase state.

2.2 Phase Split

For phase split we follow Jindrová and Mikyška [11]. Let us assume that the mixture is unstable and splits into two phases. The problem is to find equilibrium mole numbers of the phases $\mathbf{N}'$, $\mathbf{N}''$ and volumes V', V''.

The equilibrium state corresponds to a global minimum of two-phase state energy a^{II}. Since the energy of single-phase state a^{I} is constant, the minimums of a^{II} and Δa are the same. Finally, the phase split problem is transformed into a constrained optimization of Δa (5)

$$\min \Delta a(\mathbf{N}', V') \quad \text{where } \mathbf{N}', V' \text{ are feasible.} \tag{7}$$

2.3 Models of Fluid

In this work, we use a cubic equation of state and CP-PC-SAFT EoS [21]. Each of them introduces a model constraint on phase size.

The general cubic EoS [3] explicitly defines pressure

$$P(\mathbf{N}, V, T) = \frac{NRT}{V - \mathcal{B}(\mathbf{N})} - \frac{\mathcal{A}(\mathbf{N}, T)}{[V + \mathcal{C}(\mathbf{N})][V + \mathcal{D}(\mathbf{N})]}, \tag{8}$$

where $N = \sum_{i=1}^{n} N_i$ is the total mole number, and $\mathcal{A}$, $\mathcal{B}$, $\mathcal{C}$, $\mathcal{D}$ are EoS coefficients. Here we focus on the coefficient $\mathcal{B} = \sum_{i=1}^{n} N_i b_i$, where b_i is covolume parameter of ith component. This coefficient introduces a constraint on size of a phase and determines feasible region of thermodynamic states. Therefore, concentrations $\boldsymbol{\eta}'$ in phase stability problem (6) must satisfy

$$\sum_{i=1}^{n} \eta_i' b_i < 1. \tag{9}$$

For the phase splitting problem (7), the EoS (8) introduces constraints on moles $\mathbf{N}'$, $\mathbf{N}''$ and volumes V', V'' of the phases

$$\sum_{i=1}^{n} N_i' b_i < V', \quad \sum_{i=1}^{n} N_i'' b_i < V''. \tag{10}$$

CP-PC-SAFT EoS explicitly defines dimensionless Helmholtz free energy of a phase

$$a = a^{\text{ideal}} + a^{\text{hs}} + a^{\text{chain}} + a^{\text{disp}}. \tag{11}$$

The energy consists of ideal gas, hard sphere, chain, and dispersion contributions. Parameters of this EoS for a pure compound can be found from its critical and triple points. For full description of the EoS see [21], but here we should note that, the EoS constrains concentration of a phase. The pressure and chemical potential are determined from thermodynamic relations:

$$P = -RT\frac{\partial a}{\partial V}, \quad \mu_i = RT\frac{\partial a}{\partial N_i}. \tag{12}$$

We now summarize implementation concerns of the models.

- The cubic EoS (8) defines pressure, which can be analytically integrated to get chemical potential (2) and energy (1). On other hand, CP-PC-SAFT (11) explicitly defines energy, whereas pressure and chemical potential can be found by differentiation.
- CP-PC-SAFT EoS is algebraically more complex than the cubic EoS, so it is suitable to calculate the derivatives (12) by automatic differentiation.
- Both EoS introduce limits for size of phases, but in case of the cubic EoS the constraints are much simpler to express analytically.

3 Numerical Approach

Initially, both phase stability (6) and phase split (7) problems are *constrained* optimization problems. Whereas equality constraints (4) were accounted analytically, inequality constraints may be accounted in *unconstrained* optimization through line search strategy. We sought for faster (Hessian-free) alternatives to Newton method and choose to adapt Broyden-Fletcher-Goldfarb-Shanno (BFGS) [17] for our purposes.

BFGS is an iterative deterministic quasi-Newton solver for unconstrained optimization. It does not need calculation of the Hessian, hence the iteration cost is lower than for Newton method. Once an initial Hessian is provided, BFGS keeps its approximation $\mathbf{B}_k$ positive-definitive guaranteed by an updating formula. BFGS involves line search, which chooses a magnitude of step towards the descent direction. The line search should be both computationally efficient and precise.

The next approximation of the solution $\mathbf{x}_{k+1}$ is found in the following steps. Firstly, the descent direction $\mathbf{d}_k$ is sought from linear system

$$\mathbf{d}_k = -\mathbf{B}_k^{-1}\nabla f(\mathbf{x}_k), \tag{13}$$

where $\nabla f(\mathbf{x}_k)$ is gradient of the objective function f.

The second stage is to find step magnitude $\alpha > 0$. It is sought from approximate scalar minimization of $(\alpha) \to f(\mathbf{x}_k + \alpha\mathbf{d}_k)$. For that we used strong backtracking line search [17] which seeks for an α^* satisfying strong Wolfe conditions in two phases. The bracketing phase locates interval of the answer, and zoom phase finds it. Here is list of our modifications.

- We added maximum allowed step $\alpha_{\max}$ in bracketing phase, so upper bound of the interval is ensured to be less than $\alpha_{\max}$. Essentially, introducing $\alpha_{\max}$ in the line search allows to account inequality constraints in the optimization.
- We included parabolic approximation [9] in both stages for numerical stability near stationary points of $\phi(\alpha)$.
- We used cubic interpolation [17] in both stages for faster convergence.

Once magnitude α^* is known, the new approximation of the solution is

$$\mathbf{x}_{k+1} = \mathbf{x}_k + \alpha^* \mathbf{d}_k. \tag{14}$$

The final step of the iteration checks a stop criterion at $\mathbf{x}_{k+1}$, e.g. norm of the gradient. If the stop criterion is satisfied, $\mathbf{x}_{k+1}$ is considered as a local minimum of the objective function f. Otherwise, the next approximation of the Hessian $\mathbf{B}_{k+1}$ is constructed by a symmetric rank-two update, which keeps positive definiteness

$$\mathbf{B}_{k+1} = \mathbf{B}_k + \frac{\mathbf{y}_k \mathbf{y}_k^\top}{\mathbf{y}_k^\top \mathbf{s}_k} - \frac{\mathbf{B}_k \mathbf{s}_k \mathbf{s}_k^\top \mathbf{B}_k^\top}{\mathbf{s}_k^\top \mathbf{B}_k \mathbf{s}_k}, \tag{15}$$

where $\mathbf{s}_k = \mathbf{x}_{k+1} - \mathbf{x}_k$, $\mathbf{y}_k = \nabla f(\mathbf{x}_{k+1}) - \nabla f(\mathbf{x}_k)$. Importantly, this update can be made directly to the Cholesky factors of $\mathbf{B}_k$.

We found that standard update on inverse of $\mathbf{B}_k$ sometimes leads to the loss of numerical positive definiteness, and the BFGS method based on (15) with the Cholesky factors of the direct Hessian approximation is more stable.

One iteration in our version of BFGS has computational complexity of $O(n^2)$. Updating (15) costs $O(n^2)$. Keeping $\mathbf{B}_k$ in (15) in the from of Cholesky factors leads to the cost of solving (13) $O(n^2)$ as well. Only initialization of the algorithm may cost $O(n^3)$, when modified Cholesky factorization is needed.

3.1 Phase Stability

In [25] we showed that BFGS can be used for solving phase stability without Hessian calculation. With proper scaling of optimization variables one can provide a standard initial guess for concentration using a supplemental equation of state and identity matrix as initial Hessian.

The physical inequality constraints ($\eta_i' > 0$) are easily applied to (14). For the general cubic EoS inequality constraint (9) leads to a quadratic inequality and gives feasible interval of α. For CP-PC-SAFT EoS we find upper bound of the step magnitude using bisection between 0 and the physical upper bound. When the bisection finds a non-throwing exception magnitude α_1, the feasible interval for magnitude is considered to be $\alpha \in (0, \alpha_1)$ for CP-PC-SAFT EoS. Therefore, one can solve both the physical and the model inequality constraints to find $\alpha_{\max}$ for the line search. When $\alpha_{\max}$ does not meet corresponding lower bound inequalities, the optimization fails.

3.2 Phase Split

The phase split is run when the phase stability indicates unstable single-phase state. For the phase split we use physical unknowns $\mathbf{x}' = [\mathbf{N}'; V']^\top$. Though, it is not the performant option, it is practically robust. Other approaches are available in the literature, to name a few [7,16]. Expressions for the gradient and Hessian of energy difference (5) can be found in [11].

The physical constraints are derived from the balance constraints (4) and positiveness of mole numbers $\mathbf{N}'$ and volume V'. Applying those to (14) gives inequalities for step magnitude α

$$0 < [\mathbf{x}'_k + \alpha \mathbf{d}_k]_i < [\mathbf{x}^I]_i, \quad i = 1, \dots, n+1,$$

where $[\mathbf{a}]_i$ means ith component of $\mathbf{a}$, and $\mathbf{x}^I = [\mathbf{N}; V]^\top = \text{const}$.

For the general cubic EoS (8) each of the model constraints (10) applied to (14) leads to a linear inequality, and can be solved analytically. In case of CP-PC-SAFT we determine $\alpha_{\max}$ numerically in a similar manner described for the phase stability.

Solution of the inequality constraints is maximum allowed magnitude of step $\alpha_{\max}$. When this magnitude does not satisfy lower bound constraints, $\mathbf{x}'_{k+1}$ can not be found and the optimization fails.

Initial guess for the unknowns is generated similar to [11]. The initial two-phase state has a phase with concentration $\boldsymbol{\eta}'$ given by the phase stability. The suitable saturation $s' = V'/V$ is found by backtracking on energy difference $(s') \to \Delta a(s' V \boldsymbol{\eta}', s' V)$ until a negative $\Delta a < 0$ is found. Once the saturation is known, initial moles $\mathbf{N}'$ and volume V' can be calculated.

The initial Hessian is explicitly calculated and factorized by modified Cholesky decomposition. Hence, a phase split run requires one calculation of the Hessian.

4 Implementation Notes

Before developing CubicEoS.jl [19] package, we had broad experience in writing physics-related software in C/C++ and Python languages. Some years ago we tried Julia language [2], and now it's our first-option tool. The key features of Julia are hierarchical dynamic type system and multiple dispatch. The Julia's compiler is known to be state-of-art producing performant programs even with untyped arguments. Julia is a notable option for fast writing fast software. It has broad built-in support of linear algebra, C-language calls, environment management, unit testing and verbose documentation. Julia natively offers coroutines, multi-threading and distributed computing. Additionally, there are ports of existing libraries for GPU and distributed computing. Though, Julia is in active development, it has friendly and responsive community. The language ecosystem consists of small packages published mostly on GitHub. Many related packages now accumulate into fine-tuning frameworks.

CubicEoS.jl defines interface for an EoS object through method overloading. After implementing the interface in dependency injection manner, a user may use the solvers. A similar pattern for custom EoS can be found in Clapeyron.jl package [24], but it lacks of VT solvers. For now CubicEoS.jl requires that, a custom EoS object must be a subtype of the CubicEoS.jl EoS object, but we consider to implement a trait-based dispatch for better decoupling of modules.

The general cubic EoS is a built-in module, which may be used as an implementation example for other EoS. In case of the cubic EoS, definitions of the necessary physical relations are analytical. But, our implementation of CP-PC-SAFT EoS [18] uses automatic differentiation [23].

CubicEoS.jl contains interface for custom scaling of optimization unknowns, which we use for research of better VT solvers. This feature is implemented by multiple dispatch as well. We reduce memory allocations using optional *buffer* argument throughout the package.

CubicEoS.jl uses ours Downhill.jl [20], which contains a collection of descent-based optimization methods. This package exploits Julia's elegant *iterate* protocol and a monad-like pattern for customization of solvers keeping a core stepping method of a solver the same. We needed our implementation of BFGS because standard Optim.jl [14] had too many allocations, thus it's expensive to use repeatedly. We also implemented modified Cholesky factorization, because PositiveFactorizations.jl [10] more suitable for large matrices.

Our experience of Julia shows that this language is flexible for numerical computations. It allows to implement effective low level operations without C-language extensions and with much less effort that C/C++ requires.

5 Results

We show results of solving phase equilibrium for a number of mixtures modelled by the general cubic EoS (8) and CP-PC-SAFT EoS (11). The flash is performed on a 100×100 uniform grid of overall concentrations $\sum_i N_i/V$ and temperatures of a mixture. The following results may be compared with [11] where the flash were performed with Peng-Robinson EoS. In the last subsection, we consider parallel computation of a phase diagram.

For the phase stability the stopping criterion is $\max_i |\mu_i - \mu_i'| < 10^{-6}RT$. A single-phase was considered unstable if one of four tries shows $D < -10^{-5}$. In that case a phase split were performed with the stopping criterion

$$\max_i |\mu_i' - \mu_i''| < 10^{-6}RT, \quad \frac{|P' - P''|V}{RT\sum_i N_i} < 10^{-6}.$$

Both the phase stability and the phase split could take no more than 1000 iterations per run.

For phase split we sorted states by phase compressibility z in post-processing manner. A phase with a lower value of z is labelled as "liquid", and the second phase is labelled as "gas". The general **c**ubic EoS is labelled as "C" and CP-PC-**S**AFT EoS is labelled as "S".

Critical points and acentric factors of the pure components were taken from NIST [12] for both EoS. The remained parameters for the general cubic EoS were taken from [1]. All parameters for CP-PC-SAFT EoS were taken from [21] except hydrogen sulfide [5]. Binary interaction parameters for CP-PC-SAFT EoS were considered zero. Also, we did not recalculate parameters of CP-PC-SAFT EoS on NIST critical and triple points.

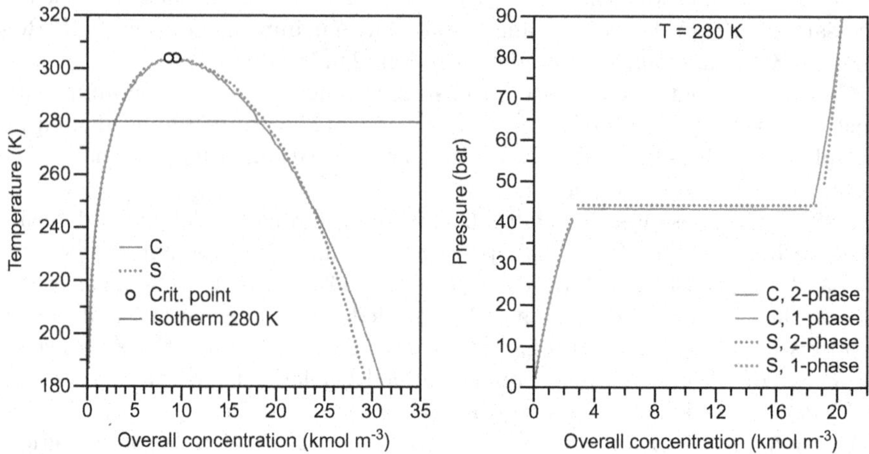

Fig. 1. Example 1 (CO_2). Approximate binodal and 280 K isotherm (left). Equilibrium pressure as a function of overall concentration at $T = 280$ K (right).

5.1 Example 1

This example shows phase equilibrium parameters of pure carbon dioxide CO_2. The binodal is shown in Fig. 1 (left). During isothermal isochoric compression, single-phase state of CO_2 becomes unstable, CO_2 splits and becomes single-phase again at a higher concentration. Corresponding pressure as a function of overall concentration is shown in Fig. 1 (right). Note that, an isobaric flash can not distinguish states within two-phase region. Mass densities of both states for $T = 280$ K are shown in Fig. 2 (left).

5.2 Example 2

This example shows phase equilibrium parameters of a binary mixture of methane C_1 (0.547413) and normal pentane nC_5 (0.452587). The approximate binodal is shown in Fig. 2 (right). Corresponding isothermal equilibrium pressure as a function of overall concentration is shown in Fig. 3 (left). Mass densities of both states at $T = 371$ K are shown in Fig. 3 (right). Molar fractions of the components are shown in Fig. 4.

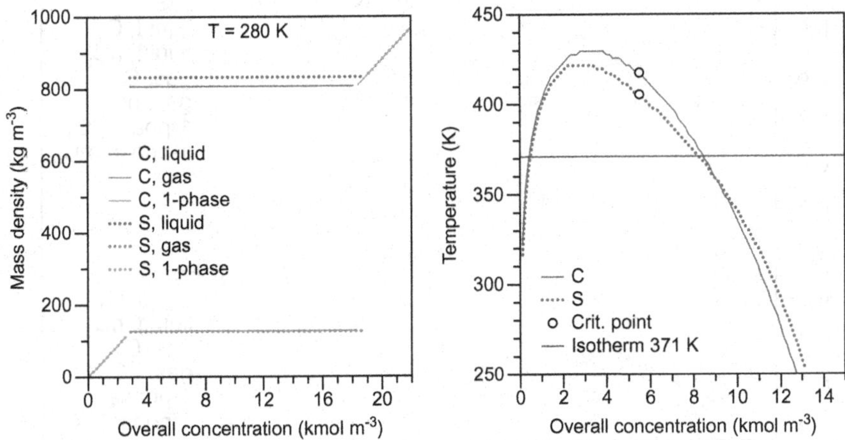

Fig. 2. Example 1 (CO_2): mass densities as function of overall concentration at $T =$ 280 K (left). Example 2 ($C_1 + nC_5$): approximate binodal (right).

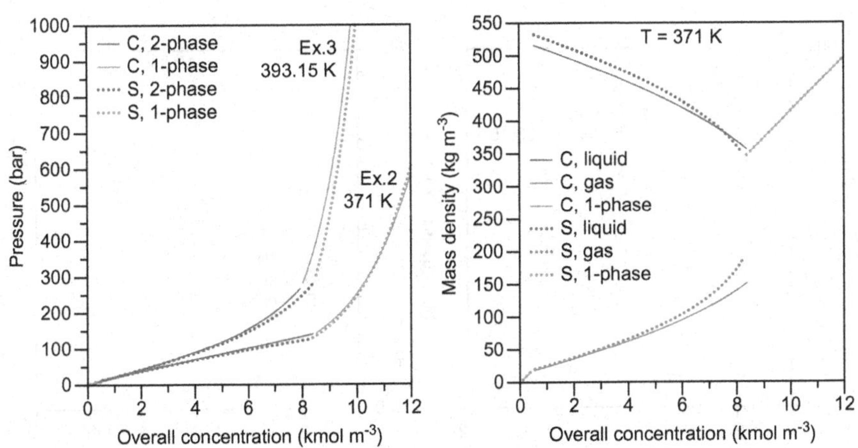

Fig. 3. Pressure as a function of overall concentration for Example 2 ($C_1 + nC_5$) at 371 K and Example 3 ($N_2 + C_1 + C_3 + nC_{10}$) at 393.15 K (left). Example 2 ($C_1 + nC_5$): mass densities as function of overall concentration at 371 K (right).

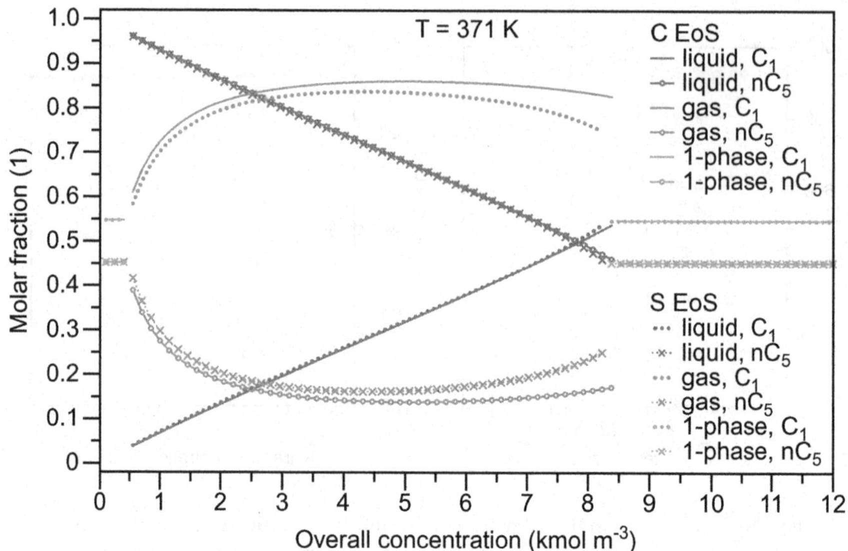

Fig. 4. Example 2 ($C_1 + nC_5$ mixture): equilibrium molar fractions as functions of overall concentration at $T = 371$ K.

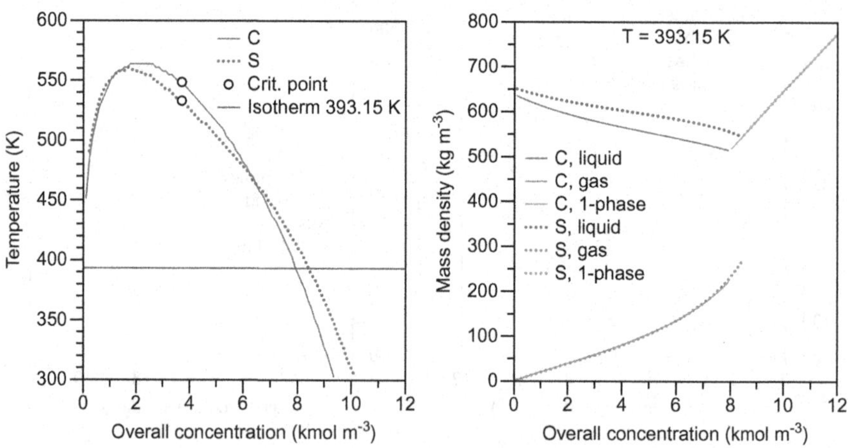

Fig. 5. Example 3 ($N_2 + C_1 + C_3 + nC_{10}$). Approximate binodal and 393.15 K isotherm (left). Equilibrium pressure as a function of overall concentration at $T = 393.15$ K (right).

5.3 Example 3

This example shows phase equilibrium parameters of a mixture of four components, namely, nitrogen N_2 (0.2463), methane C_1 (0.2208), propane C_3 (0.2208) and normal decane nC_{10} (0.3121). The approximate binodal is shown in Fig. 5 (left). Corresponding equilibrium pressure as a function of overall concentration is shown in Fig. 3 (left). Mass densities of both states for T = 393.15 K are shown in Fig. 5 (right).

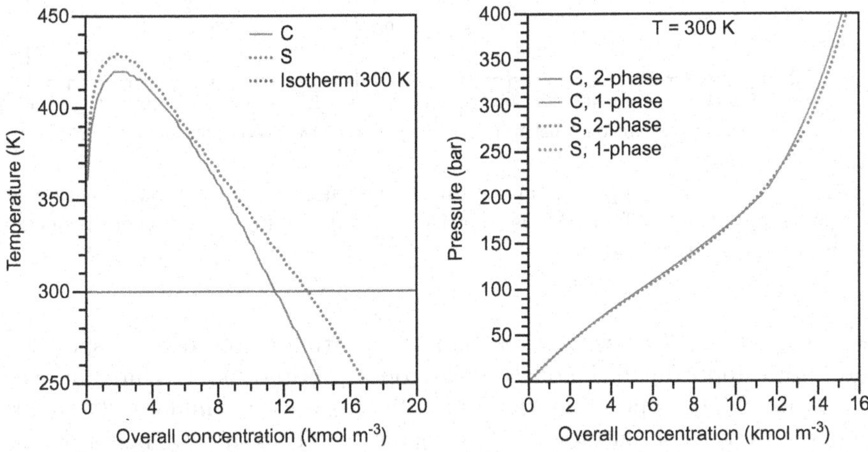

Fig. 6. Example 4 (7-component mixture). Approximate binodal and 300 K isotherm (left). Equilibrium pressure as a function of overall concentration at T = 300 K (right).

5.4 Example 4

This example shows phase equilibrium parameters of a mixture of seven components, namely, nitrogen N_2 (0.00325), carbon dioxide CO_2 (0.01556), hydrogen sulfide H_2S (0.03329), methane C_1 (0.82829), propane C_3 (0.08552), normal hexane nC_6 (0.01725) and normal decane nC_{10} (0.01684). The approximate binodal is shown in Fig. 6 (left). Corresponding isothermal equilibrium pressure as a function of overall concentration is shown in Fig. 6 (right). Gaseous phase molar fractions at different temperatures and mass densities of both states at T = 300 K are shown in Fig. 7. Both EoS predict retrograde behavior of the mixture.

5.5 Multi-Threaded Computation of Phase Diagram

In this section we consider efficiency of multi-threaded VT flash computations. We tested two parallel strategies on all mixtures from the examples above in

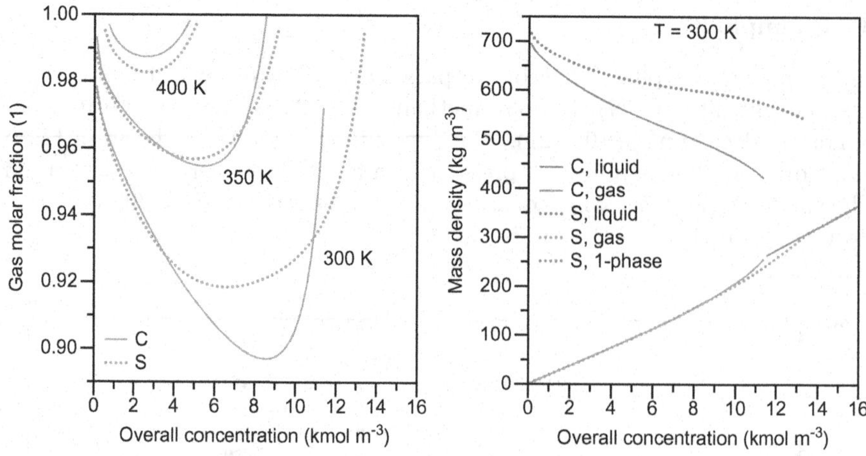

Fig. 7. Example 4 (7-component mixture). Equilibrium gas phase molar fraction at different temperatures (left) and mass densities (right) as a function of overall concentration at $T = 300$ K (right).

the ranges of overall concentrations and temperatures given on corresponding figures with approximate binodals. The stopping criteria and volume are the same as for the examples, but the grid is finer, we used a uniform 200×200 grid of the overall concentration and temperature. The tests were performed on a single CPU AMD EPYC 7351P with 16 cores and 64 GB of RAM.

We compare two parallel strategies. The first ("cold") performs the flashes independently on available threads. We prepare and shuffle 40000 tasks to distribute work between the threads better.

The second ("hot") strategy uses wave pattern from minimum of to maximum of concentration and temperature, e.g. from bottom left corner to top right corner in Fig. 6 (left). First three runs are performed serially, then a new chunk of calculations is performed in parallel with precondition on available data from previous two chunks. Precisely, for a (η, T) point we obtain initial guess from three neighbors. The initial guess for a stability run is average $\boldsymbol{\eta}'^*$ of concentrations with the lowest D from neighboring stability runs. Then we check value of $D(\boldsymbol{\eta}'^*)$ and only if it's positive, performs a stability run with standard initial guesses (see Sect. 3.1). For the split, we calculate averages of $\mathbf{N}'$, $\mathbf{N}''$ and V', V'' of neighboring split runs and choose for initial guess $\mathbf{N}^*$ and V^*, which correspond to a phase with larger total moles. If the stability indicates non-stable single phase state, we try to perform a split from initial estimates $\mathbf{N}^*$ and V^*. If the split fails, we perform the usual split from concentration given by the stability. In perfect scenario, $D(\boldsymbol{\eta}'^*)$ is negative, stability is not performed, and split converges in few iterations from $\mathbf{N}^*$ and V^*.

The results for the mixtures have similar trends, so we consider only cases of Examples 2 and 4. Total duration of the flashes versus number of threads are shown in Fig. 8 for both EoS and the strategies. Efficiency of both "cold" and

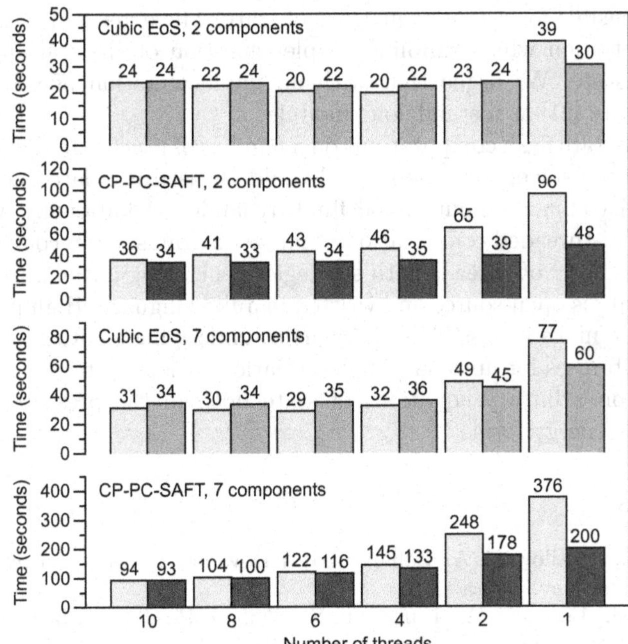

Fig. 8. Comparison of multi-threaded VT flash efficiency. Each bar corresponds to a total duration of 4×10^4 VT flashes in ranges of overall concentration and temperature for Examples 2 and 4. The orange and blue bars correspond to calculations with cubic EoS and CP-PC-SAFT EoS, respectively. Translucent and opaque bars correspond to "cold" and "hot" strategies, respectively. (Color figure online)

"hot" strategies saturates at 4–6 threads for the cubic EoS, and at higher number of threads for CP-PC-SAFT EoS. This may be caused by higher algebraic complexity of CP-PC-SAFT EoS. The "hot" strategy reduces number of BFGS iterations and is faster on small number of threads. It is especially efficient for CP-PC-SAFT EoS.

We suppose that the problem reaches memory bounds on few threads. For a simple EoS there is no need of large number of threads. For a complex EoS the number of threads should be chosen carefully. When a single thread is used, strategies producing initial guesses are preferable. For example, flash results from a previous time layer should be used in a non-stationary hydrodynamic simulation.

6 Conclusion

We implemented CubicEoS.jl package for isothermal-isochoric two-phase fluid-fluid phase equilibrium computations. The flash is based on minimization of Helmholtz free energy. The package ships with a general cubic equation of state

[3] and is extensible for custom equations of state. The extensions can use automatic differentiation which simplifies implementation of algebraically complex equations of state. We argue that with an implementation of CP-PC-SAFT equation of state [21] as a standalone module.

We demonstrate flash computations on a number of practically used mixtures. The implemented solvers are robust and could be used in related applications, e.g. in control-volume computational fluid dynamics. Additionally, we present results for multi-threaded computation of phase diagrams and recommend usage of moderate number of threads with strategies generating initial guesses.

Our software is open-source and written in Julia language. High performance of the language make it possible to implement underlying algorithms directly in Julia. Using libraries for automatic differentiation, it is easy to extend the flash computation on arbitrary equations of state both in the pressure-explicit or Helmholtz free energy forms.

References

1. Batalin, O., Brusilovskij, A., Zaharov, M.: Fazovye ravnovesija v sistemah prirodnyh uglevodorodov. Nedra (1992)
2. Bezanson, J., Edelman, A., Karpinski, S., Shah, V.B.: Julia: a fresh approach to numerical computing. SIAM Rev. **59**(1), 65–98 (2017). https://doi.org/10.1137/141000671
3. Brusilovsky, A.: Mathematical simulation of phase behavior of natural multicomponent systems at high pressures with an equation of state. SPE Res. Eng. **7**(01), 117–122 (1992). https://doi.org/10.2118/20180-pa
4. Chen, Z., Huan, G., Ma, Y.: Computational Methods for Multiphase Flows in Porous Media. SIAM, Philadelphia (2006)
5. Chiko, A., Polishuk, I., Cea-Klapp, E., Garrido, J.M.: Comparison of CP-PC-SAFT and SAFT-VR-Mie in predicting phase equilibria of binary systems comprising gases and 1-alkyl-3-methylimidazolium ionic liquids. Molecules **26**(21), 6621 (2021). https://doi.org/10.3390/molecules26216621
6. Ciotta, F., Trusler, J.M., Vesovic, V.: Extended hard-sphere model for the viscosity of dense fluids. Fluid Phase Equilib. **363**, 239–247 (2014). https://doi.org/10.1016/j.fluid.2013.11.032
7. Cismondi, M., Ndiaye, P.M., Tavares, F.W.: A new simple and efficient flash algorithm for T-v specifications. Fluid Phase Equilib. **464**, 32–39 (2018). https://doi.org/10.1016/j.fluid.2018.02.019
8. Gerasimov, A., Alexandrov, I., Grigoriev, B.: Modeling and calculation of thermodynamic properties and phase equilibria of oil and gas condensate fractions based on two generalized multiparameter equations of state. Fluid Phase Equilib. **418**, 204–223 (2016)
9. Hager, W.W., Zhang, H.: A new conjugate gradient method with guaranteed descent and an efficient line search. SIAM J. Optim. **16**(1), 170–192 (2005). https://doi.org/10.1137/030601880
10. Holy, T.: PositiveFactorizations.jl (2020). https://github.com/timholy/PositiveFactorizations.jl
11. Jindrová, T., Mikyška, J.: Fast and robust algorithm for calculation of two-phase equilibria at given volume, temperature, and moles. Fluid Phase Equilib. **353**, 101–114 (2013). https://doi.org/10.1016/j.fluid.2013.05.036

12. Linstrom, P.: NIST chemistry WebBook, NIST standard reference database 69 (1997). https://doi.org/10.18434/T4D303
13. Mikyška, J., Firoozabadi, A.: A new thermodynamic function for phase-splitting at constant temperature, moles, and volume. AIChE J. **57**(7), 1897–1904 (2010). https://doi.org/10.1002/aic.12387
14. Mogensen, P.K., Riseth, A.N.: Optim: a mathematical optimization package for Julia. J. Open Source Softw. **3**(24), 615 (2018). https://doi.org/10.21105/joss.00615
15. Nichita, D.V.: Fast and robust phase stability testing at isothermal-isochoric conditions. Fluid Phase Equilib. **447**, 107–124 (2017). https://doi.org/10.1016/j.fluid.2017.05.022
16. Nichita, D.V.: New unconstrained minimization methods for robust flash calculations at temperature, volume and moles specifications. Fluid Phase Equilib. **466**, 31–47 (2018). https://doi.org/10.1016/j.fluid.2018.03.012
17. Nocedal, J., Wright, S.J.: Numerical Optimization. Springer Series in Operations Research, 2nd edn. Springer, New York (2006). https://doi.org/10.1007/978-0-387-40065-5
18. Pisarev, V., Zakharov, S.: CP_PC_SAFT.jl. https://github.com/stepanzh/CP_PC_SAFT.jl
19. Pisarev, V., Zakharov, S.: CubicEoS.jl. https://github.com/vvpisarev/CubicEoS.jl/
20. Pisarev, V., Zakharov, S.: Downhill.jl. https://github.com/vvpisarev/Downhill.jl/
21. Polishuk, I.: Standardized critical point-based numerical solution of statistical association fluid theory parameters: the perturbed chain-statistical association fluid theory equation of state revisited. Ind. Eng. Chem. Res. **53**(36), 14127–14141 (2014). https://doi.org/10.1021/ie502633e
22. Polívka, O., Mikyška, J.: Compositional modeling in porous media using constant volume flash and flux computation without the need for phase identification. J. Comput. Phys. **272**, 149–169 (2014)
23. Revels, J., Lubin, M., Papamarkou, T.: Forward-mode automatic differentiation in Julia (arXiv:1607.07892) (2016). https://doi.org/10.48550/arXiv.1607.07892
24. Walker, P.J., Yew, H.W., Riedemann, A.: Clapeyron.jl: an extensible, open-source fluid thermodynamics toolkit. Ind. Eng. Chem. Res. **61**(20), 7130–7153 (2022). https://doi.org/10.1021/acs.iecr.2c00326
25. Zakharov, S.A., Pisarev, V.V.: Quasi-newton single-phase stability testing without explicit hessian calculation. Math. Models Comput. Simul. **15**(5), 894–904 (2023). https://doi.org/10.1134/S2070048223050137

Efficiency and Accuracy of High-Performance Calculations of the Electrostatic Energy of Thin Films Atomistic Clusters

Fedor Grigoriev(✉), Vladimir Sulimov, and Alexander Tikhonravov

Research Computing Center, M.V. Lomonosov Moscow State University, Moscow 119234, Russia

fedor.grigoriev@gmail.com, vs@dimonta.com, tikh@srcc.msu.ru

Abstract. A study of the efficiency and accuracy of calculations of the electrostatic energy of atomistic clusters of thin films of silicon dioxide is presented. Electrostatic energy is calculated using the Particle Mesh Ewald method using the GROMACS program. The parallel efficiency is calculated for the number of cores from 8 to 64. The dependence of the results on two main parameters of the Particle Mesh Ewald method - fourierspacing and interpolation order - is studied. It is found that the density profiles of growing films are sensitive to the interpolation order.

Keyword: Atomistic modeling · Silicon dioxide films · High-performance simulations · Particle mesh Ewald

1 Introduction

Modern optical coatings are widely used mirrors, photovoltaic cells, filters, antireflecting coatings and other optical devices [1]. These coatings consist of several tens dielectric layers with different refractive indices. Choice of the number of the layers, their material and thickness depends on the device in which the coating is used.

One of the problems occurring in the design and manufacture of the coatings relates to the significant dependence of the film's properties on the fabrication conditions. For instance, in the physical vapor deposition method the density of the fabricated films depends significantly on the energy of the arriving to the substrate atoms [1]. Also, the structure and properties of films, which are important for applications, are affected by the substrate temperature, the deposition angle, the pressure and composition of the gas in the vacuum chamber, and the geometry of the coating device [2]. Studying of the dependencies between the fabrication conditions and film characteristics is the challenge task due to strong nonequilibrium character of the film growth process and large number of parameters, acting process.

At present, mathematical modeling is widely used to study film growth and calculate its characteristics depending on production conditions [3, 4]. The most fundamental level of this modeling is the atomistic one, which includes classical molecular dynamics (MD),

V. Voevodin et al. (Eds.): RuSCDays 2023, LNCS 14388, pp. 74–85, 2023.
https://doi.org/10.1007/978-3-031-49432-1_6

Monte Carlo and quantum methods. Classical methods are used to calculate the structural and mechanical parameters of films [5–7] quantum methods - for calculating optical and electronic parameters and studying the formation of point defects [8]. In atomistic modeling, the film is represented by clusters ranging in dimension from nanometers to tens of nanometers with the number of atoms from several hundred (quantum methods) to several million. The dimension of the cluster depends on the modeling task and the available computing power.

The numerical efficiency of the modeling using the classical methods significantly depends on the force field describing the interatomic interactions. It's important that as a rule the optical coatings are formed from the two- and more component materials, such as SiO_2, TiO_2, HfO_2, ZnO and so on. Due to difference in the electronegativity of the chemical elements, the partial charges occur in the atoms. These charges produce the long-range electrostatic interactions in film forming materials, that should be taken into account in frame of force fields used for the classical simulation. Since the large number of atoms are involved in these interactions, the numerical efficiency reduces. This is why the maximum number of atoms when simulating optical films is on the order of millions, while when simulating single-component materials such as metal, the number of atoms can exceed tens of millions.

Today the Particle Mesh Ewald (PME) [9] method is widely used for the calculation of the electrostatic component of the energy of the interatomic interaction. In this method the sum of the pair interactions is divided in two parts. First of them is calculated directly (short-range term) while the second part (long-range term) is calculated using the fast Fourier transform method. In the present work we study the accuracy and numerical efficiency of the PME method at the simulation of the atomistic clusters of silicon dioxide films. The two main parameters, fourierspacing and interpolation order that control the calculation of the long-range term are varied [10]. The number of cores in the parallel computing changes from 8 to 64.

2 Method of the Simulation

The deposited film is a macroscopic object, which in atomistic modeling is represented by a microscopic cluster (Fig. 1). In a real technological process, the substrate thickness is, as a rule, much greater than the film thickness. To reduce the number of atoms during simulation, the substrate is represented by a thin layer with a thickness of the order of several nanometers (Fig. 1, right side). Periodic boundary conditions (PBC) are applied in a plane parallel to the substrate [11]. In the direction of film growth, a rigid wall approach can be applied to restrict the movement of atoms, as well as PBC.

As it mentioned in the Introduction, the dimensions of the clusters depend on the simulation task. To calculate the density, radial distribution function (RDF), distribution of the structural rings over the number of atoms, distribution of the valence angle, bulk modulus, Poisson ration, Young's modulus the relatively small clusters with dimensions of several of nanometers are sufficient [12]. Investigation of the surface roughness, porosity of the films, deposited by the low-energy methods, stresses, occurring in the films during their growth, requires the larger since these characteristics depends both on the films thickness and in-plane dimensions [3]. Also, the ratio of L and H (Fig. 1, right side) depends on the calculated characteristics. For instance, the stresses in the normal deposited films depend more on the films thickness than on in-plane dimensions[13], while the surface roughness of the high-porous films can be underestimated in the simulation with small L.

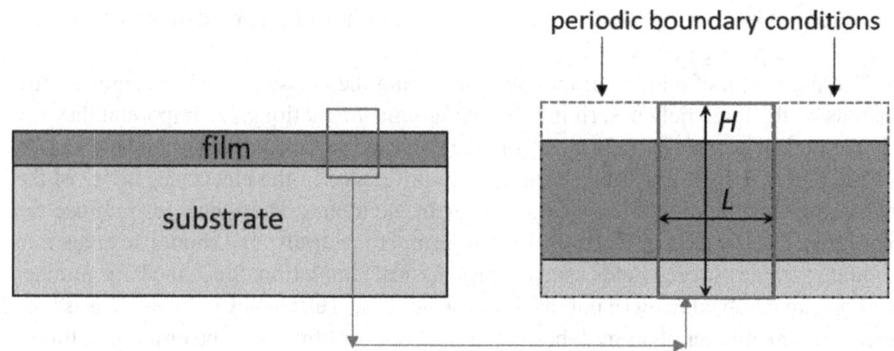

Fig. 1. Representation of the film and substrate in the atomistic simulation.

The clusters with largest dimensions are required to study the anisotropic films, produced by the deposition at large angles. This method of thin films producing is called glancing angle deposition (GLAD). GLAD films are characterized by the formation of the separated structures of different shapes [14]. The dimensions of these structures vary from several nanometers to several tens of nanometers. Thus, for atomistic modeling of these structures, clusters with a dimension of at least several tens of nanometers are required.

Simulation of the process of thin film deposition begins with the preparation of the substrate structure. Both crystalline and amorphous phases of materials are used in experiments [1]. In the first case, the structure of the substrate can be generated using the crystallographic coordinates of the atoms in the unit cell of the chosen polymorph of the substrate materials. In the second case, the MD quenching–melting method can be used to amorphize the initial crystal structure [15].

The simulation of the films growth is carried out using the step-by-step procedure [16]. In each step the specified number of the atoms inserted in the top of the simulation box. Coordinates of the atoms are chosen randomly, and their initial velocities are specified accordingly to the deposition conditions. It should be noted that LAMMPS program [17] has the special functionality for the simulation of the deposition process which makes modeling easier from a technical point of view.

The present paper considers the simulation of silicon dioxide thin films. The potential energy of the interaction between all of the atoms in the simulation area is calculated using the non-polarizable pairwise DESIL force field [16]:

$$U = q_i q_j / r_{ij} + A_{ij} / r_{ij}^{12} - B_{ij} / r_{ij}^{6} \tag{1}$$

where $q_{i(j)}$ is the charge of the $i(j)$-th atom, $q_O = -0.65e$, $q_{Si} = 1.3e$, A_{ij} and B_{ij}, are parameters of the Lennard-Jones potential for the van der Waals interaction, r_{ij} is the interatomic distance, $A_{SiO} = 4.6 \cdot 10^{-8}$ kJ·(nm)^{12}/mol, $A_{SiSi} =$

$A_{OO} = 1.5 \cdot 10^{-6}$ kJ·(nm)^{12}/mol, $B_{SiO} = 4.2 \cdot 10^{-3}$ kJ·(nm)^6/mol, $B_{SiSi} = B_{OO} = 5 \cdot 10^{-5}$ kJ·(nm)^6/mol, e is the value of the elementary charge.

The substrate temperature is keep constant using the Berendsen thermostat [18]. The simulation was performed using the equipment of the shared research facilities of HPC computing resources at Lomonosov Moscow State University [19]. The processors with following characteristics are used: Intel Xeon Gold 6126, 2.6 GHz, 12 cores, 16 GB (queue «pasçal» in the supercomputer "Lomonosov-2"). The GROMACS program [20] is used for the MD simulation.

3 Results and Discussion

The clusters of the two different dimensions, obtained as described in the **Method** section, are used in the simulation (Fig. 2). The total number of the atoms in the first and second clusters are equal to $1.8 \cdot 10^5$ and $2.1 \cdot 10^6$, respectively. The "small" cluster represents the dense homogeneous film, which is formed by the high-energy normal deposition. The "large" cluster represents the high porous anisotropic GLAD film (see the previous section for the details). So, these clusters allow to study the dependencies of efficiency and accuracy of PME method on the size of the simulation clusters and film density. Both clusters are deposited at room temperature, $T = 300$ K. The energy of the deposited Si atom is equal to 10 eV, and energy of oxygen atoms is equal to 0.1 eV. The low energy of oxygen atoms takes into account that the arriving to the substrate Si atoms are oxidizes by the gas in the vacuum chamber.

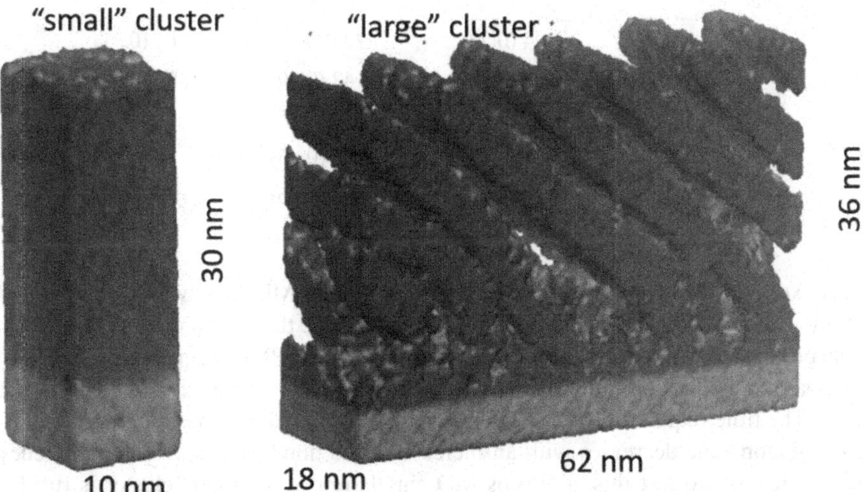

Fig. 2. Atomistic clusters of deposited silicon dioxide films, used in the simulation.

The results of the simulation are presented in Tables 1, 2 and Figs. 2 a, b. The dependence of the simulation time of the 20 ps MD trajectory on the one of the key PME parameters, PME order, and number of the computational cores is presented in

Table 1. The PME order = 4 means that the cubic interpolation is applied in the calculation of the reciprocal part of the electrostatic energy. The increase in the interpolation order increases the accuracy of the computational procedure but makes it more time-consuming. The parallel efficiency is defined as follows:

$$e(N) = 8t_8/(Nt_N), \tag{2}$$

where N is the number of cores, t_8 and t_N are the simulation time using 8 and N cores, respectively. Values of *e(N)* are also presented in Table 1.

Table 1. The dependence of the simulation time (s) on the number of computational cores N and value of the PME order parameter for both clusters (Fig. 2). Values in the parentheses are the values of the parallel efficiency *e(N)*, see Eq. (2).

PME order	*N*			
	8	16	32	64
"large" cluster				
4	1446	820 (0.88)	451 (0.80)	352 (0.51)
6	4106	2278 (0.90)	1224 (0.84)	682 (0.75)
8	6207	3337 (0.93)	1732 (0.90)	970 (0.80)
10	10352	5932 (0.87)	2920 (0.89)	1498 (0.86)
12	18037	9391 (0.96)	5120 (0.88)	2594 (0.87)
"small" cluster				
4	151	104 (0.73)	72 (0.53)	61 (0.31)
6	393	264 (0.74)	142 (0.69)	93 (0.53)
8	535	312 (0.86)	178 (0.75)	122 (0.55)
10	942	487 (0.97)	285 (0.83)	165 (0.71)
12	1716	871 (0.99)	497 (0.86)	289 (0.74)

As expected, the simulation time increases with the PME order value. The parallel efficiency decreases as the number of cores increases (see the last column in Table 1). It should be noted that the decrease in e(N) at a low value of the PME order is associated with an increase in the proportion of operations not related to the calculation of electrostatic energy. The time required for these operations is approximately constant, therefore, as the simulation time decreases with an increase in the number of cores, the efficiency value decreases. To test this, a 100 ps MD simulation of a "small" cluster is run for PME order = 4. The calculated value of e(64) is increased to 0.72 from 0.51 for a 20 ps simulation.

These results should be taken into account when choosing the number of cores when modeling the deposition process. The duration of one deposition cycle is about 10 ps [16], so the weight of nonparallel operations can become relatively large with an increase in the number of cores. On the other hand, simulations of annealing, stress calculations, and mechanical properties such as Young's modulus, bulk modulus, and thermal conductivity required trajectories hundreds of picoseconds long. In this case, the number of computational cores can be increased without loss of the efficiency of the performance. It should be noted that these results refer to simulations using the GROMACS program. As mentioned above, the LAMPPS program has special functionality for modeling the deposition process, which can potentially increase the parallel efficiency.

Not only the efficiency, but also the simulation results depend on the PME order parameters (Fig. 3). The density profiles shown in Fig. 3 are calculated as follows. The deposited film is divided into layers parallel to the plane of the substrate and having a thickness of 1 nm. The horizontal dimensions of the layers are equal to the dimensions of the substrate. Next, the density of each layer is calculated as follows:

$$\rho = (N_{Si}\mu_{Si} + N_O\mu_O)/(N_A h L_x L_y), \tag{3}$$

where N_{Si} and N_O are number of silicon and oxygen atoms in the layer, $\mu_{Si} = 28$ g/mol and $\mu_O = 32$ g/mol are the molar weights of Si and O, N_A is the Avogadro number, $h =$ 1 nm is the layer thickness, L_x and L_y are the horizontal dimensions of the substrate.

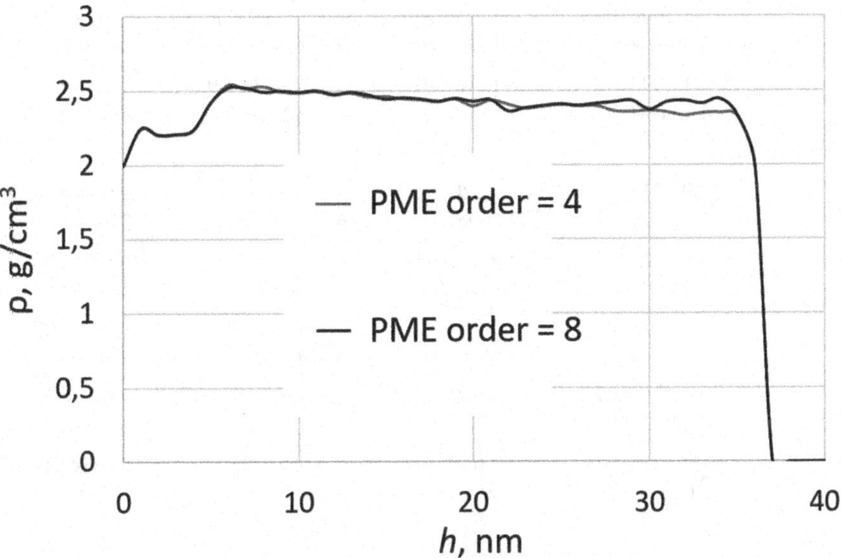

Fig. 3. The density profiles of the "small" cluster, deposited at two different values of PME order. Other simulation parameters are the same.

As it seen from the plots in Fig. 3, the difference in the density can achieve $\Delta\rho = 0.1$–0.2 g/cm^3. This value of $\Delta\rho$ is close to the difference in density between "as deposited" and annealed silicon dioxide films [21]. Thus, when studying the dependencies of the structural properties of normal deposited films, the PME order = 8 should be used to prevent the occurring of the noticeable inaccuracy.

The results of the calculations of the electrostatic component of the potential energy of interatomic interaction, averaged over 20 ps simulation trajectory, are presented in Table 2.

Table 2. Electrostatic components of the energy of the clusters. The upper value in the cell is the short-range term, lower value is the long-range term (kJ/mol), N is the number of computational cores.

PME order	*N*			
	8	16	32	64
"large" cluster				
4	−1.109e+09 4.941e+05	−1.109e+09 5.447e+05	−1.109e+09 3.949e+05	−1.109e+09 5.700e+05
6	−1.109e+09 3.403e+05	−1.109e+09 4.170e+05	−1.109e+09 4.272e+05	−1.109e+09 4.848e+05
8	−1.109e+09 3.810e+05	−1.109e+09 3.393e+05	−1.109e+09 3.621e+05	−1.109e+09 5.131e+05
10	−1.109e+09 3.666e+05	−1.109e+09 2.151e+05	−1.109e+09 7.836e+05	−1.109e+09 4.485e+05
12	−1.109e+09 4.434e+05	−1.109e+09 5.539e+05	−1.10983e+09 8.09825e+05	−1.109e+09 5.084e+05
"small" cluster				
4	−9.621e + 07 3.922e + 04	−9.620e+07 2.369e+04	−9.621e+07 4.033e+04	−9.624e+07 6.310e+04
6	−9.621e+07 3.983e+04	−9.628e+07 1.077e+05	−9.621e+07 4.098e+04	−9.624e+07 6.582e+04
8	−9.621e+07 3.988e+04	−9.619e+07 1.765e+04	−9.621e+07 4.0211e+04	−9.624e+07 6.604e+04
10	−9.624e+07 6.626e+04	−9.619e+07 1.534e+04	−9.624e+07 6.866e+04	−9.624e+07 6.614e+04
12	−9.638e+07 2.097e+05	−9.639e+07 2.098e+05	−9.638e+07 2.096e+05	−9.638e+07 2.097e+05

Based on the results presented in Table 2, the following conclusions can be drawn:

1. The short-range term is much larger than the long-range term. This relationship between two terms of the electrostatic energy of the interaction is observed for all values of PME order parameter and for both clusters. The short-range term in all cases is negative while the long-range term is positive. The sum of these terms is negative.
2. The total value of the electrostatic energy is proportional to the number of the particles in the clusters. Indeed, the ratio of the number of the atoms in "large" and "small" cluster is equal to $2.1 \bullet 10^6/1.8 \bullet 10^5 = 11.7$, that close to the corresponding ratio of

the electrostatic energy 1.11e+09/9.6e+07 = 11.5. It corresponds to the experimental fact the atomization energy of the mater is proportional to the number of particles.

3. The value of long-range term essentially fluctuates with change in the number of computational cores and value of PME order parameter with exception of one case – "large" cluster with PME order = 12 (bottom line in Table 2). The amplitude of fluctuation is not decreases with increase of the value of PME order parameter.
4. As stated in the GROMACS manual [10], the relative accuracy of calculating electrostatic forces with default parameters is about 2–3 · 10^{-4}. As can be seen from the data in Table 1, the relative fluctuation of the long-range component, which dominates the electrostatic energy, is about 10^{-4}, which corresponds to the indicated force fluctuations.

Summing up, we can say that the relative inaccuracy of the calculation of the electrostatic energy is about 10^{-4}. This inaccuracy slightly depends on the PME order parameter and number of the computational cores in parallel computing.

The main components of the pressure tensor are listed in Table 3. The calculations are performed in the NVT (constant number of the particles, volume and temperature, T = 300 K) ensemble. This type of the simulation used, for instance, to study the dependencies of the stresses in the growing films on the deposition conditions [13]. Data are listed only for the values of PME order parameter equal to 4 and 12 since the pressure depends slightly on this parameter. As can be seen from Table 3, the relative fluctuations of p_{xx} and p_{yy} components are of the order of several percent.

The difference of the pressure values for "small" and "large" clusters is explained as follows. The "small" clusters formed by the normal high-energy deposition. At these conditions the dense film grows. Due to collisions with incoming high-energy silicon atoms the structure of dense film tends to expand in the substrate plane, perpendicular to the flow of incoming atoms. For fixed dimensions of the simulated cell (NVT ensemble), this leads to occurrence of the pressure at the cell boundaries. Since the normal deposited films has the homogeneous and isotopic structure, the p_{xx} and p_{yy} components differ insignificantly.

At the same time the "large" cluster formed by the glancing angle deposition, when the high-porous anisotropic film growth. In this case the film can expand into pores, so the high pressure on the cell boundaries is not observed. Taking into account the relationship $p_{xx(yy)} = -\sigma_{xx(yy)}$, where $\sigma_{xx(yy)}$ are the main components of the stress tensor, the positive values of $p_{xx(yy)}$ mean the occurring the compressive stress, the negative ones – the tensile stress. The significant difference in the p_{xx} and p_{yy} component for the case of the "large" cluster is explained by the strong asymmetry of the structure, see Fig. 2.

The dimensions of the grid, that are used in the calculation of the reciprocal part (long-range term) of electrostatic energy are controlled in the GROMACS by the fourierspacing parameter. The default value of this parameter is equal to 0.1 nm for the cubic interpolation, that corresponds to the PME order = 4. In the GROMACS manual is recommended to decrease the grid dimensions (fourierspacing) while increasing interpolation (PME order).

The values of the simulation time of the 20 ps MD trajectory for the "small" cluster are listed in Table 4. As can be seen from these data, the increase in the fourierspacing parameters from 0.05 nm to 0.2 nm significantly decreases the simulation time. For the

Table 3. The main components of the pressure tensor (atm), the upper value in the cell is the p_{xx} component, lower value is the p_{yy} component, coordinate axes are in the substrate plane.

PME order	*N*			
	8	16	32	64
"large" cluster				
4	7.600e+01 −1.114e+02	7.660e+01 −1.109e+02	7.682e+01 −1.11807e+02	7.595e+01 −1.143e+02
12	7.006e+01 −1.114e+02	7.308e+01 −1.087e+02	7.484e+01 −1.078e+02	7.095e+01 −1.102e+02
"small" cluster				
4	1.755e+03 1.742e+03	1.742e+03 1.745e+03	1.766e+03 1.749e+03	1.755e+03 1.749e+03
12	1.748e+03 1.754e+03	1.742e+03 1.729e+03	1.755e+03 1.752e+03	1.755e+03 1.749e+03

PME order = 4,6,8 the increase of fourierspacing from 0.05 to 0.2 reduces the simulation time by three times. In the case of PME order = 12 the simulation time reduces by about half.

Table 4. The dependence of the simulation time (s) on the fourierspacing and PME order parameters for "small" cluster. Number of the computational cores is equal to 32.

fourierspacing, nm	PME order			
	4	6	8	12
0.05	172	228	451	734
0.1	182	159	333	507
0.2	55	110	153	397

The results of the calculations of the electrostatic energy are listed in Table 5. The number of cores *N* is indicated because the electrostatic components of the energy depend on *N* (see Table 3). As can be seen from the data, the increase in the fourierspacing results in the growth of long-range electrostatic term. This tendency is observed for all values of the PME order parameter and indicates the increase of the inaccuracy in the calculation of the electrostatic energy. So, while the increase in the fourierspacing allows to significantly reduce the computational time, the accuracy of the computing also reduces. It means that the simulation with large values of fourierspacing can be performed for the fast estimation the impact of deposition conditions for the structural and mechanical properties of the films.

The main components of the pressure tensor $p_{xx(yy)}$ also are calculated for the difference values fourierspacing parameter. It is found that the relative fluctuations of $p_{xx(yy)}$ values are about of several percents.

Table 5. Electrostatic components of the energy of the small "clusters". The upper value in the cell is the short-range term, lower value is the long-range term (kJ/mol). Number of the computational cores is equal to 32.

fourierspacing, nm	PME order			
	4	6	8	12
0.05	−9.618e+07 1.099e+04	−9.618e+07 7.578e+03	−9.621e+07 3.601e+04	−9.621e+07 3.409e+04
0.1	−9.623e+07 6.114e+04	−9.623e+07 6.169e+04	−9.623e+07 6.160e+04	−9.624e+07 6.359e+04
0.2	−9.623e+07 5.012e+04	−9.624e+07 6.604e+04	−9.640e+07 2.158e+05	−9.640e+07 2.195e+05

4 Conclusions

In the present work the investigation of the efficiency and accuracy of the MD simulation of silicon dioxide thin films for the different parameters of Particle Mesh Ewald (PME) method is performed using the GROMACS program. Two clusters, representing the isotropic dense and anisotropic porous films, are used for the simulations. It is revealed that increase of the fourierspacing parameter from 0.05 to 0.2 nm reduces the simulation time by 2–3 times. This reducing is accompanied by the growth of the long-range term of the electrostatic energy. The growth of the interpolation order from 4 (default value) to 12 leads to an increase in simulation time by about an order of magnitude. So, the high value of the interpolation order should be used only when the high accuracy of the simulation is required. For all of values of the investigated PME parameters the short-range term is negative. The long-term is positive and is hundredths of a percent of short-range term. The values of the main components of the pressure tensor vary within a few percent when the fourierspacing and interpolation order parameters change in the investigated interval.

The parallel efficiency of computing decreases insignificantly with increase of the number of the computational cores from 8 to 64.

The work was supported by the Russian Science Foundation (Grant no. 23-11-00047).

References

1. Angela Piegari, F.F. (ed.): Optical Thin Films and Coatings. Elsevier, Amsterdam (2018)
2. Hawkeye, M.M.; Brett, M.J.: Glancing angle deposition: fabrication, properties, and applications of micro- and nanostructured thin films. J. Vac. Sci. Technol. A Vacuum Surfaces Film **25**, 1317 (2007). https://doi.org/10.1116/1.2764082
3. Grigoriev, F.V., Sulimov, V.B.: Atomistic simulation of physical vapor deposition of optical thin films. Nanomaterials **13**, 1717 (2023)
4. Turowski, M., Jupé, M., Ehlers, H., Melzig, T., Pflug, A., Ristau, D.: Simulation in thin film technology. In: Proceedings of the Proc. SPIE, 23 September 2015, vol. 9627 (2015)
5. Tait, R.N., Smy, T., Brett, M.J.: Modelling and characterization of columnar growth in evaporated films. Thin Solid Films **226**, 196–201 (1993). https://doi.org/10.1016/0040-6090(93)90378-3
6. Sundararaman, S., Ching, W.-Y., Huang, L.: Mechanical properties of silica glass predicted by a pair-wise potential in molecular dynamics simulations. J. Non Cryst. Solids **445–446**, 102–109 (2016). https://doi.org/10.1016/j.jnoncrysol.2016.05.012
7. Badorreck, H., et al.: Correlation of structural and optical properties using virtual materials analysis. Opt. Express **27**, 22209–22225 (2019). https://doi.org/10.1364/OE.27.022209
8. Turowski, M., Amotchkina, T., Ehlers, H., Jupé, M., Ristau, D.: Calculation of optical and electronic properties of modeled titanium dioxide films of different densities. Appl. Opt. **53**, A159–A168 (2014). https://doi.org/10.1364/AO.53.00A159
9. Darden, T., York, D., Pedersen, L.: Particle mesh Ewald: an N·log(N) method for ewald sums in large systems. J. Chem. Phys. **98**, 10089–10092 (1993). https://doi.org/10.1063/1.464397
10. https://manual.gromacs.org/current/user-guide/mdp-options.html
11. Allen, M.P., Tildesley, D.J.: Computer Simulation of Liquids (2017)
12. Dai, Y., Chu, X., Gao, F.: Molecular dynamics simulation investigation on thermal stability and repetitive tensile performance of TiO2. Mater. Res. Express **6**, 85053 (2019). https://doi.org/10.1088/2053-1591/ab1ef8
13. Grigoriev, F.V., Sulimov, V.B., Tikhonravov, A.V.: Atomistic simulation of stresses in growing silicon dioxide films. Coatings **10**, 220 (2020). https://doi.org/10.3390/coatings10030220
14. Barranco, A., Borras, A., Gonzalez-Elipe, A.R., Palmero, A.: Perspectives on oblique angle deposition of thin films: from fundamentals to devices. Prog. Mater. Sci. **76**, 59–153 (2016). https://doi.org/10.1016/j.pmatsci.2015.06.003
15. Grigoriev, F.V., Sulimov, V.B., Tikhonravov, A.: V Application of a large-scale molecular dynamics approach to modelling the deposition of TiO2 thin films. Comput. Mater. Sci. **188**, 110202 (2021). https://doi.org/10.1016/j.commatsci.2020.110202
16. Grigoriev, F.V., Sulimov, A.V., Kochikov, I., Kondakova, O.A., Sulimov, V.B., Tikhonravov, A.V.: High-performance atomistic modeling of optical thin films deposited by energetic processes. Int. J. High Perform. Comput. Appl. **29**, 184–192 (2014). https://doi.org/10.1177/1094342014560591
17. Plimpton, S.: Fast parallel algorithms for short-range molecular dynamics. J. Comput. Phys. **117**, 1–19 (1995). https://doi.org/10.1006/jcph.1995.1039
18. Berendsen, H.J.C., Postma, J.P.M., Van Gunsteren, W.F., Dinola, A., Haak, J.R.: Molecular dynamics with coupling to an external bath. J. Chem. Phys. **81**, 3684–3690 (1984). https://doi.org/10.1063/1.448118
19. Voevodin, V.V., et al.: Supercomputer Lomonosov-2: large scale, deep monitoring and fine analytics for the user community. Supercomput. Front. Innov. **6**(2) (2019)

20. Abraham, M.J., et al.: GROMACS: high performance molecular simulations through multi-level parallelism from laptops to supercomputers. SoftwareX **1–2**, 19–25 (2015). https://doi.org/10.1016/j.softx.2015.06.001
21. Grigoriev, F.V., Katkova, E.V., Sulimov, A.V., Sulimov, V.B., Tikhonravov, A.V.: Annealing of deposited SiO2 thin films: full-atomistic simulation results. Opt. Mater. Express **6**, 3960–3966 (2016). https://doi.org/10.1364/OME.6.003960

Field-Split Iterative Solver Vs Direct One for Quasi-Static Biot Equation

Sergey Solovyev[1](✉) and Vadim Lisitsa[2]

[1] Institute of Mathematics SB RAS, Novosibirsk, Russia
solovevsa@ipgg.sbras.ru
[2] Institute of Petroleum Geology and Geophysics SB RAS, Novosibirsk, Russia
lisitsavv@ipgg.sbras.ru

Abstract. Using the Biot equation in scope of the frequency domain and quasi-static state, we can model low-frequency loading and obtain strain-stress relations that vary with frequency for fluid-filled poroelastic materials. To solve the linear algebraic equations resulting from the finite difference discrectisation of the Biot equation, we propose an approach based on the BCSGStab iterative solver and a preconditioner technique based on a field-split approach. In this study, we calculate the approximate amount of floating point operations needed for the suggested technique as well as a direct method. Despite the direct solver's superior OMP scalability over the iterative one, numerical experiments show that the iterative technique quickly converges and is advantageous for big Biot problems.

Keywords: Poroelasticity · Biot equation · quasi-static state · finite-differences · iterative methods · SLAE direct solvers · field-split preconditioner · scalability

1 Introduction

Solving systems of linear algebraic equations (SLAEs) arising from differential problems is computationally expensive and requires expertise in mathematical algorithms and programming for HPC systems (high performance computing). In this research, we develop solvers for SLAEs derived from the Biot equation in the frequency domain and quasi-static state to model low-frequency loading and obtain strain-stress relations for fluid-filled poroelastic materials. A finite difference (FD) approximation [9,10] on staggered grids and partial separation of variables and equations is applied [2]. The resulting SLAE can be solved using either direct or iterative algorithms with preconditioner techniques. Various preconditioning approaches can be applied: ILU0, multigrid [13], filed-split [7], etc. To distinguish between equations and variables relating to solid deformation and fluid movement, we employ a split field preconditioner. First, we describe our numerical upscaling algorithm for estimating the effective properties of media. The low frequency regime and fractured porous isotropic materials

V. Voevodin et al. (Eds.): RuSCDays 2023, LNCS 14388, pp. 86–99, 2023.
https://doi.org/10.1007/978-3-031-49432-1_7

are considered. Then, we suggest a finite difference (FD) method that makes use of staggered grids and equation/variable partial separation. The result is a SLAE that can be solved using either *Direct* or *Iterative* algorithms with preconditioner techniques. Both direct (based on optimized LU factorization [3,8], [6]) and preconditioned iterative (BCGStab [14]) solvers are described. A special section is devoted to the construction of the field-split preconditioner. The section with the experiments includes the measures of memory and time consumption. They show that the direct approach is more efficient for smaller problems, while the iterative approach with preconditioning is more effective for larger models.

2 Problem Overview

2.1 Biot Equations in Quasistatic State

This study starts by introducing the Biot equations describing the pressure diffusion process in poroelastic media in a quasi-static regime. [4,5]:

$$\frac{\partial}{\partial x}\left[C_{11}\frac{\partial u_x}{\partial x}+C_{13}\frac{\partial u_z}{\partial z}\right]+\frac{\partial}{\partial z}\left[C_{55}\left(\frac{\partial u_x}{\partial z}+\frac{\partial u_z}{\partial x}\right)\right]+\frac{\partial}{\partial x}\left[\alpha M\left(\frac{\partial w_x}{\partial x}+\frac{\partial w_z}{\partial z}\right)\right]=0, \tag{1}$$

$$\frac{\partial}{\partial x}\left[C_{55}\left(\frac{\partial u_x}{\partial z}+\frac{\partial u_z}{\partial x}\right)\right]+\frac{\partial}{\partial z}\left[C_{13}\frac{\partial u_x}{\partial x}+C_{33}\frac{\partial u_z}{\partial z}\right]+\frac{\partial}{\partial z}\left[\alpha M\left(\frac{\partial w_x}{\partial x}+\frac{\partial w_z}{\partial z}\right)\right]=0, \tag{2}$$

$$\frac{\partial}{\partial x}\left[\alpha M\left(\frac{\partial u_x}{\partial x}+\frac{\partial u_z}{\partial z}\right)\right]+\frac{\partial}{\partial x}\left[M\left(\frac{\partial w_x}{\partial x}+\frac{\partial w_z}{\partial z}\right)\right]-i\omega\frac{\eta}{k}w_x=0, \tag{3}$$

$$\frac{\partial}{\partial z}\left[\alpha M\left(\frac{\partial u_x}{\partial x}+\frac{\partial u_z}{\partial z}\right)\right]+\frac{\partial}{\partial z}\left[M\left(\frac{\partial w_x}{\partial x}+\frac{\partial w_z}{\partial z}\right)\right]-i\omega\frac{\eta}{k}w_z=0. \tag{4}$$

In this equation, $\boldsymbol{u}=(u_x,u_z)^T$, $\boldsymbol{w}=(w_x,w_z)^T$ are the solid and relative fluid velocity vectors; ω is the time frequency; C_{11}, C_{33}, C_{13}, C_{55}, M, α are the materials properties: components of the matrix stiffness tensor, fluid storage coefficient and the Biot-Willis coefficient.

The symmetry of the stiffness, strain, and stress tensors allows us to state Hooke's law in a more straightforward manner even if the stiffness tensor is a fourth order tensor.:

$$\begin{pmatrix}\sigma_{xx}\\ \sigma_{zz}\\ \sigma_{xz}\end{pmatrix}=\begin{pmatrix}C_{11} & C_{13} & 0\\ C_{13} & C_{33} & 0\\ 0 & 0 & C_{55}\end{pmatrix}\begin{pmatrix}\varepsilon_{xx}\\ \varepsilon_{zz}\\ \varepsilon_{xz}\end{pmatrix},\quad \begin{matrix}\varepsilon_{xx}=\frac{\partial u_x}{\partial x},\\ \varepsilon_{zz}=\frac{\partial u_z}{\partial z},\\ \varepsilon_{xz}=\frac{1}{2}\left(\frac{\partial u_z}{\partial x}+\frac{\partial u_x}{\partial z}\right).\end{matrix}$$

The Neumann (or second-type) boundary conditions are used for the system of Eqs. (1)–(4):

$$\begin{aligned} \sigma \cdot \boldsymbol{n}|_{\partial D} &= \boldsymbol{\sigma}_0 \\ \boldsymbol{w} \cdot \boldsymbol{n}|_{\partial D} &= 0. \end{aligned} \tag{5}$$

The numerical upscaling algorithm for estimating the effective properties of fractured porous isotropic media (Fig. 1) is to reconstruct the frequency dependent viscoelastic differential Eq. (6), (7) with boundary condition (8) similar to the initial (1–4) and (5). The "similar" means that the average solution should be the same for both systems.

$$\frac{\partial}{\partial x}\left[\hat{C}_{11}(\omega)\frac{\partial \hat{u}_x}{\partial x} + \hat{C}_{13}(\omega)\frac{\partial \hat{u}_z}{\partial z}\right] + \frac{\partial}{\partial z}\left[\hat{C}_{55}(\omega)\left(\frac{\partial \hat{u}_x}{\partial z} + \frac{\partial \hat{u}_z}{\partial x}\right)\right] = 0, \tag{6}$$

$$\frac{\partial}{\partial x}\left[\hat{C}_{55}(\omega)\left(\frac{\partial \hat{u}_x}{\partial z} + \frac{\partial \hat{u}_z}{\partial x}\right)\right] + \frac{\partial}{\partial z}\left[\hat{C}_{13}(\omega)\frac{\partial \hat{u}_x}{\partial x} + \hat{C}_{33}(\omega)\frac{\partial \hat{u}_z}{\partial z}\right] = 0, \tag{7}$$

$$\hat{\sigma} \cdot \boldsymbol{n}|_{\partial D} = \boldsymbol{\sigma}_0 \tag{8}$$

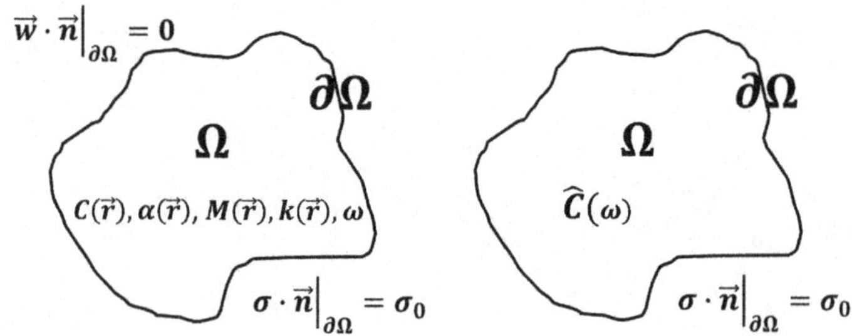

Fig. 1. Computational domain, media properties and boundary conditions: original poroelastic fluid-saturated model on the left; reconstructed effective frequency-dependent viscoelastic model on the right. The $\boldsymbol{n}$ – vector of outer normal, and $C(\boldsymbol{r}), \alpha(\boldsymbol{r}), M(\boldsymbol{r}), k((\boldsymbol{r}))$ – space dependent parameters of the Eqs. (1)–(4).

In order to handle with this problem we solve the SLAE with the three right-hand sides generated by a system of equations in a domain with three separate boundary conditions. Details of the reconstruction algorithm are described in [11,12]. Now we describe how to approximate and solve SLAE with 3 right hand sides (RHS).

2.2 Discretization the Biot Equations

To approximate the Biot Eqs. (1)–(4) we utilizes a rectangular grid with N_x by N_z mesh points. The discretization mesh and computational domain are illustrated in Fig. 2 (right).

Figure 2 (left) shows the positions of the variables on the mesh. At the center of x-direction edges the u_z, w_z vectors components are defined and Eqs. (2), (4)

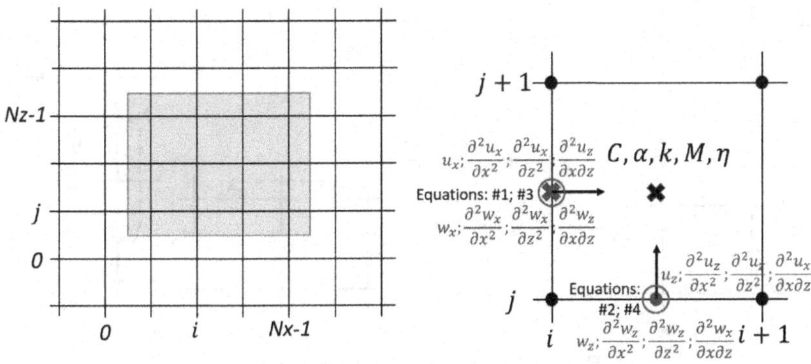

Fig. 2. Left: discretization mesh and the computational domain. Right: mesh positions of Biot equation parameters, solution components, derivatives location, and nodes, where equations are approximated.

are approximated. Whereas the u_x, w_x vectors components and approximation of the Eqs. (2), (4) are defined at the center of z-direction edges. The coefficients of the equations (materials properties) are defined at half-integer points in the x and z directions (the centers of cells).

The Biot differentiation equations are discretized both inside of the computational domain and at its boundary.

The number of FD (finite-difference) approximations for (1) and (3) is $N_z(N_x - 1)$; and number of FD approximations for (2) and (4) is $(N_z - 1)N_x$. Thus the number of SLAE unknowns (N)is

$$2N_z(N_x - 1) + 2(N_z - 1)N_x \approx 4N_zN_x.$$

The details of such FD approximation of the Biot differentiation equations has been discussed in [11], but we are highlighting the main features of the resulting SLAE. Firstly, such matrix A has a general form: not symmetric, not Hermitian complex sparse squared matrix. Secondly, the boundary conditions of Neumann-type for Eq. (5) make the matrix ill-conditioned or singular. In addition, the matrix's non zero elements number,denoted by $NNZ(A)$, depends on the finite-difference rules used for the approximation. Figure 3 shows the stencil for approximation the Biot equations. Eqs. (1) and (2) require 16 mesh points, while Eqs. (3) and (4) require 14 mesh points, resulting in approximately $60N_xN_z$ non-zero elements in A.

3 Algorithms of SLAE Solution

Any algorithm of SLAE solution should satisfy the following factors:

- **Accuracy**. It can be a small relative error of the solution. But in practice there is no exact solution of SLAE to compute the error, so the popular criterion of a good solution is the small norm of the relative residual $r = ||b - Ax||/||b||$.

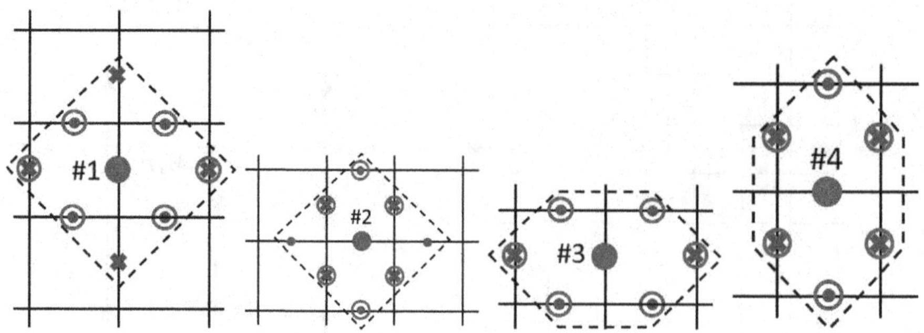

Fig. 3. Stencils for Biot equations.

- **Performance**. The proposed algorithm is expected to resolve SLAE within an acceptable timeframe. In theory, floating-point (FLOPS) operations should be estimated and kept to a minimum.
  However, in practice, the computation time is the ultimate criterion for the performance of the algorithm. The implementation of the algorithm should therefore take advantage of high performance features such as parallelisation and the use of libraries with optimized math functions.
- **Memory usage**. All computational data should be minimised to fit the available memory (RAM).

To solve a SLAE resulting from differential equation discretization, two main approaches can be used: direct methods and iterative methods. In the context of solving Biot problem, we will explore both methods.

3.1 Direct Solver

Such solvers provide the best accuracy, not so good performance and huge memory consumption. They are usually based on LU factorization algorithms. For the SLAEs with sparse matrices there are advanced algorithms to increase the poor performance and memory usage, such as reordering the elements of the SLAEs matrix, using multifrontal and super-nodal factorization, etc. A lot of Sparse Direct Solvers contain such algorithms: MUMPS [3], SuperLU [8], PARDISO [6], etc. Hovewer direct solvers could not solve the large problem. In our experiments on a system with 512GB RAM (see below), the maximum number of mesh points for the Biot discretization is about 2000×2000, while the iterative solution can handle a 4000×4000 problem.

In this paper we use the PARDISO solver from the Intel MKL library. Investigation of reconstruction of effective viscoelastic media is presented in [11]. Here we investigate this solver in the context of scalability and performance in comparison with the proposed iterative solver. The number of float point operations $Flops(Dir)$ and memory consumption $Mem(Dir)$ of the "black box" solver Intel MKL PARDISO will be estimated.

The majors SLAE solving stages of any sparse direct solver are showed in the (9).

1) Permutation of the intial matrix A to decrease number of non zeros while factorization in factors (Reordering)
2) LU factorization of the permiuted matrix $\hat{A} = \hat{L}\hat{U}$(Factorization)
3) Resolving the SLAEs $\hat{L}y = b$ and $\hat{U}x = y$ (Solving).

(9)

Table 1. Differential equations of the "Field-Split" preconditioner B.

$\frac{\partial}{\partial x}\left[C_{11}\frac{\partial u_x}{\partial x} + C_{13}\frac{\partial u_z}{\partial z}\right] + \frac{\partial}{\partial z}\left[C_{55}\left(\frac{\partial u_x}{\partial z} + \frac{\partial u_z}{\partial x}\right)\right]$	$+0$		$=0$
$\frac{\partial}{\partial x}\left[C_{55}\left(\frac{\partial u_x}{\partial z} + \frac{\partial u_z}{\partial x}\right)\right] + \frac{\partial}{\partial z}\left[C_{13}\frac{\partial u_x}{\partial x} + C_{33}\frac{\partial u_z}{\partial z}\right]$	$+0$		$=0$
$\frac{\partial}{\partial x}\left[\alpha M\left(\frac{\partial u_x}{\partial x} + \frac{\partial u_z}{\partial z}\right)\right]$	$+\frac{\partial}{\partial x}\left[M\left(\frac{\partial w_x}{\partial x} + \frac{\partial w_z}{\partial z}\right)\right]$	$- i\omega\frac{\eta}{k}w_x$	$= 0$
$\frac{\partial}{\partial z}\left[\alpha M\left(\frac{\partial u_x}{\partial x} + \frac{\partial u_z}{\partial z}\right)\right]$	$+\frac{\partial}{\partial z}\left[M\left(\frac{\partial w_x}{\partial x} + \frac{\partial w_z}{\partial z}\right)\right]$	$- i\omega\frac{\eta}{k}w_z$	$= 0,$

Graph partitioning algorithms are used in the Reordering step to reorder the elements of the original matrix prior to factorization This process is usually performed using integers and is faster than the factorization step. We will not take it into account to estimate the FLOPS (number of floating point operations) $Flops(Dir)$, but will measure its timing in experiments:

$Flops(Dir) = Flops(Fct) + Flops(Slv)$.

The estimation of $Flops(Slv)$ can be based on counting non zero elements in $\hat{L}$ and $\hat{U}$ factors (below we write $\hat{L}$ and $\hat{U}$ without a "hat"). This is because each element requires two operations: a multiplication "$*$" and an addition "$+$". Since the matrix A of the SLAE is structurally symmetric, the pattern of L is the same as that of U, resulting in $NNZ(LU) = 2 * NNZ(L)$. Three different loads provide three RHS which should be considered in FLOPS. So the formula for $Flops(Slv)$ is: $(3\ RHS) * (2\ operations\ per\ one\ element) * (NNZ(L\&U))$.

The total FLOPS can be calculated as $Flops(Dir) = Flops(Fct) + 6 * NNZ(L\&U)$.

Parameters $Flops(Fct)$ and $NNZ(L\&U)$ are obtained experimentally using the Intel MKL PARDISO solver in the next sections.

Parameters $Flops(Fct)$ and $NNZ(L\&U)$ are obtained experimentally by using Intel MKL PARDISO solver in the next sections.

3.2 Iterative Solver

The main benefit of iterative methods is their small memory usage. Despite this fact, they may not achieve the same level of accuracy as direct methods and convergence may be slow. However, this can be overcome by choosing a suitable iterative solver and developing a suitable preconditioner.

Using a preconditioner B provides the SLAE: $\hat{A}x = \hat{b}$ where $\hat{A}x = B^{-1}Ax$, $\hat{b} = B^{-1}b$.

We will use the BCSGStab algorithm [14] to solve the SLAE with the matrix $\hat{A}$, which has general properties:

1) *set* x_0
2) *set* $j_{restart}$
3) *reorder/factorize* B *(will use in product* $\hat{A}x = B^{-1}Ax$*)*
4) *get* $\hat{b} = B^{-1}b, ||\hat{b}||$
5) $r_0 := \hat{b} - \hat{A}x_0$
6) $p_0 := r_0$
7) For $j = 0, 1, \ldots,$ until convergence Do :
8) $a_j := \frac{(r_j, r_0^*)}{(\hat{A}p_j, r_0^*)}$
9) $s_j := r_j - a_j \hat{A}p_j$ (10)
10) $\omega_j := \frac{(\hat{A}s_j, s_j)}{(\hat{A}s_j, \hat{A}s_j)}$
11) $x_{j+1} := x_j + \alpha_j p_j + \omega_j s_j$
12) $r_{j+1} := s_j + \omega_j \hat{A}s_j$
13) If remainder $(j/j_{restart}) = 0$ Then $r_{j+1} := \hat{b} - \hat{A}x_{j+1}$
14) $\beta_j := \frac{(r_{j+1}, r_0^*)}{(r_j, r_0^*)} \frac{\alpha_j}{\omega_j}$
15) $p_{j+1} := r_{j+1} + \beta_j(p_j - \omega_j \hat{A}p_j)$
16) End Loop

To calculate the FLOPS required by BCGStab, we should count the scalar product (**dot**), the operations named as "vector plus a vector times a constant" (**axpy**) and the $\hat{A}x$ product, which takes the most time. The inversion of the preconditioner B (**inv**) and the matrix-vector product of the initial matrix A (**mv**) form the $\hat{A}x$ product.

Table 2. Main mathematical operations in BCGStab, number of FLOPS; recall that $N = 4 * n^2$ and $NNZ(A) = (2 * 16 + 2 * 14) * n^2 = 15N$.

Operation type	FLOPS per one operation	FLOPS per one step
axpy	2N	6
dot	2N-1	4
mv	2*NNZ(A)	2
inv	TBD	2

Therefore (considering the FLOPS of these operations given in the Table 2) the total FLOPs for the BCGStab is:

$Flops(Itr) = N_{iter}[80N + 2Flops(invB)]$.

The next subsection describes the preconditioner B and the counting of $Flops(invB)$.block low-triangular preconditioner

block low-triangular preconditioner

3.3 Construct SLAE Preconditioner

The main criteria for the construction of a preconditioner: it should be easy to invert.

However, the inversion of the preconditioner should be quite fast. Our experiments show that wel-known preconditioners such as Jacoby, Block-Jacoby, and Zeidel are not suitable for this purpose. The BICGStab with these does not converge with adequate accuracy.

We propose to use the "Field-Split" approach to construct the preconditioner. The idea is to remove the operators $\frac{\partial}{\partial x}\left[\alpha M\left(\frac{\partial}{\partial x}+\frac{\partial}{\partial z}\right)\right]$ and $\frac{\partial}{\partial z}\left[\alpha M\left(\frac{\partial}{\partial x}+\frac{\partial}{\partial z}\right)\right]$ associated with the unknown variable w from Eqs. 1 and 2. By using the FD approximation in equations from the Table 1, a block low-triangular preconditioner B can be obtained.

Therefore algorithm of solution SLAE $B\begin{bmatrix} x_0 \\ x_3 \end{bmatrix} = \begin{bmatrix} y_0 \\ y_3 \end{bmatrix}$ is:

1. Solve $A_0 x_0 = y_0$
2. Set $y_3 = y_3 - A_2 x_0$
3. Solve $A_3 x_3 = y_3$.

The block representation of matrices A, B and vectors x, y is shown in the (11).

$$A = \begin{bmatrix} A_0 & A_1 \\ A_2 & A_3 \end{bmatrix}, B = \begin{bmatrix} A_0 & 0 \\ A_2 & A_3 \end{bmatrix}, x = \begin{bmatrix} x_0 \\ x_3 \end{bmatrix}, y = \begin{bmatrix} y_0 \\ y_3 \end{bmatrix} \tag{11}$$

The differential operators for matrices A_0, A_2, A_3 and stencils for their approximations are showed in the Table 3 and Fig. 4.

Using the introduced notations the number of FLOPs for inverting the preconditioner is:

$Flops(invB) = Flops(invA_0) + 14n^2 + Flops(invA_3)$.

The primary advantage of inverting A_0 and A_3 instead of the full matrix A is that they are smaller than A, allowing it to be factorized quickly and done it once before the iterative process.

So, the number of FLOPs for inversion B is:

$Flops(invB) = [Flops(FctA_0) + Flops(SlvL_0)] + 14n^2 + [Flops(FctA_3) + Flops(SlvL_3)]$.

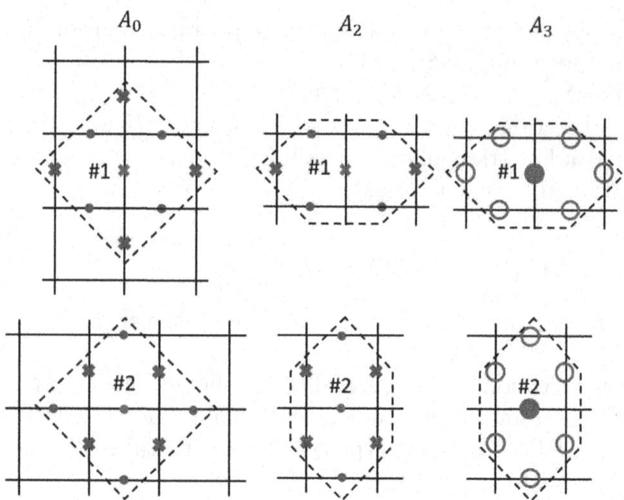

Fig. 4. Approximation stencils for operators: A_0 on the left, A_2 on the center, A_3 on the right.

Table 3. Blocks of the preconditioner B.

A_j block of B	Differential operator	Number non zeros of A_j
A_0	$\frac{\partial}{\partial x}\left[C_{11}\frac{\partial}{\partial x}+C_{13}\frac{\partial}{\partial z}\right]+\frac{\partial}{\partial z}\left[C_{55}\left(\frac{\partial}{\partial z}+\frac{\partial}{\partial x}\right)\right]$	$2*9*n^2$
	$\frac{\partial}{\partial x}\left[C_{55}\left(\frac{\partial}{\partial z}+\frac{\partial}{\partial x}\right)\right]+\frac{\partial}{\partial z}\left[C_{13}\frac{\partial}{\partial x}+C_{33}\frac{\partial}{\partial z}\right]$	
A_2	$\frac{\partial}{\partial x}\left[\alpha M\left(\frac{\partial}{\partial x}+\frac{\partial}{\partial z}\right)\right]$	$2*7*n^2$
	$\frac{\partial}{\partial z}\left[\alpha M\left(\frac{\partial}{\partial x}+\frac{\partial}{\partial z}\right)\right]$	
A_3	$\frac{\partial}{\partial x}\left[M\left(\frac{\partial}{\partial x}+\frac{\partial}{\partial z}\right)\right]-i\omega\frac{\eta}{k}$	$2*7*n^2$
	$\frac{\partial}{\partial z}\left[M\left(\frac{\partial}{\partial x}+\frac{\partial}{\partial z}\right)\right]-i\omega\frac{\eta}{k}$	

The $Flops(SlvL_0)$ and $Flops(SlvL_3)$ are estimated througth the structure of factors L_0 and L_3 like was done in previous section:

$Flops(SlvL) = 12Nnz(L)$.

The number of FLOPs for the iterative process is:

$Flops(Itr) = Flops(FctA_0) + Flops(FctA_3) + N_{iter}[80N + 2*12Nnz(L_0) + 14n^2 + 2*12Nnz(L_3)]$.

The factorization FLOPS and the number of nonzero elements in L-factors are determined by experimental computations in the next sections.

4 Implementation of the Direct and Iterative Algorithms

In this section we share some details of the implementation two proposed algorithms.

The direct solver PARDISO is taking from the Intel MKL library as a "black box". Three steps (9) of it are described in the MKL manual [1].

The bottleneck of the direct algorithm is the second step "Factorize". The third one ("Solve") takes less FLOPS; the first one ("Reordering") contains only int operations and performance will be estimated below from the experiments.

The major bottleneck of the iterative BCGStab algorithm could be the preliminary steps "Reorder/Factorize B", "$B^{-1}b$", "$\hat{A}p_j$" or two products "$\hat{A}p_j$;" "$\hat{A}s_j$" computed at each iterative step. When there are many iterations, the time required for the $\hat{A}\{p_j, s_j\}$ operation may be longer than the factorization time. The number FLOPS of other iterative operations such as dot products, sum of vectors and scalar-vector products contain are significantly less FLOPS and were coded without any optimization.

To perform both Reordering/Factorize and Solve step we use Intel MKL PARDSIO as in the direct solver. By the way, the complexity of using PARDSIO for preconditioner B is less than for A due to the special structure of B (need factorze just A_0 and A_2).

Therefore in numerical experiments would be nice to look at the memory consumption, time profiling of both solvers and the number of steps for iterative process.

The described Field-split solver was implemented in C and compiled by Intel compiler with default optimization for using on Intel Xeon hardware with CPU E5-2690 and 20cores×3.00 GHz, 512 G RAM.

5 Numerical Experiments to Estimate Complexity of the Direct and Iterative Approaches

In the numerical experiments we compare direct and iterative solvers on Biot problems discretized on various meshs: 500×500,1000×1000,2000×2000 and 4000×4000. The number of FLOPS, memory usage, scalability and performance are measured.

The model of Biot problem is fractured, squared domain 5, the coefficient of Biot equations in bone and cracks are presented in the Table 4.

The number of SLAE unknowns N, non-zero elements NNZ in matrices A, A_0, A_3 and in their LU-factors for different problem sizes are shown in the Table 5. The table shows that the number of nob-zeros elements in LU-factors is $10 \dots 25$ times more than in the initial matrix and the size of factors of preconditioner B about two times less than size of A. Another good result for the iterative solver is that number of iterations N_{iter} does not depend on task size of the problem and equal 4 to reach the residual $||\hat{b} - \hat{A}x_0||/||\hat{b}||$ less than threshold 10^{-10}. It is sufficient to determine the effective tensor $\hat{C}$ with an error of less than 1%.

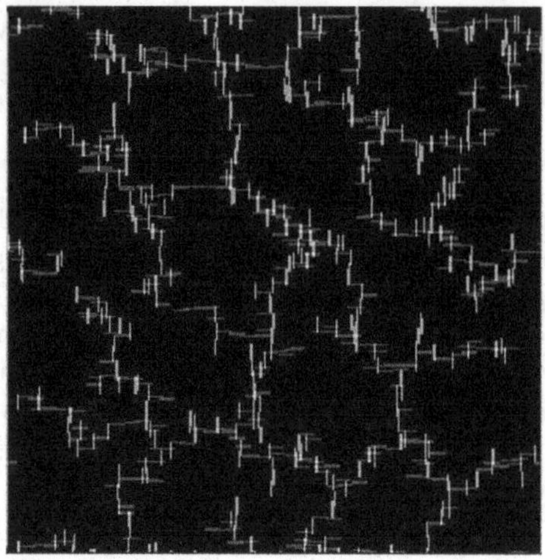

Fig. 5. Fractured model.

Table 4. Bone and cracks coefficients of the fractured model.

Koeff	Bone	Crack
C_{11}	$69.10 * 10^9$	$38.96 * 10^9$
C_{12}	$7.159 * 10^9$	$32.67 * 10^9$
C_{22}	$69.10 * 10^9$	$38.96 * 10^9$
C_{33}	$30.97 * 10^9$	$22.62 * 10^9$
M	$20.10 * 10^9$	$9.330 * 10^9$
αM	$5.953 * 10^9$	$6.854 * 10^9$
$\frac{\eta}{k}$	$1000 * 10^9$	$0.007 * 10^9$

Table 5. SLAEs characteristics, number of non-zero elements in the initial matrices and in their L/U-factors.

Problem index	$n = n_x = n_z$	$N * 10^6$	NNZ $*10^9$					
#	mesh size	$\hat{A} \| B$	$\hat{A}$	$\hat{L}\&\hat{U}$	A_0	$L_0\&U_0$	A_3	$L_3\&U_3$
1	500	1	0.015	0.233	0.004	0.070	0.003	0.039
2	1000	4	0.060	1.079	0.018	0.340	0.014	0.181
3	2000	16	0.240	4.954	0.072	1.540	0.056	0.869
4	4000	64	0.960	N/A	0.288	7.422	0.224	3.930

The Table 6 contains experimental data to calculate the FLOPS of the direct and iterative solvers and the total number of FLOPS, calculated by the formula (12). This table shows that the iterative process should be more than 3 times faster than the direct one. Moreover the largest problem (#4) could not be solved by the direct one because of the high memory usage.

$$\begin{aligned} &Flops(Dir) = Flops(FctA) + 6 * NNZ(\hat{L}\&\hat{U}) \\ &Flops(Itr) = Flops(FctA_0) + Flops(FctA_3) + \\ &+N_{iter}[80N + 2 * 6Nnz(L_0\&U_0) + 14n^2 + 2 * 6Nnz(L_3\&U_3)] \end{aligned} \tag{12}$$

Table 6. Number of the FLOPS for matrices factorization and total FLOPs of the direct and iterative solvers.

Problem index	$n = n_x = n_z$	$N * 10^6$	GFLOPS number				
#	mesh size	$\hat{A}\|B$	$FctA$	$FctA_0$	$FctA_3$	Direct	Iterative
1	500	1	655	136	36	656	178
2	1000	4	531	1241	304	5318	1572
3	2000	16	45119	11178	3445	45149	14744
4	4000	64	N/A	93872	28881	N/A	123318

However the time measurements are more correct indicator for comparing these solvers. The Table 7 shows the memory usage and time profiling of direct solver. The main result is that the scalability of time-consuming Factorization stage is significantly better than the scalability Reorder of Solve stage, so on 16 cores (OMP threads) Factorization stage is about 10 times slower than the Solve one.

Profiling the iterative solver (8) shows the similar behaviour of scalability for Reordering, Factorization and Solve stages.

It leads to the fact that the time of $\hat{A}p_j$,$\hat{A}p_j$ (for 4 iterations) are the similar as Reordering and Factorize (performed before iteration process) on 16 cores. Other operations $(4), 5), 8) - 15))$ take little time despite the fact that they are not parallelized.

The summary of the time comparison between two solvers is shown in the Table 9. It shows that the FLOPS estimates are correlated with the time behaviour in non-parallel mode (the iterative solver is faster than the direct one). The scalability of the direct solver is better than the iterative so it is faster than the Iterative on problems that fit RAM. However the performance gap between the solvers closes to 0 while increasing the problem size. Also, the iterative solver can handle the large problems than the direct one because of its lower memory consumption (Tables 7 and 8). The memory usage grows 4–5 times while increasing problem size for both the direct and the iterative solvers. But for the proposed iteative solver it more than twice less due to using direct one for factorizing preconditioner blocks instead factorizing full matrix A in the direct solver. It can be additionally reduced by using other approaches of inversing blocks of the matrix preconditioner instead of direct one. But this work is out of scope of this paper and i will be researched in a scope of solving 3D Biot problem.

Table 7. Direct solver: number of FLOPS for factorization matrix A, memory usage, computational time for various SLAE sizes N and strong scalability from 1 to 16 OMP threads.

Problem #	1			2			3			4		
GFLOPS												
Factorize A	655			5312			45119			N/A		
Memory usage, G.												
$A + LU$	≈ 4			≈ 18			≈ 83			Not fit 512 RAM		
Time, s. ; Scalability												
NOMP	1	16	$\frac{1}{16}$	1	16	$\frac{1}{16}$	1	16	$\frac{1}{16}$	1	16	$\frac{1}{16}$
Reorder A	5.9	3.0	×2.0	24.3	12.1	×2.0	107.0	53.6	×2.0	N/A	N/A	N/A
Factorize A	35.3	3.5	×10.2	265.6	24.9	×10.7	2359.7	205.7	×11.5	N/A	N/A	N/A
Solve A	1.7	1.0	×1.7	7.4	4.5	×1.7	32.2	17.5	×1.8	N/A	N/A	N/A

Table 8. Iterative solver: number of FLOPS for factorization preconditioner B, memory usage, computational time for 4 iterations for various SLAE sizes N and strong scalability from 1 to 16 OMP threads.

Problem #	1			2			3			4		
GFLOPS												
$Fct(A_0) + Fct(A_3)$	172			1545			14623			122753		
Memory usage, G.												
$A_0 + A_3 + LU_0 + LU_3$	≈ 2			≈ 9			≈ 41			≈ 190		
Time, s. ; Scalability												
NOMP	1	16	$\frac{1}{16}$	1	16	$\frac{1}{16}$	1	16	$\frac{1}{16}$	1	16	$\frac{1}{16}$
3) Reoder+Factorize A_0,A_3	14.5	3.2	×4.6	95.1	15.6	×6.1	756.5	97.4	×7.8	6656.6	673.0	×9.9
4) *get* $\hat{b} = B^{-1}b$, $\|\|\hat{b}\|\|$	2.0	1.4	×1.4	7.6	5.4	×1.4	31.9	26.2	×1.2	232.8	97.7	×2.4
5) $r_0 := \hat{b} - \hat{A}x_0$	3.4	2.2	×1.6	14.1	9.0	×1.6	59.4	37.2	×1.6	435.4	160.2	×2.7
$\hat{A}p_j$,$\hat{A}p_j$ (×4*iter*)	13.2	8.3	×1.6	56.4	34.4	×1.6	237.3	141.3	×1.7	1740.2	629.7	×2.8
8)—15) **dot**, **axpy** (×4*iter*)	1.0	1.1	×1.0	4.1	4.4	×0.9	16.2	17.0	×1.0	108.0	93.8	×1.2

Table 9. Total time of direct and iterative solvers; strong scalability from 1 to 16 OMP threads; direct vs. iterative time ratio.

Problem #	1			2			3			4		
Total time, s. ; Scalability												
NOMP	1	16	$\frac{1}{16}$	1	16	$\frac{1}{16}$	1	16	$\frac{1}{16}$	1	16	$\frac{1}{16}$
Direct solver	42.9	7.5	×5.7	297.3	41.5	×7.2	2498.9	276.7	×9.0	N/A	N/A	N/A
Iterative solver	34.2	16.2	×2.1	177.2	68.8	×2.6	1101.3	319.0	×3.5	9173.0	1654.4	×5.5
Direct/Iterative ratio	1.3	0.5	—	1.7	0.6	—	2.3	0.9	—	N/A	N/A	N/A

6 Conclusion

We proposed the field-split preconditioned BCSGStab iterative solver to handle with Biot problem and compared it with the highly-optimized Intel MKL PARDSIO direct solver. Performance investigation showed the direct solver has time advantages on small problems in parallel mode on 16 cores. On large systems, the performance of the proposed iterative field-split solver achieves the direct one. The memory measurements also show that the iterative solver uses more than twice as less memory as the direct solver. Therefore, the iterative field-split solver can be used to solve large 2D and 3D Biot problems. Further optimization of both performance and memory usage will be continue in the context of solving large 3D Biot problems.

Acknowledgements. The research was supported by the Russian Science Foundation grant no. 22-11-00104, https://rscf.ru/project/22-11-00104/.

References

1. Intel math kernel library documentation. https://software.intel.com/en-us/intel-mkl/
2. Alekseev, A.S., Mikhailenko, B.G.: Solution of dynamic problems of elastic wave propagation in inhomogeneous media by a combination of partial separation of variables and finite difference methods. Geophysics **48**, 161–172 (1980)
3. Amestoy, P.R., Duff, I.S., Koster, J., L'Excellent, J.-Y.: A fully asynchronous multifrontal solver using distributed dynamic scheduling. SIAM J. Matrix Anal. Appl. **23**(1), 15–41 (2001)
4. Biot, M.A.: Theory of propagation of elastic waves in a fluid-saturated porous solid. ii. higher frequency range. J. Acoust. Society America **28**, 179–191 (1956)
5. Biot, M.A.: Theory of propagation of elastic waves in fluid-saturated porous solid. i. low-frequency range. J. Acoust. Society America **28**, 168–178 (1956)
6. Bollhöfer, M., Schenk, O., Janalik, R., Hamm, S., Gullapalli, K.: State-of-the-art sparse direct solvers. In: Grama, A., Sameh, A.H. (eds.) Parallel Algorithms in Computational Science and Engineering. MSSET, pp. 3–33. Springer, Cham (2020). https://doi.org/10.1007/978-3-030-43736-7_1
7. Ke, G., Calandrini, S., Aulisa, E.: A field-split preconditioning technique for fluid-structure interaction problems with applications in biomechanics. Int. J. Numer. Method Biomed. Eng. **36**(3), e3301 (2020)
8. Xiaoye, S.L.: An overview of SuperLU: algorithms, implementation, and user interface. ACM Trans. Math. Softw. **31**(3), 302–325 (2005)
9. Masson, Y.J., Pride, S.R., Nihei, K.T.: Finite difference modeling of biot's poroelastic equations at seismic frequencies. J. Geophys. Res.: Solid Earth **111**(B10), 305 (2006)
10. Quintal, B., Steeb, H., Frehner, M., Schmalholz, S.M.: Quasi-static finite-element modeling of seismic attenuation and dispersion due to wave-induced fluid flow in poroelastic media. J. Geophys. Res. **116**, B01201 (2011)
11. Solovyev, S., Novikov, M., Lisitsa, V.: Numerical solution of anisotropic biot equations in quasi-static state. In: Gervasi, O., Murgante, B., Misra, S., Rocha, A.M.A.C., Garau, C. (eds.) Computational Science and Its Applications – ICCSA 2022 Workshops: Malaga, Spain, July 4–7, 2022, Proceedings, Part II, pp. 310–327. Springer International Publishing, Cham (2022). https://doi.org/10.1007/978-3-031-10562-3_23
12. Solovyev, S.A., Novikov, M.A., Lisitsa, V.V.: Numerical solution of anisotropic biot equations of poroelastic fluid-saturated media in quasi-static state for numerical upscaling. Num. Methods Programm. (Vychislitel'nye Metody i Programmirovanie) **24**(75), 67–88 (2023)
13. Stuben, K.: A review of algebraic multigrid. J. Comput. Appl. Math. **128**(1–2), 281–309 (2001)
14. Saad, Y.: Iterative Methods for Sparse Linear Systems. PWS Publishing, New York (1996)

GPU-Accelerated Matrix Exponent for Solving 1D Time-Dependent Schrödinger Equation

Yea Rem Choi[1(✉)] and Vladimir Stegailov[1,2]

[1] HSE University, Moscow, Russia
e.choj@hse.ru
[2] Joint Institute for High Temperatures of RAS, Moscow, Russia
stegailov@jiht.ru

Abstract. Non-adiabatic electron-ion quantum dynamics is still an area of many unresolved problems even for such simple systems as the H_2^+ molecular ion. Mathematical modelling based on time-dependent Schrödinger equation (TDSE) is an important method that can provide better understanding of these phenomena. In this work, we present TDSE solution for 1D TDSE that describes non-adiabatic electron-ion quantum dynamics for the simplified H_2^+ model. For solving TDSE, we use the real-space representation and the matrix exponent method that is quite computationally expensive but is free from usual symmetry-based simplifications. For this purpose, we make use of the very high performance of modern Nvidia V100/A100 GPUs and deploy our parallel multi-GPU matrix multiplication algorithm.

Keywords: TDSE · Non-adiabatic quantum dynamics · Hydrogen molecular ion · Soft-core Coulomb potential · Parallel computing

1 Introduction

Despite the significant progress in the understanding of the quantum processes many phenomena even in such simple systems as molecular hydrogen are still objects of active experimental and theoretical studies, e.g. the dynamics of attosecond photoionization of H_2^+ [1] and H_2 [2]. Despite the simplicity, the models of electronic structure of such molecules still have such approximations as, for example, the use of the soft-core Coulomb potential [3]. The description of the non-adiabatic electron-ion quantum dynamics of these molecules is beyond the capabilities of the analytical solutions of TDSE and requires the high performance computing methods. Since we consider the time evolution of isolated systems the finite-difference time domain (FDTD) approach for solving TDSE seems to be a reasonable choice. For example, the FDTD approach was successfully applied for solving TDSE of quantum dots [4].

In this work, we report our attempt to use the FDTD method based on the matrix exponent for solving TDSE. The matrix exponent approach is one of the most generic methods for solving differential equations. The calculation of

V. Voevodin et al. (Eds.): RuSCDays 2023, LNCS 14388, pp. 100–113, 2023.
https://doi.org/10.1007/978-3-031-49432-1_8

the matrix exponent has been a computationally hard problem for a long time. Various approaches of acceleration for particular matrix were developed [5,6]. The development of the corresponding computational tools provided new appeal to the matrix exponent-based FDTD calculations [7].

2 Related Works

TDSE for simple systems have been considered in the context of the interaction of an atom or a molecule with ultrashort atomic pulses. In the paper of Lugovskoy and Bray an almost sudden perturbation of a quantum system by a ultrashort pulse has been considered [8]: the analytical theory has been compared with numerical solution of TDSE. Different scenarios of He ionization have been considered by numerically solving 1D TDSE by Yu and Madsen [9,10]. Non-adiabatic quantum dynamics of H_2^+ and HD^+ excited by single one-cycle laser pulses linearly polarized along the molecular axis have been studied within a three-dimensional model by Paramonov et al. [11]. Strong laser field interactions with He, H_2^+, and H_2 have been modelled by Majorosi et al. [12].

In several papers, the authors used the simplified 1D approximation with soft-core Coulomb potentials [8–10,12]. This type of electron-ion potentials is used in different atomic models (e.g., see the recent paper of Truong et al. [13]). The most accurate 3D model of molecular hydrogen based on the exponential split operator method [14] was used by Paramonov et al. [11]. The method presented in this work is free from the any symmetry assumptions and can be used with any form of potentials. The method is extendable to 3D geometry too. With our computational algorithm we have obtained the first results on the non-adiabatic vibronic energy transfer of energy from moving ions to electron subsystem: to the best of our knowledge this process was not considered before at the TDSE level of theory.

3 1D TDSE Model of a H_2^+ Molecular Ion

In this work we consider 1D TDSE for a single electron

$$i\hbar\frac{\partial\psi}{\partial t} = H(t)\psi, \tag{1}$$

where i is the imaginary unit, $\hbar$ is the Planck constant, ψ is the wave function, and $H(t)$ is the Hamiltonian matrix that can depend on time and has kinetic (T) and potential (V) parts as follows

$$H = T + V = -\frac{\hbar}{2m}\frac{\partial^2}{\partial r^2} + V(r,t). \tag{2}$$

In the spatial form TDSE can be approximated by the second order finite-difference scheme as [15]

$$i\hbar\frac{\partial}{\partial t}\psi_i = H\psi_i = -\frac{\hbar^2}{2m}\left(\frac{\psi_{i+1} - 2\psi_i + \psi_{i-1}}{\Delta r^2}\right) + V(r_i)\psi_i, \tag{3}$$

that can be written in the matrix form as

$$H = -\frac{\hbar^2}{2m\Delta r^2}\begin{pmatrix} -2 & 1 & & & \\ 1 & -2 & 1 & & \\ & \ddots & \ddots & \ddots & \\ & & 1 & -2 & 1 \\ & & & 1 & -2 \end{pmatrix} + \begin{pmatrix} V(r_0) & & & & \\ & \ddots & & & \\ & & V(r_i) & & \\ & & & \ddots & \\ & & & & V(r_N) \end{pmatrix}. \quad (4)$$

The finite-difference solution of TDSE (1) can be expressed using the matrix exponent as

$$\psi(r, t + \Delta t) = \exp\left[iH\Delta t\right]\psi(r, t), \quad (5)$$

where the exponent of a matrix A is defined as the infinite series

$$\exp A = I + \frac{1}{1!}A + \frac{1}{2!}A^2 + \frac{1}{3!}A^3 + \dots. \quad (6)$$

In (3) and (4) the Planck constant ($\hbar$) and the mass (m) are defined as 1 in our calculations to avoid the work with huge or tiny numbers. The absorbing boundary conditions are implemented.

The 1D hydrogen models with a soft-core Coulomb of electron-nucleus interaction is considered

$$V(r) = \frac{-Z}{\sqrt{r^2 + a}}. \quad (7)$$

To mimic the ionic vibration we have implemented the movement of the ion centers

$$V(r, t) = \frac{-Z}{\sqrt{(r - \alpha \sin(\beta t))^2 + a}}, \quad (8)$$

where Z is the soft-core Coulomb interaction strength, a is the softening parameter [9], α and β are some constants.

The stationary state of the wave function can be found by the time-independent equation

$$H\psi(r) = E\psi(r). \quad (9)$$

Here E is a constant value, so ψ in stationary state is the eigenvector of Hamiltonian matrix H and E is the eigen energy of the corresponding state (see Fig. 1).

4 Remarks About the Matrix Exponent Calculation

The matrix exponent algorithm used in this work for solving of TDSE (5) was developed based on our multi-GPU GEMM algorithm [16] that shows high performance for rather big matrices. So we took the attempt to build the program which does not use any assumptions about the matrix structure and calculates the matrix exponent for comparatively big matrix sizes.

Our multi-GPU GEMM algorithm uses only GPU devices for computation and data store, because it was aimed to the platforms with high speed links

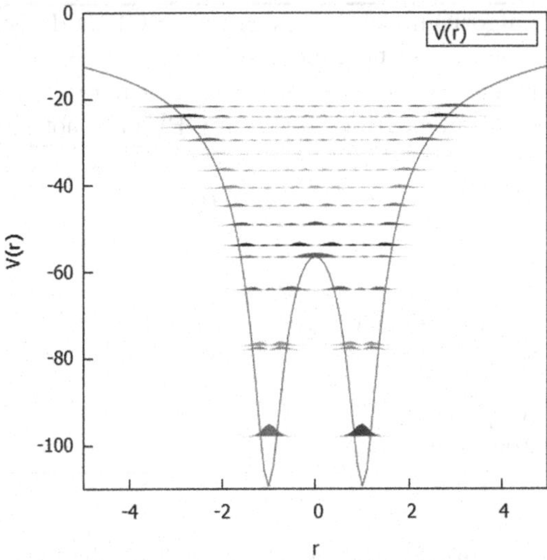

Fig. 1. The example of electron density distributions $|\psi_n(r)|^2$ for several bound states on the corresponding energy level positions in the soft-core Coulomb potential of two ions (7) ($Z = 30, a = 0.1$).

between GPUs (e.g., NVLink). The algorithm works asynchronously and reaches its high performance by overlapping computation and communication. It shows the performance rate rather close to the theoretical peak performance when it works with big matrices.

However, the proposed algorithm for solving TDSE has parts executed on CPU as well. In the beginning, the initial state ψ_0 is set in CPU memory and sent to GPUs. Also, the time-dependent potential $V(r,t)$ on each time step is defined in CPU memory then supplied to GPUs. The output operation of storing ψ at the specified moments of time into data files goes through CPU as well.

Yet, the most part of the algorithm is executed on GPU devices. The potential V in the Hamiltonian matrix is reinitialized each time step. The real and imaginary parts of matrices are stored in GPUs memory. The following objects are stored in GPU memory: the initialized complex matrix, the k-th term, and the resulted matrix to which each $(k+1)$-th term is added. To find the next term of the complex matrix 4 matrix multiplications are used: two for the real part $(Re * Re - Im * Im)$ and two for the imaginary part $(Re * Im + Im * Re)$. Also, the matrix-to-vector multiplication $(\exp H\psi)$ is done on GPUs, identically, two operations for the real part and two operations for the imaginary part at each time step. The algorithm scheme is shown at Algorithm 1.

The matrix exponent series (6) converges exponentially fast [17], so we have the question, when the convergence is reached and we can stop the computing and adding the subsequent terms due their small impact on the result. One method is to check the matrix elements if they are lesser than some fixed ϵ (this method may be applied in next version of the program). Currently, the selection

Algorithm 1. The algorithm scheme executed in GPUs during one time step, ψ is the wave function, H is the generated Hamiltonian matrix, $\exp A$ is the resulted matrix exponent. All operations are done separately for real and imaginary matrices. The communications between GPUs are not shown.

```
receive (potential V);
build Hamiltonian matrix (H = T + V), A = iHΔt;
exp A = I + A;
for k = 2 to rank do
    α = 1/k;
    Multi-GPU GEMM (A^k = αAA^(k−1));
    exp A = exp A + A^k;
end for
GEMV (ψ_j = exp A ψ_(j−1));
send (ψ_j); //for output in file
```

of the number of terms in the series is determined by the biggest row (column) of the matrix to which we apply the exponential. The matrix (4) is symmetric, so the biggest row (column) determines the slowest converging element of the series.

From (3) and (4) we see that the matrix exponent in TDSE has only an imaginary part, so the series can be transformed as

$$\exp iA = \left(I + \frac{i^2}{2!}A^2 + \ldots\right) + \left(\frac{i}{1!}A + \frac{i^3}{3!}A^3 + \ldots\right) = \cos A + i \sin A. \quad (10)$$

In such way we can make the algorithm simpler by separating the real and imaginary parts (till this moment the program has been developed for the general case). For optimization we take into some features of trigonometric matrices [18]. Since we have to get trigonometric matrices it could be anticipated that the elements of the resulted matrix should be in the range of $[-1, 1]$. As the matrix is symmetric (4), if the absolute value of the element is bigger than a natural k, then all terms till the k-th would be definitely bigger than 1 ($(a_{ij})^k/k!, a_{ij} > k$). Then, if we suppose that there are not much elements with comparably big values, the $k+1$ term and the following terms would decrease exponentially fast. Such "hump" phenomenon is known to cause some problems [6]. Accordingly, the margin of error increases dependent on the maximal value of the summing floating points. So, if the elements of the original matrix are much bigger than 1, then after the computation we can receive the margin of error comparable to 1. Here is one of the restrictions on the time step value (the smaller is the time step Δt, the smaller are the values of the matrix elements). Thus, if we would use a small time step, then, firstly, the series would start decreasing faster, and, secondly, we would have better accuracy, but, it would be required to compute more iteration for the same time period.

Talking about the distance step Δr, reducing it causes increase of kinetic energy part of the matrix (4). In other words, scaling up can matter the issues mentioned above as well, reasoning the necessity of the time step decrease as $\Delta r \sim \Delta t^2$.

There are some issues with allocating GPU memory. In GPUs we need to allocate memories of four complex matrices: the initial one, the k-th term, the $(k+1)$-th term and the resulted one. The real and imaginary parts can be stored separately in different devices, so they can be spread up to eight GPUs. Memory allocation size of one matrix is needed on devices with the resulted matrices (real and imaginary) to receive the data of k-th term and to do summation. Storing complex wave functions (ψ_j and ψ_{j+1}) and the vector of potential energy (V) requires much less memory. Additionally, during the multi-GPU GEMM execution there are needed temporary memory dependent on size of tile matrices [16]. This volume would be smaller for small tile size, but, it is recommended to choose optimal one dependent on the platform parameters [19,20].

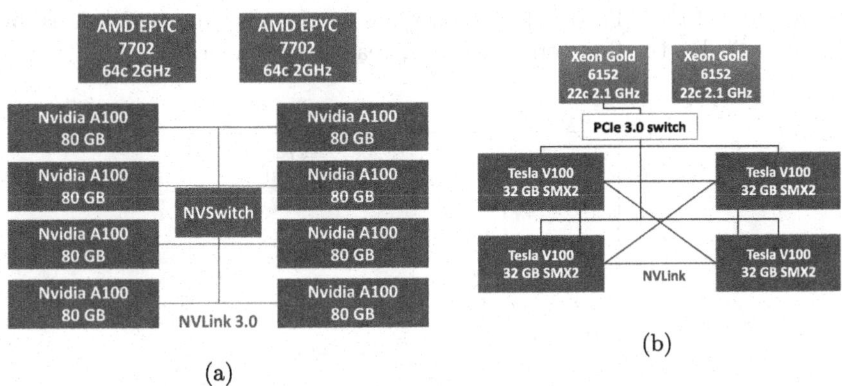

Fig. 2. The topology of the A100-equipped node of the cHARISMa supercomputer with two CPUs and eight Nvidia A100 GPUs by NVLink 3.0 (a) and the V100-equipped node of the cHARISMa supercomputer with two CPUs and four Nvidia V100 GPUs by NVLink 2.0, configuration K (type A, B) (b).

5 Testing Platforms

The results reported in this study are obtained on the nodes of the cHARISMa supercomputer at HSE University [21,22]. The first kind of nodes are based on the 8x Nvidia A100 GPU "type E" platform with NVSwitch (Fig. 2a). Each GPU has 80 Gb of HBM2 memory, and the eight GPUs are connected by NVLINK 3.0 via NVSwitch.

The second kind of nodes are based on the 4x Nvidia V100 GPU "type A, B, C" platform (Fig. 2b). Each GPU has 32 Gb of HBM2 memory, and the four GPUs are connected by NVLINK 2.0. Between GPUs there are no differences for configuration K (types A and B) and configuration M (type C).

The benchmarking studies were carried out using the standard HPC software stack based on CentOS Linux release 7.9.2009, GNU compilers 8.3.0, and CUDA Version 11.7.64 with the driver ver. 515.43.04.

6 Analysis of Numerical Experiments

The computations are performed with single precision numbers (FP32). One of the reason for this choice is that while using the tensor core technology (TF32) the performance rate increases greatly in comparison to double precision (TF64), but certain problem is the accuracy. As it is described in Sect. 4, we limit the maximal value of matrices by 8 (and better by 1) by regulating the time step. Then in the case of 8 the last 30-th ($k = 30$) term would be $\max a_{ij}^k \lesssim 8^{30}/30! \approx 4.7 * 10^{-6}$ and in the case of 1 the last 10-th ($k = 10$) term would be $\max a_{ij}^k \lesssim 1^{10}/10! \approx 2.8 * 10^{-7}$. The simple non-matrix example of the sequence behavior is illustrated in Fig. 3. The sequence converges to a number in range $[-1, 1]$, but has a "hump" due the first terms which increases the error rate.

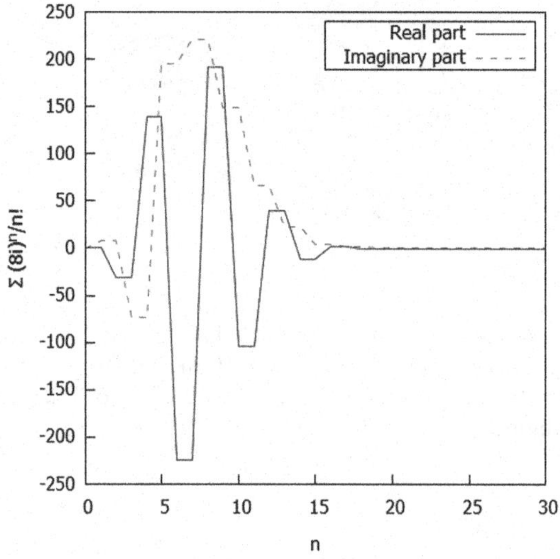

Fig. 3. The behavior of function $\sum_n \frac{(8i)^n}{n!}$ that illustrates the typical convergence of the matrix exponent elements.

In the experiments the number of distance points were set to $N = 8192$, consequently the matrices have $N^2 = 8192^2$ elements. For this size of matrices the GPUs do not show the best performance with tensor cores, that to share the workload between all GPUs we have to take the size of tiles $N_i = 2048$ or less for four V100 GPUs, and $N_i = 1024$ or less for eight A100 GPUs. This issue would go away with sufficient increase of the matrices size (e.g., in 2D or 3D geometries), but, as we have also pointed out the memory requirements pose their limitations. A possible further development of the algorithm is to execute several multiplications in parallel. It means that the GPUs can be split into groups (of two or four) where each group would compute the different real and image parts combinations of complex multiplication. In such way the bigger tile size can be used of sharing the workload between all devices in the group. Now with the studied size of matrices, the GPUs show about 70% of utilization on four V100 GPUs and 10% of utilization on eight A100 GPUs which is not efficient enough.

The approximate average execution time for 15000 time steps ($\Delta t = 0.002$) of series with 10 terms ($k = 10$) are shown in Table 1. For the same number of GPUs, A100 works faster than V100. But, with 8 GPUs the performance of A100 falls down. This is because between 8 GPUs the data transfer mapping becomes more complicated, but computation load is still low for our multi-GPU GEMM algorithm. Then, the necessary time of data transfer increases, thus, overall time increases as well.

Table 1. Average execution times on different platforms.

Number of GPUs	4xV100	4xA100	8xA100
Time (sec)	24700	17550	44850
Time per one iteration (sec)	1.65	1.17	2.99

The execution time dependence on the matrix size for A100 and V100 GPUs are illustrated in Fig. 4. Because of the memory limitations in the case of V100 GPUs it was impossible to launch the size of $N = 65536$.

In Fig. 5 the profiles by Nsight Systems are illustrated for $N = 16384$. In scaled up Fig. 5b there is shown that the multi-GPU GEMM algorithm works in best form, but, the barriers make some intervals between the kernel calls. However, these intervals would be smaller for bigger matrix sizes.

7 Results

Figure 6 and Fig. 7 illustrate the numerical results obtained with our TDSE model for the H_2^+ ion with $Z = 30, a = 0.1$. The ground state wave function is chosen to be the initial condition for TDSE. One can notice (see Fig. 1) that there are two nearly degenerate states with the lowest energy: one is in the left Coulomb potential well and other is in the right well.

In Fig. 6 the evolution of the wave is shown for the fixed distance between the nuclei. In this case, the Hamiltonian matrix does not change in time. It is the confirmation that the initial condition is indeed the stationary solution and the corresponding probability density does not depend on time.

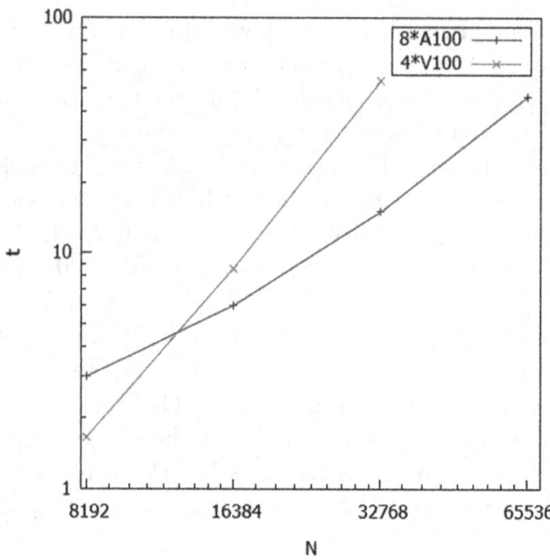

Fig. 4. The execution time (sec) per one time iteration versus the matrix size N.

Figure 7 shows the results for the model with two moving nuclei (8). In this case, the Hamiltonian matrix does change in time and our TDSE GPU-accelerated algorithm brings its benefit in high-speed recalculation of $\exp(iH\Delta t)$.

The change of $V(r,t)$ due to the nuclear motion with time displaces the wave function from the stationary state. Two effects are clearly visible. The electron probability becomes localized at both nuclei and the wave function obtains a node (i.e. the point with zero probability). It means that we observe the non-adiabatic process of electron excitation due to energy transfer from the moving nuclei to the electron subsystem.

8 Discussion

The proposed method for solving TDSE with the usage of the GPU-accelerated matrix exponent can be generalized to 2D and 3D geometries since there are no assumptions on the structure of Hamiltonian matrix. There are no assumptions on the symmetry of the model that open a way to study, for example, the collisions of a single proton on the hydrogen molecular ion. The method can be generalized for 2 electrons (with opposite spins) as well. The major challenge for such modification is the increase of memory for storing the Hamiltonian matrix. Several optimizations options are not been used at this moment: the use of the memory of all GPUs involved in the computation, the saving one half of the total memory taking into account the symmetry of the Hamiltonian matrix. Moreover, with the development of the APUs with unified memory (e.g., such as AMD MI300 or Nvidia Grace Hopper Superchip) one can expect that larger volumes of memory will be directly available for GPU-accelerated algorithms

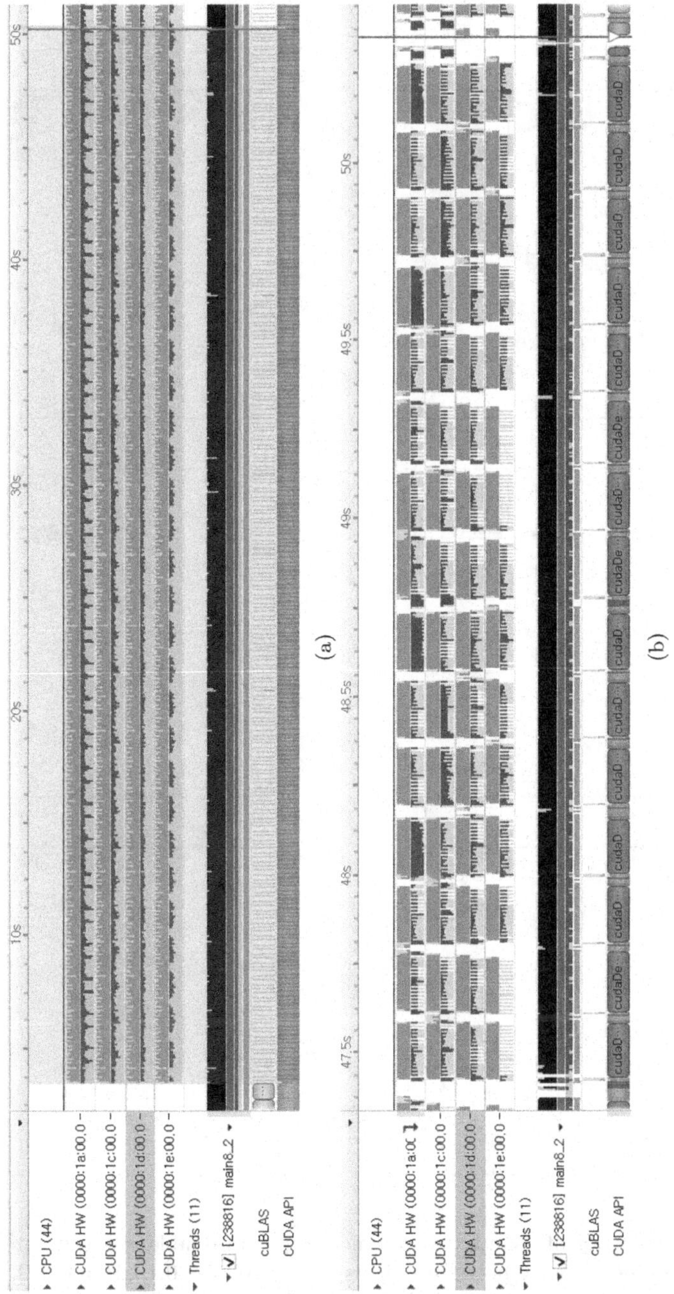

Fig. 5. The profiles on 4 V100 GPUs. The number of distance elements is $N = 16384$ and the tile size is $N_i = 2048$. The blue bars are the computation kernels in GPUs, and the brown bars are the peer-to-peer data transfer operations between GPUs. In (a) the computation during one iteration is marked by green. By the long vertical blue line we show the wave function data supply to CPU for output operation. In (b) the scaled up fragment is shown. (Color figure online)

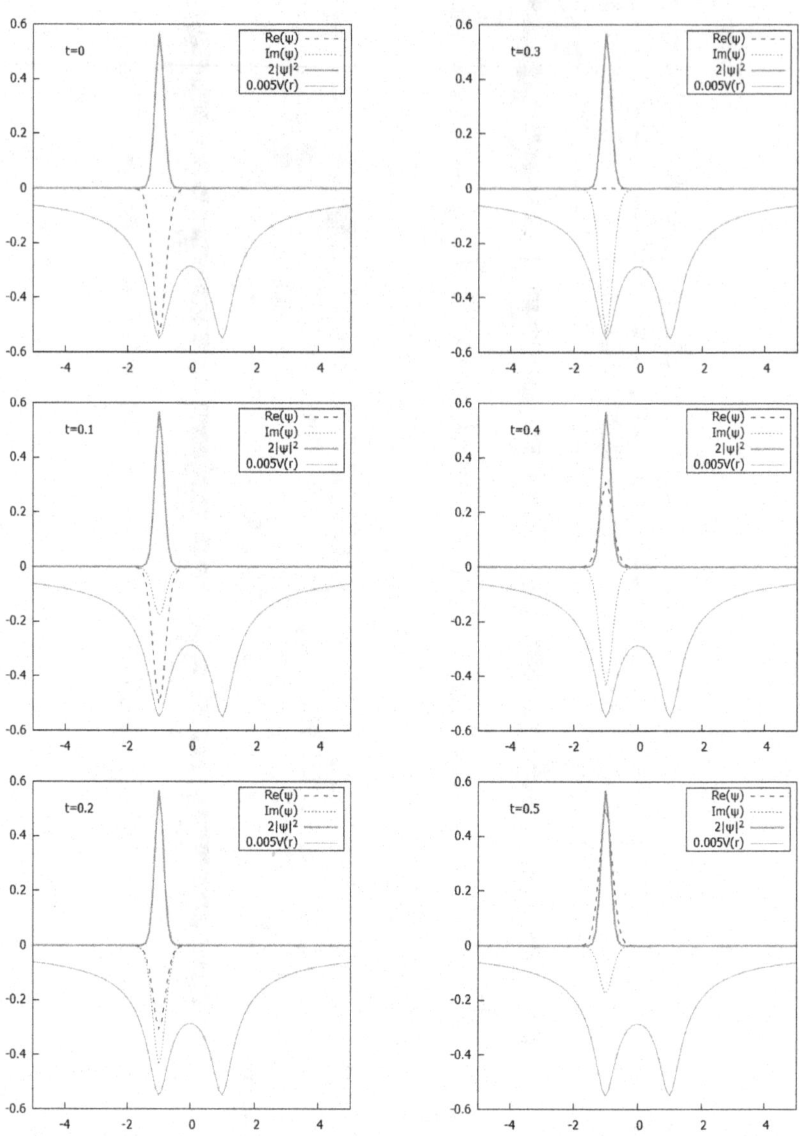

Fig. 6. The behavior of complex wave function (ψ) in double well soft-core Coulomb potential (7) (the distance between wells is 2, $Z = 30, a = 0.1$, $\Delta t = 0.002$, $\Delta r = 0.1$, $k = 10$). The time moments are 0, 0.1, 0.2 in the left block, and 0.3, 0.4, 0.5 in the right block. The results show that the probability density remains stationary in time for the initial ground state wave function.

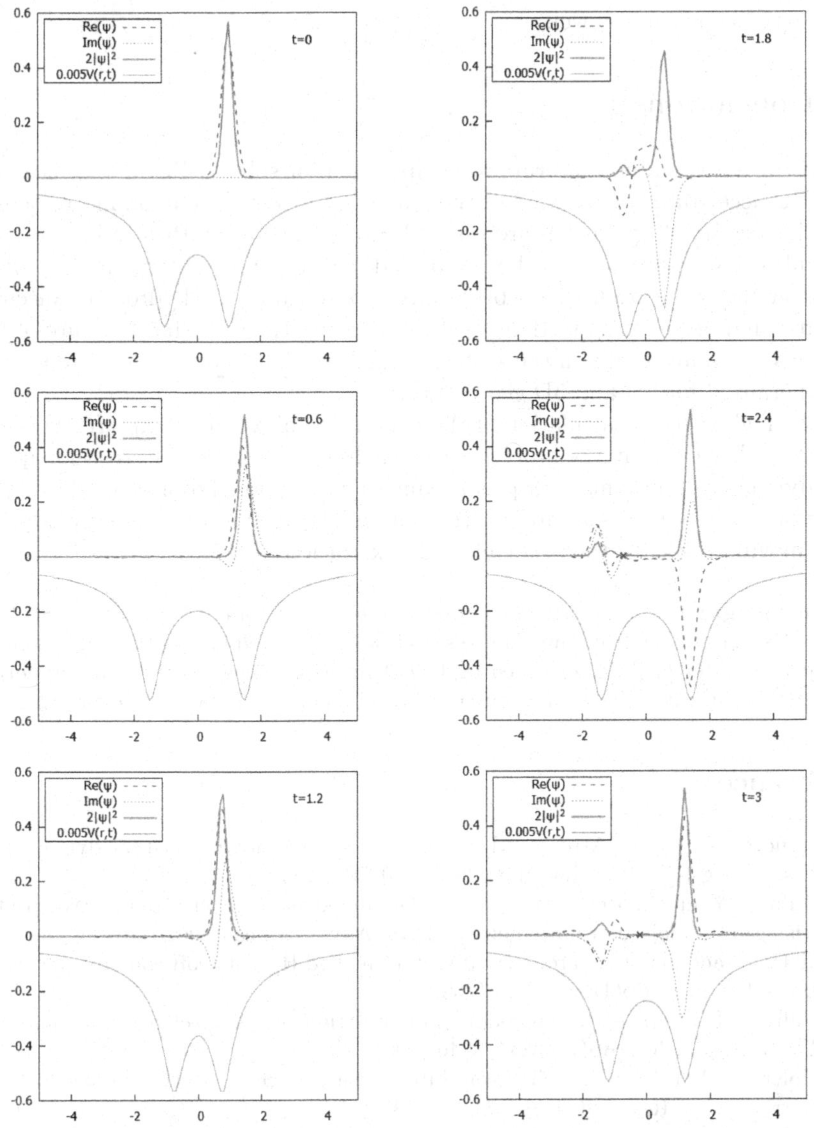

Fig. 7. The behavior of complex wave function (ψ) in the sinusoidally moving double well soft-core Coulomb potential (8) (the same parameters as in Fig. 6 with $\alpha = 0.5$ and $\beta = 3$). The cross shows the node of the wave function that appears after the excitation from the ground state.

that will make easier the deployment of the algorithms like the one considered in this work. In principle, the presented multi-GPU accelerated matrix exponent approach can be applicable not only for solving TDSE but other types of differential equations as well.

9 Conclusions

In this work, we propose a brute-force approach for solving TDSE that is based on GPU-accelerated calculation of the matrix exponent. The main motivation is that floating point operations are very "cheap" on modern GPUs and the matrix multiplication operations can be performed very quickly for large matrix sizes. We show the application of this brute-force approach for 1D hydrogen molecular ion. It is important to note that we use no assumptions on the structure of the Hamiltonian matrix and on the system symmetry that is why this approach can be generalized for 2D and 3D geometries.

The high speed recalculation of the Hamiltonian exponent $\exp(iH\Delta t)$ opens the possibility to study the processes that include the coupled electron-ion quantum dynamics. Using this high-performance computational tool we modelled (for the first time as we are aware of) the non-adiabatic (vibronic) energy transfer from moving nuclei to the single electron excitation of H_2^+.

Acknowledgments. The article was prepared within the framework of the HSE University Basic Research Program. This research was supported in part through resources of supercomputer facilities provided by HSE University. This research was supported in part through computational resources of HPC facilities at HSE University [22].

References

1. Staudte, A., et al.: Attosecond strobing of two-surface population dynamics in dissociating H_2^+. Phys. Rev. Lett. **98**(7), 073003 (2007)
2. Bello, R.Y.,et al.: Reconstruction of the time-dependent electronic wave packet arising from molecular autoionization. Sci. Adv. **4**(8), eaat3962 (2018)
3. Li, C.: Exact analytical ground state solution of 1d H_2^+ with soft coulomb potential. J. Math. Chem. **60**(1), 184–194 (2022)
4. Sullivan, D., Citrin, D.: Time-domain simulation of two electrons in a quantum dot. J. Appl. Phys. **89**(7), 3841–3846 (2001)
5. Moler, C., Van Loan, C.: Nineteen dubious ways to compute the exponential of a matrix. SIAM Rev. **20**(4), 801–836 (1978)
6. Moler, C., Van Loan, C.: Nineteen dubious ways to compute the exponential of a matrix, twenty-five years later. SIAM Rev. **45**(1), 3–49 (2003)
7. Ramadan, O.: Unified matrix-exponential FDTD formulations for modeling electrically and magnetically dispersive materials. Comput. Phys. Commun. **183**(5), 1101–1106 (2012)
8. Lugovskoy, A., Bray, I.: Almost sudden perturbation of a quantum system with ultrashort electric pulses. Phys. Rev. A **77**(2), 023420 (2008)

9. Yu, C., Madsen, L.B.: Sequential and nonsequential double ionization of helium by intense xuv laser pulses: revealing ac stark shifts from joint energy spectra. Phys. Rev. A **94**(5), 053424 (2016)
10. Yu, C., Madsen, L.B.: Above-threshold ionization of helium in the long-wavelength regime: examining the single-active-electron approximation and the two-electron strong-field approximation. Phys. Rev. A **95**(6), 063407 (2017)
11. Paramonov, G.K., Klamroth, T., Lu, H., Bandrauk, A.D.: Quantum dynamics, isotope effects, and power spectra of H_2^+ and HD^+ excited to the continuum by strong one-cycle laser pulses: Three-dimensional non-born-oppenheimer simulations. Phys. Rev. A **98**(6), 063431 (2018)
12. Majorosi, S., Benedict, M.G., Bogár, F., Paragi, G., Czirják, A.: Density-based one-dimensional model potentials for strong-field simulations in he, h 2+, and h 2. Phys. Rev. A **101**(2), 023405 (2020)
13. Truong, T.D., et al.: Soft parameters in coulomb potential of noble atoms for non-sequential double ionization: classical ensemble model and simulations. Comput. Phys. Commun. **276**, 108372 (2022)
14. Bandrauk, A.D., Shen, H.: Exponential split operator methods for solving coupled time-dependent schrödinger equations. J. Chem. Phys. **99**(2), 1185–1193 (1993)
15. Viklund, L., Augustsson, L., Melander, J.: Numerical approaches to solving the time-dependent schrödinger equation with different potentials (2016)
16. Choi, Y.R., Nikolskiy, V., Stegailov, V.: Matrix-matrix multiplication using multiple GPUs connected by NVLink. In: 2020 Global Smart Industry Conference (GloSIC), pp. 354–361. IEEE (2020)
17. Anthonisse, J.M., Tijms, H.: Exponential convergence of products of stochastic matrices. J. Math. Anal. Appl. **59**(2), 360–364 (1977)
18. Alonso, P., Ibáñez, J., Sastre, J., Peinado, J., Defez, E.: Efficient and accurate algorithms for computing matrix trigonometric functions. J. Comput. Appl. Math. **309**, 325–332 (2017)
19. Choi, Y.R., Nikolskiy, V., Stegailov, V.: Tuning of a matrix-matrix multiplication algorithm for several GPUS connected by fast communication links. In: Sokolinsky, L., Zymbler, M. (eds.) Parallel Computational Technologies: 16th International Conference, PCT 2022, Dubna, Russia, March 29–31, 2022, Revised Selected Papers, pp. 158–171. Springer International Publishing, Cham (2022). https://doi.org/10.1007/978-3-031-11623-0_12
20. Choi, Y.R., Stegailov, V.: Multi-GPU GEMM algorithm performance analysis for Nvidia and AMD GPUs connected by NVLink and PCIe. In: Balandin, D., Barkalov, K., Meyerov, I. (eds.) Mathematical Modeling and Supercomputer Technologies: 22nd International Conference, MMST 2022, Nizhny Novgorod, Russia, November 14–17, 2022, Revised Selected Papers, pp. 281–292. Springer Nature Switzerland, Cham (2022). https://doi.org/10.1007/978-3-031-24145-1_23
21. Kondratyuk, N., et al.: Performance and scalability of materials science and machine learning codes on the state-of-art hybrid supercomputer architecture. In: Voevodin, V., Sobolev, S. (eds.) Supercomputing: 5th Russian Supercomputing Days, RuSCDays 2019, Moscow, Russia, September 23–24, 2019, Revised Selected Papers, pp. 597–609. Springer International Publishing, Cham (2019). https://doi.org/10.1007/978-3-030-36592-9_49
22. Kostenetskiy, P.S., Chulkevich, R.A., Kozyrev, V.I.: HPC resources of the higher school of economics. J. Phys.: Conf. Series **1740**, 012050 (Jan 2021). https://doi.org/10.1088/1742-6596/1740/1/012050

How to Make Lanczos-Montgomery Fast on Modern Supercomputers?

Dmitry Zheltkov[1(✉)], Nikolai Zamarashkin[1,2], and Sergey Matveev[1,2]

[1] Marchuk Institute of Numerical Mathematics of the Russian Academy of Sciences, Moscow, Russia
dmitry.zheltkov@gmail.com
[2] Lomonosov Moscow State University, Moscow, Russia

Abstract. This paper deals with the performance analysis of the INM RAS implementation of the block Lanczos-Montgomery method that was used to accomplish the factorization of the RSA-232 number. Other steps of RSA-232 factorization carried out by CADO-NFS open source library are also mentioned. Further adaptation of parallel block Lanczos-Montgomery method for the modern supercomputers is discussed, including implementation of basic operations of the method on GPUs.

Keywords: finite fields · linear systems · parallel computation · Lanczos-Montgomery · integer factorization · RSA-232 · GPGPU

1 RSA-232 Factorization

One of the most popular cryptosystems is RSA [1]. Its cryptographic strength is based on the hardness of the integer factorization problem. The RSA Factoring Challenge is a challenge devoted to research of a practical difficulty of the large integer factorization. One of the most difficult steps of integer factorization algorithms is solution of huge sparse linear system over GF(2). Such systems can be solved by parallel block Lanczos-Montgomery method [2,3]. In this paper factorization of the RSA-232 number of the RSA Factoring Challenge is described. To solve the linear system, INM RAS implementation of the parallel block Lanczos-Montgomery method has been used.

The RSA-232 number has 232 decimal digits and it was the smallest number from the RSA Factoring Challenge that had not been factored by the start of this experiment in December 2018. However, this number is of the same size (in bits or decimal digits) as the RSA-768 number which was the largest factored number at that time. As of June 2023 the RSA-232 and the RSA-768 numbers

RSA-232 factorization was supported by the Moscow Center of Fundamental and Applied Mathematics at INM RAS (Agreement with the Ministry of Education and Science of the Russian Federation No. 075-15-2022-286), block Lanczos performance analysis and its improvements research was supported by the Russian Science Foundation project № 19-11-00338, https://rscf.ru/en/project/19-11-00338/.

V. Voevodin et al. (Eds.): RuSCDays 2023, LNCS 14388, pp. 114–128, 2023.
https://doi.org/10.1007/978-3-031-49432-1_9

are the third largest (in bits or decimal digits) factored RSA numbers with the RSA-250 number (that has 250 decimal digits) being the largest one.

Factorization was performed using the generalized number field sieve (GNFS) algorithm [4], all stages of the algorithm except the solution of a linear system over GF(2) were accomplished by CADO-NFS open source library [5]. Below all stages of the algorithm are briefly described and then the performance of INM RAS implementation of block Lanczos-Montgomery method is analyzed.

1.1 GNFS Stages

The GNFS algorithm consists from 5 stages:

- Selection of irreducible polynomial that provides "good" extension of rational number field.
- Lattice sieving that finds ideals that are completely factored by prime ideals of norm less then some bound.
- Filtering that performs removal of duplicates and reduction of the size of a linear system using "greedy" "smart" Gauss elimination.
- Solution of a linear system over GF(2).
- Square root computation.

Polynomial Selection. Polynomial selection was performed in December 2018 using CADO-NFS library on Zhores supercomputer of Skolkovo Institute of Science and Technology. All the parameters were used are default CADO-NFS parameters that are in file *parameters/factor/params.c230* of that library. Computational cost was about 1.5 coreyears. The final polynomials are

$$f(x) = 2468070000x^6 - 181228069236569685x^5 - 543698239577082532987336x^4 +$$
$$114867654265258359415108217588 2x^3 - 1403545065887564178311798720022944 4x^2 -$$
$$93492026266785457363678158624735511106195 2x -$$
$$28007552266611184983113738168774066463910177280$$
$$g(x) = 980398213587383664 7687x - 168027075241687571943114310982734190 07.$$

Lattice Sieving. Lattice sieving was performed from December 2018 till March 2019. About 80% of sieving was done on Lomonosov supercomputer of Lomonosov Moscow State University supercomputer center and 20% was done using Zhores supercomputer of Skolkovo Institute of Science and Technology. All the parameters were the default parameters of CADO-NFS that are in file *parameters/factor/params.c230* except that for Lomonosov supercomputer range I was reduced to fit RAM.

If all the computations were done using nodes of Zhores supercomputer that has Intel Xeon Gold 6136 processor, total computational cost would be about 550 coreyears. Total number of collected relations is about 5.7 billions.

Filtering. Filtering was done in June 2019 using CADO-NFS library on single node of Arcuda cluster of Skolkovo Institute of Science and Technology. Total computational cost was less than 0.1 coreyears, but required more than 1 TB of RAM on single node. After duplicate removal 4.4 billions relations left, after singleton removal there were only 1.8 billions relations. Clique removal reduced number of relations to 1.15 billions and after the merge step a final matrix of size about 317 millions and average number of nonzero entries per row equal to 170 was obtained.

Linear System Solution. Solution of linear system was done from December 2019 till January 2020 on Zhores supercomputer of Skolkovo Institute of Science and Technology using INM RAS implementation of the block Lancsos-Montgomery method. Different node configurations (from 20 to 40) nodes were used during computations and solution was obtained in 38 days.

If all computations were done on 20 nodes solution would take 47 days and total computational cost was about 62 core years with 90% of time (about 56 coreyears) spent on the matrix by block product and 21% of that time (about 11.5 coreyears) spent on the communications between nodes. About 10% of total time (about 6.2 coreyears) spent on the dense operations.

Square Root Computation. Square root computation was done in February 2020 on *m1-megamem-96* instance of Google Cloud service using CADO-NFS library. Total computation cost was less than 0.1 coreyears but computations required more than 200 GB of RAM for each square root. Luckily, the first square root allowed us to obtain factorization:

RSA-232 =

2966909333208360660361779924242630634742946262521852394401857157419437019472326239074491011257180427449407445275189 1

$*$

3403816175197563438006609498491521420547121760734723172735163413276050706174852650644314432514808888111508386301 7669

2 Parallel Block Lanczos-Montgomery Method

In order to analyze performance of INM RAS implementation of the parallel block Lanczos-Montgomery method let us describe the method and estimate complexity of its parts. The block Lanczos-Montgomery method [2] is in essence the Lanczos method [6] that performs all possible iterations to find a solution and uses blocks instead of vectors and longer recurrence for A-orthogonalization to address the issue that matrices over GF(2) are often singular.

The Lanczos algorithm for a linear system solution is very similar to the well known conjugate gradient algorithm [7] (and obtains on each step the same approximation of the solution if computations are exact) with the difference that new direction vector is obtained not by A-orthogonalization of the current residual but by A-orthogonalization of the product of the matrix and current direction vector.

2.1 The Algorithm

There are two main resources of parallelism of the method: distribution of the sparse matrix across nodes and the block factor [3].

Matrix Distribution. Assume that computations are performed on s nodes. For simplicity let matrix A sizes M and N be divisible by s, $m = M/s$, $n = N/s$.

It is evident that if a nontrivial solution $\hat{X}$ such that $P_1AP_2\hat{X} = 0$ have been obtained, where P_1 and P_2 are permutation matrices, than $X = P_2\hat{X}$ is nontrivial solution of $AX = 0$.

Assume that the matrix have been permuted in a way that

$$A = \begin{bmatrix} A_{11} & \dots & A_{1\,s} \\ \vdots & \vdots & \vdots \\ A_{s1} & \dots & A_{ss} \end{bmatrix},$$

blocks A_{ij} are of sizes $m \times n$ and have approximately the same number of nonzero elements. Note that existence of such permutation hasn't been proved, but for the matrices that arise in the GNFS algorithm there is a simple greedy algorithm that allows to obtain such permutations in practice.

Let us introduce two dimensional grid $s_r \times s_c$ of nodes ($s = s_r s_c$). Each node now corresponds to pair of indices $\{j_1, j_2\}, i = \overline{1 \dots s_r}, j = \overline{1 \dots s_c}$. Block $A_{IJ}, I = \overline{1 \dots s}, J = \overline{1 \dots s}$ is stored on the node $\{\left\lceil \frac{I-1}{s_c} \right\rceil, \left\lceil \frac{J-1}{s_r} \right\rceil\}$. Let us denote block A_{IJ} that is stored on the node $\{j_1, j_2\}$ as $A_{kl}^{\{j_1,j_2\}}$, where $k = 1 + ((I-1) \mod s_c), l = 1 + ((J-1) \mod s_r)$. Then

$$A^{\{j_1,j_2\}} = \begin{bmatrix} A_{11}^{\{j_1,j_2\}} & \dots & A_{1s_r}^{\{j_1,j_2\}} \\ \vdots & \vdots & \vdots \\ A_{s_c1}^{\{j_1,j_2\}} & \dots & A_{s_cs_r}^{\{j_1,j_2\}} \end{bmatrix}$$

is the part of matrix stored on the node $\{j_1, j_2\}$.

Blocks by which the matrix is multiplied are also distributed across all nodes. Consider $N \times b$ block

$$V = \left[V_1^T \dots V_s^T\right]^T$$

with $n \times b$ blocks $V_J, J = \overline{1 \dots s}$. Block V_J is stored on the node

$$\{1 + ((J-1) \mod s_r), \left\lceil \frac{J-1}{s_r} \right\rceil\},$$

so each node stores just a single part. Denote the part stored on the node $\{j_1, j_2\}$ as $V^{\{j_1,j_2\}}$. With that notation

$$V = \left[\left(V^{\{1,1\}}\right)^T \dots \left(V^{\{s_r,1\}}\right)^T \dots \left(V^{\{s_r,s_c\}}\right)^T\right]^T$$

Algorithm 1 computes the product $W = AV$, with the result stored distributed across the nodes

$$W = \left[\left(W^{\{1,1\}}\right)^T \dots \left(W^{\{1,s_c\}}\right)^T \vdots \left(W^{\{s_r,s_c\}}\right)^T\right].$$

Algorithm 1. Distributed matrix by block product

Require: Nodes grid $s_r \times s_c$, $A^{\{j_1,j_2\}}$ and $V^{\{j_1,j_2\}}$ on the node $\{j_1, j_2\}$
Ensure: Resulting $m \times b$ block part $W^{\{j_1,j_2\}}$ on node $\{j_1, j_2\}$
1: **for** k from 1 to s_c **do**
2: $\quad T_k^{\{j_1,j_2\}} \leftarrow 0_{m\times b}$
3: **end for**
4: **for** l from 1 to s_r **do**
5: $\quad l \leftarrow 1 + ((j_1 + l - 2) \mod s_r)$
6: $\quad$ **for** k from 1 to s_c **do**
7: $\qquad T_k^{\{j_1,j_2\}} \leftarrow T_k^{\{j_1,j_2\}} + A_{kl}^{\{j_1,j_2\}} V^{\{l,j_2\}}$
8: $\quad$ **end for**
9: **end for**
10: $W^{\{j_1,j_2\}} \leftarrow 0_{m\times b}$
11: **for** k from 1 to s_c **do**
12: $\quad W^{\{j_1,j_2\}} \leftarrow W^{\{j_1,j_2\}} + T_{j_2}^{\{j_1,k\}}$
13: **end for**

Cycle in lines 4–8 of Algorithm 1 multiplicates block columns of locally stored matrix by a part of the block starting with the part that is locally stored. On each iteration it cyclically sends and receives part of the block across the first dimension of the nodes grid.

Cycle in lines 11–13 of Algorithm 1 corresponds to *MPI_Reduce_scatter* operation across second dimension of the nodes grid, it computes on each node corresponding part of the sum of vectors that are stored across nodes.

Multiplication of transposed matrix by a block is very similar. On input it has block distributed as output of Algorithm 1 and produces block distributed as its input.

Total size of data transfers of the Algorithm 1 is $2b((s_r - 1)n + (s_c - 1)m)$ bits per node.

Block Factor. Assume there is $s_r \times s_c \times p$ nodes. Let us have block of sizes $N \times bp$ distributed across all the nodes:

$$\left[V\right]_{j_1 j_2 j_3} = V^{\{j_1,j_2,j_3\}}$$

Each part $V_j^{\{j_1,j_2,j_3\}}$ is stored on the node j_1, j_2, j_3 and has sizes $n \times pb$, where $n = N/(s_r s_c p)$.

Algorithm 2 is the algorithm for computation of product of the distributed block by the matrix, each subgrid of size $s_r \times s_c$ node stores its own distributed copy of the matrix. Lines 1 and 4 of Algorithm 2 correspond to *MPI_Alltoall* operation along third dimension. Such operation performs redistribution of data. After line 1 each of p subgrids of size $s_r \times s_c$ has its own distributed block of total size $N \times b$ across all nodes. Therefore *distributed_matvec* and *transposed_distributed_matvec* are Algorithm 1 for the matrix and transposed matrix, and have communications only across such subgrid. And line 4 return resulting block to the same distribution around whole grid as input block had.

Thus, for the fat tree topology (fat tree topology required at least along third dimension of nodes grid to have desired performance of *MPI_Alltoall* operation) total size in bits of exchanged data per node for this algorithm (including data transfers of Algorithm 1) is

$$\frac{4b}{s_r s_c p}\left((p-1)N + p(s_r - 1)N + p(s_c - 1)M\right).$$

Algorithm 2. Multiplication of matrix by the distributed block

Require: $s_r \times s_c \times p$ nodes, $A^{\{j_1,j_2\}}$ and $V^{\{j_1,j_2,j_3\}}$ on the node $\{j_1, j_2, j_3\}$.
Ensure: $\frac{N}{s_r s_c p} \times bp$ part $U^{\{j_1,j_2,j_3\}}$ of the product.

1: $P^{\{j_1,j_2,j_3\}} \leftarrow \left[\left[V^{\{j_1,j_2,1\}^T}\right]_{j_3} \dots \left[V^{\{j_1,j_2,p\}^T}\right]_{j_3}\right]^T$
2: $W^{\{j_1,j_2,j_3\}} \leftarrow$ distributed_matvec$(A^{\{j_1,j_2\}}, P^{\{j_1,j_2,j_3\}})$
3: $P^{\{j_1,j_2,j_3\}} \leftarrow$ transposed_distributed_matvec$(A^{\{j_1,j_2\}}, P^{\{j_1,j_2,j_3\}})$
4: $U^{\{j_1,j_2,j_3\}} \leftarrow \left[P^{\{j_1,j_2,1\}} \dots P^{\{j_1,j_2,p\}}\right]$

Using the Algorithm 2 it is easy to construct the parallel block Lanczos-Montgomery Algorithm 3 with block factor p and matrix distribution among $s_r \times s_c$ nodes. Here *combined_matvec* is the Algorithm 2, *matvec* — similar algorithm that performs multiplication only by the matrix and returns on each node distributed block part of sizes $M/(ps_r s_c) \times bp$.

Procedure *distributed_LU* performs distributed LU decomposition of matrix X with full pivoting

$$X = P_1 L \left[U_{11}\ U_{12}\right] P_2$$

with $r \times r$ nonsingular triangular matrix U_{11}, r is the rank of matrix X and P_1, P_2 are permutation matrices of corresponding sizes. Symbol '$\sim$' means that corresponding output is not used.

Lines 4, 9, 18 correspond to *MPI_Allreduce* operation that computes sum across all the nodes and then provides the copy of the result to all the nodes. All variables without superscript in Algorithm 3 have the same values for all the nodes.

The function

$$[Z_i^+, S_i, r_i] \leftarrow \text{inverse}(Z_i, S_{i-1}, r_{i-1})$$

finds rank r_i of symmetric matrix Z_i and computes $pb \times r$ matrix

$$S_i = P \begin{bmatrix} I_{r_i \times r_i} \\ 0_{(pb-r_i)\times r_i} \end{bmatrix}$$

for some permutation matrix P. Matrix S_i selects nonsingular $r_i \times r_i$ symmetric submatrix $S_i^T Z_i S_i$ of the matrix Z_i, with additional requirement that

$$(I_{pb\times pb} - S_i S_i^T)(I_{pb\times pb} - S_{i-1}S_{i-1}^T) = 0$$

if r_i is not zero. That means that columns that were not selected by S_{i-1} should be selected by S_i.

Matrix Z_i^+ is $pb\times pb$ matrix that contains the inverse of the selected submatrix in corresponding positions and zeros elsewhere

$$Z_i^+ = S_i \left(S_i^T Z_i S_i\right)^{-1} S_i^T.$$

If $N \gg p^2 s_r s_c b$ then the algorithm requires slightly more than

$$(5N + M)b/(s_r s_c)$$

bits of memory per node.

On the fat tree topology total amount of sent and received data per node is equal to

$$\frac{4M}{s_r s_c p}\left(\frac{p-1}{p}N + s_r(s_r - 1)N + s_c(s_c - 1)M + p(s_r s_c p - 1)b\right)$$

Computations of the algorithm require

$$M\left(10\frac{N}{s_r s_c} + 17p^2 b\right) b + o\left(\frac{MNb}{s_r s_c}\right)$$

bit operations per node and $2M/pb$ multiplications of $M/s_r \times N/s_c$ sparse submatrix by a block of b columns.

Note that at the Algorithm 3 formula for computation of F_{i+1} differs from the original paper [2], but it is just a straightforward simplification. It is also easy to see that if $r_{i-1} = r_i = pb$ (and therefore $S_i = I_{pb\times pb}, Z_i^+ = Z_i^{-1}$) then the algorithm is just the parallel block Lanczos algorithm.

2.2 Implementation Details

Block Lanczos-Montgomery method is implemented on **C** language with handwritten assembler functions for the performance critical functions. Implementation uses **MPI** (message passing interface) library for distributed memory parallelism and **OpenMP** (open multi-processing) extension for the parallelism on the shared memory.

Current implementation does not make use of GPUs or other accelerators.

Algorithm 3. Parallel Block Lanczos-Montgomery method

Require: Block size b, Nodes grid $s_r \times s_c \times p$, $A^{\{j_1,j_2\}}$ on the node $\{j_1, j_2, j_3\}$.
Ensure: Part $X^{\{j_1,j_2,j_3\}}$ of the block X s.t. $AX = 0$, number of columns n of X.

$X_0^{\{j_1,j_2,j_3\}} \leftarrow$ random block
$V_1^{\{j_1,j_2,j_3\}} \leftarrow \text{combined_matvec}(A^{\{j_1,j_2\}}, X_0^{\{j_1,j_2,j_3\}})$
$G_1^{\{j_1,j_2,j_3\}} \leftarrow \left(V_1^{\{j_1,j_2,j_3\}}\right)^T V_1^{\{j_1,j_2,j_3\}}$
$G_1 \leftarrow \sum_{l_1=1}^{s_r} \sum_{l_2=1}^{s_c} \sum_{l_3=1}^{p} G_1^{\{l_1,l_2,l_3\}}$
$r_0 \leftarrow pb, S_0 \leftarrow I_{pb\times pb}, k \leftarrow 0, i \leftarrow 1$
while $k < M$ **do**
  $V_{i+1}^{\{j_1,j_2,j_3\}} \leftarrow \text{combined_matvec}(A^{\{j_1,j_2\}}, V_i^{\{j_1,j_2,j_3\}})$
  $Z_i^{\{j_1,j_2,j_3\}} \leftarrow \left(V_i^{\{j_1,j_2,j_3\}}\right)^T V_{i+1}^{\{j_1,j_2,j_3\}}$
  $Z_i \leftarrow \sum_{l_1=1}^{s_r} \sum_{l_2=1}^{s_c} \sum_{l_3=1}^{p} Z_i^{\{l_1,l_2,l_3\}}$
  $[Z_i^+, S_i, r_i] \leftarrow \text{inverse}(Z_i, S_{i-1}, r_{i-1})$
  if r_i is zero **then**
    break
  end if
  $H_i \leftarrow Z_i^+ G_i$
  $X_i^{\{j_1,j_2,j_3\}} \leftarrow X_{i-1}^{\{j_1,j_2,j_3\}} + V_i^{\{j_1,j_2,j_3\}} H_i$
  $G_{i+1} \leftarrow 0$
  $Y_i^{\{j_1,j_2,j_3\}} \leftarrow \left(V_{i+1}^{\{j_1,j_2,j_3\}}\right)^T V_{i+1}^{\{j_1,j_2,j_3\}} S_i S_i^T$
  $Y_i \leftarrow \sum_{l_1=1}^{s_r} \sum_{l_2=1}^{s_c} \sum_{l_3=1}^{p} Y_i^{\{l_1,l_2,l_3\}}$
  if $i > 2$ and $r_{i-1} < b$ **then**
    $F_{i+1} \leftarrow E_i D_i - Z_{i-2}^+ Y_{i-1}$
    $V_{i+1}^{\{j_1,j_2,j_3\}} \leftarrow V_{i+1}^{\{j_1,j_2,j_3\}} + V_{i-2}^{\{j_1,j_2,j_3\}} F_{i+1}$
    $G_{i+1} \leftarrow G_{i+1} + F_{i+1}^T G_{i-2}$
  end if
  if $i > 1$ **then**
    $E_{i+1} \leftarrow -Z_{i-1}^+ Z_i$
    $V_{i+1}^{\{j_1,j_2,j_3\}} \leftarrow V_{i+1}^{\{j_1,j_2,j_3\}} + V_{i-1}^{\{j_1,j_2,j_3\}} E_{i+1}$
    $G_{i+1} \leftarrow G_{i+1} + E_{i+1}^T G_{i-1}$
  end if
  $D_{i+1} \leftarrow I_{b\times b} - Z_i^+(Y_i + Z_i)$
  $V_{i+1}^{\{j_1,j_2,j_3\}} \leftarrow V_{i+1}^{\{j_1,j_2,j_3\}} S_i S_i^T + V_i^{\{j_1,j_2,j_3\}} D_{i+1}$
  $G_{i+1} \leftarrow S_i S_i^T G_{i+1} + D_i^T G_i$
  $i \leftarrow i + 1, k \leftarrow k + r_i$
end while
$W^{\{j_1,j_2,j_3\}} = \text{matvec}(A, X_{i-1}^{\{j_1,j_2,j_3\}})$
$[\sim, \sim, U_{11}, U_{12}, P_2, r] \leftarrow \text{distributed_LU}(W^{\{j_1,j_2,j_3\}})$
$X^{\{j_1,j_2,j_3\}} \leftarrow X_{i-1}^{\{j_1,j_2,j_3\}} P_2^T \begin{bmatrix} -U_{11}^{-1} U_{12} \\ I_{(b-r)\times(b-r)} \end{bmatrix}$
$[P_1, X^{\{j_1,j_2,j_3\}}, \sim, \sim, n] \leftarrow \text{distributed_LU}(X^{\{j_1,j_2,j_3\}})$
$X^{\{j_1,j_2,j_3\}} \leftarrow P_1^T X^{\{j_1,j_2,j_3\}}$

Matrix Storage. Current implementation stores two matrices, $A^{\{j_1,j_2\}}$ and $\left(A^{\{j_1,j_2\}}\right)^T$, both in CSR (compressed sparse row) format [8]. Two matrices are stored to obtain better performance, as multiplication by the transposed matrix in CSR format is much slower, especially for multithreaded multiplication.

Block Size. An important question is how to chose block size b, as the complexity of dense operations grows with b. But larger block size allows to use wider vector instructions. Hence if b is equal to the minimal size of vector for which optimal performance of the computational device achieved, then the time on dense operations is also close to optimal.

However, for the matrices that arise at GNFS algorithm [4] the complexity of dense operations is usually far from the greatest concern. This matrices are huge — the order is hundreds of millions for the record factorizations [9,10], and are extremely sparse — 200–300 nonzero elements per row on average. Moreover, the sparsity pattern of such matrices is very random. That means that caching is almost totally ineffective especially for the CSR storage as it does not optimize cache usage. Thus, for almost each nonzero element a row of block will be read from RAM, performance of matrix by block product is bound be memory bandwidth and such memory accesses should be optimized.

If program access some element in memory, then whole cache line is loaded from it. If cache line contains several rows of the block than the probability that any of this rows will be reused before eviction from the cache is negligibly low. Thus, a row should be a multiple of the cache line size. Increasing block size more than the cache line size is useless as the only positive result is that the matrix itself loaded less times from memory. But the complexity of dense operations grows and probability of cache hit drops.

So the optimal size for the sparse matrix by block multiplication is equal to the cache line size. For the vast majority of the modern CPUs cache line size is 64 bytes, so optimal $b = 512$. Moreover, many modern HPC CPUs has support of AVX-512 instruction set, including ones of the supercomputer was used to solve the system that have arisen during RSA-232 factorization. Such instructions are for 512-bit vectors, so for the dense operations $b = 512$ is also good.

Dense Operations. Dense operations are implemented not optimally. Firstly, symmetry of bilinear forms is not used so complexity is approximately 2 times higher. Secondly, unsimplified formulas are implemented leading to 4 more $b \times b$ matrix multiplications per iteration. Total complexity of implemented algorithm is

$$M\left(12\frac{N}{s_r s_c} + 25p^2 b\right)b + o\left(\frac{MNb}{s_r s_c}\right)$$

bit operations per node.

From the other hand, method of four Russians [11] is used for matrix multiplication and Coppersmith algorithm [12] is used for bilinear form computation. In theory that allows to reduce complexity by the $\log_2(pb)$ factor. However, these algorithms use lookup tables during computations and performance is optimal when such tables fit L1 cache. Therefore such algorithms may reduce complexity only by a constant factor and this constant is not very large.

An estimate for naive algorithm is used to analyze if INM RAS implementation of faster algorithms work better than naive algorithm at the peak performance of CPU.

2.3 Analysis of INM RAS Implementation Performance

At first let us notice that performance of the method is better than performance of CADO-NFS implementation of block Wiedemann-Coppersmith algorithm. The linear system was larger (and complexity is about 20% higher) than the one obtained during RSA-240 factorization [10] and was solved faster (62 coreyears versus 82 coreyears) on the similar hardware. But is this performance good enough? In order to answer this question let us analyze performance of each of 3 different types of operations that are used in block Lancsos-Montgomery method.

Matrix by Block Product. Both matrix and transposed matrix are stored in CSR (compressed sparse row) format. Matrix by block product for this format is performed row by row: at first product of the first matrix row by vector is computed, then the second and so on. That means that intermediate results for each row can be stored on the registers, so result for each row is stored in RAM just once.

Let us assume that there is not any other caching except for registers. To perform multiplication matrix itself should be loaded from memory, that for CSR format leads to $8\,N+4\rho N$ bytes loaded, where N is the order of the matrix and ρ is average number of nonzero elements. For each nonzero element a row from a block should be loaded from the RAM. With blocks being 512 bits in size that leads to load of $64\rho N$ bytes in total. Result block of N rows is stored back to memory that is additional $64N$ bytes stored. For the transposed matrix an estimate is the same, therefore to perform multiplication of block by the matrix and transposed matrix no more then $144\,N+136\rho N$ bytes of data transferred from and to memory is required.

Total number of iterations is $N/512$ thus total number of memory transfers is $(18+17\rho)N^2/64$ bytes.

For the RSA-232 factorization matrix has $N=3.17*10^8$ rows and $\rho=170$. Memory bandwidth per core for Intel Xeon Gold 6136 processor about $1,066*10^{10}$ bytes per second. Then expected computational cost of such operation is about 13.6 coreyears and in the experiment about 42 coreyears were obtained. That means that sparse matrix by block operation can be greatly improved.

Communications. An estimate on Sect. 2 suggest that combined matvec has $\frac{4b}{s_r s_c p}\left((p-1)N+p(s_r-1)N+p(s_c-1)M\right)$ bits of data transferred per node.

In total there are M/bp iterations. So total data exchanges per node is

$$\frac{4M}{s_r s_c p^2}\left((p-1)N + p(s_r-1)N + p(s_c-1)M\right).$$

For the 20 nodes parameters are $s_r = 5, s_c = 4, p = 1$. Matrix size is $N = 3.17 \cdot 10^8$ and Zhores supercomputer has $2 \cdot 10^{11}$ bidirectional bandwidth bits per second per node. Thus, total cost of communications can be estimated as 10.7 coreyears. It is well correlated with obtained results.

Dense Operations. Total complexity of dense operations is

$$M\left(12\frac{N}{s_r s_c} + 25p^2 b\right) b$$

bit operations per node. Each core of Intel Xeon Gold 6136 processor could perform 2048 bit operations per clock, leading to about $6 \cdot 10^{12}$ bit operations per second. Thus, total cost estimate for that operations with $s_r = 5, s_c = 4, M = N = 3.17 \cdot 10^8, p = 1, b = 512$ is about 3.2 coreyears and there was more than 6 coreyears in the experiment. Therefore current implementation of four Russians method is twice slower than naive algorithm at peak performance of the CPU.

Summary. Total time can be estimated as 27.5 coreyears that is more than twice less than 62 coreyears obtained in practice. The implementation can be greatly improved by speed up of sparse matrix by block and dense block operations, while communications are close to optimal.

3 How to Make the Method Fast?

There are three types of improvements that can be considered: optimization of operations implementation on CPU, implementation of operation on GPU and general method improvement.

3.1 Optimizations on CPU

Sparse Matrix Multiplication. Sparse matrix storage can be improved for both memory usage and performance of matrix by block multiplication. Reduction of memory allows to use split matrix into smaller parts leading to better scalability. The sparse matrix by block multiplication is the most time consuming operation, therefore improvement of its performance leads to significantly smaller time for the whole algorithm.

In this section the matrix is considered to be stored on the single node (it might be the part of the matrix that is stored on this node, of course). At first, the reasons of the bad performance of multiplication in CSR format should be found. They are:

1. TLB (translation lookaside buffer) misses.
   For the matrices arising in the GNFS algorithm nonzero elements are distributed randomly and matrices are very large. That mean that corresponding rows of dense block are stored in different memory pages with high probability. Thus, there are a lot of misses in TLB cache, that stores correspondence of virtual page addresses to physical ones.
2. Prefetching.
   CPUs try to prefetch data if data access has some regular pattern. With nonzero elements distributed quite randomly there are short sequences that could be assumed to have regular pattern, but next required element with high probability does not fit the pattern and prefetching of such element is wasteful.

Secondly, for CSR format both A and A^T should be stored to have good performance. Hence, there is a question if there is a way to store only matrix A and have similar or better performance.

Note, that matrices arising in the GNFS algorithm are very different from matrices arising in other applications, because there are huge and have nonzero elements distributed randomly. Hence, standard approaches for caching are not very suitable. Let use suggest the following storage format for such matrices:

- Split matrix into $K \times K$ parts, where K – amount of rows of the dense block that fit L2 cache.
  With L2 cache size for the modern CPUs being 1–2 MB and $b = 512$ that means $K = 16384$–32768. For the matrix that was obtained during RSA-232 factorization number of such blocks is about matrix size, and number of nonzero element of each block is about average number of nonzero element per row of the matrix.
- To store nonzero element within such block row and column indices of element are used. With K of the considered sizes only 2 bytes are required to store each index leading to 4 bytes in total for each nonzero element. It is the same as for CSR where only one index stored but it could be large and 4 bytes are required to store it.
- All blocks of sparse matrix are stored continuously in a single array, But also there is another array containing offsets of starting position for each block. Number of nonzero elements in block is just the difference of the offset for the next block and for the current block. Each element of such array is of size 8 byte just as row offsets in CSR format. The size of this array is the number of blocks of sparse matrix. And as was noted above it is close to matrix size. So amount of memory required to store this array is comparable to amount required to store similar array in CSR format.

How to perform multiplication in this format? It is easy to see that it is very similar for the matrix and for the transposed matrix:

- If we denote $K \times K$ blocks as A_{ij} then for the multiplication by matrix itself at each step multiply by i-th block row of this matrix by computing products

of blocks A_{i1}, A_{i2} and so on by corresponding part of dense block.
For the transposed matrix multiply by the j-th block row of transposed matrix, blocks A^T_{1j}, A^T_{2j} and so on are multiplied by corresponding part of dense block.
- For the loads from the dense block loads with non-temporary hints are used. That means that such load does not pollute the cache and does not allow prefetching.

The result for each step of such multiplications is a dense block of K rows. It fits L2 cache. So if loads from dense block do not pollute cache it will not be evicted from cache. It means that resulting vector will be stored to RAM just ones. The estimate of memory transfers will be the same as was for CSR.

The suggested format requires twice less memory (as transposed matrix is not stored) for the same estimate of memory transfers for multiplication by both A and A^T. Moreover, it lead to significantly less TLB misses – hugepages are of size 2 or 4 MB, thus multiplication by one $K \times K$ block is guaranties to not have TLB miss.

Dense Operations. Following the ideas of M4RI library [13] for the four Russians method 16 tables of 2^4 rows are constructed with each row being 512 bit. Such tables require 16 KB of memory and fit L1 cache of modern CPUs.

The test shows that for the multiplication of two matrices of order 65536 such implementation is $5 - 6$ times faster than the one used during RSA-232 experiment. On the Intel Core i9-7900X multiplication of such matrices with new implementation takes 3 s instead of 16. Thus, such implementation is $2.5 - 3$ times faster that naive multiplication at peak performance of the CPU. That means that such implementation of four Russians method is reasonable. The same ideas are used for the Coppersmith algorithm.

GPU Implementation of Operations. Modern supercomputers very often have GPU accelerators. For the block Lanczos-Montgomery method to work fast on modern supercomputers operations of the method should be implemented on GPUs. That can be easily done.

In differ from CPU, for GPU multiplication of the sparse matrix in CSR format works fast, with the performance even a bit better than the theoretical estimate (it is possible, as the estimates do not takes caching into account). And as memory bandwidth of GPUs is much higher that memory bandwidth of CPUs, GPUs perform such multiplication much faster. Let us describe in short such algorithm:

- Row of dense blocks are of size 1024 bit, which equal to 128 bytes which is cache line size on GPUs.
- Each computational block performs multiplication of one row of the sparse matrix.
- Each computational block consist of 32 threads. Each thread performs computation of its 4 bytes of the result.

Four Russians (and Coppersmith) method also could be implemented on GPUs, using shared memory to store lookup tables [14]. Performance of such method is about $1.5-2$ times better than theoretically best performance of naive algorithm. And theoretically best performance for naive algorithm on GPU is much higher than on CPUs.

The only problem is that GPUs have less memory. And both matrix and transposed matrix required to be stored, while on CPU a way to avoid this is suggested. Splitting matrix to more parts allow to operate on GPU, but further research for the possibility to reduce amount of required memory is necessary.

3.2 General Improvements

As E. Thomé showed [15] the method may store one dense block less, saving about 16% of memory. Though in practice memory usage is dominated by the matrix, such an improvement is very nice, especially for GPUs.

The method has three types of operations: sparse matrix by dense block multiplications, dense operations and communications. This operations are bounded by different type of resources: memory bandwidth, computational power and interconnect bandwidth.

If such operations are performed simultaneously, they affect performance of each other only slightly. And there is a way to perform at least the part of such operations asynchronously, that is especially useful for GPUs, as they support asynchronous computation by the design. It is easy to see that the most of the communications can be performed simultaneously with computation of sparse matrix by dense block multiplication (matvec). Update of X could also be delayed and performed during matvec on the next iteration and computation of $V_{i-2}F_{i+1}$ (if it is required) can be done during matvec. So even without modification of the algorithm there are a lot of options to do computations asynchronously. But further research using the ideas for the pipelined conjugate gradient method [16] may lead to even more operations to be performed asynchronously.

4 Conclusion

The INM RAS implementation of block Lanczos-Montgomery method was tested on the close to record factorization of RSA-232 number. A performance analysis shows that critical operations work far from optimal. A ways to obtain close to optimal performance of this operations on CPU are suggested. Besides, the performance analysis shows that the method should work much faster on GPUs. Also, asynchronous computations are suggested to improve performance further.

References

1. Rivest, R.L., Shamir, A., Adleman, L.: A method for obtaining digital signatures and public-key cryptosystems. Commun. ACM **21**(2), 120–126 (1978). Association for Computing Machinery, New York, NY, USA. https://doi.org/10.1145/359340.359342
2. Montgomery, P.L.: A block Lanczos algorithm for finding dependencies over GF(2). In: Guillou, L.C., Quisquater, J.-J. (eds.) EUROCRYPT 1995. LNCS, vol. 921, pp. 106–120. Springer, Heidelberg (1995). https://doi.org/10.1007/3-540-49264-X_9
3. Zamarashkin, N., Zheltkov, D.: Block Lanczos–montgomery method with reduced data exchanges. In: Voevodin, V., Sobolev, S. (eds.) RuSCDays 2016. CCIS, vol. 687, pp. 15–26. Springer, Cham (2016). https://doi.org/10.1007/978-3-319-55669-7_2
4. Lenstra, A.K., Lenstra, H.W., Manasse, M.S., Pollard, J.M.: The number field sieve. In: Lenstra, A.K., Lenstra, H.W. (eds.) The development of the number field sieve. LNM, vol. 1554, pp. 11–42. Springer, Heidelberg (1993). https://doi.org/10.1007/BFb0091537
5. CADO-NFS Homepage. https://gitlab.inria.fr/cado-nfs/cado-nfs. Accessed 30 Apr 2023
6. Lanczos, C.: Solution of systems of linear equations by minimized iterations. J. Res. Natl. Bur. Stand. **49**, 33–53 (1952). https://doi.org/10.6028/jres.049.006
7. Hestenes, M.R., Stiefel, E.: Methods of conjugate gradients for solving linear systems. J. Res. Natl. Bur. Stand. **49**(6), 409–436 (1952). https://doi.org/10.6028/jres.049.044
8. Saad, Y.: Iterative methods for sparse linear systems. Soc. Ind. Appl. Math. (2003). https://doi.org/10.1137/1.9780898718003
9. Kleinjung, T., et al.: Factorization of a 768-Bit RSA modulus. In: Rabin, T. (ed.) CRYPTO 2010. LNCS, vol. 6223, pp. 333–350. Springer, Heidelberg (2010). https://doi.org/10.1007/978-3-642-14623-7_18
10. Boudot, F., Gaudry, P., Guillevic, A., Heninger, N., Thomé, E., Zimmermann, P.: Comparing the difficulty of factorization and discrete logarithm: a 240-digit experiment. In: Micciancio, D., Ristenpart, T. (eds.) CRYPTO 2020. LNCS, vol. 12171, pp. 62–91. Springer, Cham (2020). https://doi.org/10.1007/978-3-030-56880-1_3
11. Arlazarov, V.L., Dinitz, Y.A., Kronrod, M.A., Faradzhev, I.A.: On economical construction of the transitive closure of an oriented graph. Dokl. Akad. Nauk SSSR **194**(3), 487–488 (1970)
12. Coppersmith, D.: Solving homogeneous linear equations over via block Wiedemann algorithm. Math. Comp. **62**, 333–350 (1994). https://doi.org/10.1090/S0025-5718-1994-1192970-7
13. Albrecht M., Bard G., Hart W.: Algorithm 898: Efficient multiplication of dense matrices over GF(2). ACM Trans. Math. Softw. **37**(1), Article 9, pp. 1–14 (2010). https://doi.org/10.1145/1644001.1644010
14. Zamarashkin, N.L., Zheltkov, D.A.: GPU acceleration of dense matrix and block operations for Lanczos method for systems over GF(2). Lobachevskii J. Math. **40**, 1881–1991 (2019). https://doi.org/10.1134/S1995080219110337
15. Thomé, E.: A modified block Lanczos algorithm with fewer vectors. arXiv preprint 1604.02277 (2016). https://doi.org/10.48550/arXiv.1604.02277
16. Ghysels, P., Vanroose, W.: Hiding global synchronization latency in the preconditioned Conjugate Gradient algorithm. Parallel Comput. **40**(7), 224–238 (2014). https://doi.org/10.1016/j.parco.2013.06.001

Multi-node GPU-Enabled Pseudo-spectral Solver for Turbulence Problems

Rodion Stepanov[1(✉)], Soumyadeep Chatterjee[2], Manthan Verma[2], and Mahendra Verma[2]

[1] Institute of Continuous Media Mechanics, Perm, Russian Federation
rodion@icmm.ru
[2] Department of Physics, Indian Institute of Technology Kanpur, Kanpur, India
{soumyade,manve,mkv}@iitk.ac.in

Abstract. Fast Fourier Transform (FFT) and pseudo-spectral codes are important applications in science and engineering. In this paper, we present the design and scaling results of our GPU-enabled multinode FFT and pseudo-spectral code, TARANG. Our FFT is in CUDA, but TARANG is in Python with `CuPy`. We find that TARANG runs about 500 times faster on the A100 GPU than on a single-core EPYC 7551 processor. We perform a two-dimensional magnetohydrodynamic turbulence simulation with TARANG and verify the Kolmogorov-like energy spectrum and flux for the flow at different grid resolutions.

Keywords: Computational fluid dynamics · Pseudo-spectral code · Fast Fourier transform · MHD turbulence · TARANG code · GPU

1 Introduction

Magnetohydrodynamic (MHD) turbulence is widely used to model astrophysical phenomena that play a crucial role in the generation of cosmic magnetic fields [5]. The concept of the two-scale dynamo suggests that small-scale interactions are necessary to drive the large-scale magnetic fields of planets, stars and galaxies. The current phenomenology for mean hydrodynamic flows agrees satisfactorily with experiment and allows the solution of several engineering problems. However, the ever-increasing complexity of the technology and the optimisation of the parameters require a more accurate prediction of the mean field characteristics. The intensive development of computer technology in recent decades has brought numerical simulations to the fore as an important research tool. This is particularly important for MHD turbulence, since it is almost impossible to perform a laboratory experiment at high magnetic Reynolds numbers [15].

At present, direct numerical simulation methods are constantly evolving. Most codes are based on numerical algorithms such as finite element, finite volume, finite difference, pseudo-spectral, etc. Among them, the pseudo-spectral method is the most accurate in approximating the spatial derivatives. In this paper, we describe a GPU-enabled pseudo-spectral code TARANG with multiple nodes. Note that the pseudo-spectral code uses the Fast Fourier Transform (FFT) to compute the nonlinear term. See Boyd [6] for details.

V. Voevodin et al. (Eds.): RuSCDays 2023, LNCS 14388, pp. 129–139, 2023.
https://doi.org/10.1007/978-3-031-49432-1_10

Turbulence simulations on large grids require parallel implementation to complete runs in a finite time. Since the FFT takes 70% to 80% of the total time in a spectral code, it is important to parallelize the FFT. For multicore systems there are a number of parallel FFT libraries, namely P3DFFT [13], FFTK [7] etc. However, there are only a handful of parallel GPU-enabled FFTs. Recently, Kiran et al. [14] reported a parallel GPU FFT. In addition, Nvidia announced a multinode cuFFTMp [12] available as part of the Nvidia HPC SDK 22.3 library. Recently, we wrote an open source multinode CUDA-based GPU FFT [18] and scaled it to 512 GPUs on a Selene cluster. We emphasise that our open-source FFT library can be ported to non-CUDA platforms (e.g. AMD GPUs, e.g. MI210), as well as independently optimised by the user community, and is therefore complementary to cuFFTMp.

Using this GPU FFT, we have transformed our C++-based spectral solver [17] into a CuPy-based GPU-enabled multi-node parallel pseudo-spectral solver, TARANG. We simulated two-dimensional (2D) MHD turbulence using this code. In this paper, we brief our results on parallel FFT and MHD turbulence. We remark that our spectral code can simulate hydrodynamic, convection, and MHD turbulence on both multicore and GPUs. However, we only present the GPU results here.

In the next section, we present some details of our GPU-enabled FFT library.

2 Multi-node Multi-GPU Fast Fourier Transform

We have designed a multi-node multi GPU FFT library CUDA [18]; we will refer to this library as GPU-FFT. Our library uses slab decomposition for numerical data, which is more efficient than pencil decomposition for a moderate number of GPUs (a few thousand). Although modern multi-core HPC systems usually prefer pencil decomposition due to the large number of available cores, we prefer slab decomposition due to our limited resources, as we currently only have access to up to 512 A100 GPUs to test the scalability of our GPU-FFT library.

Our GPU-FFT library performs FFT of real-space data in several steps. Initially, the data is divided into p slabs along the x axis and distributed across p GPUs using `cudaMemcpy`. Each GPU then performs a forward 2D real-to-complex (R2C) FFT to all yz planes of the slab using batched `cufft`. The data is then aligned along the x direction in the GPUs through `Alltoall` communication, which is achieved using a combination of asynchronous `MPI_Isend` and `MPI_Irecv` operations, as well as `MPI_Waitall` and `cudaMemcpy`. Finally, a 1D strided and batched complex-to-complex (C2C) FFT is executed along the x axis using `cufft`. Note that these steps are employed in reverse order for the inverse FFT. To optimize memory usage, the same workspace pointer is utilized for the real-to-complex, complex-to-complex, and complex-to-real Fourier transforms. In addition, GPUDirect RDMA and CUDA-aware MPI [10] are used to minimize unnecessary data transfers between the device and the host, resulting in faster communication. Refer to Verma et al. [18] for more details on the implementation.

We perform a scaling study of our single and double precision GPU-FFT on NVIDIA's *Selene* supercomputer, which holds the ninth spot on the November 2022 Top500 list [1]. The system has a massive 1120 TB of system memory and consists of 540 DGX boxes, each equipped with two Rome processors and 8 A100 GPU cards, each with 80 GB of VRAM. The GPUs in each DGX box communicate with each other via high-speed NVlink with a bandwidth of 600 GB/sec. Communication between different nodes is enabled by a Fast Mellanox HDR Infiniband switch with an average bisection bandwidth of 200 Gb/sec/node. We compute the timings for performing forward and backward FFT of the following real space field:

$$f(x, y, z) = 8\sin(x)\sin(2y)\sin(3z) + 8\sin(4x)\sin(5y)\sin(6z), \tag{1}$$

on 1024^3, 2048^3, and 4096^3 grids using 8 to 64, 8 to 128, and 64 to 512 GPUs respectively. Using `MPI_Wtime`, we recorded the timings of multiple operations in the FFT, averaging the results over 10 to 100 FFT pairs to minimize timing errors.

Figure 1(a, b) exhibits the computation and communication times as a function of number of GPUs, p, for a different number of grid points, N^3, and for double-precision (DP) and single-precision (SP) FFTs. We employ 1024^3, 2048^3 and 4096^3 grids. For the three grids, we observe that

$$T_{\text{comp}} = C_1 p^{-\gamma_1}, \tag{2}$$

$$T_{\text{comm}} = C_2 p^{-\gamma_2}, \tag{3}$$

$$T = C p^{-\gamma}, \tag{4}$$

where T_{comp}, T_{comm}, T are the computation, communcation, and total times respectively; γ_1, γ_2, γ are the corresponding exponents, and C_1, C_2, C are constants. We compute the above coefficients and exponents using linear regression, and their values are listed in Table 1.

Table 1. FFT scaling on Selene: The exponents γ_1 for the computation time (T_{comp}) scaling, γ_2 for the communication time (T_{comm}) scaling, and γ for the total time (T) scaling. Here, we present single precision (SP) and double precision (DP) results.

Grid size	γ_1		γ_2		γ	
	SP	DP	SP	DP	SP	DP
1024^3	0.98 ± 0.01	0.97 ± 0.01	0.12 ± 0.11	0.11 ± 0.15	0.35 ± 0.05	0.34 ± 0.07
2048^3	1.00 ± 0.01	1.00 ± 0.002	0.27 ± 0.12	0.30 ± 0.10	0.49 ± 0.06	0.48 ± 0.05
4096^3	1.00 ± 0.02	1.00 ± 0.02	0.69 ± 0.16	0.64 ± 0.13	0.75 ± 0.13	0.71 ± 0.11

We observe that the exponent γ_1 is almost unity, implying linear scaling for the computation time. However, the communication scaling lags behind the

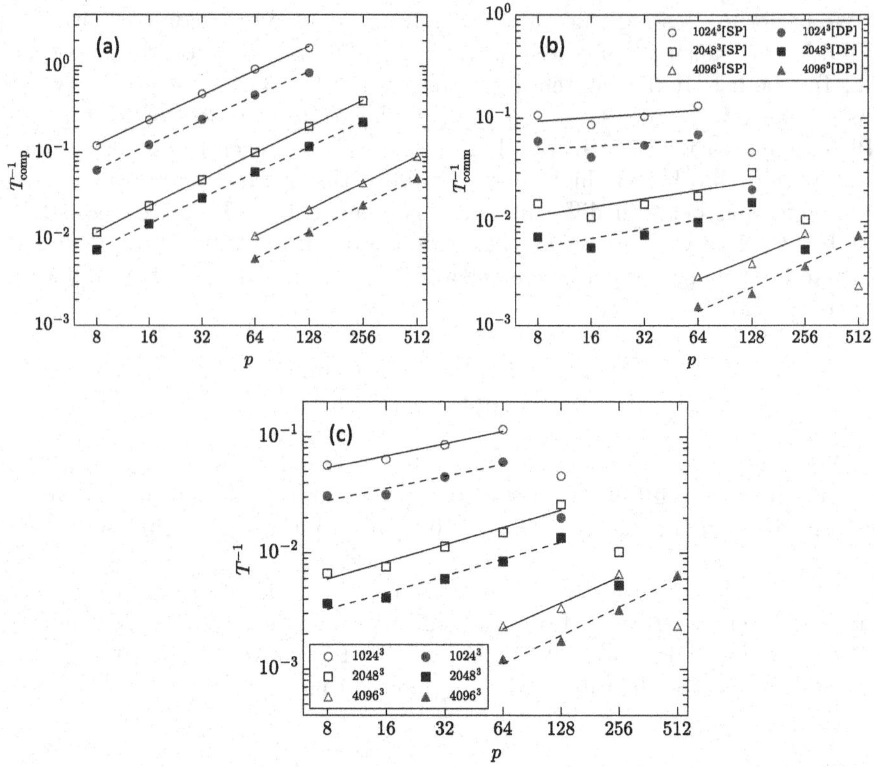

Fig. 1. (a, b) Plots of the inverse computation time, T^{-1}_{comp}, and the inverse communication time, T^{-1}_{comm}, as a function of the number of GPUs, denoted by p, for 1024^3, 2048^3, and 4096^3 grids on *Selene*. (c) Plots showing the strong scaling (T^{-1} vs. p) for single precision (empty symbols) and double precision (filled symbols) FFTs for the same grid sizes. Note that T_{comp}, T_{comm} and T are the reported times in milliseconds for a forward-inverse FFT pair.

computation scaling due to the large data transfers in the FFT. Excellent communication scaling is achieved for 4096^3 grid size, while poor scaling is observed for the 1024^3 grid size. This occurs because of efficient communication scaling provided by NVLink and NVSwitch within a DGX box. As shown in Fig. 1(b), the communication performance drops suddenly for the last plot points, except for 4096^3(DP). We observe that the chunk or packet size is 1 MB for the 5 plot points where the communication performance degrades considerably. The small packet size seems to be the reason for the drop in the inter-GPU communication performance [9]. For large packets, GPUDirect RDMA and 3rd Gen NVLink are expected to provide efficient communication. Thus, due to the high communication cost (also in Table 1), the strong scaling exponent, γ, falls between 0.34 to 0.75. Another important observation is that the communication time is typically larger than computation time. However, $T_{\text{comp}} \approx T_{\text{comm}}$ for a single DGX box. Hence, a GPU-FFT in a single DGX box is the most efficient.

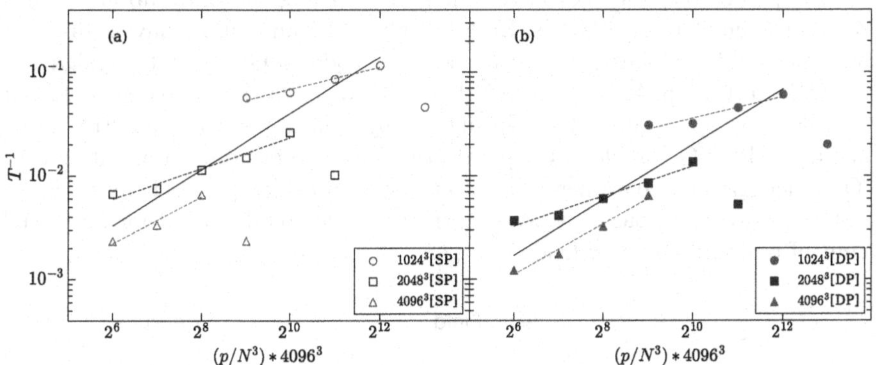

Fig. 2. Plots portraying the weak scaling (T^{-1} vs. $(p/N^3)4096^3$) for (a) single-precision and (b) double-precision FFTs on *Selene* for 1024^3, 2048^3, and 4096^3 grids.

The weak scaling of our GPU-FFT is shown in Fig. 2(a, b), where T^{-1} is plotted against $(p/N^3) \times 4096^3$ for SP and DP FFTs. The data points do not collapse into a single curve, but the behavior is similar to strong scaling in some segments (see Fig. 1(c)). An approximate fit to all points results in a weak scaling exponent of about 0.9, but this exponent is not an accurate representation of the FFT performance. Verma et al. [18] performed a performance comparison of our library with other existing GPU FFT libraries [2–4, 8, 11, 14, 19] and showed that our FFT implementation achieves comparable performance to the other libraries. See Verma et al. [18] for details.

We also compare our GPU-FFT with FFTK (C++-based FFT). We observe that we achieve a similar performance on 128 A100 GPUs of Selene as those achieved on Shaheen II (Cray XC40) with 196608 Intel Haswell cores (or 12288 processors). The improved performance on Selene is attributed to the fast computation of A100 GPUs, and the efficient inter-GPU communication facilitated by NVlink and NVSwitch.

In the next section, we present our GPU-enabled pseudo-spectral solver TARANG.

3 Structure of TARANG, a Pseudo-spectral Solver

In the pseudo-spectral scheme, the fluid equations are solved in spectral space given initial condition [6]. However, the products of the nonlinear computation are computed in real space in the FFT in order to avoid convolution. Thus, the time complexity of a pseudo-spectral solver is $\mathcal{O}(M \log M)$, where M is the total number of grid points. After computing of the nonlinear term and the pressure term (using the nonlinear and force terms), we time-advance the equations using the fourth-order Runge-Kutta (RK4) method to reach the final state. The dissipative terms (viscous and Joule) are computed using the exponential trick [7,17].

We implement the above scheme in Python using the `CuPy` library, which allows our code to run on GPUs. Interestingly, `CuPy` and `NumPy` have significant similarities, which makes the transition of our code to GPUs quite straightforward. We use the `mpi4py` library for the MPI implementation. We also use our CUDA FFT wrapped in Python (using the `pybind` library) for our FFT functions. In TARANG, we cleanly separate the parameters from the input/output (I/O) functions. The parameters, e.g., grid size, time-stepping schemes, viscosity, etc., are stored in `para.py`. We use the versatile HDF5 format for input and output of real and complex fields.

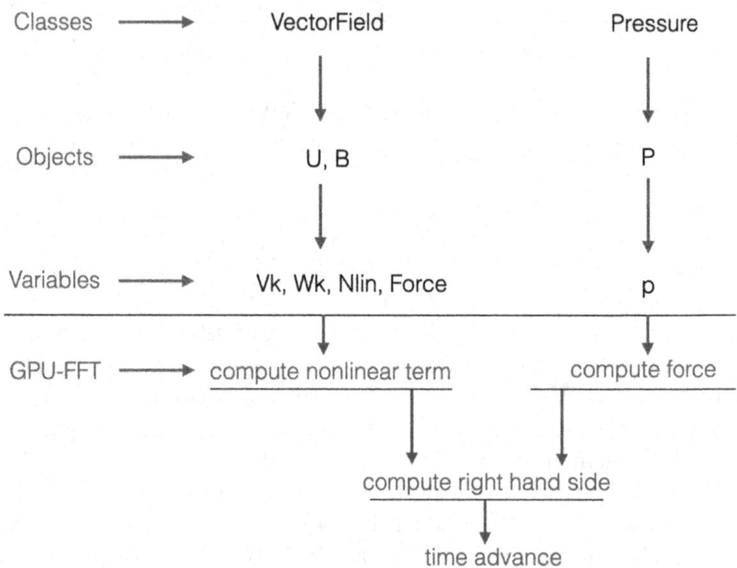

Fig. 3. Schematic structure of the TARANG spectral solver.

We use object-oriented features that allow our solver to solve different types of problems, such as hydrodynamics, thermal convection, and MHD. This flexibility is a key feature of TARANG. A schematic diagram of TARANG's structure is shown in Fig. 3. In MHD, the velocity and magnetic fields are the `VectorField` class, while the pressure is the `Pressure` class. The Vector class contains several arrays that store the real and Fourier space fields, as well as the nonlinear term and the forcing (see Fig. 3).

4 Solving 2D MHD Turbulence Using TARANG

We simulate forced 2D MHD turbulence with TARANG. We force the Elsässer variables $\mathbf{z}_+$ and $\mathbf{z}_-$ with injection rates $\epsilon_+ = 0.3$ and $\epsilon_- = 0.1$ respectively. We force the fields at wavenumber k_f. In this scheme, the magnetic field is forced, so we avoid the **anti-dynamo theorem** and reach steady states. In addition, we use hyperviscosity ($\nu_{\text{hyper}}\nabla^4\mathbf{u}, \eta_{\text{hyper}}\nabla^4\mathbf{b}$) and hypoviscosity ($\nu_{\text{hypo}}\nabla^{-12}\mathbf{u}, \eta_{\text{hypo}}\nabla^{-12}\mathbf{b}$), which are effective at large and small wavenumbers, respectively. We ran our simulations on 1024^2 and 4096^2 grids with the reduced hyperviscosity to demonstrate the dependence on resolution.

Using the numerical data under steady state, we compute the spectrum and fluxes of the Elsässer variables $\mathbf{z}_{\pm}$ and the vector potential A. The spectra are denoted by $E_{+}(k), E_{-}(k), E_A(k)$ respectively, and the corresponding fluxes are $\Pi_{+}(k), \Pi_{-}(k), \Pi_A(k)$. We illustrate these fluxes and spectra for simulations on 1024^2 in Fig. 4. As shown in Fig. 4(a), $\Pi_A(k)$ is negative and constant for $k < k_f$; in this band, $E_A(k) \sim k^{-5/3}$, which is consistent with the dimensional analysis (compare with the arguments for passive scalar [16]).

As shown in Fig. 4(b), the energy fluxes $\Pi_{+}(k)$ and $\Pi_{-}(k)$ are unequal but constants in the inertial range. In this band of wavenumbers we observe that $E_{+}(k) \sim k^{-5/3}$ and $E_{-}(k) \sim k^{-5/3}$. These results clearly demonstrate the Kolmogorov-like phenomenology for 2D MHD turbulence. Interestingly, the energy cascades for $\mathbf{z}_{\pm}$ variables are forward for 2D and 3D MHD turbulence, which allows us to test the turbulence phenomenology of MHD turbulence. Furthermore, we obtain the inverse cascade $\mathbf{z}_{\pm}$, which is the result of the inverse cascade A^2 (expected for 2D MHD) and its dissipation on large scales.

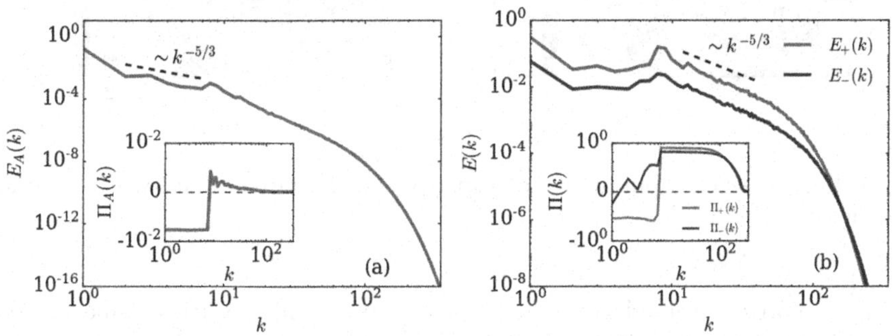

Fig. 4. (a) The spectrum ($E_A(k)$) and flux ($\Pi_A(k)$) of the magnetic vector potential A, obtained for the ratio of injection rate ($\epsilon_{+}/\epsilon_{-} = 3$), grid size of 1024^2, and $k_f = 8$. (b) The spectrum ($E_{\pm}(k)$) and fluxes ($\Pi_{\pm}(k)$) of Elsässer variables, $\mathbf{z}_{\pm}$. Note that $\nu_{\text{hypo}} = \eta_{\text{hypo}} = 8 \times 10^{-6}$, and $\nu_{\text{hyper}} = \eta_{\text{hyper}} = 8 \times 10^{-8}$.

We have performed simulations on 4096^2 grid to check the spectral slopes in extended inertial ranges of scales. For this purpose, we set our forcing to a smaller scale and reduced the hypo- and hyperviscosity (see Fig. 5). You can see that the spectrum with the forward energy cascade has been extended to smaller scales but in the infrared part, the spectrum of A^2 has become steeper. Typical velocity and magnetic field patterns are shown in Fig. 6. One can see that the field structures are partially correlated implying a high degree of cross-helicity.

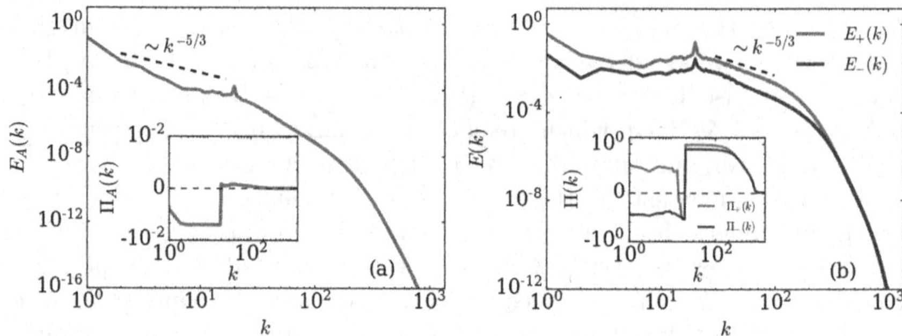

Fig. 5. (a) The spectrum ($E_A(k)$) and flux ($\Pi_A(k)$) of the magnetic vector potential A, obtained for the ratio of injection rate ($\epsilon_+/\epsilon_- = 3$), grid size of 4096^2, and $k_f = 20$. (b) The spectrum ($E_\pm(k)$) and fluxes ($\Pi_\pm(k)$) of Elsässer variables, $\mathbf{z}_\pm$. Note that $\nu_{\text{hypo}} = \eta_{\text{hypo}} = 1 \times 10^{-6}$, and $\nu_{\text{hyper}} = \eta_{\text{hyper}} = 1 \times 10^{-8}$.

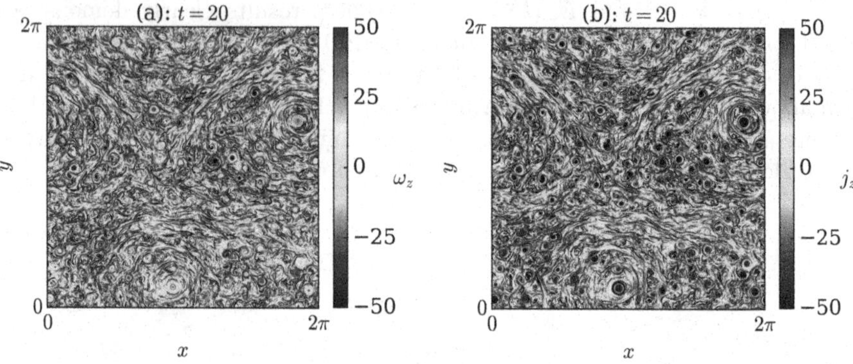

Fig. 6. Real space distributions of (a) vorticity and (b) current density at $t = 20$ for case shown in Fig. 5.

We also present the relative speed of our code on leading GPUs, namely A100, V100, K40, and RTX 3090Ti. We compute the timings per step per grid point for 2D MHD simulations on grid sizes of 1024^2, 2048^2, 4096^2, and 8192^2, and present them in Table 2. Our data are average values over 2000 time steps. Note that A100 is about 3 times faster than V100 on the 8192^2 grid. In addition, the RTX 3090Ti delivers comparable performance to the V100; this is useful information because the RTX 3090Ti is much cheaper than the V100 GPU card. In addition to the above tests, we also compared the timings of the A100 card with a single-core performance on an AMD Naples processor (AMD EPYC 7551). We observe that our Python-based TARANG code is about 500 times faster on the A100 compared to a single-core performance on the AMD Naples processor (AMD EPYC 7551). This provides an estimate of the minimum number of CPUs required to achieve equivalent performance on a single GPU

Table 2. Scaling of TARANG: We show the timings (in secs) per step per grid point on different GPUs for different grid sizes.

Grid size	on A100	on V100	on K40s	on RTX 3090Ti
1024^2	3.4×10^{-8}	4.9×10^{-8}	1.3×10^{-7}	5.3×10^{-8}
2048^2	1.8×10^{-8}	2.6×10^{-8}	1.0×10^{-7}	3.3×10^{-8}
4096^2	1.47×10^{-8}	2.6×10^{-8}	1.1×10^{-7}	3.2×10^{-8}
8192^2	1.43×10^{-8}	3.9×10^{-8}	-	4.3×10^{-8}

5 Conclusions

In this paper, we present the implementation and speed-up of our multi-node GPU-enabled FFT and the pseudo-spectral code, TARANG. A summary of our results is given below:

1. Compared to a multi-core cluster, we observe a significant performance boost on GPUs for a spectral code. For example, TARANG on A100 GPU is 500 times faster than a single core of AMD Naples processor (AMD EPYC 7551). Our GPU-based FFT on 128 A100 GPUs of Selene is as fast as 196608 Intel Haswell cores of Shaheen II (Cray XC40).
2. FFT is a communication intensive library. On a multi-core cluster, we observe that communication takes about 98% of the total time [18]. In comparison, communication is comparable to computation on a single DGX box. For multiple DGX boxes, communication dominates computation, but the ratio is much smaller than for multicore systems. The above gain is due to thousands of cores in GPUs, fast VRAM and efficient communication via NVlink.

In summary, using a multi-node GPU FFT approach is an effective strategy for performing spectral simulations on large grids. Our Python-based pseudo-spectral code, TARANG, is useful for solving a variety of problems. We plan to further optimise our code in the future.

Acknowledgements. We thank Kiran Ravikumar, P. K. Yeung, Manish Modani, Preeti Malakar, Anando Chatterjee, Anish Saxena, Bharatkumar Sharma, Gaurav Garg, Nishant Arya, and Shashi Kumar for useful discussions. We thank Nvidia for an access to *Selene*, where scaling studies were performed. Soumyadeep Chatterjee is supported by INSPIRE fellowship (IF180094) of Department of Science & Technology, India. This work is supported by Project No. 6104-1 from Indo-French Centre for the Promotion of Advanced Research (IFCPAR/CEFIPRA). We thank the Supercomputing Centers of Lomonosov Moscow State University and N.N. Krasovskii Institute of Mathematics and Mechanics UB RAS for support of GPU performance tests.

References

1. Highlights, November 2022. https://www.top500.org/lists/top500/2022/11/
2. Ayala, A., Tomov, S., Haidar, A., Dongarra, J.: *heFFTe*: highly efficient FFT for exascale. In: Krzhizhanovskaya, V.V., Závodszky, G., Lees, M.H., Dongarra, J.J., Sloot, P.M.A., Brissos, S., Teixeira, J. (eds.) ICCS 2020. LNCS, vol. 12137, pp. 262–275. Springer, Cham (2020). https://doi.org/10.1007/978-3-030-50371-0_19
3. Ayala, A., et al.: Impacts of multi-gpu mpi collective communications on large fft computation. In: 2019 IEEE/ACM Workshop on Exascale MPI (ExaMPI), pp. 12–18 (2019). https://doi.org/10.1109/ExaMPI49596.2019.00007
4. Bak, S., et al.: OpenMP application experiences: porting to accelerated nodes. Parallel Comput. **109**, 102856 (2022)
5. Biskamp, D.: Magnetohydrodynamic Turbulence. Cambridge University Press, Cambridge (2003)
6. Boyd, J.P.: Chebyshev and Fourier Spectral Methods. Dover Publications, New York, 2nd revised edn. (2003)
7. Chatterjee, A.G., Verma, M.K., Kumar, A., Samtaney, R., Hadri, B., Khurram, R.: Scaling of a Fast Fourier Transform and a pseudo-spectral fluid solver up to 196608 cores. J. Parallel Distrib. Comput. **113**, 77–91 (2018)
8. Czechowski, K., Battaglino, C., McClanahan, C., Iyer, K., Yeung, P.K., Vuduc, R.: On the communication complexity of 3D FFTs and its implications for Exascale. In: Proceedings of the 26th ACM international conference on Supercomputing, pp. 205–214. ACM, New York, June 2012
9. Doerfler, D., Brightwell, R.: Measuring mpi send and receive overhead and application availability in high performance network interfaces, vol. 4192, pp. 331–338, Sept 2006. https://doi.org/10.1007/11846802_46
10. Faraji, I.: Improving Communication Performance in GPU-Accelerated HPC Clusters. Ph.D. thesis, Queen's University, Queen's University, Kingston, Ontario, Canada (2018)
11. Gholami, A., Hill, J., Malhotra, D., Biros, G.: AccFFT: a library for distributed-memory FFT on CPU and GPU architectures. arXiv e-prints arXiv:1506.07933, June 2015. https://doi.org/10.48550/arXiv.1506.07933
12. Nvidia: Multinode multi-gpu: Using nvidia cufftmp ffts at scale. https://developer.nvidia.com/blog/multinode-multi-gpu-using-nvidia-cufftmp-ffts-at-scale/
13. Pekurovsky, D.: P3dfft: A framework for parallel computations of fourier transforms in three dimensions. SIAM J. Sci. Comput. **34**, January 2012. https://doi.org/10.1137/11082748X
14. Ravikumar, K., Appelhans, D., Yeung, P.K.: GPU acceleration of extreme scale pseudo-spectral simulations of turbulence using asynchronism. In: SC '19: Proceedings of the International Conference for High Performance Computing, Networking, Storage and Analysis. SC '19. Association for Computing Machinery, New York, NY, USA (Nov 17–22 2019). https://doi.org/10.1145/3295500.3356209. https://doi.org/10.1145/3295500.3356209
15. Verma, M.K.: Statistical theory of magnetohydrodynamic turbulence: recent results. Phys. Rep. **401**(5), 229–380 (2004)
16. Verma, M.K.: Energy Transfers in Fluid Flows: Multiscale and Spectral Perspectives. Cambridge University Press, Cambridge (2019)
17. Verma, M.K., Chatterjee, A.G., Yadav, R.K., Paul, S., Chandra, M., Samtaney, R.: Benchmarking and scaling studies of pseudospectral code Tarang for turbulence simulations. Pramana-J. Phys. **81**(4), 617–629 (2013)

18. Verma, M., et al.: Scalable multi-node fast fourier transform on gpus (2022). arXiv:physics.comp-ph/2202.12756
19. Wang, C., Chandrasekaran, S., Chapman, B.M.: cusfft: a high-performance sparse fast fourier transform algorithm on gpus. In: 2016 IEEE International Parallel and Distributed Processing Symposium (IPDPS), pp. 963–972 (2016)

Multicriteria Optimization of Chemical Reactions Using Interval Analysis. Parallel Scheme for Implementing the Computational Process

Kamila Koledina[1,2(✉)], Irek M. Gubaydullin[1,2], and Sergey Koledin[2]

[1] Institute of Petrochemistry and Catalysis of Russian Academy of Sciences, Ufa, Russia
koledinakamila@mail.ru
[2] Ufa State Petroleum Technological University, Ufa, Russia

Abstract. An algorithm for determining the permissible interval values of variable parameters in solving the problem of multi-criteria optimization of conditions for a multi-stage chemical process is considered. The mathematical model of kinetics is given in the form of an interval problem, according to the intervals of kinetic parameters, and its solution is carried out by a two-line method. This approach makes it possible to take into account possible fluctuations in the reaction conditions and their influence on the values of the optimality criteria. This is especially important for industrial processes and must be taken into account when modeling laboratory reactions with subsequent introduction into production. The object of research in this work is the catalytic reaction of hydroalumination of olefins in the presence of triisobutyl aluminum, the product of which are higher aluminogranic compounds. The developed kinetic model of the process takes into account possible parameter intervals, due to fluctuations in the reaction temperature. And the solution of the multi-criteria optimization problem makes it possible to take into account the optimal conversion interval of the initial olefin. To assess the adequacy of the solution, a comparison is made with experimental data and according to the criteria for evaluating the quality of Pareto approximation. The algorithm of parallelization of calculations for the task of multi-criteria optimization using interval analysis is proposed.

Keywords: Chemical kinetics · Mathematical model · Multi-criteria interval optimization · Two-way method · Olefin hydroalumination reaction · Parallel scheme

1 Introduction

The object of the study is complex chemical reactions, namely the modeling of the kinetics of processes. The uncertainty of such models is associated with the lack of information content of the chemical experiment: not all substances

V. Voevodin et al. (Eds.): RuSCDays 2023, LNCS 14388, pp. 140–151, 2023.
https://doi.org/10.1007/978-3-031-49432-1_11

are observable, the error of measuring instruments, etc. This uncertainty of the mathematical model further affects the result of solving the problem of multicriteria optimization of process conditions [1], due to the uncertainty in the values of kinetic parameters. In work [2] the problem of multicriteria optimization of temperature conditions of induction heating of metal plates under conditions of interval uncertainty is given. Researchers [3] consider an interval optimization problem for a linear programming problem. Authors [4] indicate the relevance of problems with interval parameters for chemical kinetics and provide an overview of existing libraries and methods implemented in them for modeling dynamic systems with interval parameters. In connection with the above, it is relevant to formulate and solve the problem of multicriteria optimization of a chemical reaction based on the interval kinetic model [5]. This paper presents the formulation and algorithm for solving the problem of multi-criteria optimization with interval kinetic parameters and solving the problem for a multi-stage catalytic process of hydroaluminating olefins with triisobutyl aluminum.

2 Formulation of the Problem of Multicriteria Optimization of Chemical Reactions Based on the Interval Kinetic Model

The kinetic model is based on a mathematical description of a chemical reaction according to the law of acting masses and is generally determined by the values of component concentrations and kinetic parameters. The model is a system of ordinary nonlinear differential equations:

$$\frac{dy_i}{d\tau} = \phi_i(y_i, k_j), i = 1, ...I, j = 1, ...J, \tag{1}$$

$$k_j = A_j^0 exp(-\frac{E_j}{RT}); \tag{2}$$

$\tau = 0, y_i(0) = y_i^0;\ \tau \in [0, \tau^*]$,
where y_i - concentrations of substances, mol/l; τ^* - time or conditional reaction time, min; ϕ_i - functional dependence on concentrations and parameters; I - number of substances; J - number of selected stages; k_j - stage rate constants; A_j - pre-exponential factors of stages of the Arrhenius equation (2); E_j - activation energy of stages, kcal/mol; R - universal gas constant, 0.002 kcal/(mol*K); T - temperature, K.

The effect of temperature changes on the model is determined by Eq. (2). If the allowable temperature range is set $T \in (\underline{T}, \overline{T})$, then the rate constants in the model will be $k_j \in (\underline{k_j}, \overline{k_j})$.

The solution of the interval system of ordinary nonlinear differential equations will be carried out using the two-way method [6,7]. The method decomposes the system into two systems, each of which calculates, respectively, the lower and upper limits of the values of the concentrations of substances [8,9].

$$\begin{cases} \frac{d\underline{y}_i}{d\tau} = \phi_i(\underline{y}_1, \underline{y}_2, ..., \underline{y}_i, \underline{\mathbf{k}}_l, \overline{\mathbf{k}}_m), \\ \frac{d\overline{y}_i}{d\tau} = \phi_i(\overline{y}_1, \overline{y}_2, ..., \overline{y}_i, \overline{\mathbf{k}}_l, \underline{\mathbf{k}}_m), \end{cases} \tag{3}$$

$\underline{y}_i(0) = \overline{y}_i(0) = y_i^0.$

The solution of the two-sided system (3) for each reaction component is the concentration change interval $y_i = [\underline{y_i}; \overline{y_i}]$. The formulation of the multi-criteria optimization problem with interval parameters is proposed. As variable parameters in the general case can be considered $X = (x_1, x_2, x_3, \ldots)$, where x_1 - reaction temperature; x_2 - initial concentrations of reagents; x_3 - reaction time, etc. With corresponding direct restrictions $X \in [X^{min}, X^{max}] : x_1 \in [x_1^-, x_1^+]; x_2 \in [x_2^-, x_2^+]; x_3 \in [x_3^-, x_3^+], \ldots]$.

Then for the vector of optimality criteria $F(X) = (f_1(X), f_2(X), f_3(X), \ldots)$ it is necessary to determine the values depending on the interval parameters. Since an interval can be uniquely defined by its midpoint and width, then for $F(X)$, $l = 1, 2$:

$$midf_l = \frac{\underline{f}_l + \overline{f}_l}{2}, \tag{4}$$

$$widf_l = \overline{f}_l - \underline{f}_l, \tag{5}$$

Here $midf_l$ - interval middle, $widf_l$ - interval width.

Then the multi-criteria optimization problem with interval parameters is defined as [10]

$$\max_{X \in D_X} F(X) = F(X^*) = F^*. \tag{6}$$

where D_X - range of acceptable values of variable parameters.

Thus, interval multi-criteria optimization of the conditions based on the kinetic model is relevant for both laboratory and industrial processes. The developed algorithm for the formulation and solution of the interval MCO problem is used to analyze the optimal conditions for the laboratory process of obtaining higher organoaluminium compounds.

3 Interval Kinetic Model of Olefin Hydroalumination Reaction in the Presence of Triisobutylaluminum

To obtain higher organoaluminum compounds, today, the process of hydroalumination of olefins with organoaluminum compounds at elevated temperature is mainly used. Catalytic olefins hydroalumination allows the researchers to obtain important organoaluminum compounds with set structure and has great industrial significance [11,12]. Based on the available manufacturing data it is necessary to elaborate DKM to calculate process optimal conditions. It is essential to solve the multiobjective optimization task as the Pareto approximation.

In reactions with metal complex catalysts, intermediate compounds are formed, often with a complicated structure. The works [13,14] present a detailed kinetic model (DKM) of the catalytic reaction of olefin hydroalumination in the presence of organoaluminum compounds.

According to the developed DKM, the schemes of chemical transformations for the general reaction of HA olefins with organoaluminum compounds triisobutyl aluminum (TIBA) are presented in the scheme Fig. 1 [15].

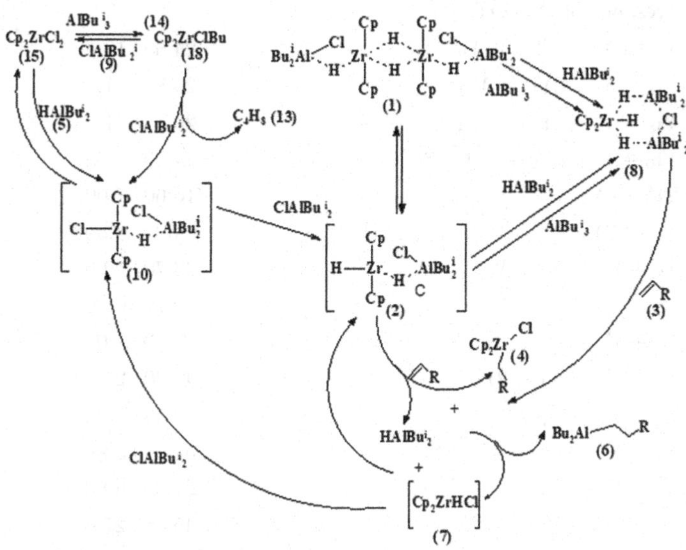

Fig. 1. Scheme of chemical transformations in the general reaction of catalytic hydroalumination of olefins with TIBA

Based on the diagram of Fig. 1, the sequence of chemical transformations of the reaction and the values of kinetic parameters [14] are shown in Table 1.

Here $Y_1 = [Cp_2ZrH_2ClAlBu_2]_2$, $Y_2 = [Cp_2ZrH_2ClAlBu_2]$, $Y_3 = CH_2 CHR$, $Y_4 = Cp_2ZrCl(CH_2CH_2R)$, $Y_5 = HAlBu_2$, $Y_6 = Bu_2Al(CH_2CH_2R)$, $Y_7 = Cp_2ZrHCl$, $Y_8 = [Cp_2ZrH_2HAlBu_2ClAlBu_2]$, $Y_9 = ClAlBu_2$, $Y_{10} = [Cp_2ZrHClClAlBu_2]$, $Y_{11} = Cl_2AlBu$, $Y_{13} = C_4H_8$, $Y_{14} = AlBu_3$, $Y_{15} = Cp_2ZrCl_2$, $Y_{18} = Cp_2ZrClBu$, $R = C_5H_{11}$, C_6H_{13}, C_7H_{15}, C_8H_{17}, $Bu = C_4H_9$, $Cp = C_5H_5$.

An interval kinetic model for the hydroalumination reaction can be set at the lower and upper temperature limits. Then according to (2) there will be different values of the velocity constants of the stages and the mathematical model will have the form of two systems of ordinary nonlinear equations for calculating the lower and upper limits of the concentrations of components according to (3). The solution of the direct interval kinetic problem was carried out using a two-way method in combination with the multistep Gear method of variable order [16,17].

Table 1. Scheme of chemical transformations of hydroalumination olefins in the presence of triisobutylaluminum and the values of kinetic parameters of the stages (A_j - pre-exponential factor in the Arrhenius equation (2), E_j - activation energies of stages)

N	Interaction of CH_2CHR with $AlBu_3^i$ in the presence of Cp_2ZrCl_2	lnA_j	E_j, kcal/mol
1	$Y_{15} + Y_{14} \rightarrow Y_{18} + Y_9$	24.60	10.6
2	$Y_{18} + Y_9 \rightarrow Y_{15} + Y_{14}$	26.60	11.5
3	$Y_{18} + Y_9 \rightarrow Y_{10} + Y_{13}$	20.1	11.6
4	$Y_{10} + Y_9 \rightarrow Y_2 + Y_{13} + Y_{11}$	24.20	10.6
5	$2Y_2 \rightarrow Y_1$	16.60	7.00
6	$Y_1 \rightarrow 2Y_2$	9.30	4.50
7	$Y_2 + Y_3 \rightarrow Y_4 + Y_5$	33.70	10.0
8	$Y_1 + Y_5 \rightarrow Y_8 + Y_2$	12.70	6.00
9	$Y_2 + Y_5 \rightarrow Y_8$	18.50	7.00
10	$Y_8 + Y_3 \rightarrow Y_4 + 2Y_5$	42.30	26.0
11	$Y_4 + Y_5 \rightarrow Y_7 + Y_6$	19.50	7.20
12	$Y_1 + Y_{14} \rightarrow Y_8 + Y_2 + Y_{13}$	5.50	3.9
13	$Y_7 + Y_5 \rightarrow Y_2$	24.20	6.60
14	$Y_7 + Y_9 \rightarrow Y_{10}$	45.40	27.0
15	$Y_{15} + Y_5 \rightarrow Y_{10}$	9.30	13.6
16	$Y_{10} \rightarrow Y_{15} + Y_5$	12.60	11.1
17	$Y_2 + Y_{14} \rightarrow Y_8 + Y_{13}$	40.50	9.2

Figures 2, 3 and 4 shows the intervals of calculated values of the measured substrates of the catalytic reaction of hydroalumination olefins. The observed substrates are the target product of the reaction a higher organoaluminium compound Bu_2AlR (Y_6), initial olefin CH_2CHR (Y_3) and the original organoaluminum compound - TIBA $AlBu_3$ (Y_{14}). The graphs show the concentration values in the temperature range [10 °C, 15 °C].

The intervals of changes in the concentration of the initial olefin (Fig. 2) and the reaction product (Fig. 3) increase with time at the specified temperature intervals. The concentrations of the initial type are not affected by the specified temperature intervals (Fig. 4).

Subsequent introduction of the process into production requires determining the optimal conditions for the reaction in order to maximize the conversion of the initial reagents. Based on the available interval kinetic model of the reaction, it is possible to formulate a multi-criteria interval optimization problem [18,19].

4 Multicriteria Optimization of the Conditions of the Olefin Hydroalumination Reaction in the Presence of Triisobutylaluminum

The formulation of the MCIO problem allows taking into account direct restrictions on them when determining variable parameters, rather than singling them out separately, as was done earlier [19]. The MCIO solution covers all permissible reaction conditions that allow reaching the extremes of the optimality criteria, but at the same time limiting changes in target functions when regime indicators change. That for practical tasks determines the entire range of acceptable values of the variable parameters.

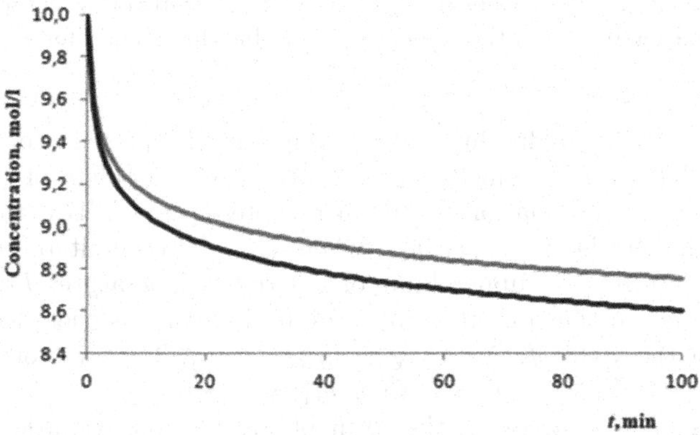

Fig. 2. Intervals of calculated values of the measured substrates of the catalytic reaction of hydroalumination olefins in the presence of triisobutylaluminum for CH_2CHR (Y_3) (black curve - the lower limit of the interval, gray - the upper limit of the interval)

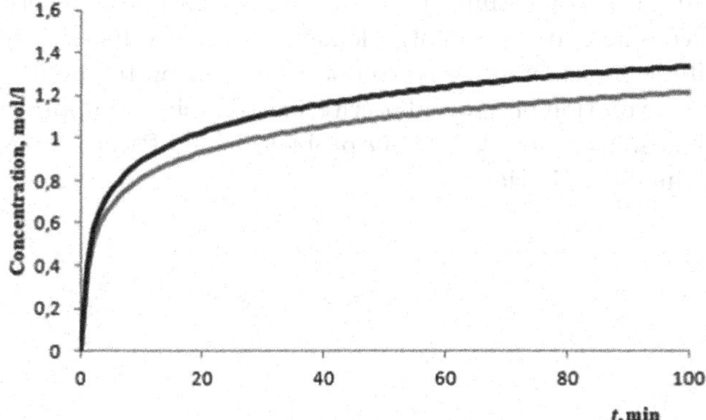

Fig. 3. Intervals of calculated values of the measured substrates of the catalytic reaction of hydroalumination olefins in the presence of triisobutylaluminum for Bu_2AlR (Y_6) (black curve - the upper limit of the interval, gray - the lower limit of the interval)

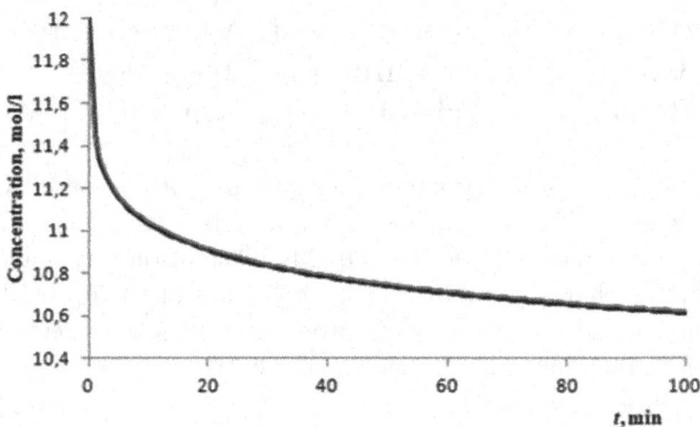

Fig. 4. Intervals of calculated values of the measured substrates of the catalytic reaction of hydroalumination olefins in the presence of triisobutylaluminum for $AlBu_3$ (Y_{14})

In the reaction of hydroalumination olefins in the presence of TIBA, the product Bu_2AlR (Y_6) is formed. Then, for the MCO problem of the reaction conditions of hydroalumination olefins in the presence of TIBA, the vector of variable parameters is $X = (x_1, x_2)$, where x_1 - lower limit of the reaction temperature, $Tmin$; x_2 - upper limit of reaction temperature, $Tmax$. As an optimality criterion, the conversion of the initial olefin was chosen in the form of minimizing the yield: $f_1(X) = y_{CH_2CHR(Y_3) \to min}$. Then vector function of optimality criteria $F(X) = (midf_1(X), widf_1(X)) \to min.$

The problem was solved in the form of Pareto approximation using the NSGA-II (Non-dominated Sorting Genetic Algorithm) multi-criteria optimization algorithm [20,21], which allows solving the problem of compromise of optimality criteria values and calculating the entire set of unimproved solutions. The choice of the NSGA-II method is dictated by its rapid convergence to a solution, the global nature of optimization, since it is based on a genetic algorithm [20]. Simultaneous and independent calculation of the values of contradictory optimality criteria makes it possible to obtain a solution to the MCO problem without using convolution of particular criteria and assigning appropriate weight parameters. The solution to the MCIO problem is the Pareto interval front in the area of optimality criteria.

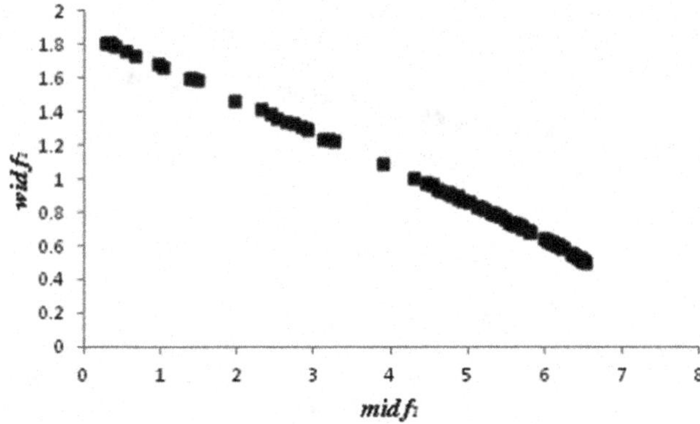

Fig. 5. Approximation Pareto front MCO problem of the reaction conditions of hydroalumination olefins in the presence of triisobutylaluminum

Figure 5 shows the dependence of the calculated values of the midpoint change in interval f_1, and the width of this interval. Moreover, with an increase in the value $midf_1$ interval width decreases $widf_1$, and vice versa. These values are not improved according to the specified criteria.

Figure 6 shows the corresponding knowledge of the Pareto set in the range of variable parameters $Tmin$ and $Tmax$. The coordinates of each point represent the allowable interval for varying the reaction temperature.

5 Parallel Scheme for Implementing the Computational Process

With sequential calculation, the solution of the problem takes several hours. Therefore, an algorithm for parallelizing calculations is proposed in this paper.

The basis for parallelization of multi-objective optimization algorithms is the decomposition and structuring of the population (sets of possible solutions). That is, splitting the original population into several subsets (subpopulations - S_i).

The paper used an island model of parallelization by the distribution of the intervals of variation of kinetic parameters.

To solve the problem of multicriteria optimization of chemical reactions based on the interval kinetic model, the NSGA-II genetic algorithm with an island model of parallelization of the computational process was applied [24]. At the input, the system receives vectors of intervals for changing the variable parameters and a list of optimality criteria. Each S_i processor selects the value of the

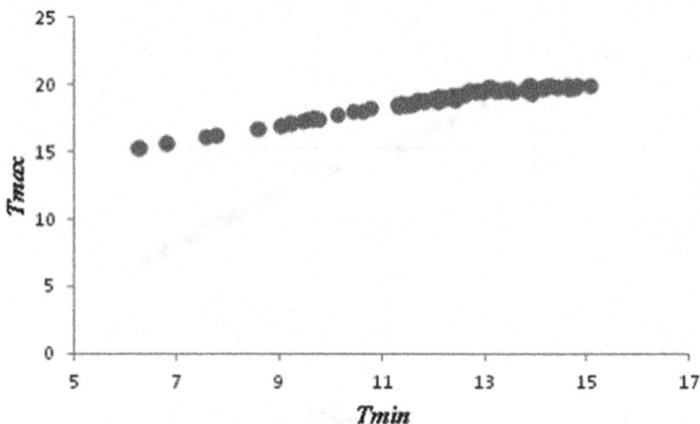

Fig. 6. Approximation Pareto set MCO problem of the reaction conditions of hydroalumination olefins in the presence of triisobutylaluminum

vector of variable parameters from its i-th interval and passes it to the solver of the two-way system dib_{low}, dib_{up}. The solver returns the values of the lower and upper bounds for the concentrations of the reaction components. Based on the calculated concentrations, the values of the optimality criteria for S_i processor. After checking the non-dominance condition for the solution, the optimal value are determined $X^{opt,i}$ and $F^{opt,i}$ on each subinterval. At the output of the computing system, the general values are determined X^{opt} and F^{opt} over the entire variation interval (Fig. 7).

Such a parallelization scheme makes it possible to effectively scale computations.

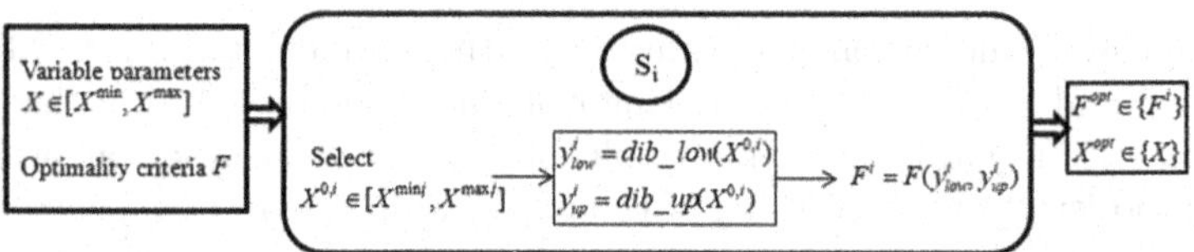

Fig. 7. The scheme of parallelization of the computational process of solving the problem of multicriteria optimization of chemical reactions based on the interval kinetic model

A computational experiment to calculate the optimal temperature change intervals of the olefin hydroaluminination reaction was carried out on a 4-core Intel Core I5 7th Gen personal computer using OpenMP parallelization technology.

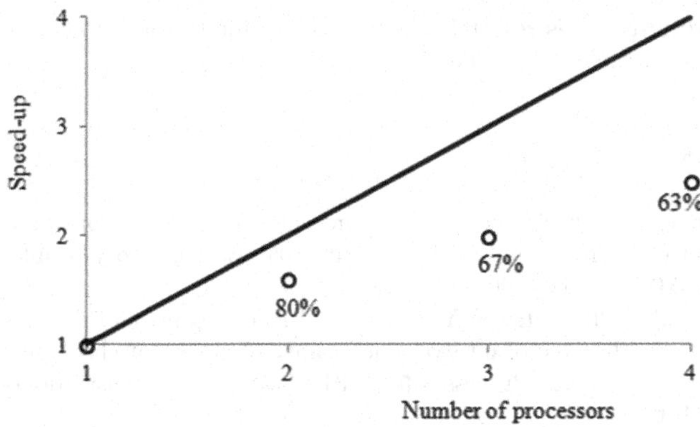

Fig. 8. The parallelization efficiency of solving the problem of multi-criteria optimization of chemical reactions based on the interval kinetic model

With an increase in the number of processors, efficiency decreases, due to the time spent on data synchronization between subpopulations (Fig. 8).

6 Conclusions

The need to study the stability of optimization problems to parameter perturbations is caused by a number of factors, such as the inaccuracy of the initial data, the inadequacy of models to real processes, the error of numerical methods, rounding errors, the need to develop algorithms for solving "close" problems, etc. [22,23]. In addition, for complex multi-stage chemical processes, including production, technological operating conditions require the determination of permissible intervals of parameter values that ensure the stability of the calculated solution with a given permissible error. The paper proposes an algorithm for determining the permissible interval values of variable parameters when solving the problem of multi-criteria optimization of conditions for a multi-stage chemical process. A mathematical model of kinetics with intervals of kinetic parameters allows taking into account possible fluctuations in reaction conditions. For the catalytic reaction of hydroalumination of olefins in the presence of triisobutylaluminum, the allowable range of temperature change was determined, which makes it possible to obtain the optimal range of change in the conversion of the initial olefin.

An algorithm for parallelization of calculations for the problem of multicriteria optimization using interval analysis is proposed. The efficiency indicator of computational experiments (63% on 4 cores of the central process) showed that in the future it is necessary to consider a larger number of optimized parameters and transition to a computing system with a large number of cores.

The considered algorithm can also be used to study fluid filtration in fractured-porous reservoirs, since they are based on similar mathematical models, but in systems of differential equations in partial derivatives [25].

Acknowledgement. This research was performed due to the Russian Science Foundation grant (project No. 21-71-20047).

References

1. Bukhtoyarov, S.E., Emelichev, V.A.: Parametrization of the optimality principle (from Pareto to Slater) and stability of multicriteria trajectory problems. J. Appl. Ind. Math. **10**(2), 3–18 (2003)
2. Rapoport, E.Y., Pleshivtseva, Y.E.: Multi-objective control of distributed parameter systems in the case of interval uncertainty of the plant characteristics. Optoelectron. Instrum. Data Process. **55**(4), 317–330 (2019). https://doi.org/10.3103/S8756699019040010
3. Abdieva, L.K., Sadykova, N.A., Taalaibekova, M.T.: Mathematical modeling of the interval optimization problem under uncertainty. Mod. Probl. Mech. **46**(4), 106–114 (2021)
4. Morozov, A.Yu., Reviznikov, D.L.: Modeling of dynamic systems with interval parameters. Review of methods and software. Model. Data Anal. **4**, 5–31 (2019). https://doi.org/10.17759/mda.2019090401
5. Koledina, K., Gubaydullin, I., Koledin, S.: Parameter analysis of stability of the Pareto front for optimal conditions of catalytic processes. Lobachevskii J. Math. **42**(12), 2834–2840 (2021). https://doi.org/10.1134/S1995080221120192
6. Rangaiah, G., Andrew, Z., Hoadley, F.: Multi-objective optimization applications in chemical process engineering: tutorial and review. Processes **8**(5), 508 (2020). https://doi.org/10.3390/pr8050508
7. Subbaramaiha, V., Srivastava, V., Mall, I.: Optimization of reaction parameters and kinetic modeling of catalytic wet peroxidation of picoline by Cu/SBA-15. Ind. Eng. Chem. Res. **52**(26), 9021–9029 (2013). https://doi.org/10.1002/aic.14017
8. Dobronets, B.S.: Interval mathematics. Study guide. Krasnoyar. State. Un-T., p. 216 (2004)
9. Koledina, K., Koledin, S., Karpenko, A., Gubaydullin, I., Vovdenko, M.: Multi-objective optimization of chemical reaction conditions based on a kinetic model. J. Math. Chem. **57**(2), 484–493 (2019). https://doi.org/10.1007/s10910-018-0960-z
10. Alonso, P., Argüeso, F., Cortina, R., Ranilla, J., Vidal, A.M.: Non-linear parallel solver for detecting point sources in CMB maps using Bayesian techniques. J. Math. Chem. **51**(4), 1153–1163 (2013). https://doi.org/10.1007/s10910-012-0078-7
11. Dzhemilev, U.M., Khusnutdinov, R.I., Tolstikov, G.A.: Synthesis of cyclobutane and cyclopentane compounds using homogeneous metal complex catalysts. J. Organomet. Chem. **409**(1–2), 15–65 (1991). https://doi.org/10.1016/0022-328X(91)86131-9
12. Dzhemilev, U.M., Vostrikova, O.S., Tolstikov, G.A.: Homogeneous zirconium based catalysts in organic synthesis. J. Organomet. Chem. **304**(1–2), 17–39 (1986). https://doi.org/10.1016/S0022-328X(00)99674-8
13. Nurislamova, L.F., Gubaydullin, I.M., Koledina, K.F.: Kinetic model of isolated reactions of the catalytic hydroalumination of olefins. Reac. Kinet. Mech. Cat. **116**(1), 79–93 (2015). https://doi.org/10.1007/s11144-015-0876-6
14. Nurislamova, L., Gubaydullin, I., Koledina, K., Safin, R.: Kinetic model of the catalytic hydroalumination of olefins with organoaluminum compounds. Reac Kinet Mech Cat. **117**(1), 1–14 (2016). https://doi.org/10.1007/s11144-015-0927-z

15. Gubaydullin, I., Koledina, K., Sayfullina, L.: Mathematical modeling of induction period of the olefins hydroalumination reaction by Diisobutylaluminiumchloride catalyzed with Cp2ZrCl2. Eng. J. **18**(1), 13–24 (2014). https://doi.org/10.4186/ej.2014.18.1.13
16. Gear, C.V.: Numerical Initial Value Problems in Ordinary Differential Equations, p. 252. Prentice-Hall, Englewood Cliffs (1971)
17. Aleksandrov, V.M.: Computing of optimal inertial control of a linear system. Num. Anal. Appl. **8**(1), 1–12 (2015). https://doi.org/10.1134/S1995423915010012
18. Lotov, A.V., Ryabikov, A.I.: Launch pad method in multi-extreme multi-criteria optimization problems. J. Comput. Math. Math. Phys. **59**(12), 2111–2128 (2019). https://doi.org/10.1134/S0965542519120145
19. Koledina, K.F., Koledin, S.N., Nurislamova, L.F., Gubaydullin, I.M.: Internal parallelism of multi-objective optimization and optimal control based on a compact kinetic model for the catalytic reaction of dimethyl carbonate with alcohols. Commun. Comput. Inf. Sci. **1063**, 242–255 (2019). https://doi.org/10.1007/978-3-030-28163-2_17
20. Deb, K., Mohan, M., Mishra, S.: Evolutionary Multi-criterion Optimization. Springer, Cham (2003). https://doi.org/10.1007/978-3-031-27250-9
21. Kalyanmoy, D., Pratap, A., Agarwal, S., Meyarivan, T.: A fast and elitist multi-objective genetic algorithm: NSGA-II. IEEE Trans. Evol. Comput. **6**(2), 182–197 (2002). https://doi.org/10.1109/4235.996017
22. Kreutz, J., Shukhaev, A., Du, W., Druskin, S., Daugulis, O., Ismagilov, R.: Evolution of catalysts directed by genetic algorithms in a plug-based microfluidic device tested with oxidation of methane by oxygen. J. Am. Chem. Soc. **132**(9), 3128–3132 (2010). https://doi.org/10.1021/ja909853x
23. Koledina, K., Koledin, S., Gubaydullin, I.: Automated system for identification of conditions for homogeneous and heterogeneous reactions in multiobjective optimization problems. Numer. Anal. Appl. **12**(2), 116–125 (2019). https://doi.org/10.1134/S1995423919020022
24. Koledin, S., Koledina, K., Gubaydullin, I.: Parallel computing in solving the problem of interval multicriteria optimization in chemical kinetics. In: Voevodin, V., Sobolev, S., Yakobovskiy, M., Shagaliev, R. (eds.) Supercomputing. RuSCDays 2022. LNCS, vol. 13708, pp. 214–224. Springer, Cham (2022). https://doi.org/10.1007/978-3-031-22941-1_15
25. Bobreneva, Y.O.: Modeling the piezoconductivity process of a two-phase fluid system in a fractured-porous reservoir. Math. Models Comput. Simul. T. **14**(4), 645–653 (2022). https://doi.org/10.1134/S2070048222040032

Parallel Numerical Implementation 3D Wave Hydrodynamics and SWAN Models

Alexander Sukhinov[1], Elena Protsenko[2], and Sofya Protsenko[2(✉)]

[1] Don State Technical University, Rostov-on-Don, Russia
[2] Chekhov Taganrog Institute (branch) of Rostov State University of Economics, Taganrog, Russia
{eapros,rab55555}@rambler.ru

Abstract. The work is devoted to the parallel implementation of the wave hydrodynamics model and the modern SWAN wind-wave model. To determine the indicators of parallel efficiency of models, the model problem of hydrodynamics was solved. The calculation of water flow rates for the area of a shallow reservoir was carried out, while using a grid with steps differing by orders of magnitude in the horizontal and vertical coordinate directions. Two parallelization strategies SWAN OpenMP and MPI are compared. The indicators of parallel implementation are determined: computing time, speed-up radio, efficiency ratio. It is shown that the MPI version is more efficient than OpenMP. The indicators for evaluating the parallel computational efficiency of a three-dimensional wave model of hydrodynamics are presented. The dependence of computational efficiency indicators on the number of processors required to solve hydrodynamic problems using MPI is shown. It was revealed that the speed-up radio reaches the highest value at 128 cores, and with a further increase in the number of computing cores, the acceleration only decreases, which is associated with an increase in the time spent on data exchange between nodes. The spatial distribution algorithm for individual processors provides load balancing for each time step, but does not guarantee that communication is synchronized, since not every calculation on each processor will require the same effort.

Keywords: SWAN · 3D wave hydrodynamics model · Coastal zone · Wave dynamics · Parallel efficiency · Computational scalability

1 Introduction

In the modern world, numerical methods play a key role in the study of complex physical phenomena, especially in the field of hydrodynamics and wave modeling. However, with the increasing complexity of problems related to three-dimensional wave hydrodynamics and SWAN (Simulating WAves Nearshore) models, it becomes necessary to use parallel computing to effectively solve these problems. In this article, we will discuss the parallel numerical implementation of three-dimensional wave hydrodynamics and SWAN models, identifying the advantages and prospects of this approach in the context of modern research in the field of marine and coastal processes.

V. Voevodin et al. (Eds.): RuSCDays 2023, LNCS 14388, pp. 152–162, 2023.
https://doi.org/10.1007/978-3-031-49432-1_12

Wave impact models such as WAM (Wave Model), SWAN (Simulating WAves Nearshore) and WaveWatch are key tools in predicting and modeling sea waves. Let's look at their pros and cons [1–3].

WAM can be used to simulate waves in a variety of marine environments, including open oceans and coastal zones. With proper tuning and calibration, WAM provides high accuracy in predicting wave height and spectral composition. The model can be demanding of computational resources, especially when working with three-dimensional wave hydrodynamics. WAM may have limited capabilities in modeling coastal processes.

SWAN specializes in wave modeling in coastal zones, which makes it an effective tool for studying the effects of waves on the coastline. SWAN provides the possibility of integration with other models, which makes it possible to more fully take into account the interaction of waves with other oceanic processes. SWAN is not always suitable for modeling open sea areas with high accuracy. Some aspects of the model may require additional data for calibration and verification.

WaveWatch is focused on global wave modeling, which makes it useful for a wide range of applications. The model integrates real data in some aspects, improving the accuracy of forecasts. WaveWatch may not be as effective in predicting waves in coastal areas where the impact of coastal processes is more significant. WAM, WaveWatch can be computationally demanding in global modeling.

Each of these models has its advantages and limitations, and the choice depends on the specific requirements and goals of the study [4–6].

The construction of a parallel numerical implementation of a three-dimensional mathematical model of hydrodynamics and the SWAN windwave model can be extremely important for several reasons. Parallel computing allows you to distribute the computational load between multiple processors or cores, which increases overall performance and reduces the execution time of complex calculations. This is especially important when modeling three-dimensional hydrodynamics and wave processes, where high spatial resolution requires significant computing resources.

Modeling of three-dimensional hydrodynamics and wave processes generates huge amounts of data. Parallel processing allows you to effectively manage this data and provide their analysis in real time or in a short time. The solution to this problem is carried out by attracting data from field studies. The three-dimensional hydrodynamic model combined with the SWAN wind-wave model can provide a more accurate and realistic representation of marine conditions. Parallel computing allows for more detailed consideration of complex interactions between various physical processes, such as currents, winds and waves.

Parallel numerical implementation is especially useful when modeling coastal zones where waves interact with the coastline, bottom and other coastal processes. These areas require high spatial resolution, which can be achieved by efficient parallel computing. Parallel numerical implementations improve not only the efficiency of modeling, but also its accuracy, which makes them important tools for research in the field of marine hydrodynamics and waves.

2 3D Wave Hydrodynamics Mathematical Model

Consider a system of Navier-Stokes equations taking into account variable density, temperature and salinity, which describes the movement of a liquid under the influence of various forces, including pressure and viscosity, as well as forces caused by the action of waves, it includes [6–8]:

the continuity equation:

$$\frac{\partial \rho}{\partial t} + \nabla \cdot (\rho \mathbf{u}) = 0, \tag{1}$$

the equations of motion:

$$\begin{aligned}
\frac{\partial u}{\partial t} + u\frac{\partial u}{\partial x} + v\frac{\partial u}{\partial y} + w\frac{\partial u}{\partial z} &= -\frac{1}{\rho}\frac{\partial P}{\partial x} + F_x - 2\Omega v \sin(\phi) + \nu\nabla^2 u, \\
\frac{\partial v}{\partial t} + u\frac{\partial v}{\partial x} + v\frac{\partial v}{\partial y} + w\frac{\partial v}{\partial z} &= -\frac{1}{\rho}\frac{\partial P}{\partial y} + F_y + 2\Omega u \sin(\phi) + \nu\nabla^2 v, \\
\frac{\partial w}{\partial t} + u\frac{\partial w}{\partial x} + v\frac{\partial w}{\partial y} + w\frac{\partial w}{\partial z} &= -\frac{1}{\rho}\frac{\partial P}{\partial z} + F_z + \nu\nabla^2 w,
\end{aligned} \tag{2}$$

the transport equation for temperature:

$$\frac{\partial T}{\partial t} + u\frac{\partial T}{\partial x} + v\frac{\partial T}{\partial y} + w\frac{\partial T}{\partial z} = Q - \frac{1}{\rho c_p}\frac{\partial (P\alpha T)}{\partial t} + \kappa\nabla^2 T, \tag{3}$$

the transfer equation for salinity:

$$\frac{\partial S}{\partial t} + u\frac{\partial S}{\partial x} + v\frac{\partial S}{\partial y} + w\frac{\partial S}{\partial z} = R - \frac{1}{\rho c_p}\frac{\partial (P\beta S)}{\partial t} + \kappa\nabla^2 S. \tag{4}$$

where ρ is the density of the liquid (variable density), P is the pressure, u, v, w are the velocity components in three directions x, y, z, F_x, F_y, F_z are the forces caused by the action of waves (for example, waves on the surface of water), Ω is the angular velocity of the Earth's rotation, ϕ is latitude, T is temperature, S is salinity, Q is the source or sink of heat, R is the source or drain of salt, α, β are the coefficients of temperature and salinity expansion, respectively, c_p is the specific heat capacity at constant pressure, κ is the coefficient of thermal conductivity.

If the grid size is chosen small enough, the average deformation rate of the cellular scale is equal to

$$\nu = C_s^2\Delta^2\frac{1}{2}\sqrt{\left(\frac{\partial \overline{u}}{\partial z}\right)^2 + \left(\frac{\partial \overline{v}}{\partial z}\right)^2},$$

where $\overline{u}$, $\overline{v}$ are the time-averaged components of the water flow velocity in the horizontal direction. This approximation makes it possible to construct a vertical coefficient of turbulent exchange that is uneven in depth based on the measured pulsations of the water flow velocity.

3 Wave Effects in SWAN

Models of spectral waves of the third generation solve the balance equation of action for the wave action density N (a function of the Cartesian coordinate x, frequency f and direction θ) as follows:

$$\frac{\mathrm{d}N}{\mathrm{d}t} = \frac{S_{\mathrm{in}} + S_{\mathrm{nl}} + S_{\mathrm{ds}} + \ldots}{\omega}, \tag{5}$$

where $N = (k, \theta, x, t) = F(k, \theta, x, t)/\omega$ is the spectrum of the density of the wave action, ω is the natural frequency (in radii), $k = |\mathbf{k}|$ is the wave number and θ is the direction of propagation of the wave energy. For deep-sea waves ω and k are related by the linear dispersion relation $\omega^2 = gk$, where g is the gravitational acceleration [4].

The right part consists of sources and absorbers of wave energy, including the wind input signal S_{in}, dissipation S_{ds}, caused by wave discontinuity, and nonlinear interactions S_{nl}. Among these physical processes S'_{nl} plays a central role in the formation of the spectrum of wind-generated waves by controlling the lowering of the spectral peak, angular propagation and high-frequency spectral tail [5, 6].

The presence of a wavy surface affects the roughness felt by the airflow. The flow of atmospheric momentum in the field of oceanic waves is denoted by τ_{in}. It is convenient to determine the friction velocity from the air side in relation to the total stress from the air side, τ_a, as

$$u_*^2 = \tau_a / \rho_a, \tag{6}$$

where ρ_a is the surface air density. The density of the wave action is related to the density of the dispersion of the wave through the ratio [8]:

$$z_0 = \alpha_{\mathrm{CH}} \frac{u_*^2}{g}, \tag{7}$$

where α_{CH} varies depending on the state of the sea, as follows

$$\alpha_{\mathrm{CH}} = \frac{\hat{\alpha}_{\mathrm{CH}}}{\sqrt{1 - \tau_{\mathrm{in}} / \tau_{\mathrm{a}}}}, \tag{8}$$

where $\hat{\alpha}_{\mathrm{CH}} = 0.006$, is the voltage caused by the wave voltage τ_{in} is related to the effect of wind on the wave field as

$$\tau_{\mathrm{in}} = \rho_{\mathrm{w}} g \int_0^{2\pi} \int_0^{\infty} \frac{\mathbf{k}}{\omega} S_{\mathrm{in}} d\omega \, d\theta. \tag{9}$$

where ρ_{w} is the density of water [9–11].

The kinetic energy of turbulence is the average kinetic energy per unit mass associated with vortices in a turbulent flow. Physically, the kinetic energy of turbulence is characterized by measured root-mean-square fluctuations of velocity. The kinetic energy of turbulence equation with Reynolds averages can be written as follows:

$$\frac{\mathrm{D}e}{\mathrm{D}t} = \frac{g}{\rho_{\mathrm{w}}} \overline{u'_3 \rho'} - \overline{u'_i u'_j} \frac{\partial \overline{u}_i}{\partial x_j} - \frac{\partial}{\partial x_j} \left(\overline{u'_j e} \right) - \frac{1}{\rho_{\mathrm{w}}} \frac{\partial}{\partial x_i} \left(\overline{u'_i \rho'} \right) - \epsilon, \tag{10}$$

where $e = q^2/2 = \overline{u_i' u_j'}/2$ is the kinetic energy of turbulence per unit mass, q is the turbulent velocity, ϵ is the scattering velocity. We will use the gradient transfer approximation, where the turbulence coefficients are proportional to the gradients in average values, the equation is obtained $\frac{\partial e}{\partial t} = K_{\text{m}} S^2 - K_\rho N^2 + \frac{\partial}{\partial z}\left(K_q \frac{\partial e}{\partial z}\right) - c_\epsilon \frac{e^{3/2}}{l_\epsilon}$.

Assuming that the buoyancy coefficient is proportional to the local Brant-Weissal frequency, we obtain: $N^2 = -\frac{g}{\rho}\frac{\partial \rho_{\text{w}}}{\partial z}$, and the magnitude of the shift is related to the shift of the average flow rate: $S^2 = \left(\frac{\partial \overline{\mathbf{u}}}{\partial z}\right)^2$.

Waves change the vertical dissipation profile compared to the traditional wall law, as they break, they significantly change the vertical dissipation profile compared to the traditional wall law, the observed scattering velocities with breaking waves are much higher. The injection of turbulent kinetic energy from incoming waves is sufficient to successfully simulate the evolution of a mixed layer, the flow of kinetic energy of turbulence is related to the water friction velocity w_* as follows: $\mathbf{\Phi}_{\text{oc}} = \rho_{\text{w}} \alpha_{\text{CB}} w_*^3$.

Thus, the flow from the breaking waves can be implemented in the model, in the form of the following boundary condition $e_0 = \frac{1}{2}(15.8\alpha_{\text{CB}})^{2/3} \frac{|\tau_{\text{oc}}|}{\rho_{\text{w}}}$.

Since that $e(z)$ changes rapidly with depth, the resulting boundary condition was modified by weighing the surface value by the thickness of the uppermost level to obtain an average value more characteristic of turbulence near the surface of the model

$$e_1 = \frac{1}{L}\int_{-L}^{0} e(z)\,\mathrm{d}z, \tag{10}$$

where $L = \Delta z_1/2$ is the depth of the T point of the first level. The average value of the boundary condition takes the form $e_1 = e_0 \frac{3}{2\lambda L}\left[1 - \exp(-2\lambda L/3)\right]$. The difference between e_1 and e_0 becomes smaller, with increasing vertical resolution.

4 SWAN Parallel Mode

The model problem of hydrodynamics was solved to determine the indicators of parallel efficiency of two models. The dynamically changing function of the water surface level was calculated using both models for a section of a shallow reservoir measuring 50 by 50 m, and a maximum depth of 2 m, using a grid with steps differing by orders of magnitude in the horizontal and vertical coordinate directions. The dimension of the grid is $100 \times 100 \times 40$ nodes, such detailed vertical resolution is due to the complex and heterogeneous bathymetry of the researched area (Fig. 1).

Two parallelization strategies are available parallel runs on distributed memory machines or shared memory systems. The indicators of parallel implementation of OpenMP and MPI were compared.

Parallel efficiency is a measure of how successfully a parallel algorithm solves a problem with an increase in the number of processors or cores. This efficiency is evaluated using various indicators. Evaluating the effectiveness of parallel computing is important for optimizing resource usage and achieving maximum performance when solving complex tasks.

The comparison of serial and parallel running of programs includes an assessment of several key aspects in order to determine the benefits of using parallel computing.

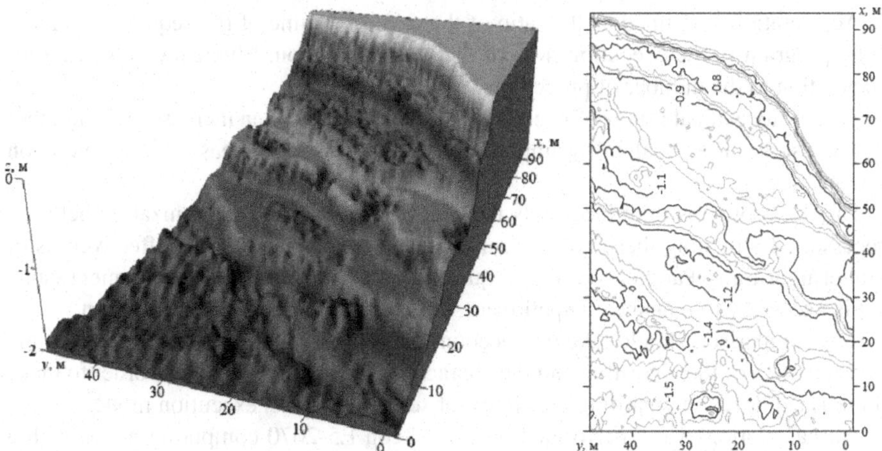

Fig. 1. Bathymetry of the researched area.

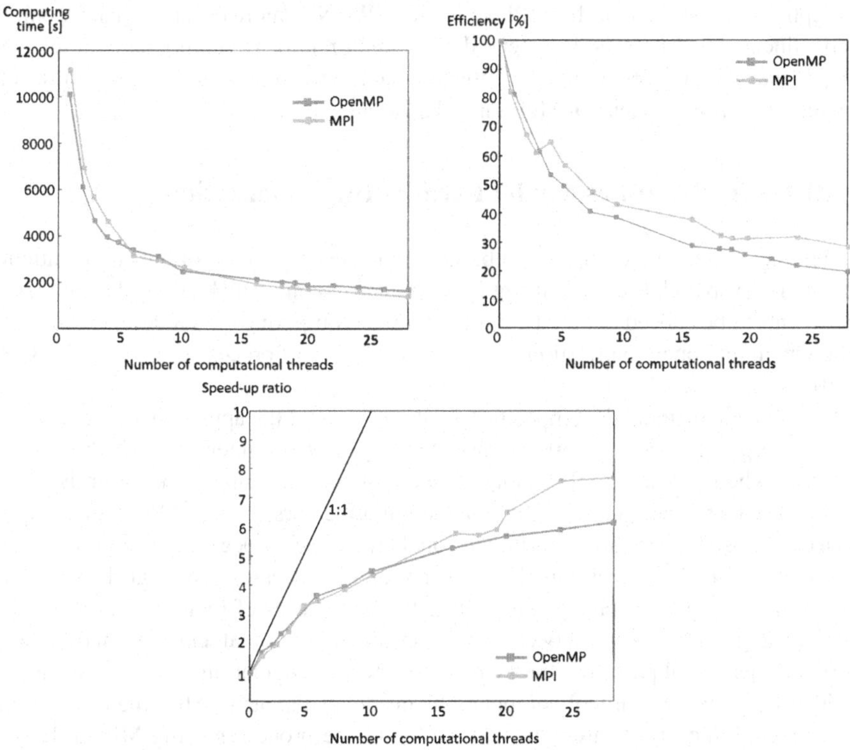

Fig. 2. Parallel computing efficiency of SWAN.

Acceleration is defined as the ratio of the execution time of the sequential version of the program to the execution time of the parallel version. Efficiency is the ratio of acceleration to the number of processors.

Scalability evaluates how efficiently a program scales with an increase in the number of processors. Good scalability implies that as processors increase, the acceleration remains high.

Parallel programs may face costs for data exchange and synchronization between processors. Estimating these costs is important for understanding the effectiveness of parallel algorithms. Parallel code may require additional efforts at the development stage, as it is necessary to manage competitiveness and ensure proper synchronization.

The comparison should take into account the specific requirements of the task, the characteristics of the algorithm and the characteristics of the hardware in order to make an informed decision regarding the choice of serial or parallel execution mode.

All calculations were performed on Intel Xeon E5-2670 computing nodes with a frequency of 2.3 GHz. Twenty-eight threads (cores) were used, each with 96 GB of RAM.

Figure 2 shows the computing time in seconds, speed-up ratio and efficiency ratio, the graphs demonstrate that the MPI version of SWAN is more efficient than OpenMP. Almost linear speed-up ratio is observed for a small number of computational threads. The calculated indicators of parallel efficiency are consistent with the research results obtained by S. Rautenbach, O. Mullarney, K. Bryan [7].

5 3D Hydrodynamics Model Parallel Implementation

Parallel implementation of algorithm based on the decomposition of the computational domain in two spatial directions using MPI was carried out, which allowed a number of experiments to be carried out on the multiprocessor computing system built on the basis of the OpenHPC open application stack, containing 1440 processor cores of 2.3 GHz and 10.24 TB of RAM.

The two-dimensional decomposition method is one of the approaches to distributed parallel computing using the MPI library (Message Passing Interface). This method is often used when solving problems that are naturally divided into blocks or grids.

MPI provides functionality for creating communicators, such as MPI_Comm_split, which can be used to organize two-dimensional grids. Each process receives a submatrix or a block of data for processing. The distribution of processes can be grid-like in two dimensions. Processes exchange data along the boundaries of their submatrices. This is the exchange of messages between processes along horizontal and vertical directions in a two-dimensional partition. Each process performs calculations on its local submatrix. This may involve parallel computations inside a submatrix. After the calculations are completed, the results are collected on one of the processes using MPI collection functions.

The advantages of the two-dimensional decomposition method include more efficient use of resources in the case of tasks that can naturally be divided into blocks in two dimensions.

Numerical solution of hydrodynamic problems on grids with steps differing by orders of magnitude in horizontal and vertical coordinate directions leads to the need to solve grid equations with poorly conditioned operators. Solving this class of problems by iterative methods requires a large number of iterations, which can reach from hundreds to tens of thousands. To reduce the counting time, it is necessary to use effective numerical methods for solving grid equations, which include the adaptive alternating-triangular iterative method. The presence of a preconditioner of the upper and lower parts of the grid equation operator can significantly reduce the number of iterations, but at the same time the processing of grid nodes is carried out in a conveyor way.

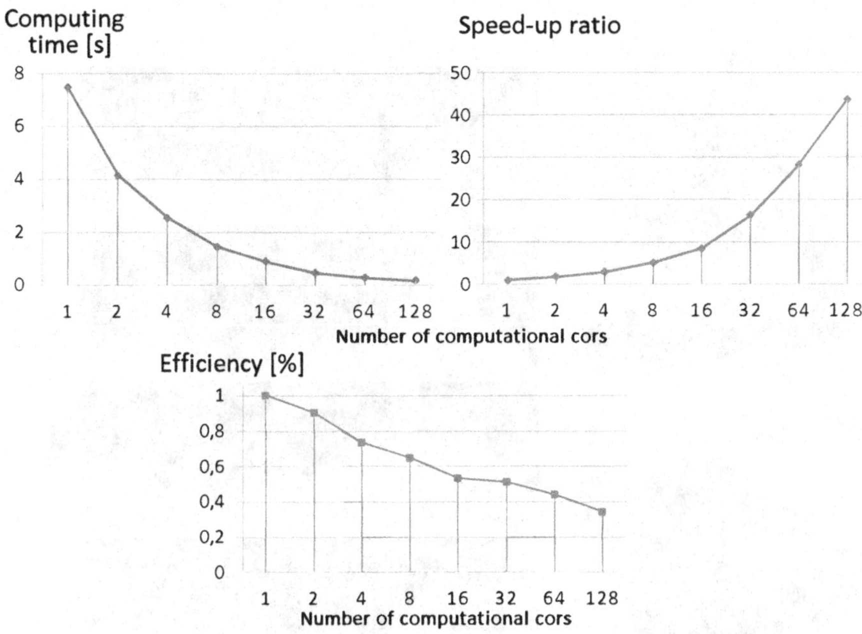

Fig. 3. Parallel computing efficiency 3D hydrodynamics mathematical model.

Figure 3 shows the dependence of computing efficiency indicators on the number of processors required to solve hydrodynamic problems on a 100 × 100 × 40 grid. The graphs show that the acceleration reaches the highest value of 43.668 with 128 cores.

Figure 4 shows the level elevation function graphs the obtained on the basis of the SWAN and 3D wave hydrodynamics model, the simulation showed similar results for the level elevation function.

Figure 5 shows the results of simulations of wave hydrodynamic processes based on 3D model. The absence of linear error growth is achieved due to the conservativeness of difference schemes. In practice, the absence of error accumulation was checked using calculations for longer periods, when the first 3–5 waves are brought ashore, a transitional process is observed, and then wave fluctuations tend to a periodic regime.

Modeling of wave hydrodynamic processes based on a three-dimensional (3D) model can provide a versatile and detailed analysis of marine conditions.

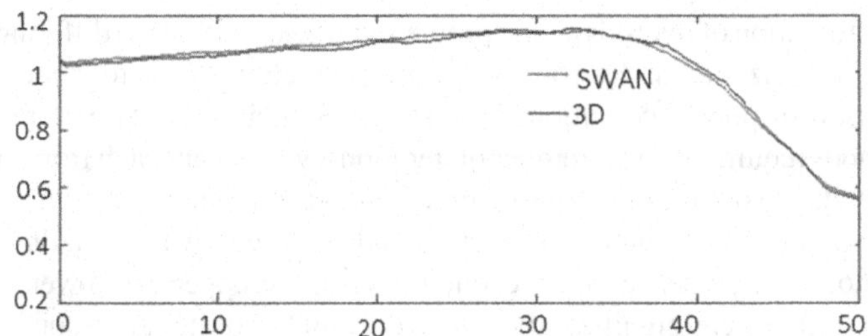

Fig. 4. Comparison of the elevation function simulation results obtained on the basis of SWAN and 3D wave hydrodynamics model.

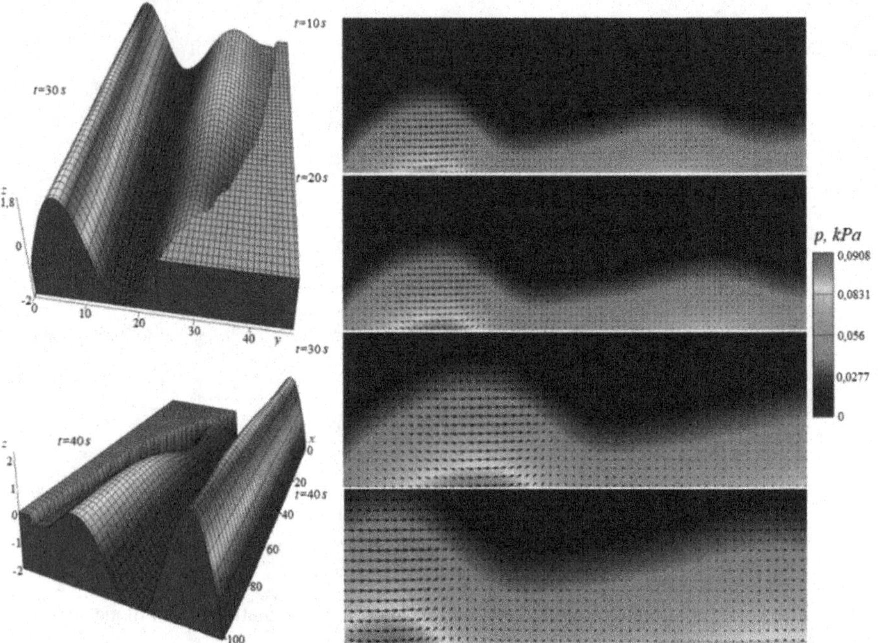

Fig. 5. Wave profiles and velocity vector fields at different time points.

Obtaining three-dimensional profiles of the height and shape of waves in space and time. This allows you to estimate changes in wave height depending on location and time.

Analysis of three-dimensional wave spectra, which gives an idea of the frequency characteristics of the wave field. This can be useful when studying wave modes and dynamics.

Estimation of wave energy parameters, such as energy density and direction of wave energy propagation. This is important for analyzing the impact of waves on coastal zones and infrastructure.

The study of the influence of waves on sea currents and, conversely, the assessment of how currents affect the characteristics of waves. This may be key to understanding marine dynamics.

Modeling of waves in coastal zones and analysis of impacts on the coastline, coastal structures and ecosystems. This is important for assessing the sustainability of coastal zones.

Investigation of the impact of waves on underwater structures, piers, bridges and other marine infrastructure. This can help in designing sustainable engineering solutions.

Modeling of extreme scenarios of strong waves and storm conditions to assess and warn of possible hazards to ships and coastal zones.

Development of early warning systems based on wave process modeling to predict and monitor changes in marine conditions.

Three-dimensional models of wave hydrodynamics allow us to study complex wave processes in depth, taking into account spatial and temporal changes. The results obtained can be used in various fields, such as engineering projects, maritime security, climate change research, etc.

6 Conclusions

The paper presents 3D wave hydrodynamics model that takes into account additive and microturbulent transport in the vertical direction in the coastal zone and, as a result, is devoid of a number of disadvantages that limit the use of SWAN-type models.

The problem of hydrodynamics was solved to determine the indicators of parallel efficiency of models. The results of numerical experiments obtained on the basis of SWAN and a three-dimensional model of wave hydrodynamics are presented, and their comparison is carried out.

Parallel implementation of 3D hydrodynamics mathematical model was based on the decomposition of the computational domain in two spatial directions. The quality indicators of the parallel algorithm were calculated: the computing time, the speed-up radio and the efficiency ratio. The dependence of computational efficiency indicators on the number of processors required to solve hydrodynamic problems by 3D model using MPI is shown.

The comparative analysis of the parallel efficiency of SWAN for a single node compared to sequential calculations in a single thread is presented. Two parallelization strategies SWAN OpenMP and MPI are compared. It is shown that the MPI version is more efficient than OpenMP.

The parallel implementations of the solution of model problems presented in the paper can be used in the study of hydrodynamic regimes in shallow-water systems, to determine the dynamics of the velocity and pressure of the aquatic environment, to analyze the possible influence of waves on the coastline and on the bottom of the reservoir.

Acknowledgments. The study was supported by the Russian Science Foundation grant No. 22-11-00295, https://rscf.ru/en/project/22-11-00295/.

References

1. Galperin, B., Sukoriansky, S., Druzhinin, O.: New analytic theory of the inertial subrange in the developed turbulence. Phys. Rev. Lett. **98**(5), 054501 (2007)
2. Gorokhovski, M., Zamansky, R.: Modeling the effects of small turbulent scales on the drag force for particles below and above the Kolmogorov scale. Phys. Rev. Fluids **3**, 034602 (2018)
3. Guedes, R.M.C., Bryan, K.R., Coco, G.: Observations of wave energy fluxes and swash motions on a low-sloping, dissipative beach. J. Geophys. Res. Oceans **118**, 3651–3669 (2013)
4. Inch, K., Davidson, M., Masselink, G., Russell, P.: Observations of nearshore infragravity wave dynamics under high energy swell and wind-wave conditions. Cont. Shelf Res. **138**, 19–31 (2017)
5. Kantha, L.H., Clayson, C.A.: Small-Scale Processes in Geophysical Fluid Flows. Academic Press, Cambridge (2000)
6. Lerma, A.N., Pedreros, R., Robinet, A., Senechal, N.: Simulating wave setup and runup during storm conditions on a complex barred beach. Coast. Eng. **123**, 29–41 (2017)
7. Palmsten, M.L., Splinter, K.D.: Observations and simulations of wave runup during a laboratory dune erosion experiment. Coast. Eng. **115**, 58–66 (2016)
8. Rautenbach, C., Mullarney, J., Bryan, K.: Parallel computing efficiency of SWAN 40.91. Geosci. Model Dev. **14**, 4241–4247 (2021). https://doi.org/10.5194/gmd-14-4241-2021
9. Smit, P., Zijlema, M., Stelling, G.: Depth-induced wave breaking in a non-hydrostatic, near-shore wave model. Coast. Eng. **76**, 1–16 (2013)
10. Stockdon, H.F., Thompson, D.M., Plant, N.G., Long, J.W.: Evaluation of wave runup predictions from numerical and parametric models. Coast. Eng. **92**, 1–11 (2014)
11. Tissier, M., Bonneton, P., Michallet, H., Ruessink, B.G.: Infragravity-wave modulation of short-wave celerity in the surf zone. J. Geophys. Res. Oceans **120**, 6799–6814 (2015)

Parallel Numerical Simulation of Sonic Log for 3D Heterogeneous TTI Media

Vladimir Cheverda[1(✉)], Victor Kostin[1], Vadim Lisitsa[2], and Galina Reshetova[1,2]

[1] Sobolev Institute of Mathematics, Novosibirsk 630090, Russia
{vova_chev,vctrkstn}@mail.ru, kgv@nmsf.sscc.ru
[2] Trofimuk Institute of Petroleum Geology and Geophysics Institute of Computational Mathematics and Mathematical Geophysics, Novosibirsk, Russia

Abstract. The paper presents an approach to the numerical simulation of sonic logging for arbitrary Tilted Transversely Isotropic (TTI) heterogeneous surrounding media. The simulation is based on the Lebedev's finite difference scheme. In order to take into account the sharpest interface of the problem, namely the interface between the fluid-filled borehole and the surrounding media, the analysis and simulation are performed in a cylindrical coordinate system. The use of this particular coordinate system causes two mathematical peculiarities: azimuth inflation of the mesh cells and singularity at the vertical axis r = 0. To solve these problems, local azimuth mesh refinement and interpolation at r = 0 are used, which are presented and verified in the paper. Another important factor in constructing an efficient and reliable method for the numerical simulation of the sonic log is the limitation of the computational domain. The use of the standard PML method for anisotropic media often leads to numerical instability. Therefore, its modification, known as MPML, is used here. The numerical simulation of acoustic wave fields in realistic borehole models requires the use of high performance computing systems with parallel architecture. For this purpose, we apply the spatial decomposition of the computational domain and organise the computations using MPI. The results of numerical experiments are presented and discussed.

Keywords: Sonic log · tilted transverse isotropy · multiaxial perfectly matched layer · finite-difference scheme · parallel computations

1 Introduction

Acoustic logging is an essential tool in the oil and gas industry for obtaining knowledge on the structure and physical features of rocks in the near borehole medium. However, the presence of drilling fluid in the well significantly affects the formation and propagation of the wave field. Biot was the first to consider this problem in an axisymmetric formulation for a homogeneous medium and analyzed the principal features of the sonic waves caused by a point source.

V. Voevodin et al. (Eds.): RuSCDays 2023, LNCS 14388, pp. 163–176, 2023.
https://doi.org/10.1007/978-3-031-49432-1_13

He derived dispersion relations for certain generated waves, which were later grouped together under the name of 'tube waves'.

In the 1970 s and 1980 s, representatives of the Leningrad school of wave propagation theory analyzed these waves in detail for specific axisymmetric models using asymptotic analysis. Their work contributed to a better understanding of the peculiarities of the processes of acoustic logging waves. However, such approaches could not describe seismo-acoustic fields for spatially inhomogeneous media, such as zones of enhanced fracturing, rock decompaction, and steep faults, which are of great practical interest for the separation and determination of mechanical properties.

The fast progress in the development of high-performance computing systems have opened the possibility of implementing numerical experiments to bring to the light the main peculiarities studies of full wave fields resulting from acoustic logging in three-dimensional heterogeneous media. On this way the people has got the possibility of taking into account anisotropy, absorption, and the presence of zones of increased fracturing and decompaction of rocks. This opens up new possibilities for accurately characterizing the subsurface, identifying potential oil and gas reservoirs, and optimizing well placement and drilling operations.

2 Mathematical Formulation

To describe the sonic waves generation and propagation we use the general elastodynamic equations:

$$\begin{cases} \varrho \dfrac{\partial \boldsymbol{u}}{\partial t} = \nabla \sigma \\ \dfrac{\partial \varepsilon}{\partial t} = \frac{1}{2}\left[\nabla \boldsymbol{u} + \nabla \boldsymbol{u}^T\right] \\ \sigma = C\varepsilon + f(t)G(\boldsymbol{x}) \end{cases} \tag{1}$$

where $\boldsymbol{u}$ is the velocity vector, and $\boldsymbol{\sigma}$, $\boldsymbol{\varepsilon}$ are stress and deformation second order tensors respectively, ϱ is the density and C is a symmetric fourth-order tensor of medium parameters. Functions $f(t)$ and $G(\boldsymbol{x})$ describe the source.

In order to take into account the sonic logging experiments geometry and approximate the sharpest interface between the well and surrounding medium we use Cylindrical coordinate system. In this system Eq. 1 are rewritung in the following form:

$$\begin{aligned} \varrho \frac{\partial u_r}{\partial t} &= \frac{\partial \sigma_{rr}}{\partial r} + \frac{1}{r}\frac{\partial \sigma_{r\theta}}{\partial \theta} + \frac{\partial \sigma_{rz}}{\partial z} + \frac{1}{r}\sigma_{rr} - \frac{1}{r}\sigma_{\theta\theta} \\ \varrho \frac{\partial u_\theta}{\partial t} &= \frac{\partial \sigma_{r\theta}}{\partial r} + \frac{1}{r}\frac{\partial \sigma_{\theta\theta}}{\partial \theta} + \frac{\partial \sigma_{\theta z}}{\partial z} + \frac{2}{r}\sigma_{r\theta} \\ \varrho \frac{\partial u_z}{\partial t} &= \frac{\partial \sigma_{rz}}{\partial r} + \frac{1}{r}\frac{\partial \sigma_{\theta z}}{\partial \theta} + \frac{\partial \sigma_{zz}}{\partial z} + \frac{1}{r}\sigma_{rz} \end{aligned} \tag{2}$$

$$\frac{\partial}{\partial t}\begin{pmatrix}\sigma_{rr}\\ \sigma_{\theta\theta}\\ \sigma_{zz}\\ \sigma_{\theta z}\\ \sigma_{rz}\\ \sigma_{r\theta}\end{pmatrix} = C_{ij}\begin{pmatrix}\frac{\partial u_r}{\partial r}\\ \frac{1}{r}u_r + \frac{1}{r}\frac{\partial u_\theta}{\partial \theta}\\ \frac{\partial u_z}{\partial z}\\ \frac{\partial u_\theta}{\partial z} + \frac{1}{r}\frac{\partial u_z}{\partial \theta}\\ \frac{\partial u_z}{\partial r} + \frac{\partial u_r}{\partial z}\\ \frac{\partial u_\theta}{\partial r} - \frac{1}{r}u_\theta + \frac{1}{r}\frac{\partial u_r}{\partial \theta}\end{pmatrix} + \boldsymbol{f(t)}\delta\left(r - r_0, \theta - \theta_0,\right) \quad (3)$$

2.1 Finite-Difference Approximation

The stiffness tensor for TTI medium has no peculiarities and, in general, all the entries are nontrivial. This leads to necessity of storing all the components of the stress tensor at the same spatial points, i.e. the stresses are coupled. To be honest, one still can use standard staggered grids finite-difference schemes for TTI and interpolate the variables to the points where they are needed but, as it was shown in [5], it cause rather strong dispersion and makes the approach inaccurate. In order to avoid these troubles we choose the Lebedev scheme ([2]). Let us introduce a grid and define two sets of indices:

$$\Omega_\sigma = \{(IJK) : I + J + K \in N\}\,;\; \Omega_u = \{(IJK)|I + J + K \in N\}\,.$$

The points belonging the first set have integer sum of indexes. There are two possibilities: all of them are integer or one is integer and the other two are fractional. The other set is composed of nodes with fractional sum of spatial indexes (all three are fractional or only one is fractional and the other two are integer). The example of the grid is presented in Fig. 1. Defining all the stresses at points (r_I, θ_J, z_K) so that $(IJK) \in \Omega_\sigma$ and all the velocities at the points (r_I, θ_J, z_K) so that $(IJK) \in \Omega_u$ one can write down Lebedev type

Due to special structure of the stiffness tensor for VTI/TTI medium the particular geometry of the grid, see Fig. 1, allows one to deal with the central differences to approximate derivatives. So, the components of the stress tensor can be spread in space. The stiffness tensor for TTI medium does not have any peculiarities and, in general, all the entries are nontrivial. This fact leads to necessity to store all the components of the stress tensor at the same spatial points. One still can use Virieux type grid for TTI and interpolate the variables to the points where they are needed but, as it was shown in [5], it cause rather strong dispersion and decrease accuracy essential. Therefore to perform numerical simulation of the system (2–3) we apply a finite-difference scheme on the base of Lebedev's grids (see Fig. 1). Defining all the stresses at points (r_I, θ_J, z_K) so that $(IJK) \in \Omega_\sigma$ and all the velocities at the points (r_I, θ_J, z_K) so that $(IJK) \in \Omega_u$ one can write down Lebedev type fds for TTI as the following:

$$
\begin{aligned}
\varrho D_t \left[u_r\right]_{IJK}^{n+1/2} &= D_r \left[\sigma_{rr}\right]_{IJK}^{n+1/2} + D_\theta \left[\sigma_{r\theta}\right]_{IJK}^{n+1/2} + D_z \left[\sigma_{rz}\right]_{IJK}^{n+1/2} + \\
&+ \qquad I_r \left[\sigma_{rr} - \sigma_{\theta\theta}\right]_{IJK}^{n+1/2}, \qquad (IJK) \in \Omega_u \\
\varrho D_t \left[u_\theta\right]_{IJK}^{n+1/2} &= D_r \left[\sigma_{r\theta}\right]_{IJK}^{n+1/2} + D_\theta \left[\sigma_{\theta\theta}\right]_{IJK}^{n+1/2} + D_z \left[\sigma_{\theta z}\right]_{IJK}^{n+1/2} + \\
&+ \qquad 2I_r \left[\sigma_{r\theta}\right]_{IJK}^{n+1/2}, \qquad (IJK) \in \Omega_u \\
\varrho D_t \left[u_z\right]_{IJK}^{n+1/2} &= D_r \left[\sigma_{rz}\right]_{IJK}^{n+1/2} + D_\theta \left[\sigma_{\theta z}\right]_{IJK}^{n+1/2} + D_z \left[\sigma_{zz}\right]_{IJK}^{n+1/2} + \\
&+ \qquad I_r \left[\sigma_{rz}\right]_{IJK}^{n+1/2}, \qquad (IJK) \in \Omega_u
\end{aligned}
\tag{4}
$$

$$
\begin{pmatrix}
D_t \left[\sigma_{rr}\right]_{IJK}^n \\
D_t \left[\sigma_{\theta\theta}\right]_{IJK}^n \\
D_t \left[\sigma_{zz}\right]_{IJK}^n \\
D_t \left[\sigma_{\theta z}\right]_{IJK}^n \\
D_t \left[\sigma_{rz}\right]_{IJK}^n \\
D_t \left[\sigma_{r\theta}\right]_{IJK}^n
\end{pmatrix}
= C
\begin{pmatrix}
D_r \left[u_r\right]_{IJK}^n \\
D_\theta \left[u_\theta\right]_{IJK}^n + I_r \left[u_r\right]_{IJK}^n \\
D_z \left[u_z\right]_{IJK}^n \\
D_\theta \left[u_z\right]_{IJK}^n + D_z \left[u_\theta\right]_{IJK}^n \\
D_r \left[u_z\right]_{IJK}^n + D_z \left[u_r\right]_{IJK}^n \\
D_r \left[u_\theta\right]_{IJK}^n + D_\theta \left[u_r\right]_{IJK}^n - I_r \left[u_\theta\right]_{IJK}^n
\end{pmatrix}
\tag{5}
$$

By standard considerations one can prove that this finite-difference scheme is conditionally stable and provides a second-order approximation of elastic wave equation for anisotropic media. Detailed analysis of the scheme one can find in [7], so we will not present it here. The principal features of the scheme to be discussed here are approximation at the axis $r = 0$ and proper introduction of sources.

2.2 Approximation on the Axis $r = 0$

Elastic wave equations in cylindrical coordinates possess mathematical singularity over line r = 0 and to compute a solution over this line one should use some additional conditions. Let us remind that it is mathematical singularity only, physical processes are regular and have no singularities there. We will not formulate these conditions for initial differential statement, instead let us introduce them directly for finite-difference scheme.

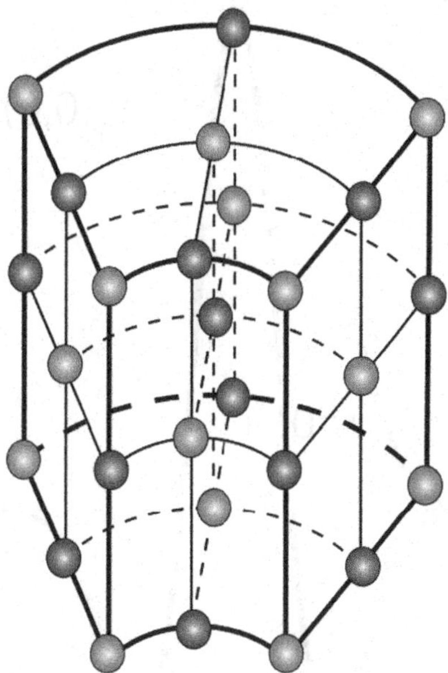

Fig. 1. The grid cell for the Lebedev type scheme. All the stresses are defined at blue circles and all the velocities are stored at red ones. (Color figure online)

Let us remind that the Lebedev grid used does not possess any knot at zero. They begin at the distance of $r = \dfrac{hr}{2}$. That means that we do not use $i = 0$ in the finite difference schemes (4–5). If we need to know functions defined at the origin $r = 0$ we use instead its interpolation computed by the following six points:

$$(3h_r, \theta, z)\,;\ (2h_r, \theta, z)\,;\ (h_r, \theta, z)\,; (h_r, \theta + \pi, z)\,;\ (2h_r, \theta + \pi, z)\,;\ (3h_r, \theta + \pi, z)\,.$$

Let us remind now that u_r, u_θ and u_z are the components of the velocity vector, that is its with coordinate vector. Singularity at r = 0 is not physical, but only the mathematical one, so vector $\boldsymbol{u}$ is be continuous there. But basis vectors $\boldsymbol{e}_r$ and $\boldsymbol{e}_\theta$ change their direction to the opposite when moving through r = 0 along the line with fixed azimuth. That follows abrupt change of component along the line of constant azimuth (see Fig. 2):

$$\lim_{\theta, r \to 0} u_r(r, \theta, z; t) = - \lim_{\theta + \pi, r \to 0} u_r(r, \theta + \pi, z; t) \tag{6}$$

The same relations take place for u_θ, $\sigma_{\theta z}$ and σ_{rz}. In order to have proper interpolation one should take this into account.

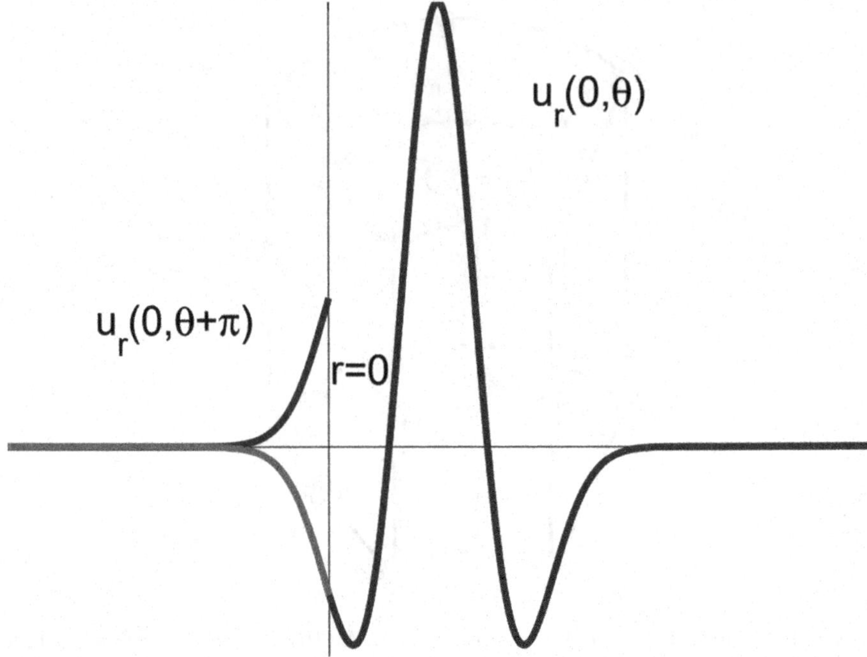

Fig. 2. Approximation of u_r at the origin

Interpolation itself is done with the help of Neville algorithm [8]. This algorithm directly computes the value of the interpolating polynomial at the target point, not the values of its coefficients. Let us briefly describe this technique. If there are $n+1$ observation points (x_i, y_i) with different x_i, the interpolating polynomial p has degree at most n and possesses the following properties:

$$p(x_i) = y_i, \quad i = 0, \cdots, n$$

Let polynomial $p_{i,j}$ has the degree $j-i$, coincides with the points (x_k, y_k) for $k = i, i+1, \cdots, j$ and satisfies the following recurrence relation

$$\begin{aligned} p_{ii}(x) &= y_i, & 0 \le i \le n \\ p_{ij}(x) &= \frac{(x-x_i)p_{i+1,j}(x) - (x-x_j)p_{i,j-1}(x)}{x-x_i}, & 0 \le i < j \le n \end{aligned} \tag{7}$$

Following this recurrence one can calculate the desired value $p_{0,n}(x)$. This is Neville's algorithm. It has the very clear representation as the following step-by-step representation:

$$
\begin{array}{llllll}
x_0 : p_0(x) & & & & & \\
 & p_{01}(x) & & & & \\
x_1 : p_1(x) & & p_{02}(x) & & & \\
 & p_{12}(x) & & p_{03}(x) & & \\
x_2 : p_2(x) & & p_{13}(x) & & p_{04}(x) & \\
 & p_{23}(x) & & p_{14}(x) & & p_{05}(x) \\
x_3 : p_3(x) & & p_{24}(x) & & p_{15}(x) & \\
 & p_{34}(x) & & p_{25}(x) & & \\
x_4 : p_4(x) & & p_{35}(x) & & & \\
 & p_{45}(x) & & & & \\
x_5 : p_5(x) & & & & &
\end{array}
$$

3 Numerical Experiments

3.1 Presentation of the Well Bore Model

We used the HTI medium with following Thomsen parameters (see [9]):

$$V_p = 2500\,\mathrm{m/s},\ V_s = 1440\,\mathrm{m/s},\ \varrho = 2000\,\mathrm{kg}/m^3,\ \varepsilon = 0.3,\ \gamma = -0.7,\ \delta = 0. \quad (8)$$

We suppose that the surrounding medium is HTI with the axis of symmetry of the model in the plane z = const and is directed along $\theta = \pi/6$. Indicatrices of the group velocities of waves for this model one can see in Fig. 3, where blue curve corresponds to qP wave, black and red are for two qS ones. On Fig. 4 one can see a snapshot of the amplitude of the wave field excited in the medium by a source of volumetric expansion. Note that the amplitude distribution in the z=0 plane coincides quite accurately with the indicatrix of the quasi-longitudinal velocity.

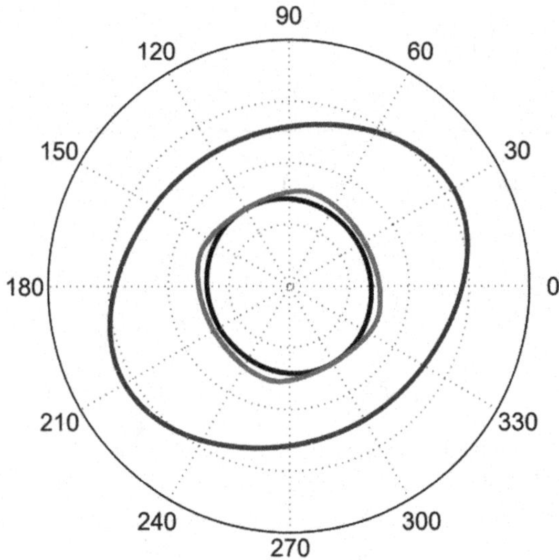

Fig. 3. Indicatrices of the group waves for the HTI model.

3.2 Approximation at R=0

To analyze a level of reflections produced by the use of interpolation at $r = 0\,\text{m}$, we did the following numerical experiment. We used not axially symmetric statement with the volumetric source point at the point $r = 0.3\,\text{m}, \theta = 0, z = 0\,\text{m}$ and placed two receivers are at points $r = 0.15\,\text{m}, \theta = 0$

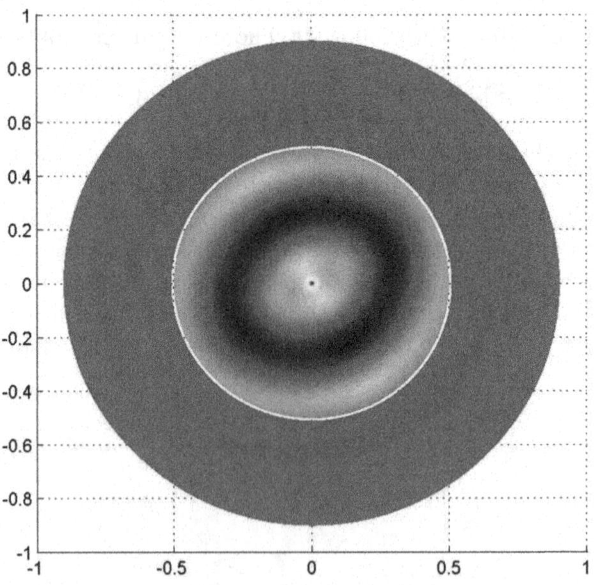

Fig. 4. Wavefield amplitude snapshot.

and $r = 0.45\,\text{m}$, $\theta = 0$ (symmetrically with respect to the source). Here and later we will call them left receiver and right receiver correspondingly. The target area is cylinder of 1m radius filled with "fluid" with velocity equals to $2400\,\text{m/s}$[1]. We used the following spatial discretization: $h_r = h_z = 0.01\,\text{m}$, $h_\theta = \pi/64$. In order to eliminate the influence of the errors associated with the use of azimuth refinement, we turned it off in these calculations. Since the receivers are at the same distance from the source, the wave which it excites reaches both of them simultaneously. So we provide only one trace, written at the left receiver (see Fig. 5). Upscaled traces for left and right receivers one can see in Fig. 6. The scale factor is 100:1. One can clearly observe two reflections on each trace. The first one corresponds to the points r = 0 and approached the left receiver faster then the right one (as expected). The second arrival is caused by use of PML which will be discussed in details later. The amplitude of both artifacts does not exceed 0.1% of the emitted wave amplitude which is acceptable for practical use.

4 Brief Description of the Code

When conducting acoustic logging, people use pulses with a predominant frequency of up to several kilohertz, that is, the characteristic length of acoustic

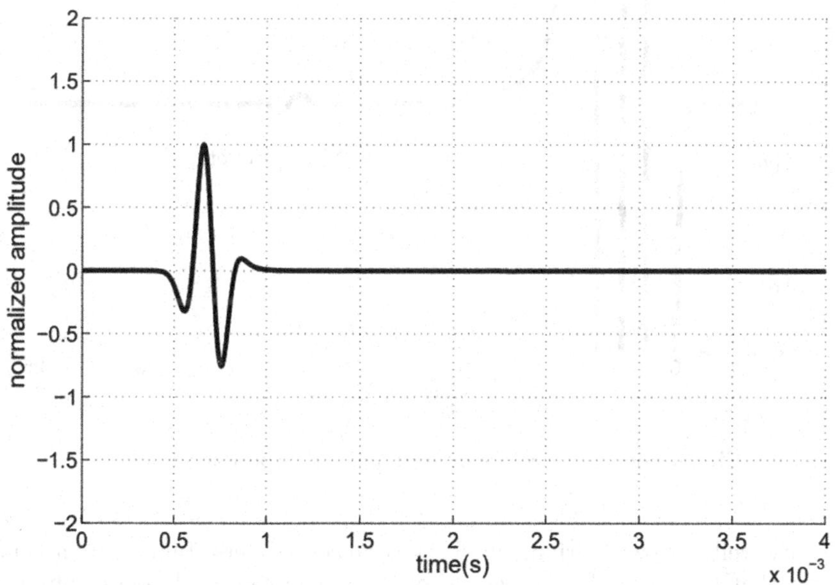

Fig. 5. Seismic trace at the left receiver

[1] We specially chose such acoustic medium to focus attention on the analysis of artifacts associated with approximation at $r = 0$.

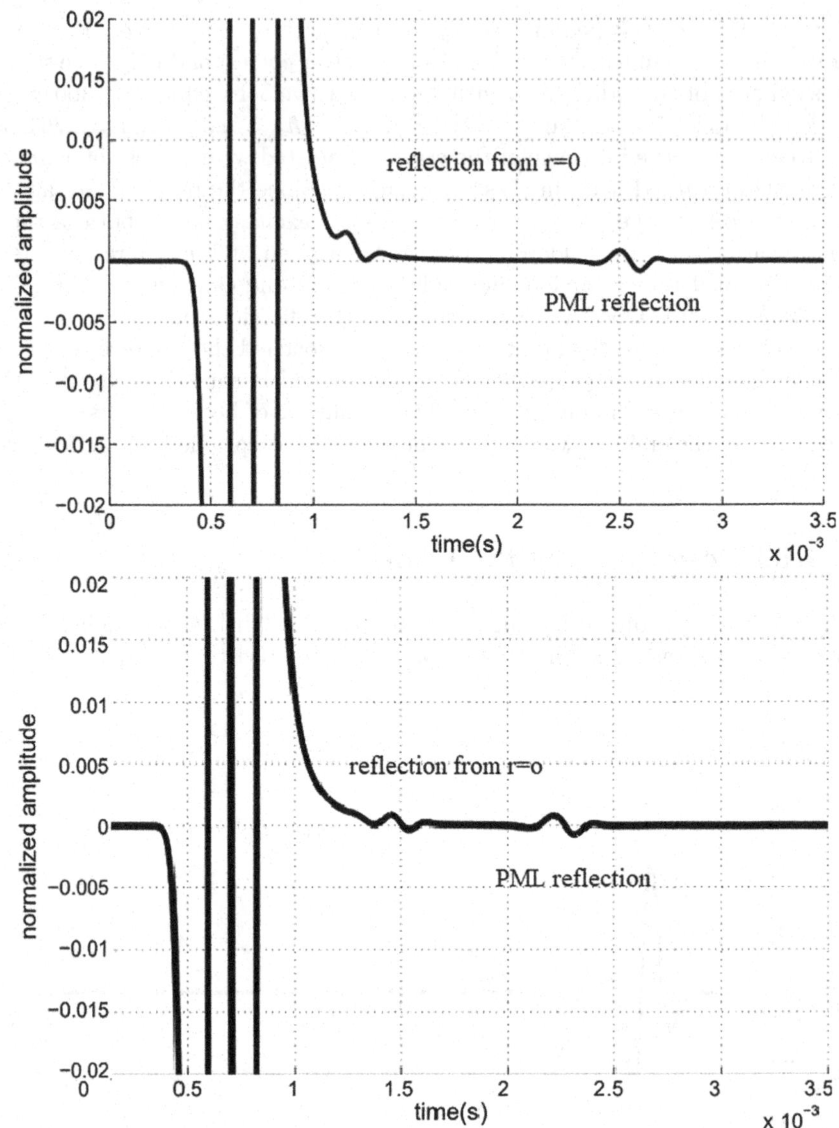

Fig. 6. Zoomed view of left (top) and right (bottom) traces.

waves in a well filled with drilling fluid is several centimeters. Taking into account the fact that to ensure the correctness of the numerical simulation results it is necessary to use grids with a step of approximately 0.1 from the dominant wavelength, we come to the use of millimeter steps in space. Considering that the dimensions of the computational area are several meters radially and several hundred meters vertically, through simple calculations we obtain an estimate of the required memory of several hundred gigabytes. Thus, full-scale numerical simulation of sonic logging for realistic 3D heterogeneous models requires the use of high-performance computing systems with parallel architecture (Fig. 7).

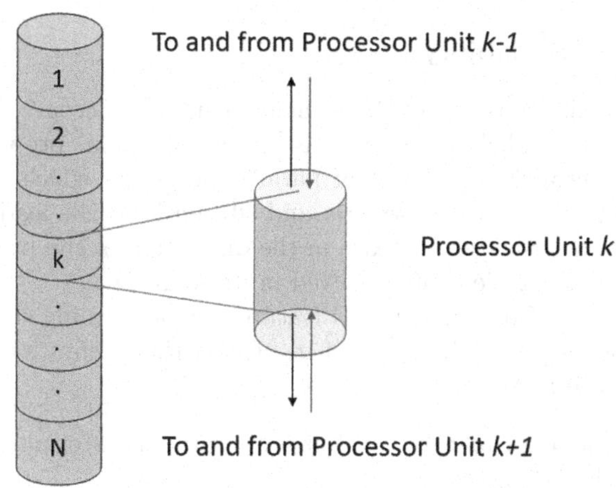

Fig. 7. Domain decomposition used for sonic log parallel simulation.

When organizing computations with distributed memory based on explicit finite-difference schemes involving decomposition of the computational domain, it is necessary to organize step-by-step transfer of data received by each of the processor elements. In the domain decomposition geometry used, implementation of such data exchange between the surfaces of the disks formed by the planes $z_k = kh_z$ and $z_{k-1} = (k-1)hz$, $z_{k+1} = (k+1)hz$, and assigned, respectively, to processor elements $k-1$ k $k+1$ is organized via MPI (Message Passing Interface).

It is worth mentioning that such transfers not only slows down the process of computations, but needs some additional resources, as it inevitably leads to waiting for its completion. In order to reduce the irrational use of computing resources, we use two approaches:

- Non-blocking commands iSend/iRecieve to exchange data;
- In each elementary computational subdomain, constructed using the decomposition of the computational domain into adjacent elementary disks, we start in the point furthest from the boundaries of the domain. This ensures that the transfer from the previous step is completed by the time the need for the next transfer arises.

4.1 Hardware Used

The developed software was debugged and tested on a high-performance computing system with parallel architecture HKC-1P at the Siberian Supercomputer Center with a peak performance of 182 TFlops and an Intel Omni-Path interconnect of 100 Gigabits per second (http://www.sscc.ru/hardware.html). To perform the numerical experiments described in the paper we used Broadwell computing nodes (CPU (2x) Intel Xeon E5-2697A v4, 2.6 GHz). The Intel Luster 200 TB parallel system was used for big data I/O.

4.2 Scalability

Scalability is one of the principal generally accepted quality criteria for a developed parallel software. It is one of the main properties of parallel programs, reflecting the features of parallel programs which refers to its ability to continue to function correctly and efficiently as the load increases. In our case, this means either an increase in the dimension of the problem, or an increase in the processing elements involved in its solution.

The most widely used features for performing such an assessment are strong and weak scalabilities. Let us present their definitions that are most widely used at the present.

- Strong scalability (SS) or acceleration is determined by the formula (Amdahl's law [1,4]):

$$SS = \frac{1}{p + \frac{1-p}{N}}$$

  Here the value p specifies the time spent by the part of the code oriented on single-processor calculations. In particular, these may be some preparatory and/or final procedures applied to all data. Then $1 - p$ determines the percentage of computation time for the parallel part of the program, and N is the number of processors.
- Weak scalability (WS) shows how the total execution time of a task changes with an increase in the number of processor elements involved in simulation with a constant load on each of them.

In order to evaluate the quality of the developed parallel software, we carried out a special series of computations for the model described in Sect. 3.1. Their main purpose was to determine quantitative parameters characterizing strong and weak scalability. To obtain the estimates we are interested in, we used up to 128 cores of the HKC-1P multiprocessor computing system. The corresponding results can be seen in Fig. 8. As one can see, the acceleration with an increase in the number of processor elements differs slightly from linear growth with a coefficient equal to one. In our opinion, this is due to the inevitable increase in overhead costs associated with data transfer when using MPI.

When studying weak scalability, its noticeable deterioration is observed at the initial values of increasing the number of processor elements. However, when more than 16 processor elements are used, it stabilizes and remains at the level of 95%.

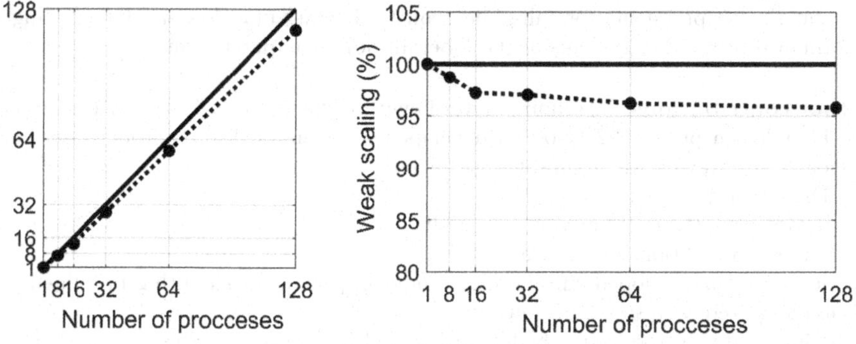

Fig. 8. Strong (left) and weak (right) scalabilities of the software developed. Solid lines ideal scalabilities, dashed lines the measured ones.

5 Conclusion

To study the processes of excitation and propagation of seismoacoustic wave fields in transversely isotropic media with a tilted symmetry axis (TTI - Tilted Transverse Isotropy), we constructed a finite-difference scheme based on Lebedev grids in a cylindrical coordinate system. The vertical axis of this coordinate system is directed along the wellbore, which provides the most accurate description of the highest contrasting boundary of the problem under consideration - the interface between the well and the surrounding elastic medium. To increase the approximation accuracy of the problem we apply adaptive meshes with azimuthal and radial step refinement. We organized parallel computations on the base of the Domain Decomposition of the target area, which was selected in the form of a cylinder with a generatrix directed along the wellbore. In this case, each of the processing elements is assigned a disk enclosed between two horizontal planes at a distance h_z from each other. Data exchanges between processing elements are organized using non-blocking iSend/iRecieve data transfer procedures. This allows us to minimize the waiting time, but requires synchronization of computations which is implemented by starting in the point furthest from the data exchange line. Thanks to this, we both strong and weak scalability at the level of 85%.

We see further development of this product in the use for more realistic models of hydrocarbon reservoirs, primarily taking into account their porosity and fluid saturation.

Acknowledgment. The study of Vladimir Cheverda and Victor Kostin are supported by Russian Science Foundation project 22-11-00104, Vadim Lisitsa was supported by Russian Science Foundation project 22-11-00004.

Galina Reshetova used the approach she developed in the framework of the RSF project 22-21-00759 to the organization of parallel computation by applying coarray fortran.

Numerical experiments for full-scale acoustic logging models were done on high-performance computing systems of the Siberian Supercomputer Center.

Author contributions. Vladimir Cheverda within the framework of the Russian Science Foundation project 22-11-00104 developed mathematical formulation describing seismoacoustic wave fields in anisotropic media:

PDE system;

MPML formulation for anisotropic media;

Boundary conditions at the axis $r = 0$.

Victor Kostin developed numerical technique of periodical azimuth grid refinement and implemented corresponding software.

Vadim Lisitsa introduced Lebedev grid for cylindrical coordinates.

Galina Reshetova implemented parallel software for numerical simulation of 3D sonic log in cylindrical coordinates and was supported by the Russian Science Foundation project 20-11-20112.

References

1. Amdahl, G.M.: AFIPS Conf. Proc. **30**, 483–485 (1967)
2. Asvadurov, S., Druskin, V., Moskow, S.: Optimal grids for anisotropic problems. Electron. Trans. Numer. Anal. **26**, 55–81 (2007)
3. Biot, M.A.: Propagation of elastic waves in a cylindrical bore containing a fluid. J. Appl. Phys. **23**(9), 997–1005 (1952)
4. Duboc, L., Rosenblum, D., Wicks, T.: A framework for modelling and analysis of software systems scalability. In: Proceedings of the 28th International Conference on Software Engineering. ICSE'06, pp. 945–948 (2006)
5. Igel, H., Mora, P., Riollet, B.: Anisotropic wave propagation through finite-difference grids. Geophysics **60**, 1203–1216 (1995)
6. Krauklis, P.V., Krauklis, L.A.: Tube waves in a well filled with a solid-fluid mixture. J. Math. Sci. **127**, 2424–2428 (2005)
7. Lisitsa, V., Vishnevsky, D.: Lebedev scheme for the numerical simulation of wave propagationin 3D anisotropic elasticity. Geophys. Prospect. **58**, 619–635 (2010)
8. Lyness, J.N., Moler, C.B.: Van der monde systems and numerical differentiation. Numer. Math. **8**, 458–464 (1966)
9. Thomsen, L.: Weak elastic anisotropy. Geophysics **51**, 1954–1966 (1986)

Quantum-Chemical Study of Some Tris(pyrrolo)benzenes and Tris(pyrrolo)-1,3,5-triazines

Vadim Volokhov[1], Elena Amosova[1(✉)], Vladimir Parakhin[1,2], David Lempert[1], and Ivan Akostelov[1,3]

[1] Federal Research Center of Problems of Chemical Physics and Medicinal Chemistry, Chernogolovka, Russian Federation
{vvm,aes,lempert}@icp.ac.ru

[2] N.D. Zelinsky Institute of Organic Chemistry, Moscow, Russian Federation
parakhin@ioc.ac.ru

[3] M.V. Lomonosov Moscow State University, Moscow, Russian Federation

Abstract. High-energy density materials are widely used in various application areas, which makes the creation of new materials and study of their properties an important task. The paper addresses to the study of properties of a number of promising high-energy tetracyclic compounds annelated with pyrrole nitro derivatives, by quantum-chemical methods within the Gaussian 09 software package. Optimized structures, enthalpies of formation, and IR absorption spectra have been calculated for existing and not yet synthesized compounds. Dependence of the enthalpy of formation on the structural parameters of the compounds has been analyzed. The energy potential of the studied compounds has been initially assessed.

Keywords: Quantum chemical calculations · High energy density materials · Tris(azolo)benzenes · Tris(azolo)azines · Enthalpy of formation

1 Introduction

Energy-intensive compounds form an important class of materials with a large amount of stored chemical energy that can be released in explosive transformation processes. Such materials serve as components of energy compositions that are widely used in civil engineering, including mining, processing, manufacturing and construction industries, pyrotechnics, but especially in rocket technology and aerospace technology [1–5]. Different purposes and tasks demand high-energy materials with different characteristics. For this reason, the creation and study of the properties of new high-energy density materials (HEDMs) is of great interest to specialists in the field of chemistry and materials science [6–12].

Over the past three decades in the world of science there has been a rapid increase in the number of scientific papers on the study of new HEDMs based

V. Voevodin et al. (Eds.): RuSCDays 2023, LNCS 14388, pp. 177–189, 2023.
https://doi.org/10.1007/978-3-031-49432-1_14

on nitrogenous heterocyclic compounds functionalized by oxidizing fragments (primarily nitro groups) and having a high enthalpy of formation ($\Delta H^0{}_f$) ($\geq$2 MJ/kg) [10,13–20].

Among energy-intensive heterocyclic compounds, it is fused polycyclic structures [21] that have recently been attracting special attention of scientists in the field of HEDMs. The most noticeable representatives of this class include still little-studied polynitrogen fused tetracyclic systems, which are a combination of three azole rings annelated with a benzene or azine ring.

The first representatives of tetracycles of the considered series to have been successfully synthesized are benzo[1,2-c:3,4-c′:5,6-c″]tris[1,2,5]oxadiazolyl-1,4,7-trioxide (**Ia**) (benzotrifuroxan, BTF) [22–26] and benzo[1,2-c:3,4-c′:5,6-c″]tris[1,2, 5]oxadiazole (**Ib**) (benzotrifurazan) [27–29] (Fig. 1). It should be noted that BTF turned out to be heat-resistant ($T_{dec.}$ > 250°C) and high-density (d = 1.901 g/cm^3) material, which has a very high enthalpy of formation ($\Delta H^0{}_f$ = 2.5 MJ/kg), which showed that tetracycles are promising.

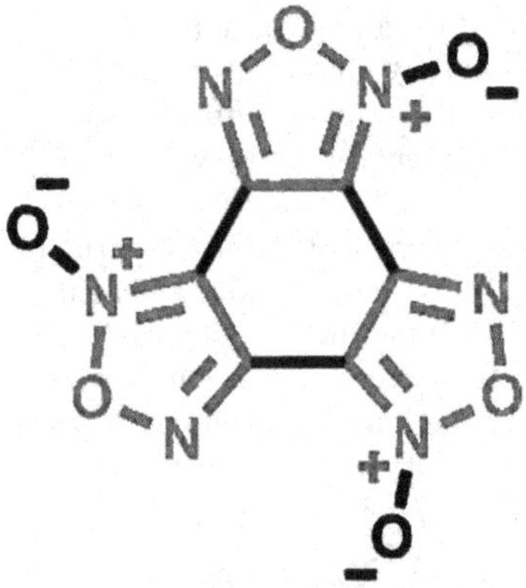

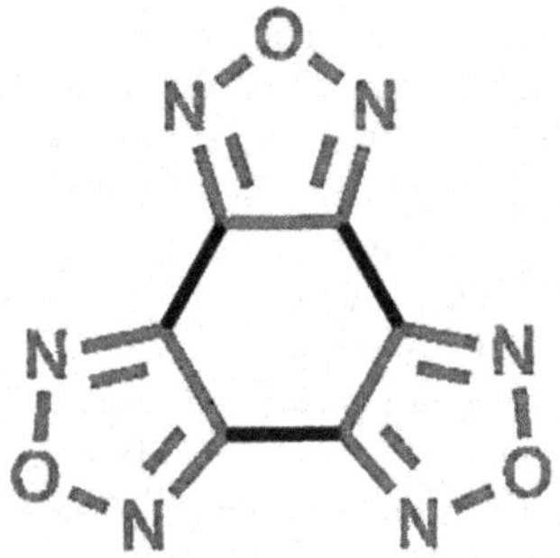

Fig. 1. The first tetracycle representatives to have been synthesized: benzotrifuroxan **Ia** and benzotrifurazan **Ib**.

Nevertheless, approaches to the synthesis of other derivatives of this type have been developed relatively recently, and a number of practically studied tetracycles is still extremely limited [30–36] due to the complexity and laboriousness of their preparation. At the same time, computer molecular design has been widely used to search for new HEDMs in the last decade. This approach allows relatively fast characterization of new structures, selection of target molecules with desired properties, or elimination of useless compounds through theoretical calculations before laboratory experiments. For example, several works on calculations of some physicochemical and energy parameters of tetracyclic compounds had been published earlier [37–39], but these studies seem to be random and fragmentary. Our approach is a systematic study of the energy potential of a wide series of tetracycles in order to identify the most promising representatives of this class. It seemed logical to start the study with tripyrrolo[1,3,5]triazines **II** and **III**, which contain the simplest nitrogenous heterocycle, i.e. pyrrole. In general, the selected objects of study consist of three pyrrole rings annelated with a central benzene or 1,3,5-triazine ring, around which the structure is built. For the primary assessment of the effect of substituents, we selected unsubstituted tetracycles **II** and their fully nitrated derivatives **III** for calculations (Fig. 2). In order to make a comparative analysis of the calculation methods and the energy level of the selected structures, we also calculated the enthalpy of formation for the already mentioned well-known tetracycles, i.e. benzotrifuroxan **Ia** and benzotrifurazan **Ib**.

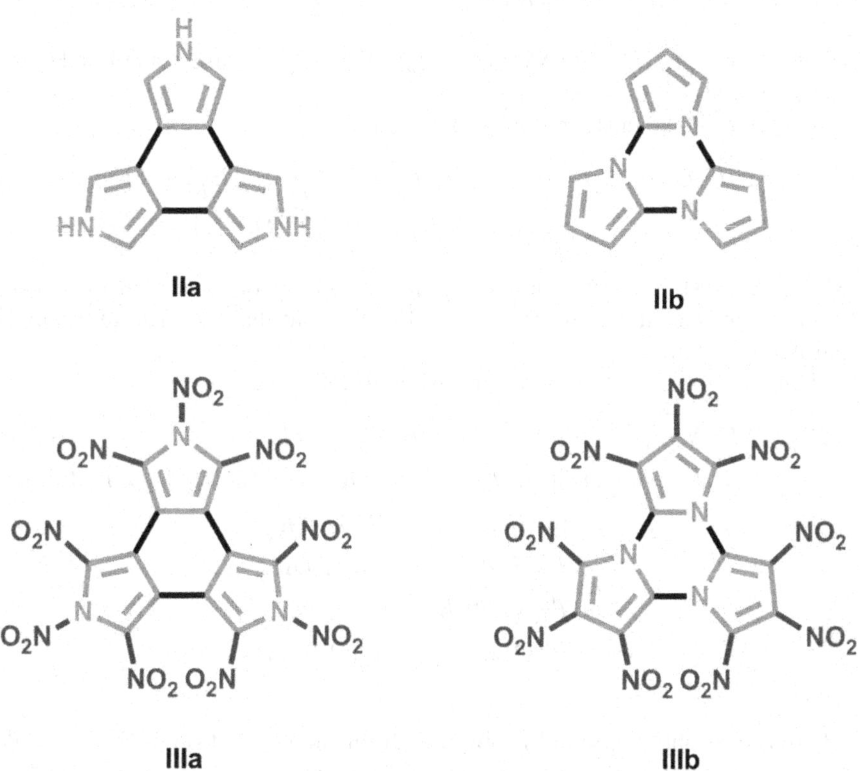

Fig. 2. A series of considered tetracyclic HEDMs **IIa,b** and **IIIa,b**.

Thus, the aim of the present work was the initial assessment of the energy capabilities of these structures by quantum-chemical calculation of their key energy parameter, the enthalpy of formation in the gas phase at a temperature of 298 K and pressure $p = 1atm$ ($\Delta H^{298}_{f(g)}$), as well as the analysis of the efficiency of calculation methods. The optimized geometry, enthalpy of formation, and IR absorption spectra of the compounds under study have been calculated by quantum-chemical methods. The influence of the structure of the compounds on their enthalpy has been analyzed.

2 Calculation Method

The enthalpy of formation of the studied substances has been calculated using the method based on the atomization reaction for the $C_wH_xN_yO_z$ molecule, which consisted of the following steps:

1. Calculation of the atomization energy

$$\sum D_0 = wE_0(C) + xE_0(H) + yE_0(N) + zE_0(O) - E_0(C_wH_xN_yO_z), \quad (1)$$

where $E_0(C), E_0(H), E_0(N), E_0(O), E_0(C_wH_xN_yO_z)$ are calculated total energies of atoms and molecule.

2. Calculation of the enthalpy of formation at $0K$

$$\begin{aligned} \Delta H_f^\circ(C_wH_xN_yO_z{,}0\,K) = w\Delta H_f^\circ(C,0\,K) + x\Delta H_f^\circ(H,0\,K) + \\ y\Delta H_f^\circ(N,0\,K) + z\Delta H_f^\circ(O,0\,K) - \sum D_0, \end{aligned} \quad (2)$$

where the first four summands are the enthalpies of formation of gaseous atomic components from the NIST-JANAF database of thermochemical parameters [40];.

3. Calculation of the enthalpy of formation at 298.15 K

$$\begin{aligned} \Delta H_f^\circ(C_wH_xN_yO_z{,}298\,K) = {} & \Delta H_f^\circ(C_wH_xN_yO_z,0\,K) + \\ & + (H^0(C_wH_xN_yO_z,298\,K) - H^0(C_wH_xN_yO_zF_p,0\,K)) - \\ & - w(H^0(C,298\,K) - H^0(C,0\,K)) - \\ & - x(H^0(H,298\,K) - H^0(h,0\,K)) - \\ & - y(H^0(N,298\,K) - H^0(N,0\,K)) - \\ & - z(H^0(O,298\,K) - H^0(O,0\,K)), \end{aligned} \quad (3)$$

where the second summand is obtained from the calculation of the molecule, the third to sixth summands are known from experiment (or calculated from experimental molecular constants).

The Gaussian 09 quantum chemical package [41] has been used for calculations. The geometry of the studied molecules has been obtained by fully optimizing all geometric parameters using the B3LYP hybrid density functional [42,43] with the 6-311+G(2d,p) basis set. The stability of the resulting configurations is confirmed by calculating the frequencies by the analytical method without taking into account the anharmonicity correction (absence of imaginary frequencies).

The enthalpy of formation of the structures under study has been also calculated using the composite G4MP2 method [44,45] for molecules consisting of 15–24 atoms (the geometry obtained previously has been used as a starting point for these calculations).

3 Results and Discussion

3.1 Enthalpy of Formation

Optimized geometries of the molecules under study are shown in Fig. 3, and the $\Delta H^{298}_{f(g)}$ calculation results are presented in Table 1.

Table 1. Results of the calculation of the enthalpy of formation of the studied tetracycles **Ia,b**, **IIa,b** and **IIIa,b**.

	Formula, (molecular mass [g/mol])	$\Delta H^{298}_{f(g)}$ [kJ/mol (kJ/kg)]			
		Literature data		Our calculation results	
		Experiment data[a]	Calculation data[b]	Calculation method	
				B3LYP/6-311+G(2d,p)	G4MP2
Ia	$C_6N_6O_6$ (251.988)	752.7±4.6 **(2987.0 ± 18.3)**	697.2 ± 7 **(2766.8 ± 27.8)**	790.64 **(3137.63)**	727.48 **(2885.65)**
Ib	$C_6N_6O_3$ (204.003)	733.9 ± 4.5 **(3597.5 ± 22.1)**	701.5 ± 6 **(3438.7 ± 29.4)**	802.54 **(3933.95)**	715.68 **(3506.44)**
IIa	$C_{12}H_9N_3$ (195.080)	–	–	531.78 **(2725.95)**	362.53 **(1856.98)**
IIb	$C_{12}H_9N_3$ (195.080)	–	–	615.55 **(3154.55)**	446.88 **(2289.04)**
IIIa	$C_{12}N_{12}O_{18}$ (599.945)	–	–	1157.86 **(1929.94)**	–
IIIb	$C_{12}N_{12}O_{18}$ (599.945)	–	–	1076.00 **(1793.50)**	–

[a] Results of experimental measurements (combustion calorimetry) [46]
[b] Calculation using the method of isodesmic reactions [47]

The results of our calculations show that tetracycles **Ia** and **Ib** have the highest enthalpy of formation among the studied structures, which can be explained by the fact that 1,2,5-oxadiazole in their structure is a powerful endothermic building block for the creation of HEDMs and makes a substantial contribution to the energy content of the molecule (217 kJ/mol in the case of furazan and 226 kJ/mol in the case of furoxan [48]). The values of the enthalpy of formation of tetracycles **Ia** and **Ib** obtained using the density functional theory significantly exceed both the enthalpies of formation obtained using the G4MP2

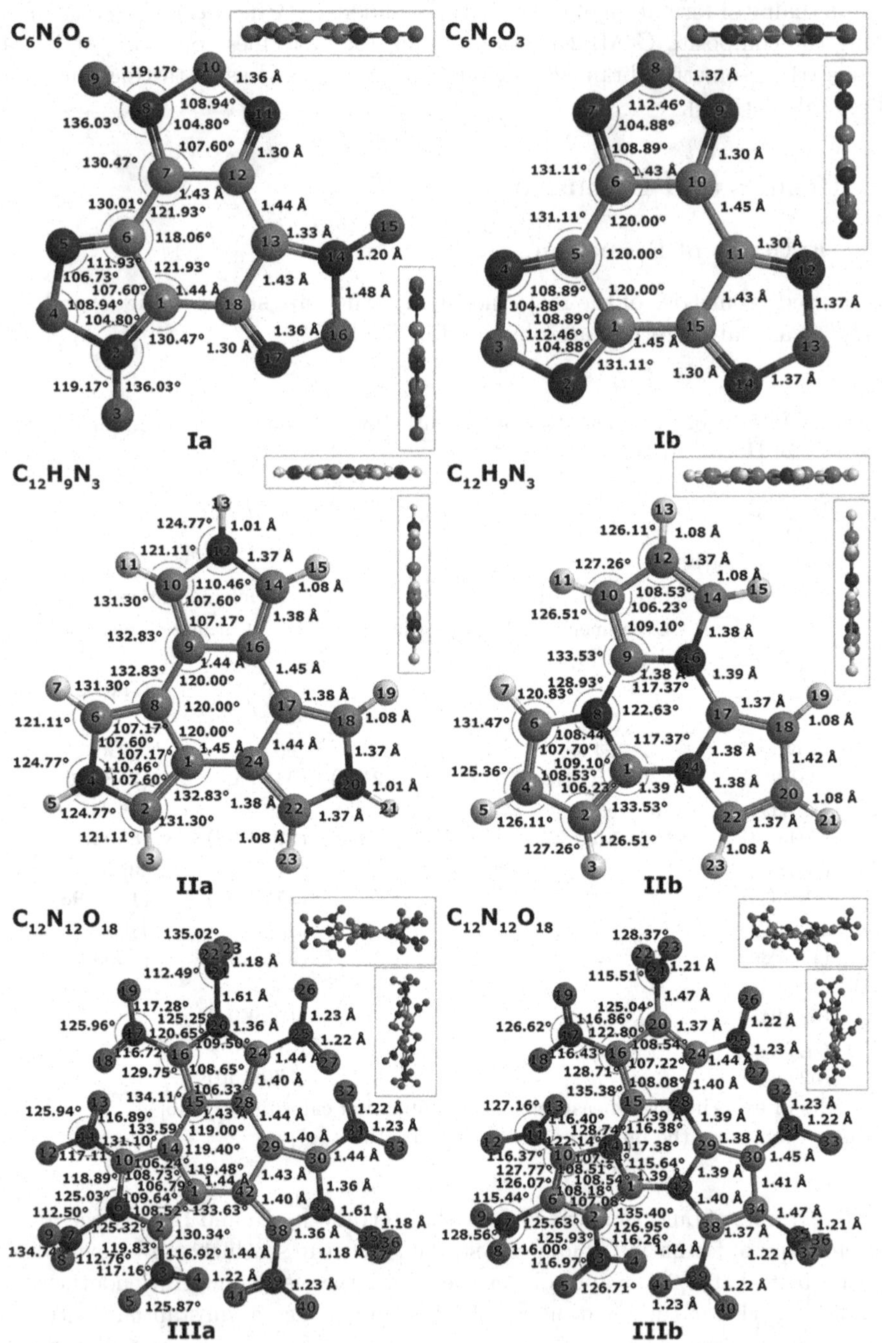

Fig. 3. Structures and geometrical parameters (in Å and °) of the studied tetracycles **Ia,b**, **IIa,b** and **IIIa,b** (at the calculation level B3LYP/6-311+G(2d,p)).

method and those given in the literature. This is due to the fact that the B3LYP hybrid functional doesn't account well enough the effects of electron correlation, which affects strongly the calculation results when using the atomization reaction to determine $\Delta H^{298}_{f(g)}$, during which the electronic structure of the system undergoes considerable transformations. The values of $\Delta H^{298}_{f(g)}$ obtained using the combined G4MP2 method are quite close to the values known from the literature, the relative deviation does not exceed 4%.

Among the unsubstituted tetracycles, the enthalpy of formation of tetracycle **IIb** based on the 1,3,5-triazine ring is 432 kJ/kg higher than that of its isomer **IIa** with a benzene ring in the center of the molecule, which is quite natural, since the compound **IIb** contains a larger number of $C-N$ bonds in its structure than its isomeric benzotricycle **IIa**.

Fully nitrated tetracycles **IIIa** and **IIIb** consist of a large number of atoms, and quantum-chemical calculations of their thermochemical properties using the composite G4MP2 method require a lot of time and resources, therefore $\Delta H^{298}_{f(g)}$ of these compounds has been calculated using only the density functional theory. Considering the difference revealed on the example of tetracycles **Ia,b** and **IIa,b** between the results of calculations using the hybrid density functional and the composite quantum chemical method, it is quite logical to assume that the values of $\Delta H^{298}_{f(g)}$ calculated by the B3LYP method, 1929.94 kJ/kg for **IIIa** structure and 1793.5 kJ/kg for **IIIb** structure, are strongly overestimated. At the same time, $\Delta H^{298}_{f(g)}$ of nitro derivatives **IIIa,b** is noticeably lower than that of unsubstituted tetracycles **IIa,b** or tris(1,2,5-oxadiazole)benzenes **Ia,b**, which is justified by a significantly higher oxygen content in compounds **IIIa,b**. It is also noteworthy that, in the case of the above mentioned nitro derivatives **IIIa,b**, it is, on the contrary, the tetracycle **IIIa** with a central benzene ring that has a higher enthalpy of formation than its isomer **IIIb** based on the 1,3,5-triazine ring. This is apparently due to the fact that the structure of the compound **IIIb** only contains $C-NO_2$ bonds, while there are three $N-NO_2$ bonds in the compound **IIIa**, which are more endothermic.

3.2 IR Absorption Spectra

Figure 4 shows the IR absorption spectra of the studied molecules calculatated at the B3LYP/6-311+G(2d,p) level.

The most intense peak in the ~1696 cm^{-1} region of the spectrum of the compound **Ia** corresponds to stretching vibrations of the $N \rightarrow O$ bond. Peaks in the region of ~908 cm^{-1} and ~1036 cm^{-1} of the **Ib** spectrum can be attributed, respectively, to the stretching and bending vibrations of the $N-O$ bonds of the azole rings. The intense peak in the region of ~409 cm^{-1} of the **IIa** spectrum is associated with bending out-of-plane vibrations, and the peak in the region of ~3676 cm^{-1} can be attributed to the stretching vibrations of the $N-H$ bonds of the pyrrole rings. An intense peak in the region of ~1676 cm^{-1} in the **IIb** spectrum corresponds to stretching vibrations of the $C-N$ bonds of the triazine ring. In the spectra of nitro derivatives **IIIa** and **IIIb**, the intense absorption

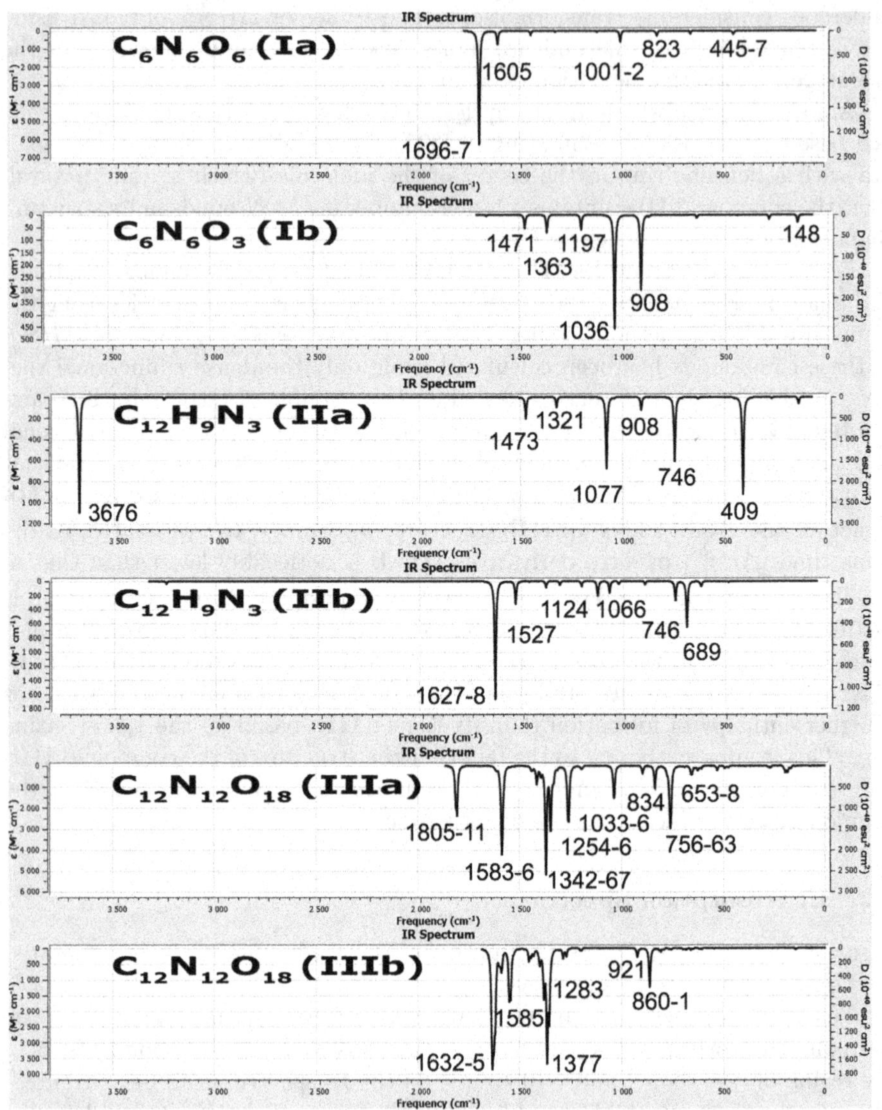

Fig. 4. IR absorption spectra of the studied tetracycles **Ia,b**, **IIa,b** and **IIIa,b**.

bands in the region of 1594–1575 cm^{-1} and 1632–1585 cm^{-1} obviously belong to asymmetric stretching vibrations of nitro groups, while the bands in the region of 1367–1342 cm^{-1} and 1398–1351 cm^{-1} — to symmetric stretching vibrations of nitro groups.

4 Computational Details

Quantum-chemical calculations were carried out using the equipment of the Center for Collective Use of Moscow State University [49,50] (project 2065 and 2312) and the computing resources of the Federal Research Center of Problems of Chemical Physics and Medicinal Chemistry of the Russian Academy of Sciences. The Gaussian software package used in the calculations employs its own Linda software for parallelizing tasks, which is not always implemented in the most efficient way. The tests carried out by the authors in the course of previous research have shown that with an extension of computing cores from 1 to 8, a noticeable increase in performance occurs, but with a further enlargement of their number, this effect subsides (Fig. 5). Therefore, for supercomputer calculations, 8 cores per task have been used.

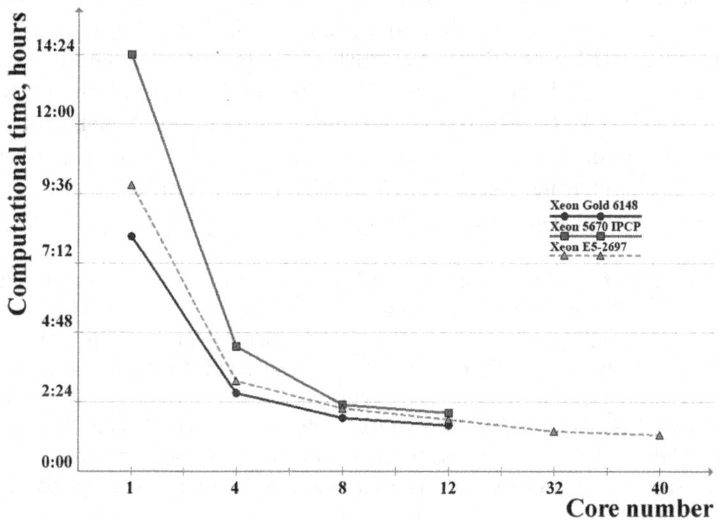

Fig. 5. Comparison of the computational time for a sample job (B3LYP/6-311+G(2d,p) optimization) in the Gaussian package on various computational configurations

Table 2 presents the calculation times for the studied molecules on the supercomputer complex. Time costs for calculation increase non-linearly with the complexity of the molecule, and for the combined G4MP2 method the computational costs become too high to use it for **IIIa,b** molecules which consist of 42 non-hydrogen atoms.

Table 2. Calculation time for the studied tetracycles **Ia,b**, **IIa,b** and **IIIa,b** (CPU*hours).

№	B3LYP/6-311+G(2d,p)	G4MP2
Ia	11	109
Ib	6	42
IIa	10	68
IIb	13	71
IIIa	506	–
IIIb	547	–

5 Conclusions

Using the B3LYP density functional theory and the combined G4MP2 method within the Gaussian 09 software package, we calculated the optimized geometry, enthalpy of formation, and IR absorption spectra of a number of tetracyclic compounds, which include both well-known tris(1,2,5-oxadiazole)benzenes and not yet synthesized tris(azolo)benzenes and tris(azolo)azines. For known substances, the results of our calculations showed a slight deviation (within 4%) from the literature data, and for new, not yet synthesized pyrrole-annelated tetracycles, the data were obtained for the first time. The dependence of the enthalpy of formation on the structure of the compounds (the number of heteroatoms, the presence of substituents and isomerism) has been established. In addition, the frequencies of the characteristic vibration bands have been assigned to the corresponding structural fragments of the compounds under study.

Acknowledgements. V.M. Volokhov and E.S. Amosova performed research in accordance with the State task, state registration No. AAAA-A19-119120690042-9. V.V. Parakhin was engaged in the formulation of a scientific problem, literature review, analysis of the results, writing and editing the article. D.B. Lempert performed work in accordance with the State task, state registration No. AAAA-A19-119101690058-9. I.I. Akostelov participated in the quantum–chemical research and the analysis of the results. Calculations on the resources of the supercomputer complex of Moscow State University were supported by the Russian Science Foundation (project No. 23-71-00005).

References

1. Mezger, M.J., Tindle, K.J., Pantoya, M., Groven, L.J., Kalyon, D.M.: Energetic materials - Advanced processing technologies for next-generation materials. CRC Press Taylor&Francis group, Boca Raton (2018)
2. Agrawal, J.P.: High Energy Materials: Propellants, Explosives And Pyrotechnics. Wiley-VCH, Weinheim (2010)
3. Patel, V.K., Katiyar, J.K., Bhattacharya, S.: Solid energetic materials-based microthrusters for space applications. In: Bhattacharya, S., Agarwal, A.K.,

Rajagopalan, T., Patel, V.K. (eds.) Nano-Energetic Materials, pp. 241–250. Springer Singapore, Singapore (2019). https://doi.org/10.1007/978-981-13-3269-2_11

4. De Luca, L.T., Shimada, T., Sinditskii, V.P., Calabro, M.: Chemical Rocket Propulsion: A Comprehensive Survey Of Energetic Materials. Springer, Switzerland (2016)
5. Singh, H., Shekhar, H.: Solid rocket propellants: science and technology challenges. Royal Society of Chemistry (2016)
6. Luo, Y., Zheng, W., Wang, X., Shen, F.: Nitrification progress of nitrogen-rich heterocyclic energetic compounds: a review. Molecules **27**, 1465 (2022). https://doi.org/10.3390/molecules27051465
7. Yount, J., Piercey, D.G.: Electrochemical synthesis of high-nitrogen materials and energetic materials. Chem. Rev. **122**, 8809–8840 (2022). https://doi.org/10.1021/acs.chemrev.1c00935
8. Tang, J., Yang, H., Cui, Y., Cheng, G.: Nitrogen-rich tricyclic-based energetic materials. Mater. Chem. Front. **5**, 7108–7118 (2021). https://doi.org/10.1039/D1QM00916H
9. Bennion, J.C., Matzger, A.J.: Development and evolution of energetic cocrystals. Acc. Chem. Res. **54**, 1699–1710 (2021). https://doi.org/10.1021/acs.accounts.0c00830
10. Zlotin, S.G., et al.: Advanced energetic materials: novel strategies and versatile applications. Mendeleev Commun. **31**, 731–749 (2021). https://doi.org/10.1016/j.mencom.2021.11.001
11. Zhou, J., Zhang, J., Wang, B., Qiu, L., Xu, R., Sheremetev, A.B.: Recent synthetic efforts towards high energy density materials: How to design high-performance energetic structures? FirePhysChem **2**, 83–139 (2021). https://doi.org/10.1016/j.fpc.2021.09.005
12. Zlotin, S.G., Dalinger, I.L., Makhova, N.N., Tartakovsky, V.A.: Nitro compounds as the core structures of promising energetic materials and versatile reagents for organic synthesis. Russ. Chem. Rev. **89**, 1–54 (2020). https://doi.org/10.1070/RCR4908
13. Churakov, A.M., Klenov, M.S., Voronin, A.A., Tartakovsky, V.A.: Energetic 1,2,3,4-Tetrazines. In: Gozin, M., Fershtat, L.L. (eds.) Nitrogen-Rich Energetic Materials, pp. 139–188. Wiley-VCH; Weinheim, Germany (2023). https://doi.org/10.1002/9783527832644
14. Singh, R.P., Gao, H., Meshri, D.T., Shreeve, J.M.: Nitrogen-rich heterocycles. In: Klapötke, T.M., et al. (eds.) High Energy Density Materials, pp. 35–83. Springer Berlin Heidelberg, Berlin, Heidelberg (2007). https://doi.org/10.1007/430_2006_055
15. Larina, L., Lopyrev, V.: Nitroazoles: Synthesis, Structure and Applications. Springer New York, New York, NY (2009). https://doi.org/10.1007/978-0-387-98070-6
16. Yongjin, C., Shuhong, B.: High energy density material (hedm) - progress in research azine energetic compounds. Johnson Matthey Technol. Rev. **63**, 51–72 (2019). https://doi.org/10.1595/205651319X15421043166627
17. Qu, Y., Babailov, S.P.: Azo-linked high-nitrogen energetic materials. J. Mater. Chem. A **6**, 1915–1940 (2018). https://doi.org/10.1039/C7TA09593G
18. Larin, A.A., Fershtat, L.L.: Energetic heterocyclic N-oxides: synthesis and performance. Mendeleev Commun. **32**, 703–713 (2022). https://doi.org/10.1016/j.mencom.2022.11.001

19. Yin, P., Zhang, Q., Shreeve, J.M.: Dancing with energetic nitrogen atoms: versatile N-functionalization strategies for N-heterocyclic frameworks in high energy density materials. Acc. Chem. Res. **49**, 4–16 (2016). https://doi.org/10.1021/acs.accounts.5b00477
20. Bakharev, V.V., Gidaspov, A.A., Parfenov, V.E.: Chemistry of (dinitromethyl)azines. Chem. Heterocycl. Compd. **53**, 659–669 (2017). https://doi.org/10.1007/s10593-017-2107-8
21. Gao, H., Zhang, Q., Shreeve, J.M.: Fused heterocycle-based energetic materials (2012–2019). J. Mater. Chem. A **8**, 4193–4216 (2020). https://doi.org/10.1039/C9TA12704F
22. Turek, O.: Le 2,4,6-trinitro-1,3,5-triazido-benzene. Nouvel explosif d'amorcage. Chimie et Industrie **26**, 781–794 (1931)
23. Bailey, A.S., Case, J.R.: 4,6-Dinitrobenzofuroxan, nitrobenzodifuroxan and benzotrifuroxan: a new series of complex-forming reagents for aromatic hydrocarbons. Tetrahedron, pp. 113–131 (1958). https://doi.org/10.1016/0040-4020(58)80003-4
24. Fogelzang, A.E., Egorshev, V.Y., Sinditsky, V.P., Dutov, M.D.: Combustion of nitro derivatives of azidobenzenes and benzofuroxans. Combust. Flame **87**, 123–135 (1991). https://doi.org/10.1016/0010-2180(91)90162-5
25. Golovina, N.I., Titkov, A.N., Raevskii, A.V., Atovmyan, L.O.: Kinetics and mechanism of phase transitions in the crystals of 2,4,6-trinitrotoluene and benzotrifuroxane. J. Solid State Chem. **113**, 229–238 (1994). https://doi.org/10.1006/jssc.1994.1365
26. Zelenov, V.P., et al.: Time for quartet: the stable 3:1 cocrystal formulation of FTDO and BTF - a high-energy-density material. CrystEngComm **22**, 4823–4832 (2020). https://doi.org/10.1039/D0CE00639D
27. Boyer, J.H., Ellzey, S.E., Jr.: Deoxygenation of Aromatic o-Dinitroso Derivatives by Phosphines. J. Org. Chem. **26**, 4684–4685 (1961)
28. Bailey, A.S., Evans, J.M.: Preparation and complex-forming ability of benzotrifurazan. Chem. Ind. **32**, 1424–1425 (1964)
29. Kondyukov, I.Z., et al.: Sulfur as a new low-cost and selective reducing agent for the transformation of benzofuroxans into benzofurazans. Russ. J. Organic Chem. **43**, 635–636 (2007). https://doi.org/10.1134/S107042800704029X
30. Thottempudi, V., Forohor, F., Parrish, D.A., Shreeve, J.M.: Tris(triazolo)benzene and its derivatives: high-density energetic materials. Angew. Chem. Int. Ed. **51**, 1–6 (2012). https://doi.org/10.1002/anie.201205134
31. Qu, Y., Zeng, Q., Wang, J., Fan, G., Huang, J., Yang, G.: Synthesis and properties for benzotriazole nitrogen oxides (BTZO) and tris[1,2,4]triazolo[1,3,5]triazine derivatives. Int. J. Mater. Sci. Appl. **7**, 49–57 (2018). https://doi.org/10.11648/j.ijmsa.20180702.13
32. Yang, X., Lin, X., Yang, L., Zhang, T.: A novel method to synthesize stable nitrogen-rich polynitrobenzenes with π-stacking for high-energy-density energetic materials. Chem. Comm. **54**, 10296–10299 (2018). https://doi.org/10.1039/c8cc05413d
33. Khisamutdinov, G.K., et al.: Synthesis and properties of 1,2,4-triazolo[4,3-d]-1,2,4-triazolo-[3,4-f]furazano[3,4-b]pyrazines. Russ. Chem. Bull. **42**, 1700–1702 (1993). https://doi.org/10.1007/BF00697044
34. Sheremetev, A.B., et al.: Oxygen-Rich 1,2,4-Triazolo[3,4-d]-1,2,4-triazolo[3,4-f]furazano[3,4-b]pyrazines as Energetic Materials. Asian J. Org. Chem. **5**, 1388–1397 (2016). https://doi.org/10.1002/ajoc.201600386

35. Lempert, D.B., Sheremetev, A.B.: Polynitromethyl derivatives of furazano[3,4-e]di([1,2,4]triazolo)-[4,3-a:3′,4′-c]pyrazine as components of solid composite propellants. Russ. Chem. Bull. **67**, 2065–2072 (2018). https://doi.org/10.1007/s11172-018-2330-1
36. Dorofeenko, E.M., Sheremetev, A.B., Lempert, D.B.: Effects of aluminum additions on the specific impulse of propellants based on high-enthalpy oxidizers containing NO_2 and NF_2 Groups. Russ. J. Phys. Chem. B **13**, 755–762 (2019). https://doi.org/10.1134/S1990793119040183
37. Yang, J.: Theoretical studies on the structures, densities, detonation properties and thermal stability of tris(triazolo)benzene and its derivatives. Polycycl. Aromat. Compd. **35**, 387–400 (2015). https://doi.org/10.1080/10406638.2014.918888
38. Zeng, Q., Qu, Y., Li, J., Huang, H.: Theoretical studies on the derivatives of tris([1,2,4]triazolo)[4,3-a:4′,3′-c:4″,3″-e][1,3,5]triazine as high energetic compounds. RSC Adv. **6**, 5419–5427 (2016). https://doi.org/10.1039/c5ra22524h
39. Maan, A., Mathpati, R.S., Ghule, V.D.: Energetic triazolo-triazolo-furazanopyrazines: a promising fused tetracycle building block with diversified functionalities and properties. ChemistrySelect **5**, 8557–8561 (2020). https://doi.org/10.1002/slct.202002440
40. NIST-JANAF Thermochemical Tables. https://janaf.nist.gov/
41. Frisch, M.J., Trucks, G.W., Schlegel, H.B. et al.: Gaussian 09, Revision B.01. Gaussian Inc, Wallingford CT (2010)
42. Becke, A.D.: Density-functional thermochemistry. III. The role of exact exchange. J. Chem. Phys., 98, pp. 5648–5652 (1993). https://doi.org/10.1063/1.464913
43. Johnson, B.J., Gill, P.M.W., Pople, J.A.: The performance of a family of density functional methods. J. Chem. Phys. **98**, 5612–5626 (1993). https://doi.org/10.1063/1.464906
44. Curtiss, L.A., Redfern, P.C., Raghavachari, K.: Gaussian-4 theory using reduced order perturbation theory. J. Chem. Phys. **127**, 124105 (2007). https://doi.org/10.1063/1.2770701
45. Curtiss, L.A., Redfern, P.C., Raghavachari, K.: Gn theory. Comput. Mol. Sci. **1**, 810 (2011). https://doi.org/10.1002/wcms.59
46. Matyushin, Y.N., Lebedev, V.P., Chironov, V.V., Pepekin, V.I.: Energy of the N-O bond in benzofuroxanes. Khim. Fiz. **21**, 58–61 (2002). (in Russian)
47. Suntsova, M.A.: Forecasting the enthalpies of formation new nitrogen-containing high-energy compounds based on quantum-chemical calculations. Candidate's Dissertation in Chemistry, Moscow (2016) (in Russian)
48. Larin, A.A., et al.: Assembly of tetrazolylfuroxan organic salts: Multipurpose green energetic materials with high enthalpies of formation and excellent detonation performance. Chem.-Eur. J. **25**, 4225–4233 (2019). https://doi.org/10.1002/chem.201806378
49. Voevodin, Vl.V., Antonov, A.S., Nikitenko, D.A., et al.: SupercomputerLomo -nosov-2: largescale, deep monitoring and fine analytics for the user community. Supercomput. Front. Innov. **6**(2), 4–11 (2019). https://doi.org/10.14529/js190201
50. Nikitenko, D.A., Voevodin, V.V., Zhumatiy, S.A.: Deep analysis of job state statistics on "Lomonosov-2" supercomputer. Supercomput. Front. Innov. **5**(2), 4–10 (2019). https://doi.org/10.14529/js180201

Reduced Precision Computations in the SL-AV Global Atmosphere Model

Mikhail Tolstykh[1,2,3(✉)], Gordey Goyman[1,2,3], Ekaterina Biryucheva[2], Vladimir Shashkin[1,2,3], and Rostislav Fadeev[1,2,3]

[1] Marchuk Institute of Numerical Mathematics RAS, Moscow, Russia
{m.tolstykh,v.shashkin}@inm.ras.ru
[2] Hydrometcentre of Russia, Moscow, Russia
[3] Moscow Institute of Physics and Technology, Dolgoprudny, Russia

Abstract. SL-AV is a global atmosphere model used for operational medium-range and long-range forecasts. Following previous successful implementation of single precision in some parts of the model dynamics solver, such computations are introduced into some parts of parameterization block of the model. Also, some memory optimizations are implemented. As a result, the elapsed time needed to compute 24-h forecast for SL-AV version with 10 km horizontal resolution and 104 vertical levels is reduced by 22% while using 2916 Cray XC40 processor cores, without detrimental effects on forecast accucacy.

Keywords: Numerical Weather Prediction · Global Atmosphere Model

1 Introduction

Numerical weather prediction as well as climate modeling is a task requiring from thousands to tens of thousands processor cores. The typical problem size is 10^9–10^{10} for the global medium range (10-days) forecast. For a forecast to be useful, it should be computed no longer than 15 min per forecast day as a maximum. Many world centers impose stronger limitation of 6 min per forecast day. The same model but with usually lower resolution is used for the medium-range ensemble prediction system that computes a set of 14-day forecasts with perturbed initial conditions and some model parameters. The typical ensemble size is about 50. The even lower resolution version of the model is also applied for the probabilistic long range forecast system with stronger requirements for ensemble size as the signal-to-noise ratio is quite small [1]. Besides, there is a trend to increase complexity for description of key diabatic processes in the atmosphere model and to couple an atmosphere model with models for Earth subsystems such as ocean, sea ice, aerosols, ozone cycle, etc. [2]. Thus, the reduction of elapsed time of a global atmosphere model is a very important task.

It seems that the idea of using reduced-precision computations was first proposed in [3]. During last decade, there are many studies [4, 9–11] on porting numerical weather prediction model codes from double to single precision. In doing so, one can expect the reduction of memory volume by a factor of two, on top of the reduction in computation

V. Voevodin et al. (Eds.): RuSCDays 2023, LNCS 14388, pp. 190–201, 2023.
https://doi.org/10.1007/978-3-031-49432-1_15

time. Besides, this approach allows in some cases a better use of multi-level processor cash memory.

Computation time reduction results in the corresponding drop of electrical power consumption. Modern supercomputers with the petaflops peak performance consume many megawatts of power so the acceleration of computations leads to a significant cost savings.

The floating-point computations are not commutative; also, single precision floating-point computations relative error has the value of about 1.e–7 instead of 1.e–15 for double precision. There are some code pieces that should remain in double precision anyway, such as the parts with some standard function computations, especially related to computations of trigonometric functions for spherical geometry. Besides, the atmosphere is intrinsically unstable so porting the code of an atmosphere model to the single precision is not an easy task. This requires a rigorous study of the impact of such porting on forecast accuracy. It was demonstrated in [10] that, while the single-precision version is 60% faster than the original version, the COSMO model's prediction accuracy is essentially unaffected by the use of single-precision computations. Similar results were found in [4], which addresses the process of transforming computations in the Integrated Forecast System model to single precision. This paper describes the way to safely switch the computations into single precision and how to analyze admissible deviation from the reference forecast. The last point is done with the example of tropical cyclone trajectory forecast. The tropical cyclone is considered as a highly unstable atmosphere feature. In particular, it is shown in [4] that tropical cyclone forecast with the single precision version of the ECMWF IFS model is very close to the forecast using the reference double precision model. Following this work, some modeling centers have also studied the impact of single precision on some parts of the atmosphere model: radiation flux computations in a climate model [5], dynamical core [6]. The impact of single precision computations was also studied for chemical kinetics block used in Earth System models [7]. The thorough study of ECMWF IFS model performance and forecast metrics using single precision arithmetic is published in [8]. Many weather prognostic centers now apply atmospheric model codes with single precision computations.

In this paper, the porting of Russian global atmosphere model SL-AV to the single precision is described. Also, some memory access optimizations are considered.

2 Global Atmosphere Model SL-AV

The global atmosphere model SL-AV [12] (Semi-Lagrangian, based on Absolute Vorticity equation) was developed at the Marchuk Institute of Numerical Mathematics RAS (INM RAS) and Hydrometcentre of Russia. It is applied for medium- and long-range forecasts at Hydrometcentre of Russia. As all the atmosphere models do, it consists of dynamical core solving the atmosphere equations set, and a set of so called parameterizations describing subgrid-scale processes. The dynamical core [13] is based on the absolute vorticity equation and has some other distinct algorithmic features. The set of parameterizations includes:

- the algorithms describing the processes of deep and shallow convection, cloud microphysics, planetary boundary layer, orographic gravity wave drag, developed by the ALADIN/LACE consortium [14];
- freeware codes for shortwave solar and longwave thermal radiation, CLIRAD SW [15] and RRTMG LW [16], respectively;
- multilayer soil model developed at INM RAS and Scientific Research Computer Center (SRCC) MSU [17], and some other parameterizations (snow albedo, subinversion cloudiness) developed at INM RAS.

The dynamical core of the SL-AV model takes about 40% of elapsed time, while the parameterizations account for the rest. The parameterizations computations can be done independently for different vertical columns and so are well parallelized. Details of parallel implementation of the SL-AV model are given in [18]. The SL-AV code has demonstrated good strong scaling at more than 13500 processor cores [19]. There is also an ongoing development of the coupled atmosphere – ocean - sea ice model on the basis of SL-AV model.

The first configuration of SL-AV model used in the study is intended for long-range forecasts and has the resolution of 0.72 × 0.9 degrees lat-lon, 96 vertical levels. The grid dimensions are 400 × 251 × 96. We will denote this version as SLAV072L96. The second version of the model is for medium-range forecast and has the resolution of 0.1 degrees (11 km) in longitude, variable resolution in latitude ranging from 8 km in the Northern hemisphere to 13 km in Southern one. This version has the vertical grid consisting of 104 levels and its grid dimensions are 3600 × 1946 × 104. This version is further denoted as SLAV10.

There were many efforts devoted to improvement of scalability and acceleration of the SL-AV code described in [20, 21] and references herein. These efforts allowed to reduce considerably the SL-AV code elapsed time for both abovementioned versions. In particular, some parts of the SL-AV dynamical core code were ported to the single precision. This allowed to accelerate to SL-AV code significantly. This paper describes further steps in this direction touching different part of the code.

3 Porting Parameterizations to Single Precision

3.1 Preliminary Analysis

First, the analysis of computational cost of subroutines was undertaken. The SLAV10 model was run at Cray XC40 computer system installed in Roshydromet Main Computing Center. The computing nodes of this system contain two 18-core Intel Xeon E2697v4 processors, the nodes are connected with Aries interconnect. In total, the system has 936 nodes, and its peak performance is 1.293 Pflops. The elapsed time for calculating the time step at 1944 processor cores was 6.8 s for the step calling solar and thermal radiation computations, and 3.5 s for other steps. (Note that the operational run of SLAV10 uses more processor cores, 2916). The result is shown in Fig. 1.

It shows that the most computationally demanding procedures except for MPI standard routines are `RRTMG_LW` (13.9%) and `DSP` (3.9%). The first of them is related to the computation of long-wave radiation flux, taking into account the maximum random overlap of clouds at various vertical levels, and the second one computes the non-orographic gravity wave drag. Therefore, it is logical to modify these routines and their dependent subroutines so that they use single precision calculations. (Note also that the relatively high amount of time taken by `MPI_BCAST` procedure is caused by the relatively short model run. This procedure is called many times at the beginning of the model run only.)

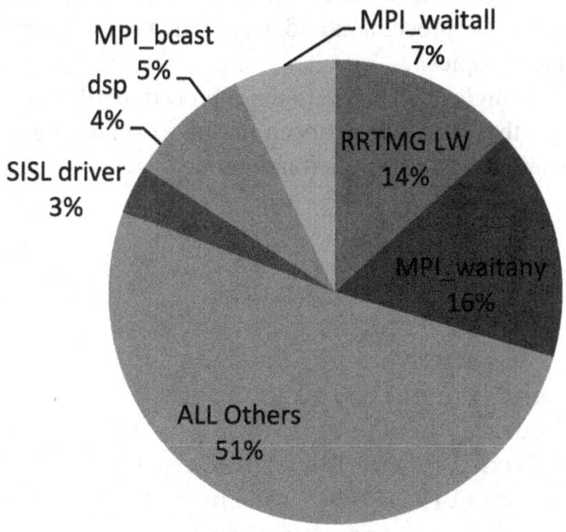

Fig. 1. Most time-consuming subroutines in SLAV10 code and their percentage of time

3.2 Code Modifications

The SL-AV model code is modified as follows. First, we introduce block specific accuracy parameter `RB` (`KIND` attribute in terms of FORTRAN source code) that is used to declare floating-point variables This allows to switch between double and single precision within a specific block, which is advantageous for backward compatibility and debugging purposes. So, all the local real variables are declared as.

```
real(kind=RB) :: var
```

instead of

```
real(kind=8) :: var
```

At the same time, in order to avoid implicit type conversions we also modify all the constants used in the code, explicitly specifying their kind, i.e.

```
a(i) = 10.0 * b(i) + 42.0_8
```

becomes

```
a(i) = 10.0_RB * b(i) + 42.0_RB
```

For the same reason, we make local copies with RB precision for double precision variables inherited from other procedures and files, so that subsequent computations can be performed using these copies.

Next, we implement single precision variants of procedures that are also called within other parts of the code that have not yet been ported to single precision. This can be implemented in convenient way using Fortran interfaces.

```
interface func
  function func_sp(a)
    real(kind=4), intent(in) :: a
    real(kind=4) :: func_sp
  end function func_sp
  function func_dp(a)
    real(kind=8), intent(in) :: a
    real(kind=8) :: func_dp
  end function func_dp
end interface
```

Historically, the SL-AV code includes some calls to double-precision vector standard functions from Intel MKL library, such as the function for raising a vector to real power VDPOWX. The conditional operator depending on RB value is introduced, calling either double precision vector function or its single-precision counterpart (VSPOWX for given example). The example of such a code is given below.

```
integer :: Len
real(kind=RB):: A(Len), B(Len), Pow_RB
...
if (RB == 4) then
  Pow_RB=Pow
  call vspowx(Len, a, Pow_RB, b)
else
  call vdpowx(Len, a, Pow, b)
end if
```

Some specific constants are used throughout the code that are sensitive to the precision. Some of these constants are simply set from computational or physical context, such as constants used to restrict quantities within physically reasonable ranges. Other constants are used to prevent floating-point arithmetic exceptions and depend on the precision in use. The latter type of constants has to be adjusted in case of single precision. Numerical constants used as limiters while calling some standard functions such as logarithm or square roots are defined now depending on `RB` value, sometimes using standard Fortran function `TINY(1._RB)`. After making all the changes outlined above, we do a sanity check to ensure that when `RB`= 8, the computations results are consistent with those of the model's original version. The procedure for consistency verification is given in the next Subsection.

In addition to changing calculations into single precision, a number of optimizations have been performed in some subroutines, aimed at increasing the proportion of vectorized loops. For example, in some cases, the conditional operator has been successfully replaced by a combination of the built-in `sign` and `max` (`min`) functions. Sometimes, a complex loop with a conditional operator depending on the loop step can be divided into several loops, and the conditional operator can be eliminated from the code.

3.3 Experiments and Results

Experiments with the low-resolution version SLAV072L96 are carried out both at the INM RAS cluster and at Cray XC40 computer system. The INM RAS cluster consists of 36 nodes each having two 20-core Intel Scalable Gold 6230 processors. The nodes are connected with InfiniBand EDR interconnect, the peak performance of this cluster is 92 Tflops. The experiments with SLAV10 model are run at Cray XC40 (its characteristics are given above), since they require at least 1944 processor cores, which exceeds the capabilities of the INM RAS cluster.

The very first evaluation is carried out based on the elapsed time analysis for individual loops in the subroutine under consideration. The SLAV072L96 version is used for this analysis. Since the elapsed time is sensitive to the INM RAS cluster load, time measurements are taken at about the same time.

The next step is to analyze the average elapsed time for the SLAV072L96 model time step using `MPI_Wtime` output data. This time turned out to be sensitive to the INM RAS cluster load, so time measurements must be made simultaneously for reference and experimental versions. Code version showing a decrease in elapsed time is then checked for forecast accuracy with a single forecast. First, the values of integrals from prognostic variables over the entire computational domain (kinetic and internal energy, integrals of wind speed components squared and humidity) are compared between experimental and reference versions.

The results of verification according to World Meteorological Organization standards are then evaluated. The mean, gradient and mean square errors are computed for 5-days (or 10-days in some cases) forecasts for the fields of mean sea level pressure, geopotential and wind speed components at 250, 500 and 850 hPa surfaces, temperature at 850 hPa surface, both for experimental and reference versions. The errors are estimated separately for the extratropical part of the Southern hemisphere (-90° – -20° S), the tropics (-20° – 20°) and the extratropical part of the Northern hemisphere (20°–90° N). Then these error metrics are compared between experimental and reference versions. If the error is recognized as admissible, a series of 10 (and in some cases, of 30) forecasts is computed, with the verification for each forecast. Then the error metrics are averaged over all forecasts computed, and these averaged errors are compared between experimental and reference codes. Depending on the variable and type of error, the range of allowable changes to these errors is usually the fourth or third significant digit. If all error changes are within these limits, the code changes are accepted for further verification with the high-resolution SLAV10 model. Three forecasts with the lead time of 5 days and initial dates for various seasons of the year are computed at Cray XC40 computer system and their error metrics are also compared similarly with errors for the original version of the model.

Using the presented methodology, we first have ported the computations of solar and thermal radiation heat flux (`SLM_RAD_DRIVER, SORAD, RRTMG`) into single accuracy. The most time-consuming routine mentioned above in Subsect. 3.1, `RRTMG_LW_RTNMR,` is among these routines. Then the computations of non-orographic gravity waves drag (subroutine `DSP`) that take the second place in time consumption are ported into the single precision.

The optimization of radiation fluxes computations has allowed to reduce the execution time of the time step with the call to radiation subroutines mentioned above by about 0.5 s, and the translation of the DSP subroutine into single accuracy allowed to win another 0.12 s. Further, porting of the diagnostic cloudiness computations into single precision allowed to gain 0.05 s more. These results are depicted in Fig. 2. The elapsed time needed to compute 24-h forecast with SLAV10 is reduced from 22.5 to 21 min.

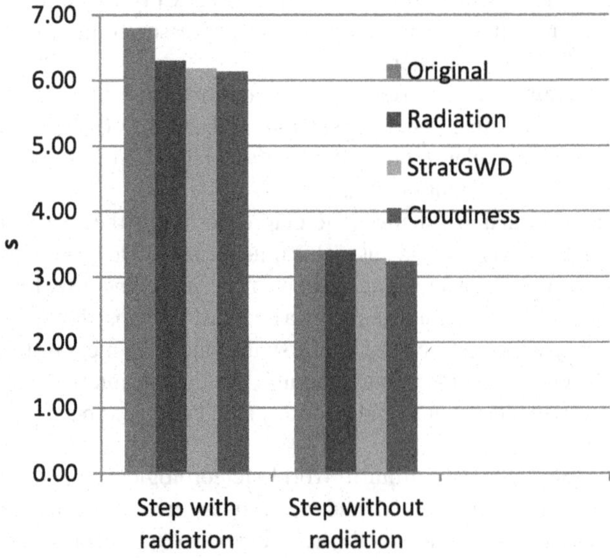

Fig. 2. Reduction of the elapsed time per time step while porting different subroutines to single precision. See the text for details

4 Memory Usage Optimization

The speed of computations using modern central processing units (CPUs) is limited in many cases by the memory bandwidth rather than the processor clock rate. As a result, a significant part of the calculation time is spent idle by the CPU while waiting for the data to be written or read from the memory. This fact is one of the reasons to use memory with a hierarchical structure in modern computer systems. Different types of memory (RAM, cache memory of different levels, processor registers) form a hierarchy where there are elements with different access times, complexity, cost and volume located at different levels of this hierarchy. By changing this structure, it is possible to speed up the computations since the algorithm at each period of time uses only some limited data set that can be placed in a faster, but expensive and therefore small, memory. Therefore, organizing algorithms to perform as many arithmetic operations on a smaller amount of data as possible often allows to significantly speed up their execution.

Previously, we managed to achieve a significant acceleration of the parameterizations for subgrid-scale physical processes of the SL-AV model by optimizing the use of the CPU cache [20, 21]. The main idea of this optimization is to divide the computational domain of the MPI process into sub-domains of a smaller fixed size and make all computations within the block for these sub-domains. This increases data localization, reduces cache misses, and improves processor memory utilization.

In this section, we present the work on further implementation of this approach for the most resource-intensive blocks of the dynamics of the SL-AV model, namely the block for calculating the right-hand sides of the semi-implicit – semi-Lagrangian algorithm and the block for the semi-Lagrangian advection algorithm. Also, we have been working on the localization of all internal arrays used in calculations in the parameterization block that allows to further increase the effect of accelerating this block by optimizing the memory use.

4.1 Controlling Vector Length

The calculation of the right-hand sides of the semi-implicit – semi-Lagrangian algorithm and the semi-Lagrangian advection block are one of the most computationally expensive parts in the dynamical core of the SL-AV model. In the subroutine for calculating these right-hand sides, the known grid functions values at the current time level are used. A detailed description of the program implementation of these blocks in the model code is given in [18].

In the original version of the SL-AV model, these blocks use parallelization of loops in longitude along OpenMP threads. Schematically, this can be represented by the following code.

```
!$omp parallel do private(ist, iend, j)
do thread_idx = 1, threads_num
  ist  = 1 + (NLON / threads_num) * (thread_idx-1)
  iend = ist + (NLON / threads_num) - 1
  do j = jbeg, jend
    call calc_rhs(ist, iend, u(1,ist,j), v(1,ist,j),…)
  end do
end do
```

Here `ist`, `iend` is the start and end index along the longitude for a given OpenMP thread, which are passed as arguments to the subroutine `calc_rhs` and determine the sizes of local arrays and the limits of the loop along the longitude within that subroutine; `jbeg, jend` are the limits of the loop in latitude, which are determined by decomposition of MPI processes. The first dimension of the arrays corresponds to the vertical direction. A similar construction is used to parallelize the OpenMP threads in the semi-Lagrangian advection block.

Thus, the computations are performed for the domain having dimensions (`NLEV, NLON/threads_num`) at each iteration of the loop in `j`, where `NLEV` is the number of vertical levels of the model, `NLON` is the dimension of the grid along the longitude. To optimize the work with the processor memory, it is proposed to use the partition of the computational domain mentioned above into sub-domains (`NLEV, NLON/blocks_num`) where `blocks_num` is the number of sub-domains at fixed latitude. The value of `blocks_num` has to be selected in such a way as to minimize the execution time of the corresponding blocks. At the same time, there are `blocks_num * (jend-jbeg+ 1)` sub-domains for each MPI process, which in turn are distributed across OpenMP threads. To introduce this change, only a small modification to the original version of the model code is required.

```
!$omp parallel do private(ist, iend, j, block_idx)
do idx = 1, blocks_num * (jend - jbeg + 1)
  j = jbeg + (idx - 1) / blocks_num
  block_idx = mod(idx - 1, blocks_num) + 1
  ist  = 1 + NLON / blocks_num * (block_idx - 1)
  iend = ist + NLON / blocks_num - 1
  call calc_rhs(ist, iend, u(1,ist,j), v(1,ist,j),...)
end do
```

To determine the optimal number of sub-domains, a series of runs with the SL-AV model are carried out where we investigated the dependence of `blocks_num` value on the execution time of the blocks of interest. The results of these calculations showed that for all considered SL-AV configurations, the choice of `NLON/num_blocks= 16` is optimal. We obtained a similar result earlier when optimizing the parameterization block [21]. At the same time, the acceleration for the routine calculating the right-hand sides is about 43% of the elapsed time with respect to the original version. For the semi-Lagrangian advection routine, the acceleration is about 28%.

4.2 Localization of Temporary Arrays in the Parameterizations Block

As noted above, we have been able to significantly speed up the SL-AV model in previous works by performing computations in this block for smaller sub-domains. Re-analysis of the code for the parameterizations block revealed that although all the computations are performed for small sub-domains as described above, a small portion of internal temporary arrays in individual subroutines is allocated with the size corresponding to the size of the original computational domain (i.e., has the size of `(NLON, NLEV)` instead of `(NLON/num_blocks, NLEV)`). As it turned out, this significantly limited

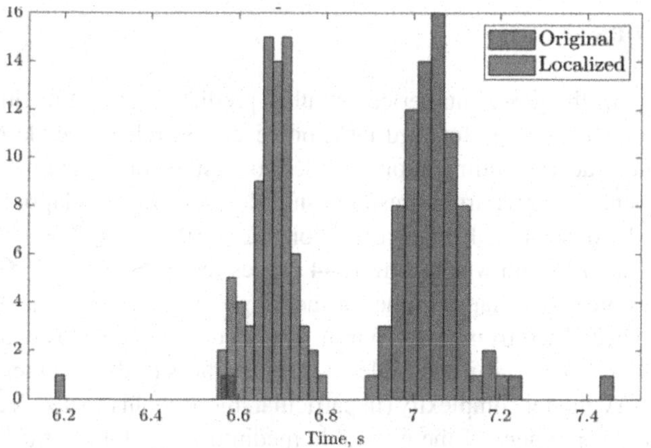

Fig. 3. Histogram for elapsed times of the SLAV10 model time step with computations of the radiation fluxes computations: original code (blue) and with memory localization (red). (Color figure online)

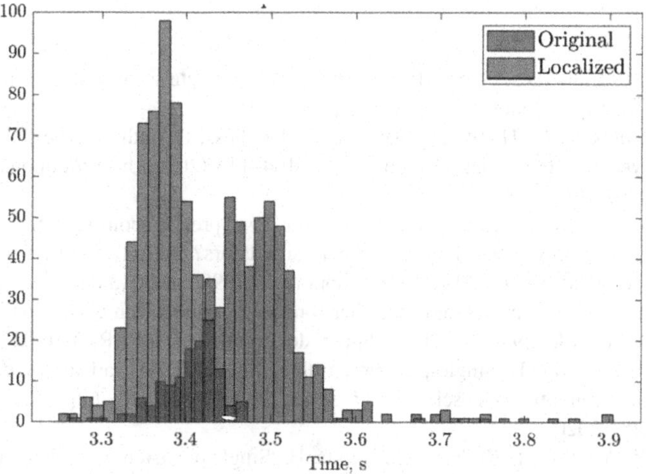

Fig. 4. Histogram for elapsed times of the SLAV10 model time step without calling radiation fluxes routines: original code (blue) and with memory localization (red). (Color figure online)

the optimization effect in these blocks, since poor memory localization of these arrays led to a slowdown in computations with their participation. We have carried out an additional work on the complete localization of all arrays participating in computations in the parameterization block. Figures 3, 4 show histograms for the elapsed time per one time step of the SLAV10 model when using 1944 cores, calling computations of solar thermal radiation heat flux (Fig. 3) and without these computations (Fig. 4). It can be seen from these figures that array localization allows, on average, to reduce the elapsed time of a time step by 0.35 and 0.15 s, respectively. The works presented in this Section are carried independently from the works described in Sect. 3.

5 Conclusions

Porting the code of the global numerical weather prediction model to single precision turned out to be not a straightforward task; however, the relevant code modifications as well as memory access optimization have led to visible computational cost savings. The works presented in this article resulted in a decrease of the elapsed time needed to compute 24-h forecast with high-resolution SLAV10 model. The elapsed time is decreased by 20% to 18 min when using 1944 process cores, and by 22.2% to 14 min at 2916 processor cores. The elapsed time for the long-range forecast with SLAV072L96 version has also decreased from 89 to 75 min. These code changes do not affect weather prediction accuracy. Thus, it is possible to redirect the saved computer resources to increase the SL-AV model complexity (in particular, more sophisticated deep convection algorithm) and development of the ensemble medium-range forecast technology with higher resolution.

This study was carried out at the Institute of Numerical Mathematics RAS and is supported with Russian Science Foundation Grant 21–71-30023.

References

1. Scaife, A.A., Smith, D.: A signal-to-noise paradox in climate science. npj Clim. Atmos. Sci. **1,** 28 (2018). https://doi.org/10.1038/s41612-018-0038-4
2. Bauer, P., Dueben, P.D., Hoefler, T., Quintino, T., Schultess, T., Wedi, N.: The digital revolution of Earth-system science. Nat. Comput. Sci. **1**, 104–113 (2021). https://doi.org/10.1038/s43588-021-00023-0
3. Palmer, T. N.: More reliable forecasts with less precise computations: a fast-track route to cloud-resolved weather and climate simulators? Phil. Trans. R. Soc. **372**(2018), A.3722013039120130391 (2014). https://doi.org/10.1098/rsta.2013.0391
4. Váňa, F., et al.: Single precision in weather forecasting models: an evaluation with the IFS. Mon. Wea. Rev. **145**, 495–502 (2017). https://doi.org/10.1175/MWR-D-16-0228.1
5. Cotronei, A., Slawig, T.: Single-precision arithmetic in ECHAM radiation reduces runtime and energy consumption. Geosci. Model Dev. **13**, 2783–2804 (2020). https://doi.org/10.5194/gmd-13-2783-2020
6. Nakano, M., Yashiro, H., Kodama, C., Tomita, H.: Single precision in the dynamical core of a nonhydrostatic global atmospheric model: evaluation using a baroclinic wave test case. Mon. Wea. Rev. **146**, 409–416 (2018). https://doi.org/10.1175/MWR-D-17-0257.1

7. Sophocleous, K., Christoudias, T.: Reduced-precision chemical kinetics in atmospheric models. Atmosphere **13**, 1418 (2022). https://doi.org/10.3390/atmos13091418
8. Lang, S., et al.: More accuracy with less precision. Q. J. Roy. Meteor. Soc. **147** (2021) https://doi.org/10.1002/qj.4181
9. Thornes, T., Düben, P.D., Palmer, T.N.: On the use of scale-dependent precision in earth system modelling. Q. J. Roy. Meteor. Soc. **143**, 897–908 (2017)
10. Russell, F.P., Niu, X., Luk, W., Palmer, T.N.: On the use of programmable hardware and reduced numerical precision in earth-system modeling. J. Adv. Model. Earth Syst. **7**, 1393–1408 (2015)
11. Rüdisühli, S., Walser A., Fuhrer O.: COSMO in single precision. Cosmo Newsl. **14**, 5–1 (2013)
12. Tolstykh, M.A., et al.: Multiscale global atmosphere model SL-AV: the results of medium-range weather forecasts. Russ. Meteorol. Hydrol. **43**, 773–779 (2018). https://doi.org/10.3103/S1068373918110080
13. Tolstykh, M., Shashkin, V., Fadeev, R., Goyman, G.: Vorticity-divergence semi-Lagrangian global atmospheric model SL-AV20: dynamical core. Geosci. Model Dev. **10**, 1961–1983 (2017). https://doi.org/10.5194/gmd-10-1961-2017
14. Termonia, P., Fischer, C., Bazile, E., Bouyssel, F., Brožková, R., Bénard, P., et al.: The ALADIN system and its canonical model configurations AROME CY41T1 and ALARO CY40T1. Geosci. Model Dev. **11**, 257–281 (2018). https://doi.org/10.5194/gmd-11-257-2018
15. Tarasova, T., Fomin, B.: The use of new parameterizations for gaseous absorption in the CLIRAD-SW solar radiation code for models. J. Atmos. Oceanic Technol. **24**(6), 1157–1162 (2007)
16. Mlawer, E.J., Taubman, S.J., Brown, P.D., Iacono, M.J., Clough, S.A.: RRTM, a validated correlated-k model for the longwave. J. Geophys. Res. **102**, 16663–16682 (1997)
17. Volodin, E.M., Lykossov, V.N.: Parametrization of heat and moisture transfer in the soil–vegetation system for use in atmospheric general circulation models: 1. Formulation and simulations based on local observational data. Izvestiya Atmos. Oceanic Phys. **34**, 402–416 (1998)
18. Tolstykh, M., Goyman, G., Fadeev, R., Shashkin, V.: Structure and algorithms of SL-AV atmosphere model parallel program complex. Lobachevskii J. Math. **39**, 587–595 (2018)
19. Tolstykh, M., Goyman, G., Fadeev, R., Shashkin, V., Lubov, S.: SL-AV model: numerical weather prediction at extra-massively parallel supercomputer. In: Voevodin, V., Sobolev, S. (eds.) RuSCDays 2018. CCIS, vol. 965, pp. 379–387. Springer, Cham (2019). https://doi.org/10.1007/978-3-030-05807-4_32
20. Tolstykh, M.A., Fadeev, R., Shashkin, V.V., Goyman, G.S.: Improving the computational efficiency of the global SL-AV numerical weather prediction model. Supercomput. Front. Innov. **8**(4), 11–23 (2021). https://doi.org/10.14529/jsfi210402
21. Tolstykh, M., Goyman, G., Fadeev, R., Travova, S., Shashkin, V.: Development of the global multiscale atmosphere model: computational aspects. J. Phys.: Conf. Ser. **1740**, 012074 (2021). https://doi.org/10.1088/1742-6596/1740/1/012074

Scalability of the INM RAS Earth System Model

Maria Tarasevich[1,2,4(✉)], Andrey Sakhno[1,2,3], Dmitry Blagodatskikh[1], Rostislav Fadeev[1,2,4], Evgeny Volodin[1], and Andrey Gritsun[1]

[1] Marchuk Institute of Numerical Mathematics of the Russian Academy of Sciences, Moscow, Russian Federation

[2] Moscow Institute of Physics and Technology, Dolgoprudny, Russian Federation

[3] National Research University of Electronic Technology, Moscow, Russian Federation

[4] Hydrometeorological Research Center of Russian Federation, Moscow, Russian Federation

mashatarasevich@gmail.com

Abstract. The paper discusses the parallel scalability of INM RAS Earth system model (INMCM). To study the parallel performance of INMCM as well as its individual components, a custom software toolkit is used. The results of the study made it possible to identify the optimal parallel configurations of the model and therefore accelerate the computations without significant redesign of the program code.

Keywords: Earth system model · INMCM · parallel scalability · software toolkit

1 Introduction

INM RAS Earth system model (INMCM) is a global climate model. There is a family of INMCM versions that have different spatial and temporal resolutions and different set of included modules. Basically, INMCM consists [1] of two general circulation models: the atmosphere model with interactive aerosol [2] and land surface [3,4] modules and the ocean model [5] with sea ice dynamics and thermodynamics module [6,7].

Two versions of the INM RAS Earth system model — INMCM5 [1] and INMCM48 [8] — are participating in the Coupled Model Intercomparison Project Phase 6 (CMIP6) [9] and show good results [10,11]. INMCM5 is capable of simulating the present-day climate [1] as well as its changes in 1850–2014 [12]. A new system of long range weather forecast based on the INMCM5 is currently under development [13–15].

The INM RAS Earth system model is constantly evolving, and the first version of the new model generation called INMCM6 has recently been released [16]. During the further INMCM6 development we expect many major upgrades both

V. Voevodin et al. (Eds.): RuSCDays 2023, LNCS 14388, pp. 202–216, 2023.
https://doi.org/10.1007/978-3-031-49432-1_16

in the mathematical model and in its implementation, including addition of some new modules, such as describing chemical processes in the upper atmosphere.

Therefore, it is crucial to provide developers with a flexible tool for evaluating the scalability and parallel efficiency of both the coupled model as a whole and its individual modules. Automatic profilers like Intel VTune [17] or Cray Performance Analysis Tool [18] can produce CPU time profiles for each subroutine of the program. However, they lack a convenient logical aggregation of the results. They also tend to analyze the program as a whole, without an ability to inspect program components separately. In addition, these tools may be unavailable in some environments (for example, Cray PAT is available only on Cray solutions) and their result data is hard to post-process due to usage of a proprietary format.

In this paper, we introduce a recently developed tool for evaluating the parallel and computational efficiency of the INMCM program code and its modules and apply it to assess the scalability of the INM RAS Earth system model. Section 2.2 of the paper describes the methodologies utilized for the developed tool for evaluating the parallel and computational efficiency. Section 3 presents the verification of developed tool results and the scalability and parallel efficiency assessment of the INMCM code. In the Sect. 4, the conclusion and discussion of the obtained results are outlined.

2 Materials and Methods

2.1 INM RAS Earth System Model

In the study we use the high resolution version called INMCM6M from the up-to-date INM RAS Earth system model generation INMCM6 [16]. The spatial resolution of its general atmosphere circulation model is $1.25° \times 1°$ in longitude and latitude and 73 in vertical σ-levels. The time step in the atmosphere dynamic core is 1.5 min for this spatial resolution. The ocean general circulation model has a horizontal resolution of $0.5° \times 0.25°$ in longitude and latitude and 40 vertical σ-levels. The time step in the ocean model is 12 min.

The atmosphere model is based on the system of the hydrothermodynamic equations with hydrostatic approximation in advective form. The interactive aerosol module [2] describing the concentration evolution of the 10 substances is included in the atmosphere model. The atmosphere general circulation model uses a semi-implicit integration scheme that requires solving an auxiliary Helmholtz-type equation at each dynamical step. The current version uses a fast Fourier transform based algorithm which parallel implementation requires global data transposing [19]. The scaling ability of this operation was studied in [20]. Different approaches that employ the multigrid method on massively parallel architectures are shown to scale better [21], but they are not used now.

The ocean model solves a set of large-scale hydrothermodynamic equations with hydrostatic and Boussinesq approximations. It includes the dynamics and thermodynamics module [6,7] for the sea ice with the elastic-viscous-plastic rheology with a single gradation of thickness. The ocean model step consists of several stages. The most computationally demanding are isopycnal diffusion and dissipation of the horizontal components of velocity. The other one is the barotropic adaptation because it requires solving a system of three implicitly discretized equations for the velocity components and the sea level. This system is solved [5] iteratively using GMRES with the block ILU(0) preconditioner from the PETSc [22] package.

The atmosphere and the ocean general circulation models and the aerosol module are implemented as independent distributed applications that exchange data using MPI (Message Passing Interface) library when working in coupled mode. Figure 1 shows INM RAS Earth system model computations and exchanges scheme. The atmosphere and the ocean models exchange a set of two-dimensional fields every two model hours. The computational grids of the atmosphere and ocean model are different, so the data is interpolated to the target model grid after the transfers.

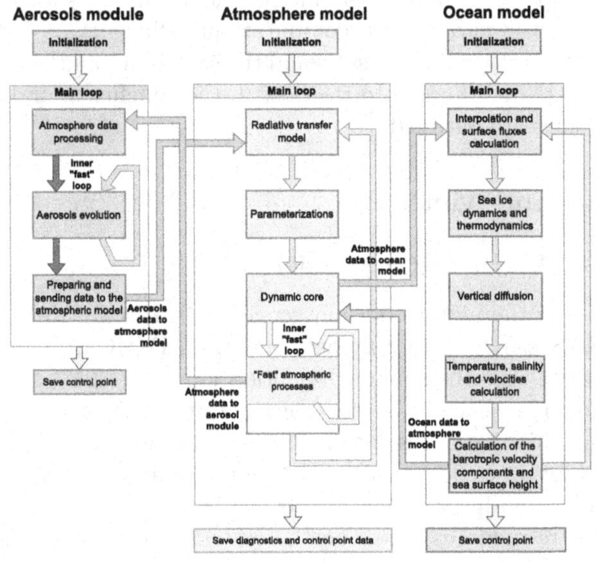

Fig. 1. INM RAS Earth system model computational scheme

The atmosphere model sends five-dimensional array of the prognostic variables state to aerosol module after each "fast" loop. The aerosol module sends the aerosols concentrations to atmosphere model every 3 h. The aerosol module works on the same grid as the atmosphere model and uses the same size of MPI communicator.

2.2 Profiler for INMCM

To analyze the parallel properties of the INMCM code, the `Mod_ParProf` module was developed, in which, by means of the `ParProf_Timer` class, the possibility of accumulating information about the counting time of the fragments of the program code of the model on each MPI process is implemented independently. The main methods of this class are `push`, `end_cycle` and `get` functions. Figure 2 shows an example of using these methods. To measure the running time of a code fragment, you need to call the `get` method before it starts, specifying the section name and the timer ID.

```
USE Mod_ParProf, ONLY: Timer => ParProf_Timer

DO      ! a loop whose scalability needs to be evaluated
    CALL Timer % push("Cycle_name", "Block_name_1")
    …   ! Code of the first block
    CALL Timer % push("Cycle_name", "Block_name_2")
    …
    CALL Timer % push("Cycle_name", "Last_block_name")
    …   ! Code of the last block
    CALL Timer % end_cycle("Cycle_name")
END DO

! Writing the results to the Name_file_out.txt file
CALL Timer % get("Cycle_name", "Name_file_out", Comm)

! Recording all results in a file
! with the name ParProf_AllX_ATMY_OCNZ.txt
CALL Timer % get(Comm)
```

Fig. 2. Listing of the `Mod_ParProf` module usage.

The object-oriented approach to the implementation of the `Mod_ParProf` module allows one to create several independent instances of the `ParProf_Timer` class that differ in the identifier. Thus, the analysis of parallel characteristics of different sections of the INMCM program code can be carried out simultaneously and independently of each other. At the end of the loop, inside which the measured block is located, it is necessary to call the `end_cycle` method with the indication of the timer ID. To record the results, there are two options for the final output: to a file with an arbitrary name and to a file whose name contains information about the number of cores in this configuration (*All* is the total number of cores, *ATM* and *OCN* are the configuration of the atmospheric and oceanic blocks of the model, respectively). After the completion of the main time cycle, profiling data is collected from all MPI processes using the `MPI_REDUCE` function (`MPI_MAX` operation), then the average running time of each fragment is calculated. A visualization system implemented for `Mod_ParProf` is written in Python.

2.3 Perftools

To verify profiling results obtained with the `Mod_ParProf`, we use `PerfTools-lite` package from Cray Performance Analysis Tool [18] suite. For profiling INMCM modules, we generate the full call graph by the `pat_report`

`-b calltable` command. The call graph data is aggregated in the same way as it is done by a set of timers from `Mod_ParProf`. The resulting data is analyzed alongside the results obtained by `Mod_ParProf`.

2.4 HPC Systems

Two high performance computing systems were used to study the scalability and parallel properties of the INMCM6M.

The first is a Cray XC40-LC massively parallel supercomputer installed at the Main Computer Center of Federal Service for Hydrometeorology and Environmental Monitoring. The Cray XC40-LC consists of 976 compute nodes interconnected via the Cray's proprietary Aries network. Each node has 128 Gb of RAM and two Intel Xeon E5-2697v4 processors with 18 CPU cores and 45 Mb of Intel Smart Cache per processor. The total number of computational cores is 35136. It is important to note that the user is able to use only 32 cores per node since 4 cores per node are reserved to maintain the distributed Lustre file system.

The second is the INM RAS cluster installed at the Marchuk Institute of Numerical Mathematics of the Russian Academy of Sciences. This HPC system has 36 compute nodes connected by Mellanox EDR MSB7800 InfiniBand with up to 100 Gb/s bandwidth. Each node has two 20-core Intel Xeon Gold 6230v2 processors with 27.5 Mb of Intel Smart Cache per processor. The total number of available CPU cores is 1440. Each compute node has 256 Gb of RAM.

The main differences between the HPC systems used are the number and performance of CPU cores (newer cores on the INM RAS cluster), the interconnect used and the file system type. We use different versions of Intel compilers to compile and build INMCM6M: 19.1.2.254 on the Cray XC40-LC and 15.0.2 on the INM RAS cluster. The compilation optimization flags are the same on both HPC systems, `-O3` for the atmosphere model and aerosol module and `-O2` for the ocean model.

3 Results

In this paper, all INMCM6M simulations are performed under the conditions of the CMIP6 piControl scenario [9]. All forcings are fixed at conditions of the year of 1850. As a part of the CMIP6, the piControl experiment is mostly used to evaluate Earth system models and to simulate the intrinsic climate variability. All simulations last for 1 model month.

3.1 Optimal Configurations for INMCM6M

Optimal configurations are sought from a pre-selected list of configurations. We used some knowledge about the internal structure of the atmosphere code. For example, the number of longitude and latitude MPI processes is chosen as such divisors of the corresponding grid sizes that each process owns almost the same number of grid cells.

For the INMCM6M atmosphere model and aerosol module, number of cells along the longitude dimension is 288 and 180 in the latitude dimension. INMCM6M uses a two-dimensional longitude-latitude communication grid and we consider the following dimensions of the MPI communicator as the feasible set:

$$\mathrm{P_{lon}} \in \{4, 6, 8, 12\}, \quad \mathrm{P_{lat}} \in \{14, 26, 30, 32, 36, 45, 60\}.$$

The requirement of P_{lon} being an even number arises from the implementation of the INM RAS Earth system model program code. We also do not consider configurations with large P_{lon} because it increases the cost of the distributed transpose operation required for the fast Fourier transform.

Table 1. Performance of INMCM6M configurations (green highlighted are the optimal) on the Cray XC40-LC and the INM RAS HPC systems.

Cray XC40-LC										INM RAS				
ATM work	ATM wait	OC work	OC wait	Total time, s	P lon	P lat	P x	P y	Total cores	ATM work	ATM wait	OC work	OC wait	Total time, s
9.81	0.41	9.50	0.72	3822.96	6	14	6	6	204	10.3	0.74	10.9	0.19	4158.05
9.74	0.37	8.88	1.23	3779.58	6	14	7	6	210	10.3	0.42	10.3	0.48	4032.70
6.99	0.89	7.71	0.17	2950.75	4	30	8	6	288	7.67	0.74	8.14	0.27	3211.82
6.18	0.34	6.05	0.47	2443.68	4	36	10	6	348	6.49	0.42	6.73	0.19	2610.20
6.15	0.36	6.28	0.23	2443.26	6	26	10	6	372					
5.62	0.63	6.08	0.17	2348.19	4	45	10	6	420					
5.16	0.32	5.20	0.29	2059.59	6	30	8	8	424	5.59	0.39	5.79	0.20	2262.59
5.65	0.29	5.24	0.71	2233.82	4	45	8	8	424					
4.91	0.31	4.89	0.33	1963.65	8	26	9	8	488	5.05	0.78	5.65	0.19	2210.90
4.63	0.62	5.08	0.17	1975.17	6	36	9	8	504					
4.65	0.29	4.54	0.40	1858.48	6	36	9	9	513	4.90	0.28	4.90	0.28	1970.35
4.70	0.30	4.58	0.42	1878.22	4	60	10	8	560					
4.32	0.45	4.60	0.18	1799.24	8	30	10	8	560					
4.26	0.31	4.37	0.19	1719.03	8	30	9	9	561	4.58	0.44	4.84	0.21	1925.02
4.33	0.30	4.39	0.25	1746.65	8	32	9	9	593	4.42	0.59	4.83	0.19	1915.72
4.00	0.71	4.54	0.17	1772.20	6	45	10	8	620					
3.99	0.38	4.20	0.18	1647.99	6	45	10	9	630					
3.86	0.28	3.78	0.36	1560.36	8	36	12	8	672	3.99	0.40	4.21	0.20	1676.23
3.64	0.26	3.33	0.58	1474.73	12	26	12	9	732	3.68	0.25	3.73	0.20	1500.01
3.68	0.43	3.93	0.18	1549.35	6	60	12	8	816					
3.37	0.66	3.86	0.19	1523.56	8	45	10	10	820					
3.22	0.37	3.42	0.18	1357.28	12	30	12	9	828					
3.38	0.31	3.51	0.18	1394.46	8	45	12	9	828					
3.42	0.25	3.22	0.45	1388.61	8	45	12	10	840					
3.01	0.34	3.17	0.18	1270.32	12	36	12	10	984					
3.14	0.22	2.63	0.74	1276.04	12	36	12	12	1008	2.80	0.28	2.90	0.21	1198.87
2.86	0.25	2.75	0.37	1183.99	8	60	15	9	1095					
2.56	0.42	2.81	0.18	1138.97	12	45	14	10	1220					
2.61	0.28	2.70	0.21	1108.26	12	45	12	12	1224	2.45	0.61	2.88	0.21	1185.13
2.49	0.23	2.40	0.34	1050.87	12	60	14	12	1608					

For the INMCM6M ocean model that works on displaced pole rotated grid, the number of cells along the x and y dimensions is 720. Therefore, we consider the following feasible values $P_{x,y} \in \{6, 7, 8, 9, 10, 12, 14, 15\}$ for the dimensions of the MPI communicator. `MPI_Dims_create` performs the domain decomposition to achieve the most "squared" decomposition and always sets $P_x \geqslant P_y$.

We call a configuration optimal if it leads to minimal total execution time and the number of used processes cannot be reduced without slowing down the running time. This is also known as Pareto optimal situation. To evaluate whether a given configuration is optimal or not, we track the total execution and wait times for the atmosphere and the ocean models using the `Mod_ParProf` module. If the execution and wait times for the atmosphere and the ocean match, then both models run with the same speed and no improvement is possible without adding more CPU resources. If the times do not match, it is possible to move some CPU cores from one model to another to slow down the former and to speed up the latter.

Table 1 summarizes the results of all experiments performed to find optimal configurations. As one can see, the INMCM6M requires significantly more processes for the atmosphere model than for the ocean model. So, to find an optimal configuration, we adjust the number of CPU cores for the ocean model ($P_x \cdot P_y$) to provide the closest match for the execution and wait times to the atmosphere model. The green highlighting indicates the configurations that were found to be optimal. Analyzing the results, we conclude that using an extremely large P_{lat} number with the small P_{lon} does not result in the best performance configurations even if they are optimal. Optimality of a configuration depends on using the particular HPC system. Only one configuration is considered optimal for both Cray XC40-LC and INM RAS clusters.

3.2 INMCM Scalability on Different HPC Systems

Figure 3 shows the results of the INMCM6M parallel scalability study. The blue squares and the orange diamonds indicate the speedup for all configurations presented in Table 1 on Cray XC40-LC and INM RAS HPC systems, respectively. On each system the speedup is calculated relative to the total execution time of the 204 CPU cores configuration. Lines join the configurations with the best performance. The black dashed line shows the linear speedup.

Figure 3 demonstrates that when the number of MPI processes is quadrupled, the speedup is close to 3, which corresponds to 70–75% of the parallelization efficiency. For less than 500 CPU cores an almost linear speedup is observed, for more cores the parallelization efficiency decreases.

Despite almost all configurations performed on the INM RAS cluster are not optimal, Fig. 3 shows that INMCM6M scales better on this HPC system compared to the Cray XC40-LC. It may be caused by usage of more recent Intel Xeon Gold 6230v2 processors (Cascade Lake family) installed in the INM RAS cluster. The equality of speedup achieved on the 1224 CPU cores configuration may be explained by the fact that this configuration is optimal for the Cray XC40-LC and is unbalanced for the INM RAS HPC system.

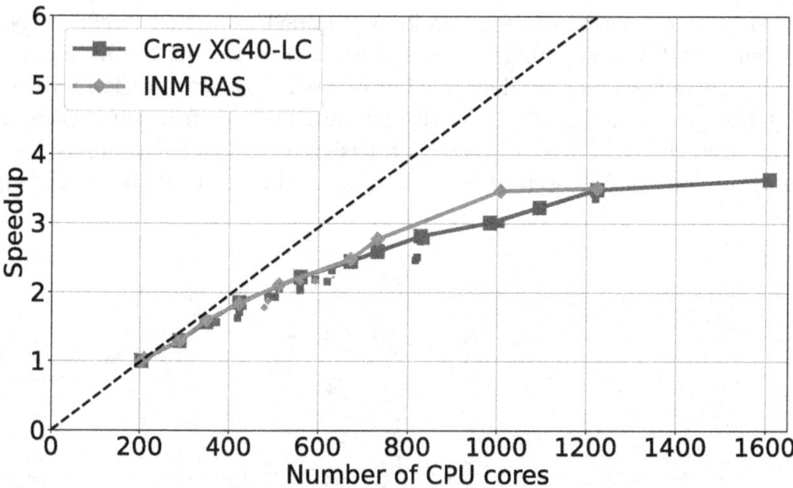

Fig. 3. INMCM6M speedup as a function of the CPU cores number for the Cray XC40-LC (blue) and the INM RAS (orange) HPC systems. (Color figure online)

The results shown in Fig. 3 are preliminary and may change slightly when the optimal INMCM6M configurations for the INM RAS HPC system are refined.

3.3 Parallel Efficiency of INMCM Modules

For a detailed analysis of the parallel scalability of the INMCM6M individual modules, a new software toolkit `Mod_ParProf` described in Sect. 2.2 was implemented in the INM RAS Earth system model. With the help of the `Mod_ParProf`, we evaluate the parallel performance of the atmosphere and the ocean models and the aerosol module. Table 2 presents the INMCM6M configurations used in the parallel efficiency study.

Table 2. Configurations of INMCM6M used in the parallel efficiency study.

	MPI communicator size					
INMCM (commworld)	288	424	561	732	1008	1224
Atmospheric model	120	180	240	312	432	540
Aerosol module	120	180	240	312	432	540
Ocean model	48	64	81	108	144	144

Atmosphere Model. First of all, the atmosphere model is studied. INM RAS Earth system model computational scheme demonstrates (see Fig. 1) that the atmosphere model has two principal loops: main loop and inner "fast" loop.

The time step fraction of the main loop obtained using `Mod_ParProf` toolkit for different INMCM6M configurations is shown in Fig. 4a for Cray XC40-LC and Fig. 4b for INM RAS cluster. The number of MPI processes of the INMCM6M model in the Fig. 4 is indicated under the column. The step fraction of each block is indicated on the right side of the bar, if it is greater than 5% compared to the computation time of one step of the main loop. Time step of the main loop is 1 h.

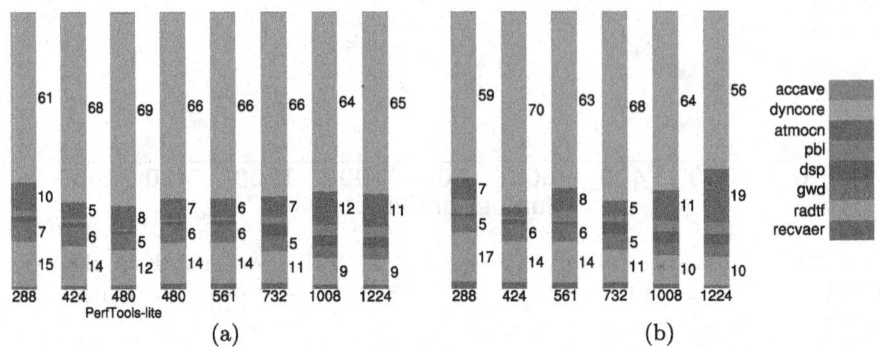

Fig. 4. Time step fraction of the most computationally demanding procedures of the INMCM6M atmosphere model obtained using the Cray XC40-LC (a) and the INM RAS cluster (b).

The main loop includes calls of the following procedures: parameterization of the gravity wave drag (`gwd` in Fig. 4); doppler-spread parameterization of gravity-wave momentum deposition in the middle atmosphere (`dsp`) also known as nonorographic forcing; planetary boundary layer, land surface and soil processes (`pbl`); radiation (long and short wavelengths) transfer (`radtf`); fast loop or dynamical core (`dyncore`); atmospheric-oceanic data exchanges and other (auxiliary) calculations (`atmocn`); accumulation of averaged characteristics of the atmosphere and surface for subsequent writing to a file (`accave`); receive data from aerosols module (`recvaer`).

Figure 4 demonstrates that the time fraction of the most computationally demanding procedures of the atmospheric model decreases with increasing number of MPI processes. This dependence corresponds to the subgrid scale processes procedures (`radtf`, `gwd`, `dsp`, `pbl`) which perform computations for each vertical column independently. The time fraction of the dynamical core (`dyncore`) is almost constant as the number of MPI processes increases. This is a good result, since dynamical core involves a large number of internal exchanges, as well as sending data to the aerosol module. It should be noted a slight increase in the time fraction of `pbl` and `dsp` procedures, as well as an increase in the time fraction of program code that implements the data processing and exchange with ocean model (`atmocn`). The exchanges between the atmosphere and ocean models are arranged as follows: data is sent from the ocean model to the atmosphere model, where they are collected by the first MPI process to perform an interpolation procedure. The data is then sent to the other MPI processes of the atmosphere model. This approach is a bottle-neck and explains the increase in (`atmocn`) procedure time fraction as the size of the MPI communicator increases.

Figure 5 shows the time fraction of the main procedures of the dynamical core (inner "fast" loop) of the INMCM6M atmosphere model for different configurations. Similar to Fig. 4, in the Fig. 5 shows the results obtained on the two computational systems: Cray XC40-LC (Fig. 5a) and INM RAS cluster (Fig. 5b).

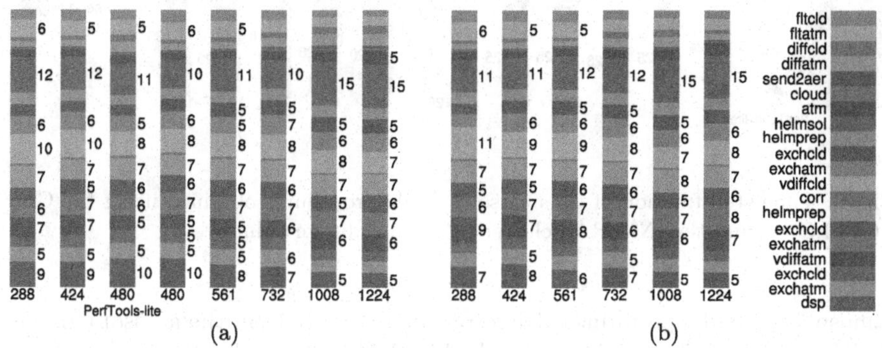

Fig. 5. Time step fraction of the INMCM6M atmosphere model dynamic core procedures obtained using the Cray XC40-LC (a) and the INM RAS cluster (b).

All dynamic core procedures can be divided into several categories: atmospheric state updates, solving the Helmholtz equation, data exchange, filtering, and vertical diffusion. The first category includes the procedures corresponding to the advancing the cloudiness `cloud` and atmospheric `atm` state. The second category includes the following procedures: prepare of the right hand side vector of the Helmholtz equation (for atmospheric and cloudiness state separately) and other necessary data `helmprep`, solve of the Helmholtz equation for atmosphere and cloudiness state together `helmsol`. Filtering category includes Asselin time filter and 8-th order diffusion scheme for cloudiness (`fltcld` and `diffcld`) as well as for atmospheric (`fltatm` and `diffatm`) state. Vertical diffusion due to turbulent processes in the boundary layer in Fig. 5 corresponds to the `vdiffatm`, `vdiffdsp` and `vdiffcld`. Procedures for exchanging data via MPI are indicated as `exch*`. Procedure `corr` implements correction of non-physical negative values of air humidity and cloudiness fraction, which may appear during calculations.

The time fractions of the inner loop procedures presented in the Fig. 5 almost do not change with increasing number of MPI processes. Therefore, the dynamic core of the INMCM6M atmospheric model is well-balanced.

Aerosol Module. The time fraction of the procedure that send atmospheric data to the aerosol model and procedure that receive data from the aerosol model is insignificant (see Figs. 5 and 4) despite the large data exchange (in both cases the procedures operate with five-dimensional arrays). Therefore, the

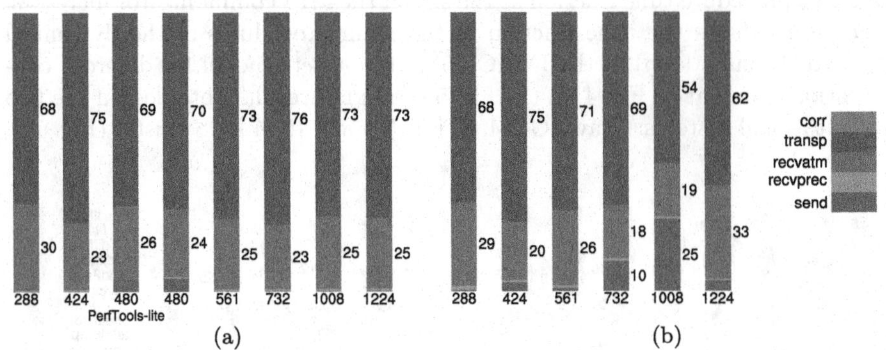

Fig. 6. Time step fraction of the aerosol module procedures obtained using the Cray XC40-LC (a) and the INM RAS cluster (b). (Color figure online)

atmospheric model performs calculations more slowly than the aerosol module.

This conclusion is confirmed by the Fig. 6, that illustrates time step fraction of the atmospheric aerosol model procedures. In the Fig. 6 one can see that a significant part of the model calculations corresponds to the procedures that implement the exchange of data with the atmospheric model. Data exchange in this figure is represented by the following functions: obtaining data on the state of the atmosphere `recvatm`, data on precipitation `recvprec` and `send` procedure that send data to the model of the atmosphere. Note that data on the state of the atmosphere (wind speed components, etc.) are transferred to the aerosol model much more often (in the dynamical core) than the atmospheric model receives data on aerosol concentrations (main loop).

According to the Fig. 6, the number of computational cores related to the aerosol module can be reduced by 25%. However, a reduction in the number of computational cores of the aerosol module will lead to changes in the decomposition of computational data in this model. Differences in the decomposition of the computational domain between MPI processes in atmospheric model and aerosol module will lead to additional exchanges. This means that the gain in the number of computational cores may not be as significant as expected.

Ocean Model. Figure 7 shows the result of applying the developed software to the ocean model. In the ocean time step loop a few stages were discerned, each one representing either a particular physical phenomenon or utility routines of the same functional purpose. Further, description of the procedures and their designation in Fig. 7 will be given.

In the `sflux` procedure 11 two-dimensional atmospheric fields defined on the longitude-latitude grid are interpolated onto the ocean grid with a displaced pole.

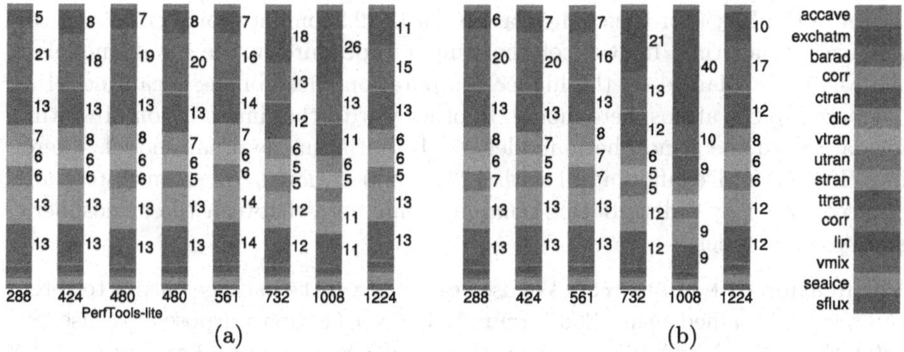

Fig. 7. Time step fraction of the ocean model procedures obtained using the Cray XC40-LC (a) and the INM RAS cluster (b). (Color figure online)

The `seaice` procedure stands for calculation of the thermodynamic processes in the sea ice and its drift by ocean currents. The turbulent mixing coefficients are defined at `vmix` stage. The metrical terms and the explicit part of the Coriolis force are treated at the stage `lin`. The advection, vertical turbulent mixing and horizontal mixing of the velocities are designated as `utran` and `vtran`. At the stages `stran`, `ttran`, `ctran` the advection, vertical and isopycnal mixing of the temperature, salinity and CO_2 are calculated.

At the `barad` stage the matrix equation for the sea surface height, the barotropic components of velocity is solved. Procedure `corr` implements correction of the non-physical values of temperature and salinity. Accumulation of average monthly values of different fields is performed in the procedure `accave` by analogy with the atmospheric model.

Since the procedure of data exchange with the atmospheric model takes a significant part of the time we analyzed its parallel characteristics with the `Mod_ParProf` toolkit. The data transferred by the atmospheric model are aggregated at the MPI master process of the ocean model, interpolated, and only then distributed to all MPI processes of the model. The results of the analysis show that about half of the procedure time is spent on distributing data to MPI processes via `MPI_BCAST` function. Therefore, there is an opportunity here for an acceleration of the INMCM6M. However, it will not be as significant as expected, since data exchange between atmospheric and oceanic models is a relatively rare event.

An interesting result is the output of the `Mod_ParProf` toolkit performed for a INMCM6M configuration with 1008 computational cores. According to Figs. 4 and 7, a significant time step fraction of the atmospheric and oceanic models (compared to configurations with 732 and 1224 computational cores) relates to the data exchange between them. This is found on both Cray XC40-LC and INM RAS computational systems which differ in the number of computational cores per node. The reasons for this deviation remain unclear and will be investigated in the future. The increased time fraction of exchanges related to the atmosphere model in the Fig. 4 for the configuration with 1224 computational cores and the relatively small time fraction of the similar procedure in the ocean model in the Fig. 7 is explained by the higher computation speed of the ocean model as compared to the atmosphere model. In other words, the time fraction of waiting for data from the atmospheric model is substantial in the ocean model. Therefore, INMCM6M configuration with 1224 computational cores can potentially be accelerated by redistributing computational cores between the atmospheric and oceanic models.

Verification of `Mod_ParProf`. We use `PerfTools-lite` package output to verify the results obtained using `Mod_ParProf`. For verification purposes, we use the 480 CPU cores INMCM6M configuration to profile using both `PerfTools-lite` and `Mod_ParProf`. The bars corresponding to the `PerfTools-lite` results in the Figs. 4a, 5a, 6a, 7a are indicated as `PerfTools-lite`. Note that the output of the `PerfTools-lite` is visualized using the `Mod_ParProf` module.

Time fractions of the model units obtained using `PerfTools-lite` and `Mod_ParProf` toolkits are close to each other. The small differences may be a consequence of the insufficient number of experiments and the potential heterogeneity of the computing system used. The overheads of these software programs may also differ. Therefore, the developed `Mod_ParProf` software toolkit can be used to study the parallel properties of the INM RAS Earth system model on the different HPC systems.

4 Discussion and Conclusion

Climate models are currently among the most resource-intensive scientific applications that require high performance computing. An important area of research in this field is the problem of efficient use of available computational resources to organize a large number of experiments for model tuning, testing and verification.

The program for examining parallel characteristics of a model like INMCM6M is therefore a useful and necessary accompanying toolkit. `Mod_ParProf` toolkit presented in this paper allows to identify slowly executing fragments of program code (bottle-necks) and to investigate the parallel characteristics of the model in detail. In our case with the help of `Mod_ParProf` we managed to find the configurations that perform 1 model month computation up to 20% faster compared to original "eye picked" configurations (for example, 41 min against 48 min for 348 CPU cores configuration) and provided guidelines for further model optimization. Other case is an optimal 672 core configuration that needs 24.5 min to complete the computation instead of 29 min and 752 CPU cores for an unbalanced configuration.

The maximum coupled model computation speed is achieved when the computational resources are distributed between the atmosphere, aerosol, and ocean models such that providing the same computation speed for each model within INMCM6M. Another parameter that affects the coupled model computation speed is the intensity of the exchanges between the INMCM6M components. Moreover, each model within INMCM6M allows for several configurations that differ in the way the computational data is decomposed. Therefore, the search of optimal INMCM6M configurations that corresponds to the maximum computation speed of the model with fixed number of computational cores is a difficult problem.

Acknowledgements. The research was carried out at the Marchuk Institute of Numerical Mathematics of the Russian Academy of Sciences. The development, implementation and verification of the INM RAS Earth system model profiler presented in Sects. 2.2 and 3.3 was supported by the Russian Federation research and technical development program in ecological strategy and climate change through grant FFMG-2023-0001 "Development of an extended version of the INM RAS Earth system model within a new computational framework". The search for optimal configurations and scalability evaluation for the INMCM6M described in Sects. 3.1 and 3.2 were carried out with the support of the Russian Science Foundation, Project 20-17-00190. All computations were performed using the HPC system of the Marchuk Institute of Numerical Mathematics of the Russian Academy of Sciences and Cray XC40-LC HPC system at the MCC of Roshydromet.

References

1. Volodin, E.M., et al.: Simulation of modern climate with the new version of the INM RAS climate model. Izvest. Atmosph. Ocean. Phys. **53**, 142–155 (2017). https://doi.org/10.1134/S0001433817020128
2. Volodin, E.M., Kostrykin, S.V.: The aerosol module in the INM RAS climate model. Russ. Meteorol. Hydrol. **41**(8), 519–528 (2016). https://doi.org/10.3103/S106837391608001X
3. Volodin, E.M., Lykosov, V.N.: Parametrization of heat and moisture transfer in the soil-vegetation system for use in atmospheric general circulation models: 1. Formulation and simulations based on local observational data. Izvest. Atmosph. Ocean. Phys. **34**(4), 405–416 (1998)
4. Volodin, E.M., Lykosov, V.N.: Parametrization of heat and moisture transfer in the soil-vegetation system for use in atmospheric general circulation models: 2. Numerical experiments in climate modeling. Izvest. Atmosph. Ocean. Phys. **34**(5), 559–569 (1998)
5. Terekhov, K.M., Volodin, E.M., Gusev, A.V.: Methods and efficiency estimation of parallel implementation of the σ-model of general ocean circulation. Russ. J. Numer. Anal. Math. Model. **26**(2), 189–208 (2011). https://doi.org/10.1515/rjnamm.2011.011
6. Yakovlev N.G.: Reproduction of the large-scale state of water and sea ice in the Arctic Ocean in 1948–2002: Part I. Numerical model. Izvest. Atmosph. Ocean. Phys. **45**(3), 357–371 (2009)
7. Yakovlev, N.G.: Reproduction of the large-scale state of water and sea ice in the Arctic Ocean from 1948 to 2002: Part II. The state of ice and snow cover. Izvest. Atmosph. Ocean. Phys. **45**(4), 478–494 (2009)
8. Volodin, E.M., Mortikov, E.V., Kostrykin, S.V., Galin, V.Y., et al.: Simulation of the modern climate using the INM-CM48 climate model. Russ. J. Numer. Anal. Math. Model. **33**(6), 367–374 (2018)
9. Eyring, V., Bony, S., Meehl, G.A., et al.: Overview of the coupled model intercomparison project phase 6 (CMIP6) experimental design and organization. Geosci. Model Develop. **9**(5), 1937–1958 (2016)

10. Kim, Y.H., Min, S.K., Zhang, X., et al.: Evaluation of the CMIP6 multi-model ensemble for climate extreme indices. Weather Climate Extremes **29**, 100269 (2020)
11. Tarasevich, M.A., Volodin, E.M.: Influence of various parameters of INM RAS climate model on the results of extreme precipitation simulation. In: International Young Scientists School and Conference on Computational Information Technologies for Environmental Sciences, 27 May–6 June 2019. IOP Conference Series: Earth and Environmental Science, p. 012012. IOP Publishing (2019)
12. Volodin, E.M., Gritsun, A.S.: Simulation of observed climate changes in 1850–2014 with climate model INM-CM5. Earth Syst. Dyn. **9**(4), 1235–1242 (2018)
13. Vorobyeva, V.V., Volodin, E.M.: Experimental studies of seasonal weather predictability based on the INM RAS climate model. Math. Models Comput. Simul. **13**(4), 571–578 (2021)
14. Vorobyeva, V., Volodin, E.: Evaluation of the INM RAS climate model skill in climate indices and stratospheric anomalies on seasonal timescale. Tellus A: Dyn. Meteorol. Oceanogr. **73**(1), 1–12 (2021)
15. Vorobeva, V.V., Volodin, E.M., Gritsun, A.S., Tarasevich, M.A.: Analysis of the atmosphere and the ocean upper layer state predictability for up to 5 years ahead using the INMCM5 climate model hindcasts. Russ. Meteorol. Hydrol. **48**, 581–589 (2023)
16. Volodin, E.M.: Simulation of present-day climate with the INMCM60 model. Izv. Atmos. Ocean. Phys. **59**(1), 16–22 (2023)
17. Intel VTune Profiler. https://software.intel.com/content/www/us/en/develop/tools/oneapi/components/vtune-profiler.html
18. Cray Performance Measurement and Analysis Tools User Guide. https://support.hpe.com/hpesc/public/docDisplay?docId=a00113917en_us. Accessed 6 June 2023
19. Gloukhov, V.: Parallel implementation of the INM atmospheric general circulation model on distributed memory multiprocessors. In: Sloot, P., Hoekstra, A., Kenneth, T., Dongarra, J. (eds.) CONFERENCE 2002, LNCS, vol. 2329, pp. 753–762. Springer, Heidelberg (2002). https://doi.org/10.1007/3-540-46043-8
20. Mortikov, E.V.: Improving scalability of the high spatial resolution earth system model soft-ware complex. In: Parallelnye vychislitelnye tekhnologii (PaVT 2015), pp. 431–435 (2015). (in Russian)
21. Mortikov, E.: The efficiency of the implementation of iterative methods for the solution of elliptic equations in atmospheric general circulation models on massively parallel systems. In: Sobolev, S., Voevodin, V. (eds.) 1st Russian Conference on Supercomputing Days 2015 (RuSCDays 2015s), CEUR Workshop Proceedings, vol. 1482, pp. 528–534. CEUR-WS (2015)
22. Balay, S., Gropp, W.D., Curfman McInnes, L., Smith, B.F.: Efficient management of parallelism in object oriented numerical software libraries. In: Modern Software Tools in Scientific Computing, pp. 163–202. Birkhäuser Press (1997)

Simulation of Free-Surface Fluid Dynamics: Parallelization for GPUs

Egor Savin, Alexander Asrankulov, Sergey Khrapov, and Alexander Khoperskov(✉)

Volgograd State University, Volgograd, Russia
{e.s.savin,khrapov,khoperskov}@volsu.ru

Abstract. Software has been developed for 3D modeling of fluid motion on an inhomogeneous terrain for problems of river hydrology. Parallelization of the Smoothed-particle hydrodynamics (SPH) method was performed using both OpenCL and CUDA for GPU computing systems. The efficiency of parallelization as a function of the number of SPH particles has been studied for various GPUs. We implemented an approach based on immobile SPH particles for setting boundary conditions on a geometrically complex surface. The digital elevation model defines such a boundary surface using standard 3D geometric solid modeling techniques. The dispersion properties of surface gravitational linear waves in the numerical model are in good agreement with the exact solution for a wide range of wavenumbers.

Keywords: Computational fluid dynamics · Parallel computing · OpenCL · Smoothed-particle hydrodynamics · Graphics processors

1 Introduction

The shallow water model (SWM) has deservedly gained widespread use for the numerical simulation of fluid dynamics over the earth's surface in a wide variety of applications. SWM is a modern basis for surface water hydrology (river and marine systems, rain flows) [1–4], descriptions of the movement of dry and wet volcanic loose flows (debris flows, snow avalanches, landslides of rock or soil, pyroclastic currents) [5], sediment transport in the study of riverbed processes [6,7], and the consequences of emergency situations [2,3,8].

The SWM based on the Saint-Venant equations and their modifications assumes several fundamental assumptions. First, the thickness of the fluid layer (H) is small compared to any inhomogeneity in the plane of motion ($L_\perp \gg H$). Strictly speaking, this condition is violated almost everywhere when modeling realistic water bodies. Secondly, all processes in the Earth's plane must occur slowly enough so that the hydrostatic vertical equilibrium has time to be established at each moment of time. Therefore, the SWM allows us to consider only vertically averaged flow characteristics and surface waves with a frequency $\omega_s = k\sqrt{gH}$ without dispersion. The above conditions for the shallow water

V. Voevodin et al. (Eds.): RuSCDays 2023, LNCS 14388, pp. 217–231, 2023.
https://doi.org/10.1007/978-3-031-49432-1_17

model are quite severe. The issue of total errors when using SWM is complex in each specific numerical experiment, and the only way to evaluate is to check on 3D models. The standard approach to model verification through calculations on finer grids has strong practical limitations due to the uncertainties of the terrain model of a particular area, the accuracy of which is insufficient when the grid is highly refined.

Three-dimensional hydrodynamic models based on the grid Euler's approach are available for modern computing systems [9,10]. The use of 3D models even for real shallow water bodies, such as the Azov Sea, shows the important role of accounting for vertical movements [11]. Engineering calculations of the impact of water flows on offshore and coastal structures require 3D modeling of a fluid with a free surface [10,12]. Finally, 3D models provide a more correct parameterization of the vertical turbulent exchange coefficient, instead of simple vertical averaging.

The aim of this work is to create an efficient parallel software package for modeling 3D hydrodynamic flows with a free surface, which can correctly describe the dispersive properties of surface waves. The used end-to-end method of setting the boundary conditions is convenient for studying water dynamics on a complex inhomogeneous terrain.

2 Basic Equations and Methods

2.1 SPH Method

This section contains mathematical and numerical models, as well as parallelization algorithms. We use the Smoothed Particle Hydrodynamics (SPH) method with the features that make it possible to simulate an incompressible fluid [4,13–15]. The basis of Smoothed Particle Hydrodynamics is the representation of an arbitrary function $f(\mathbf{r},t)$ as a convolution with a smoothing kernel W [13]

$$f(\mathbf{r},t) = \int f(\mathbf{r}',t) \cdot W(|\mathbf{r}-\mathbf{r}'|,h)\,dV', \qquad \int W(|\mathbf{r}-\mathbf{r}'|,h)\,dV = 1, \tag{1}$$

where W is the smoothing kernel depending on the smoothing length h, $|\mathbf{r}-\mathbf{r}'|$ is the distance between the point $\mathbf{r}'$ and the center of the particle. Any hydrodynamic characteristic must be represented as (1). We used some smoothing kernels, in particular, the cubic spline [14,16]

$$W(q) = \zeta_g \times \begin{cases} \frac{2}{3} - q^2 + \frac{1}{2}q^3, & \text{if} \quad q \le 1 \\ \frac{1}{6}(2-q)^3, & \text{if } 1 < q \le 2, \\ 0, & \text{if} \quad q > 2 \end{cases} \tag{2}$$

and Debrun's spiky kernel

$$W(q) = \zeta_g \times \begin{cases} (2-q)^3, & \text{if } q \le 2 \\ 0, & \text{if } q > 2, \end{cases} \tag{3}$$

where $q = |\mathbf{r}_i - \mathbf{r}_j|/h$ is the dimensionless distance between two particles, the parameter ζ_s depends on the dimension of the problem and is determined by the normalization condition (1). There are a significant number of different ways of constructing smoothing functions, the choice is largely determined by the specifics of the task [13]. We use the kernel (2) for the density and (3) for calculating the forces.

The equations of hydrodynamics in SPH notation have the form [14,16,17]:

$$\frac{d\rho_i}{dt} = \sum_{j=1,\, j\neq i}^{N^{(f)}} m_j \mathbf{u}_{ij} \nabla_i W_{ij}\,, \tag{4}$$

$$\frac{d\mathbf{u}_i}{dt} = -\sum_{j=1,\, j\neq i}^{N^{(f)}} m_j \left(\frac{p_j}{\rho_j^2} + \frac{p_i}{\rho_i^2} + \Pi_{ij} \right) \nabla_i W_{ij} + \mathbf{F}_i^{(visc)} + \mathbf{f}_i\,, \tag{5}$$

where $W_{ij} = W(|r_{ij}|/h)$, $|\mathbf{r}_i - \mathbf{r}_j|$ is the distance between i-th and j-th particles, $N^{(f)}$ is the number of "living" particles, simulating the fluid, $\rho_i = \sum\limits_j m_j W_{ij}$ is the density of the i-th particle, $\mathbf{u}_i$, ε_i, p_i, $\mathbf{f}_i$ are the velocity, internal energy, pressure, specific external force of the i-th particle, respectively, $\mathbf{u}_{ij} = \mathbf{u}_i - \mathbf{u}_j$, $|\mathbf{f}| = g = 9.8\ \text{m}\cdot\text{sec}^{-2}$ is the acceleration of gravity. The tensor Π_{ij} defines an artificial shear and bulk viscosity [14,16,18]

$$\Pi_{ij} = \begin{cases} \dfrac{1}{\bar{\rho}_{ij}}(-\alpha\bar{c}_{ij}\mu_{ij} + \beta\mu_{ij}^2), & \text{if } \mathbf{u}_{ij}\cdot\mathbf{r}_{ij} < 0 \\ 0, & \text{if } \mathbf{u}_{ij}\cdot\mathbf{r}_{ij} \geq 0\,, \end{cases} \tag{6}$$

where $\bar{\rho}_{ij}$ is the average density, $\bar{c}_{ij}$ is the characteristic average velocity as an analogue of the sound speed, the parameters α and β characterize the value of viscosity, $\mu_{ij} = \dfrac{h\,\mathbf{u}_{ij}\cdot\mathbf{r}_{ij}}{\mathbf{r}_{ij}^2 + 0.01h^2}$ for an incompressible medium with low Reynolds Number [18]. The gradient operator in (4) – (5) is calculated from the coordinates of the i-th particle.

The closure of the system of equations (4) – (5) requires an state equation. We use the following equation [15,17,18]

$$p = \begin{cases} B\left[\left(\dfrac{\rho}{\rho_0}\right)^{\gamma} - 1\right], & \text{if } \rho > \rho_0 \\ 0, & \text{if } \rho \leq \rho_0\,, \end{cases} \tag{7}$$

where $\gamma = 7$, B is the coefficient that determines the sound speed for a quasi-incompressible fluid. The problem of improving the incompressibility of SPH models is solved by applying the so-called δ-SPH and δ-plus-SPH methods by refining the divergence-free velocity condition [12].

The choice of the time integration step Δt in the numerical scheme is limited by a number of conditions [16,19]: 1) the stability of the explicit scheme of a partial differential equation is determined by the Courant condition – Friedrichs

– Lewy $CFL < 1$; 2) the value of Δt is limited by the acceleration of particles and 3) by the action of viscous forces. This imposes the following condition on the integration step of equations (4) – (5):

$$\Delta t \leq CFL \cdot \min(\Delta t_1, \Delta t_2)\,, \tag{8}$$

where

$$\Delta t_1 = \min_i \left(\frac{h}{c_i + 1.2\alpha c_i + 1.2\beta \max\limits_j \mu_{ij}} \right), \quad \Delta t_2 = \min_i \left(\frac{h}{\sqrt{|d\mathbf{u}_i/dt|}} \right).$$

An analysis of the fulfillment of the conditions in (8) shows that the integration step can be defined as Δt_1 or Δt_2 depending on the physical flow conditions or the choice free parameters of the numerical model.

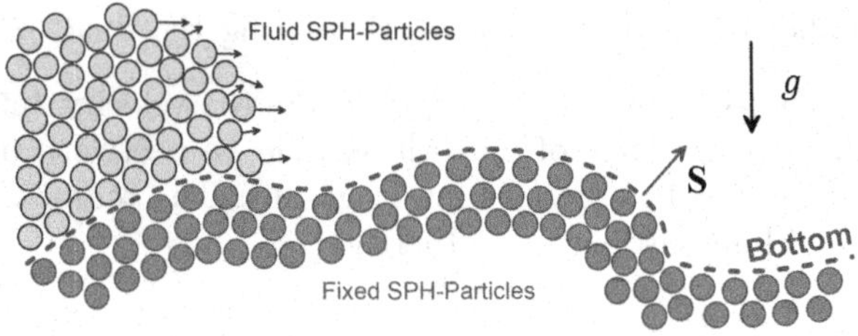

Fig. 1. Different types of SPH particles. "Fixed SPH-Particles" define the bottom surface **S**.

2.2 Boundary Conditions

The presence of solid surfaces in the flow region requires setting the boundary condition of impermeability on a given surface $\mathbf{S}(\mathbf{r})$. The complex shape of the boundary creates certain difficulties for numerical grid methods. These problems are exacerbated in the presence of moving boundaries. The particle method allows one to define arbitrarily complex surfaces $\mathbf{S}(\mathbf{r})$. We use layers of special fixed SPH particles to define the hard-solid surface $\mathbf{S}(\mathbf{r})$ (Fig. 1). Standard technologies for constructing a 3D solid body model (CAD) make it easy to replace such models with a particles system. The total number of particles N includes liquid particles ($N^{(f)}$) and solid boundary particles ($N^{(b)}$): $N = N^{(f)} + N^{(b)}$.

The advantages of this approach are, firstly, end-to-end calculations, when there is no check and selection of those liquid particles that are in close proximity to the boundary. Secondly, the way to define such solid surfaces is based on convenient 3D solid modeling technologies using CAD. The number of layers, their mutual arrangement and the distances between immobile particles are determined by the prohibition on the infiltration of liquid particles through the boundary. The disadvantage may be the requirement of large resources for fixed SPH-particles. The most optimal method for setting boundary conditions is to calculate the additional repulsive force for fixed SPH-particles in the form [15,20]:

$$\mathbf{F}_{ij}^{(rp)} = \begin{cases} D\left[\left(\frac{r_b}{r_{ij}}\right)^{\alpha_1} - \left(\frac{r_b}{r_{ij}}\right)^{\alpha_2}\right]\frac{\boldsymbol{r}_{ij}}{r_{ij}^2}, & \text{if } r_{ij} \le r_b \\ 0, & \text{if } r_{ij} > r_b\,, \end{cases} \tag{9}$$

where r_{ij} is the distance between the centers of two particles, $\alpha_1 = 12$, $\alpha_2 = 4$, D and r_b are the free parameters. Using the Formula (9) saves computational resources because it requires fewer particles $N^{(b)}$.

An additional advantage of this approach to setting boundary conditions is the simplicity of describing moving solid surfaces $\mathbf{S}(\mathbf{r}, t)$. This makes it possible to simulate surface flows on a changing terrain in the presence of sediment transport [6,7].

3 Parallelization on GPUs

3.1 Parallel Sorting Algorithm

The particle sorting algorithm is an essential part of the SPH method because it is applied for every particle at every integration step. We use a grid approach, combining different algorithms [21–24].

Parallel sorting algorithm on the GPU is based on the creation of a set of arrays in shared memory. This data is used for faster execution of the parallel reduction algorithm when finding partial sums only for neighboring particles in the CUDA block. Thus, the allocation of K integer arrays occurs at each sorting iteration [25]. The dimension of these arrays is equal to N/K.

A summary is given below using the following notation:

1. `grid[max_part]` – the array of particle numbers;
2. `cells[max_cells]` – index of first particle in the cell in the array `grid` ;
3. `neighbours[max_neigh, max_part]` – list of neighbor particles;
4. `max_part` – the total number of particles;
5. `max_cells` – the maximum number of grid cells;
6. `max_neigh` – the maximum number of neighboring particles.

Figure 2 demonstrates the algorithm for finding nearest neighbors:

1. The array `grid` contains the indexes of the particles.
2. Using a parallel sorting algorithm (such as radix sorter) when the particle is in a cell whose number is the key to compare particle positions (Listing 1.1).

Listing 1.1. Comparison operation: grid[i] < grid[i + 1]

```
bool less(__global const float2* r,
    __global const uint* grid, uint i)
{ return get_cell_idx(r[grid[i]]) <
get_cell_idx(r[grid[i+1]]) }
```

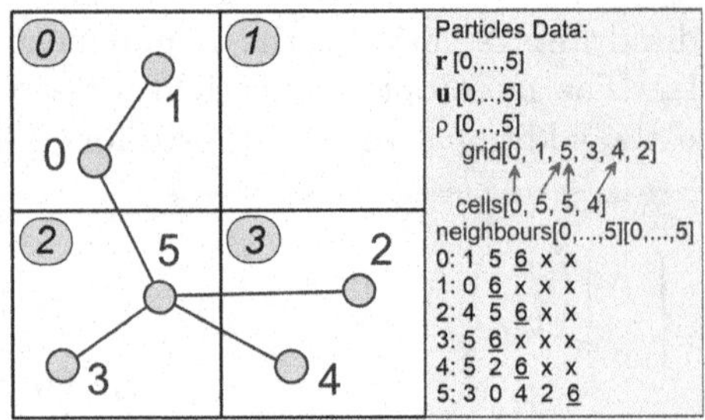

Fig. 2. Scheme of the algorithm for searching for pairs of nearest interacting particles (six blue circles in four cells). (Color figure online)

As a result, the indices of particles from one cell are arranged sequentially.

3. Binary Search for the index in `grid` allows you to get the index of the first particle in a given cell using only the cell number `cell_idx` (Listing 1.2).

Listing 1.2. Traversal method for all particles in a cell `cell_idx`

```
for (uint grid_i = cells[cell_idx];
    grid_i < cells[cell_idx + 1]; ++grid_i)
  { uint part_idx = grid[grid_i]; ... }
    // use particle index
```

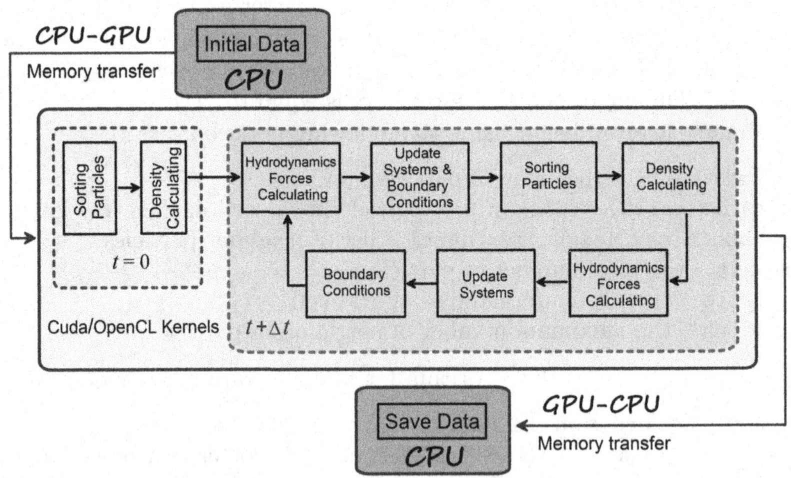

Fig. 3. Data flow diagram for the CPU and GPU.

The array `cells` points to the place in the `grid`, where to look for particles from the i-th cell. If the particle is not in the cell, then the index of the particle from the next cell is set.

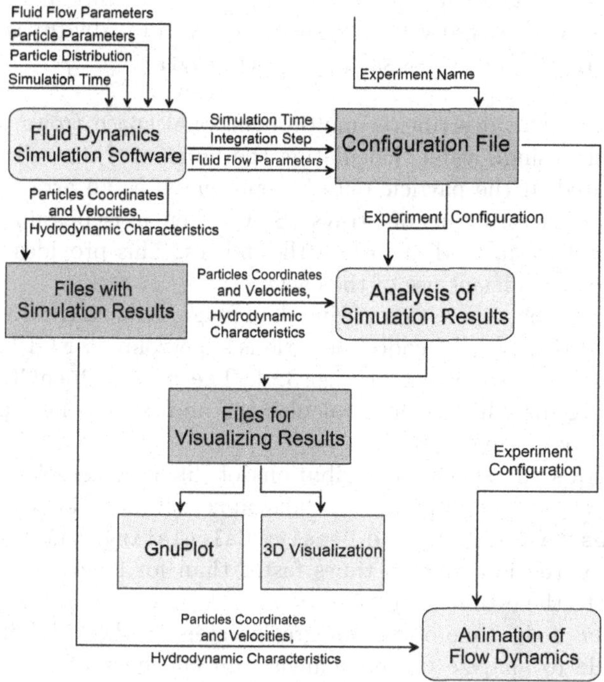

Fig. 4. Software Data Flow Diagram (DFD).

Filling the arrays `grid` and `cells` provides a simple algorithm for finding all pairs of interacting particles on the grid for neighboring cells. All such close particles are checked by the condition

$$r_{ij} \leq r_{\min} , \tag{10}$$

where $r_{\min} = (1-3)h$ depending on the chosen kernel function. Each particle has a spare memory for `max_neigh` neighbors, which allows different threads to work with non-overlapping memory regions. The criterion for the end of the list of neighbors is the appearance of a fictitious particle with the number `max_part`. The quantities W and ∇W are calculated immediately upon adding a neighboring particle.
Listing 1.3 shows an example of calculating the density of the j-th particle by iterating over the generated list of neighbors.

Listing 1.3. Way to bypass all neighbors for j-th particle

```
#define at(n,j) ((n) + max_neigh * (j))
```

```
uint j; // current particle
...
uint i; // neighbour particle
for (uint n = 0; // neighbour id
    i = neighbours[at(n, j)], i != max_part; ++n)
{   float vij_dwdr = dot(v[i]-v[j], dwdr[at(n,j)]);
    drho[j] += mass[i] * vij_dwdr;    }
```

The Morton curve describes a multidimensional space (rows and columns of a table) with a single value, calculating the number of the cell in which the particle is located. If the particle data is represented as an array of structures (AoS) instead of a structure of arrays (SoA), then it is possible to sort the particles themselves, instead of sorting the indices. This provides faster access to them due to the efficient use of the cache.

We use both the Open Computing Language (OpenCL) framework and CUDA when writing parallel codes for various supercomputer GPUs [23,24,26]. Data flow diagrams are shown in Figs. 3, 4. The use of OpenCL can solve a number of problems when scaling calculations and organizing simulations on heterogeneous computing clusters.

Figure 5 shows the specific contributions of different kernels using CUDA. The vast majority of computation time falls on kernel execution times `Hydrodynamics Forces Calculating` and `Density Calculating`. The time for kernel `Sorting Particles` is about 10 times faster than for `Density Calculating`, which is close to the estimate in [25].

Comparison of the time of one integration step for the CPU and GPU versions was made to analyze the implementation efficiency of the parallel algorithm. Figure 6 shows the dependence of the execution time on the number of particles (red line is the CPU, blue line is the GPU). Curve 1 has a monotonic profile, demonstrating a slowdown in growth as the number of particles increases. Dependence 2 shows monotonic growth with jumps, where there are singular points. This is due to the CUDA architecture of graphics accelerators, when each coprocessor contains a certain number of streaming multiprocessors (SMs) on which CUDA blocks are physically executed. If the task size (in CUDA blocks) is greater than the number of SMs, then control is transferred to the Thread Block Scheduler. This scheduler first starts the first portion of blocks, and after they are completed, transfers the next portion for processing. Thus, the magnitude of the jump corresponds to the execution time of the first portion of blocks.

Let's consider the influence of the configuration of model parameters on the parallelization efficiency using the CUDA technology as an example. Figure 7 shows the dependence of the execution time t_{GPU} on the number of SPH particles N and the number of sorting blocks on different GPUs. The number of such blocks can vary along three different directions (K_x, K_y, K_z). Our test calculations in Fig. 7*b* are limited to the case of $K_x = K_y = K_z = K$. The dependence $t_{GPU}(N)$ demonstrates a power-law growth with N. The nature of the dependencies of $t_{GPU}(N)$ turns out to be similar for different GPUs. However, the transition to the next NVIDIA GPU generations reduces the computation time by 2.5 – 3.4 depending on N and K. An increase in the number of blocks K makes it possible to significantly reduce t_{GPU} due to a decrease in the number of potential nearest neighbors at the sorting stage. Sorting blocks for small K contain a large number of particles that are not closest by the criterion (10), but increase the time t_{GPU}. This effect saturates at some K, depending on the total number of particles N and the features of the simulated flow. Figure 7*b* demonstrates such saturation at $K = 64$, when the block size does not exceed $2h$.

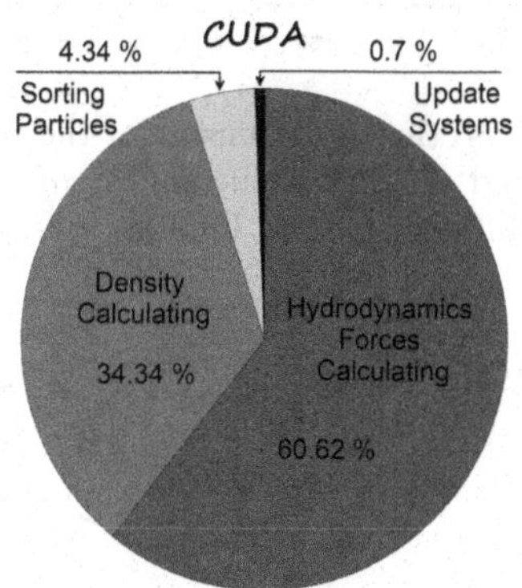

Fig. 5. Diagrams of execution time distribution by different kernels for CUDA and OpenCL.

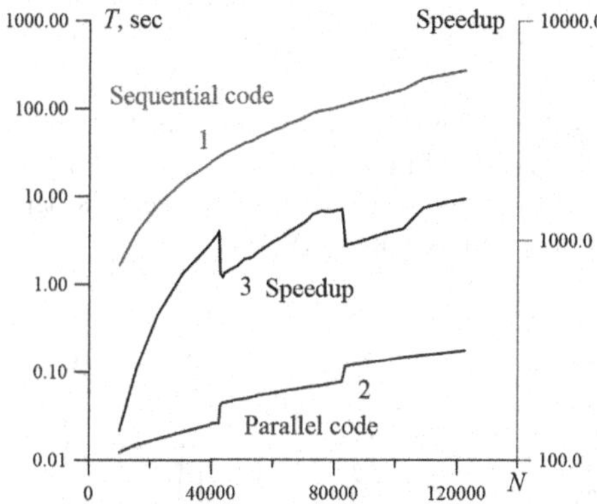

Fig. 6. Dependences of the calculation time of the average integration step Δt for parallel and sequential codes (left axis, lines 1, 2) and the speedup of parallel computations (line 3, right axis) on the number of particles N.

4 Numerical Model Verification

4.1 Dispersion of Surface Gravity Waves in Linear Approximation

The dynamics of linear waves of the form $\propto \sin(kx - \omega t)$ is determined by the dispersion equation $\omega^2 = (c_0^{(s)} \cdot k)^2$ in the shallow water model (k is the wavenumber). The quantity $c_0^{(s)} = \sqrt{gH_0}$ is the characteristic velocity of surface gravity waves. The phase velocity $V_{ph} = \omega/k = c_0^{(s)}$ is independent of the wavelength $\lambda = 2\pi/k$, so SWM does not describe the wave-packet dispersion.

Linearization of the hydrodynamic equations of an incompressible stationary fluid of thickness H_0 gives the following dispersion equation for gravitational surface waves [27]

$$\omega = \sqrt{kH_0}\,\frac{c_0^{(s)}}{H_0}\left(\tanh(kH_0)\right)^{1/2}, \tag{11}$$

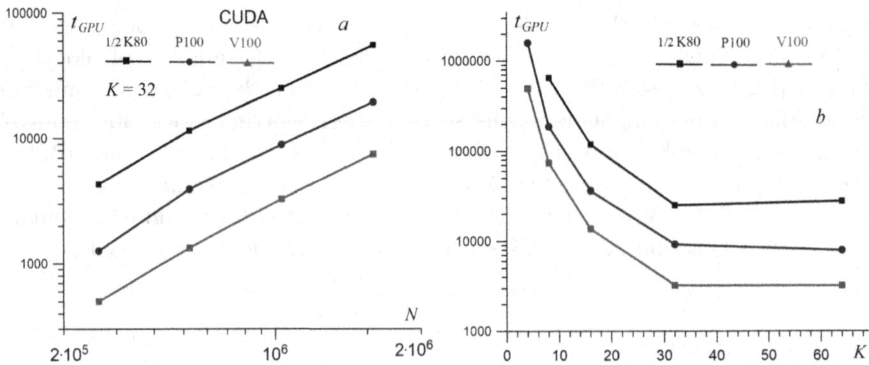

Fig. 7. *a*) The execution time on GPUs t_{GPU} [sec] vs. the total number of the particles N for different GPUs ($\frac{1}{2}$K80, P100, V100) and different values of K. *b*) The execution time on GPUs t_{GPU} [sec] vs. the K for different ($\frac{1}{2}$K80, P100, V100), the number of particles is $N = 2^{20}$.

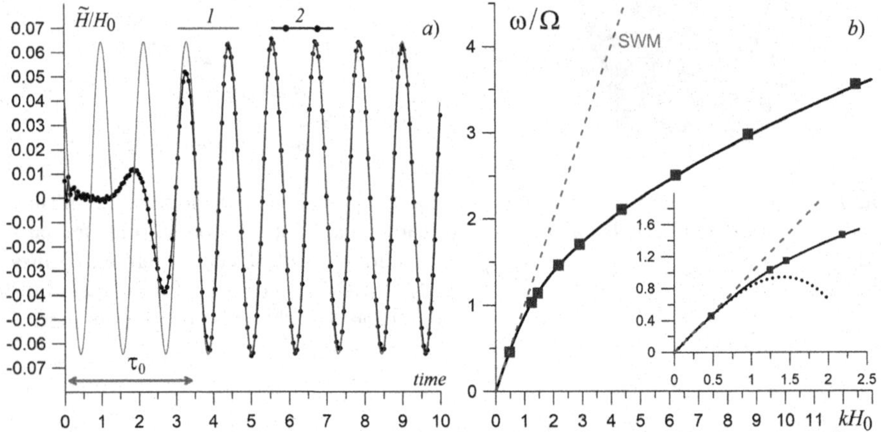

Fig. 8. Modeling of linear waves. *a*) Wave profiles versus time at a fixed point for the exact solution (*1*, red line) and numerical solution (black line *2*, symbols). *b*) Dependences of the dimensionless frequency ω/Ω ($\Omega = \sqrt{g/H_0}$) on the dimensionless wavenumber kH_0: the blue symbols are numerical experiments, the solid black line is the dispersion Eq. (11), the dashed green line is the dispersion relation for SWM. The inset shows only the long wavelength region.

where $c_0^{(s)} = \sqrt{gH_0}$. The limiting case $kH_0 \gg 1$ in (11) gives $\omega = \sqrt{kg}$. The frequency in the inverse long-wavelength limit ($kH_0 \ll 1$) is

$$\omega \simeq kc^{(s)} \left(1 - (kH_0)^2/6\right) . \tag{12}$$

Thus, waves in the long-wavelength limit (small wavenumber) do not have dispersion, which begins to appear approximately at $kH_0 > 1/2$.

Figure 8a shows the result of generating a surface wave of small amplitude $\tilde{H}$ propagating from left to right with frequency of $\omega = 5.48$ Hz. The green arrow highlights the initial interval of wave formation from the generator to the measurement points. The dispersion curves $\omega(k)$ are compared in Fig. 8b. The numerical SPH model reproduces well the exact solution for all kH_0. There is agreement with the shallow water model only for long waves $kH_0 \leq 1/2$ (green dashed line in Fig. 8b). The approximation (12) is shown as a dotted black line in Fig. 8b.

A correct description of the short-wavelength dispersion ($kH > 1/2$) is necessary for modeling nonlinear waves such as soliton solutions, tsunamis, bora. An example of the evolution of a dam break followed by reflection from a wall is depicted in Fig. 9. The color shows the distribution of pressure within the flow. Dynamic features are highlighted in Fig. 9 (See also works [17,28]), such as rising water at the right wall to a height of about $1.5H_0$ and the subsequent wave breaking on the liquid surface. As a result, an inner tube is formed in the form of an empty space inside the wave. Wave breaking leads to the birth of a characteristic liquid jet. Its subsequent fall into the water spawns another tube (See time $t = 1.5$ sec in Fig. 9).

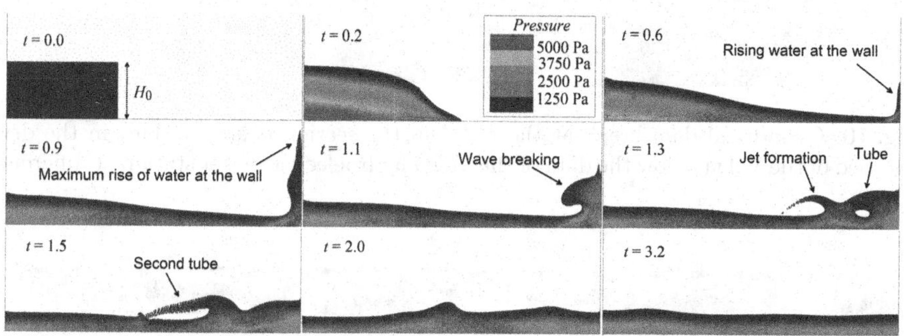

Fig. 9. The evolution of dam break flow over a dry horizontal bed and impact on the right wall, $[t] = \text{sec}$.

4.2 Placement of Immobile SPH Particles on Solid Surface

Let's briefly discuss the features of setting the boundary of the underlying surface (See Fig. 1). Such a boundary should not allow liquid particles to pass through it, which is the most important requirement for boundary conditions. In addition, the solution to the problem of saving computational resources requires the minimum number of particles $N^{(b)}$. We carried out a series of rigorous numerical experiments with different ways of defining the surface $\mathbf{S}$ by SPH particles and varying the initial impact on the bottom, including the water flow falling onto the surface from a great height and other problems. An example of such an impact is shown in Fig. 10 as an initial evolution of a circulation dam on a realistic terrain model. The total number of SPH particles is 2^{25}, including

3.4 million fluid particles for water dynamics simulations. The bottom is determined by more than 30 millions of immobile particles. Figure 11 shows the result of modeling water dynamics after a rapid decline of a fragment of the bottom by 40 m downward, which describes an earthquake. Pressure distributions for four time points after the earthquake give a complex picture of the initial formation of the tsunami after the impact.

Our analysis confirms that the three-layer staggered structure with an average distance between particles $r_0^{(b)} \simeq h$ ensures complete tightness of the bottom surface. The additional setting of the potential using (9) is a good part of defense-in-depth. One-layer or two-layer structures can pass liquid particles even at $r_0^{(b)} \ll h$.

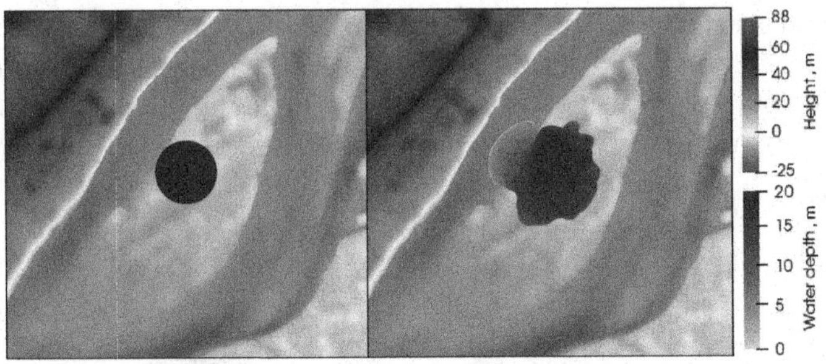

Fig. 10. Cylindrical dam-break at the DEM in the section (6 km × 6 km) in the dry riverbed of the Volga below the dam of the Volga hydroelectric power station at different times.

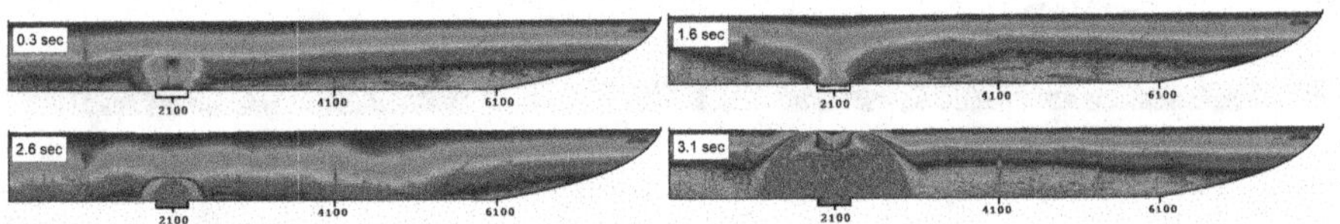

Fig. 11. Initial stage of tsunami formation. The water depth is 400 m. The source of the earthquake is localized in the vicinity of $x = 2100$ m.

5 Discussion and Conclusion

Numerical 3D models of surface water dynamics are still difficult to use over the entire range of motions with scales from $\lambda \ll H_0$ to $\lambda \gg H_0$. Modeling real extended water bodies, for example, river floodplains [23,30] requires too much resources. Traditional shallow water models have formal constraints $\lambda \ll H_0$, which requires error estimates. The result of this study is the creation of tools for verifying models of the SWM type and estimating errors for such calculations. A complete transition from SWM to full-fledged 3D models requires huge resources and is too expensive for engineering hydrology of extended water systems. Therefore, the main purpose of such 3D SPH models in hydrological applications is the verification of shallow water models.

Higher performance on the GPU compared to the CPU [23,29] ensures a wider distribution of codes for GPUs. However, problematic trends in the use of GPUs are found, such as lack of RAM, reduced code flexibility, and other reasons for performance degradation [29]. We have used two parallelization technologies on GPUs. First, there is CUDA as a native technology for NVIDIA Graphics Processing Units. Additionally, OpenCL was used as a more universal one, which allows expanding the list of GPUs.

We varied the number of SPH particles, the number of sorting blocks on different GPUs in order to evaluate the efficiency of parallelization. It should be emphasized that the efficiency of calculations can depend not only on the total number of particles, but also on the fraction of particles for specifying solid boundary surfaces, which in turn is completely determined by the features of the flow under study. At the same time, it is very important to choose the optimal number of sorting blocks, which can reduce the time of a computational experiment on the same GPU by several times.

A detailed study of the dispersion properties of surface gravity waves in the numerical SPH model has been carried out. Our computational experiments made it possible to construct dispersion curves ($\omega(k)$) both in the long-wavelength region ($kH \ll 1$) and in the short-wavelength limit ($kH \gg 1$). Satisfactory agreement with exact solutions of wave dynamics for an incompressible fluid is shown.

Acknowledgments. This work supported by the Russian Science Foundation (grant no. 23-71-00016, https://rscf.ru/project/23-71-00016/). The research is carried out using the equipment of the shared research facilities of HPC computing resources at Lomonosov Moscow State University.

References

1. Voronin, A.A., Vasilchenko, A.A., Klikunova, A.Y., Vatyukova, O.Y., Khoperskov, A.V.: The problem of safe evacuation of large floodplains population during flooding. Adv. Syst. Sci. Appl. **22**(4), 65–78 (2022)
2. Belikov, V.V., Vasil'eva, E.S.: Numerical modeling of a hydrodynamic accident at an earth-and-rockfill dam on the dyurso river. Power Technol. Eng. **54**, 326–331 (2020). https://doi.org/10.1007/s10749-020-01210-1
3. Belikov, V.V., Aleksyuk, A.I., Borisova, N.M., Glotko, A.V., Rumyantsev, A.B.: Estimation of the level of floodplain inundation in the lower don under the effect of economic activity. Retrospective hydrodynamic modeling. Water Resources **49**, 941–949 (2022). https://doi.org/10.1134/S0097807822060021
4. Violeau, D.: Fluid Mechanics and the SPH Method: Theory and Applications. Oxford University Press, Oxford (2012). https://doi.org/10.1093/acprof:oso/9780199655526.001.0001

5. Neglia, F., Sulpizio, R., Dioguardi, F., Capra, L., Sarocchi, D.: Shallow-water models for volcanic granular flows: a review of strengths and weaknesses of TITAN2D and FLO2D numerical codes. J. Volcanol. Geoth. Res. **410**, 107146 (2021). https://doi.org/10.1016/j.jvolgeores.2020.107146
6. Khrapov, S.S., Khoperskov, A.V.: Application of graphics processing units for self-consistent modelling of shallow water dynamics and sediment transport. Lobachevskii J. Math. **41**(8), 1475–1484 (2020)
7. Khrapov S.S., et al.: Numerical modeling of self-consistent dynamics of shallow waters, traction and suspended sediments: I. Influence of commercial sand mining on the safety of navigation in the channel of the Volga river. Math. Phys. Comput. Simulat. **5**(3), 31–57 (2022). https://doi.org/10.15688/mpcm.jvolsu.2022.3.3
8. Adityawan, M.B., et al.: Numerical modeling of dam break induced flow through multiple buildings in an idealized city. Results Eng. **18**, 101060 (2023)
9. Sukhinov, A.I., Chistyakov, A.E., Kuznetsova, I.Y., Atayan, A.M., Nikitina, A.V.: Regularized difference scheme for solving hydrodynamic problems. Math. Models Comput. Simul. **14**, 745–754 (2022). https://doi.org/10.1134/S2070048222050155
10. Sukhinov, A., Chistyakov, A., Protsenko, S.: 3D Model of wave impact on shore protection structures and algorithm of its parallel implementation. Commun. Comput. Inf. Sci. **1331**, 3–14 (2020). https://doi.org/10.1007/978-3-030-64616-5_1
11. Sukhinov, A.I., Chistyakov, A.E., Alekseenko, E.V.: Numerical realization of the three-dimensional model of hydrodynamics for shallow water basins on a high-performance system. Math. Models Comput. Simul. **3**(3), 562–574 (2011). https://doi.org/10.1134/S2070048211050115
12. Khayyer, A., Shimizu, Y., Gotoh, T., Gotoh, H.: Enhanced resolution of the continuity equation in explicit weakly compressible SPH simulations of incompressible free-surface fluid flows. Appl. Math. Model. **116**, 84–121 (2023). https://doi.org/10.1016/j.apm.2022.10.037
13. Liu, M.B., Liu, G.R., Lam, K.Y.: Constructing smoothing functions in smoothed particle hydrodynamics with applications. J. Comput. Appl. Math. **155**(2), 263–284 (2003). https://doi.org/10.1016/S0377-0427(02)00869-5
14. Liu, G.R., Liu, M.B.: Smoothed Particle Hydrodynamics: A Meshfree Particle Method. World Scientific Publishing Company, Singapore (2003). https://doi.org/10.1142/5340
15. Monaghan, J.J.: Simulating Free Surface Flows with SPH. J. Comput. Phys. **110**(2), 399–406 (1994)
16. Monaghan, J.J.: Smoothed particle hydrodynamics. Ann. Rev. Astron. Astrophys. **30**(1), 543–574 (1992). https://doi.org/10.1146/annurev.aa.30.090192.002551
17. Valizadeh, A., Monaghan, J.J.: A study of solid wall models for weakly compressible SPH. J. Comput. Phys. **300**, 5–19 (2015). https://doi.org/10.1016/j.jcp.2015.07.033
18. Morris, J.P., Fox, P.J., Zhu, Yi.: Modeling low Reynolds Number incompressible flows using SPH. J. Comput. Phys. **136**(1), 214–226 (1997). https://doi.org/10.1006/jcph.1997.5776
19. Courant, R., Friedrichs, K., Lewy, H.: Über die partiellen Differenzengleichungen der mathematischen Physik. Math. Ann. **100**, 32–74 (1928). https://doi.org/10.1007/BF01448839
20. Barbosa, D.A., Piccoli, F.P.: Comparing the force due to the Lennard-Jones potential and the Coulomb force in the SPH method. J. Ocean Eng. Sci. **3**(4), 310–315 (2018). https://doi.org/10.1016/j.joes.2018.10.007

21. Morillo, D., Carmona, R., Perea, J.J., Cordero, J.M.: A more efficient parallel method for neighbour search using CUDA. In: Workshop on Virtual Reality Interaction and Physical Simulation, pp. 101–109 (2015). https://doi.org/10.2312/vriphys.20151339
22. Morikawa, D.S., Tsuji, K., Asai, M.: Corrected ALE-ISPH with novel Neumann boundary condition and density-based particle shifting technique. J. Comput. Phys.: X **17**, 100125 (2023). https://doi.org/10.1016/j.jcpx.2023.100125
23. Dyakonova, T., Khoperskov, A., Khrapov, S.: Numerical model of Shallow Water: the use of NVIDIA CUDA graphics processors. Commun. Comput. Inf. Sci. **687**, 132–145 (2016)
24. Green, S.: Particle Simulation using CUDA. In: NVIDIA, Particle Simulation Using CUDA, 1st edn. NVIDIA, 9 (2013)
25. Khrapov, S., Khoperskov, A.: Smoothed-particle hydrodynamics models: implementation features on GPUs. Commun. Comput. Inf. Sci. **793**, 266–277 (2017)
26. Voevodin, V.V., et al.: Supercomputer lomonosov-2: large scale, deep monitoring and fine analytics for the user community. Supercomput. Front. Innov. **6**(2), 4–11 (2019). https://doi.org/10.14529/jsfi190201
27. Landau, L.D., Lifshitz, E.M.: Fluid mechanics, 2ed edn. Pergamon Press, Oxford (1987)
28. Marrone, S., Antuono, M., Colagrossi, A., Colicchio, G., Touze, D.L., Graziani, G.: δ-SPH model for simulating violent impact flows. Comput. Methods Appl. Mech. Eng. **200**(13–16), 1526–1542 (2011). https://doi.org/10.1016/j.cma.2010.12.016
29. Gorobets, A.: CFD simulations on hybrid supercomputers: gaining experience and harvesting problems. In: Voevodin, V., Sobolev, S., Yakobovskiy, M., Shagaliev, R. (eds.) Supercomputing: 8th Russian Supercomputing Days (RuSCDays 2022), Moscow, 26–27 September 2022, Revised Selected Papers. LNCS, vol. 13708, pp. 63–76. Springer, Cham (2022). https://doi.org/10.1007/978-3-031-22941-1_5
30. Isaeva, I.I., Voronin, A.A., Khoperskov, A.V., Kharitonov, M.A.: Modeling the territorial structure dynamics of the northern part of the Volga-Akhtuba floodplain. Computation **10**(4), 62 (2022)

Software Package USPARS for Large Sparse Systems of Linear Equations

Dmitry Bykov[1], Victor Kostin[1,2(✉)], and Sergey Solovyev[1,2]

[1] Novosibirsk Center of Informatics Technologies "UNIPRO", Novosibirsk, Russia
{dbykov,ssoloviev}@unipro.ru, vctrkstn@mail.ru

[2] Trofimuk Institute of Petroleum Gas Geology and Geophysics, Novosibirsk, Russia

Abstract. In this work, we present the software package USPARS, developed by us for solving sparse linear systems of equations using the Gaussian elimination method. The package is conceptually similar to existing packages, but there are also differences. It includes its own component for matrix reordering to reduce the fill-in of triangular factors, as well as Python interfaces that extend the package's capabilities using Python libraries. A component for solving symmetric eigenvalue problems was developed based on the linear system solver. Through careful performance optimization, the package is competitive with popular solvers, as confirmed by numerical examples presented in the article.

Keywords: Linear Algebraic Solvers · Sparse Systems of Linear Equations · Software Packages · Software Optimization

1 Motivation

The USPARS project, developed by our team at UNIPRO, aims to develop a multiplatform software package for solving systems of linear equations with large sparse coefficient matrices using the Gauss method. The package is optimized for modern processor architectures, including those produced in Russia, and aims to become a worthy competitor to existing packages for solving sparse linear systems. The project is primarily aimed at the internal Russian market, and the team is committed to providing maximum technical support to users.

2 Theoretical Background

USPARS uses the Gauss method for solving sparse linear systems of equations, in which the coefficient matrix is decomposed into a product of triangular factors, after which the problem is reduced to solving linear systems of equations with triangular coefficient matrices. Depending on the type of matrix, a certain type of factorization is applied. In the case of a symmetric positive definite matrix, this is the Cholesky factorization $A = LL^T$. For a symmetric matrix, the factorization $A = LDL^T$ is used. Finally, for a matrix without symmetry properties, the LU factorization $A = LU$ is used. In the

V. Voevodin et al. (Eds.): RuSCDays 2023, LNCS 14388, pp. 232–244, 2023.
https://doi.org/10.1007/978-3-031-49432-1_18

complex case, the Cholesky decomposition takes the form $A = LL^H$, and an additional Hermitian case with factorization $A = LDL^H$ is added to the list. In these formulas, L is a lower triangular matrix, D is block-diagonal with small-sized blocks, and U is an upper triangular matrix. The superscripts ^{T} and ^{H} denote transposition and Hermitian conjugation, respectively.

After the matrix A is factorized, the procedure for solving the SLAE $AX = F$ reduces to solving systems of linear equations with triangular and block-diagonal matrices. The formula covers the case of multiple right-hand sides, where F and X are rectangular matrices.

Storing the triangular factors obtained from the factorization of a sparse matrix often requires significantly more memory than the original matrix, which is a significant complication when using the Gaussian method. The amount of required memory depends on the structure of the nonzero elements of the matrix. Effective methods for reordering the coefficient matrix (see, for example, [1]) applied before factorization can significantly reduce the memory requirements. USPARS uses its own original development for reordering the matrix to reduce the required memory. Rearranging the elements of the matrix before factorization, undertaken to reduce the fill-in of the triangular factors, is an optimization step aimed at reducing the number of nonzero elements in the result and therefore reducing the number of arithmetic operations required to obtain the result.

Functions of factorization and solving steps are threaded using OpenMP, the threading effect see in Sect. 4.

Arithmetic operations with floating-point numbers are subject to rounding errors, which affect the final result in the sense that the obtained solution is a solution of a system which can be considered as a perturbation of the original. Both the elements of the coefficient matrix and the elements of the right-hand side matrix are subject to perturbation. There is extensive literature devoted to studying the behavior of rounding errors when solving linear systems of equations (see, for example, [2–4] and citations therein). Errors that arise during calculations due to rounding tend to accumulate. Depending on the rate of their accumulation, calculations can be stable or unstable. Standard techniques called **scaling** and **matching** are applied in the USPARS package to improve the stability of calculations.

Another technique, called **pivoting**, is worth mentioning. The technique comes from LU factorization algorithms developed for dense matrices. However, it has its own specifics when applied to sparse matrices. The purpose of pivoting is to rearrange rows to ensure that a sufficiently large modulus element of the current column lands on the diagonal. In algorithms for dense matrices, the maximum modulus element of the column can be placed in the leading position, but this approach is not suitable for sparse matrices because it violates the matrix structure achieved at the stage of reordering aimed to reduce the fill-in of triangular factors. Violation of this structure can lead to increased fill-in and excessive memory and machine time consumption. Therefore, USPARS uses local pivoting, which rearranges rows within the current diagonal block and does not worsen the fill-in of the triangular factor.

Local pivoting is limited in its search for the maximum element and is unable to find the maximum element of a column outside of the given block. This can lead to calculations being unable to continue because the pivot is zero. The situation can be somewhat mitigated but not fully resolved by using full pivoting within the given block - the entire block may turn out to be zero, even though the initial matrix is well-conditioned. The USPARS package implements full pivoting. More specifically, it uses full local pivoting, which means that it is performed within diagonal blocks. The sizes of the diagonal blocks are small compared to the order of the matrix - this observation justifies the replacement of partial pivoting with full pivoting.

Local full pivoting improves stability, but not always - for example, the diagonal block may be close to zero. This is called a 'zero pivot'. To overcome this difficulty, USPARS has developed workarounds. When using the workaround, (very) small in absolute value diagonal elements are replaced with some perturbations that are large enough to allow calculations to continue. When continuing calculations, a zero pivot may be encountered again - the same technique is applied to it. At the end of this process, we obtain triangular factors, but obviously, these factors will correspond not to the original matrix, but to some perturbation of it. It is intuitively clear that in order for the perturbation of the original matrix to be minimal in some sense, the diagonal perturbations introduced must be limited not only from below, but also from above.

It is clear that using the obtained triangular factors in the step of solving systems with triangular coefficient matrices will lead to a perturbation of the solution, which may be unacceptable. To correct this situation, we can use the classical method of iterative refinement, in which successive approximations are computed by solving systems of equations with triangular coefficient matrices obtained as the result of factorization step and special right-hand side vectors. These right-hand side vectors are computed as residuals of the original system on vectors successively obtained during the iterative refinement process. The process is terminated if the relative norm of the residual reaches a certain threshold. If the original matrix was not too ill-conditioned and the diagonal perturbations introduced during the factorization stage are not too large, then the described process will converge.

3 Extended Functionality

PyUSPARS. In order to expand the functionality of the USPARS package, a Python package called PyUSPARS has been developed as an extension to it. This package is convenient as a tool for prototyping and testing new functionality. It provides compatibility with the standard Python format for sparse matrices, SciPy Sparse CSR, and access to all of the optimized operations on sparse matrices built into SciPy. The user is provided with the ability to use compatible visualizations, data manipulation methods, and read/write capabilities with this format. There is backward compatibility with the interfaces of direct sparse solvers, allowing USPARS to be used instead of standard SciPy methods by replacing the import, as shown in Fig. 1.

The additional functionality provided by this interface includes:

- Calculation of the residual in the numerical solution of a SLAE;
- Estimation of the condition number of the coefficient matrix of a SLAE;
- Visualization of the "non-zero element pattern" of a sparse matrix;
- Calculation of the error in the numerical solution in cases where the exact solution is known (e.g. for accuracy testing);

```
from pyuspars_package.solver import PyUspars
from pyuspars_package.solver import FACTORIZE_TYPE as ftype
from pyuspars_package.scipy import factorized, spsolve
import numpy as np
from scipy import sparse
from scipy.io import mmread
import matplotlib.pylab as plt
```

```
#from scipy.sparse import spsolve
from pyuspars_package.scipy import spsolve
```

Fig. 1. Import substitution

- Various optimizations based on user experience and related to automatic parameter selection and factorization type.

A user-friendly interface is provided, with a simple syntax for specifying solution requests, and automatic control over the allocation and release of dynamic memory (see example in Fig. 2).

UFEAST/PyUFEAST. An extension for solving the generalized symmetric eigenvalue problem has been developed using PyUSPARS. The development is based on the FEAST algorithm [5, 6], whose main idea is to approximate spectral projectors, defined as Riesz integrals, using Gauss-Legendre quadrature formulas.

A more detailed explanation for the classical formulation of the eigenvalue problem is as follows. The input information for the algorithm is an interval $(\lambda_{\min}, \lambda_{\max})$ on the real axis, where the eigenvalues of a symmetric $n \times n-$ matrix B, as shown in Fig. 3 on the left, are to be found. In this figure, C is the circle constructed on the segment $[\lambda_{\min}, \lambda_{\max}]$ as its diameter. The matrix $P_C(B)$ computed using integration along the contour

$$P_C(B) = \frac{1}{2\pi i} \oint\limits_C (zI - B)^{-1} dz$$

represents an orthogonal projector onto the invariant subspace $\mathcal{L}$ of B corresponding to the eigenvalues lying inside the circle. Thus, for a given rectangular $n \times m-$ matrix Y, the columns of the product $P_C(B)Y$ lie in $\mathcal{L}$. Assume the columns of matrix Y are in general position with respect to the invariant subspaces of B and $m \geq p$ where p is the number of eigenvalues of matrix B in the the interval $(\lambda_{\min}, \lambda_{\max})$. Then the rank of the product $P_C(B)Y$ achieves its possible maximal values p. Use QR decomposition to get a represent $P_C(B)Y = QR$ of matrix $P_C(B)Y$. Here Q is an $n \times p-$ matrix with orthonormal columns and R is an upper-trapezoidal $p \times m-$ matrix. The columns of matrix R form an orthonormal basis in the invariant subspace $\mathcal{L}$. The eigenvalues of the matrix $Q^t BQ$ represent a complete set of eigenvalues of matrix B in the interval (λ_min, λ_max).

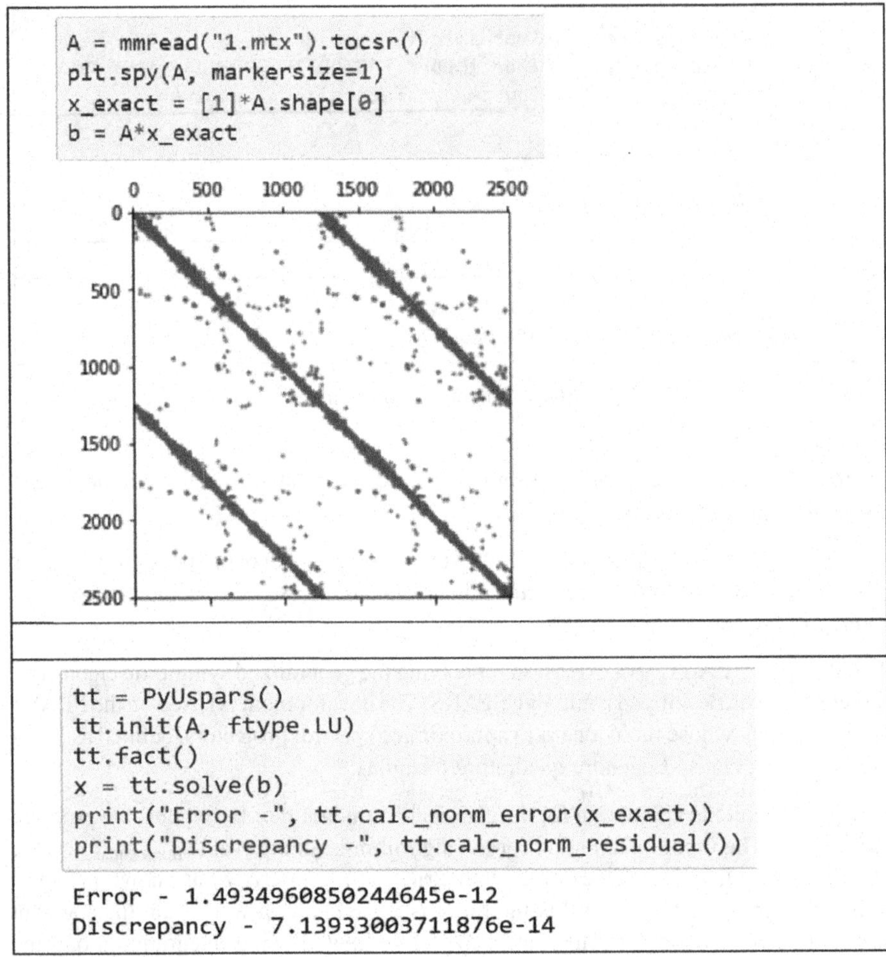

Fig. 2. An example of SLAE solution with matrix portrait visualization

To approximate matrix $P_C(B)Y$ we use the Gauss-Legendre quadrature of order q

$$P_C(B)Y \cong \sum_{j=1}^{q} w_j \left(z_j I - B\right)^{-1} Y, \tag{1}$$

where z_j are the nodes of the quadrature formula located on the circle C, w_j are the corresponding weights. The values of w_j and z_j are provided by the theory of quadrature formulas, which we do not specify here. To calculate z_j, the zeros of the Legendre polynomial of degree q are used. For $q = 8$, the right picture in Fig. 3 illustrates the location of z_j along the circle. The reality of the elements of matrix B allows reducing the number of nodes by half, using only the upper half of the circle.

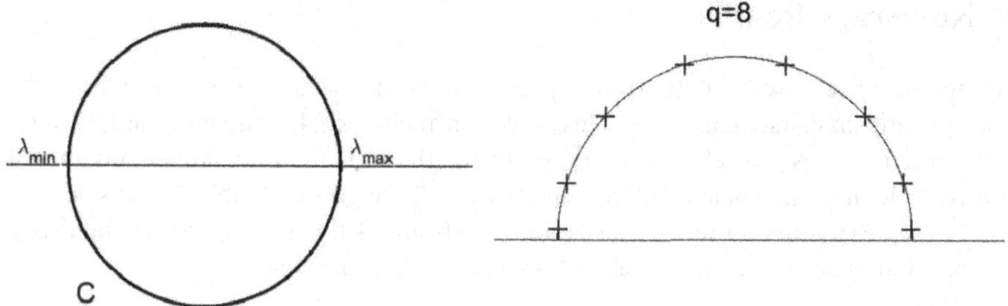

Fig. 3. Left – a circle constructed to evaluate the Riesz integral, right – a half-circle with quadrature nodes.

To compute matrices $X_j = \left(z_j I - B\right)^{-1} Y$ in formula (1), one has to solve systems of linear equations

$$\left(z_j I - B\right) X_j = Y. \tag{2}$$

Due to the complexity of z_j, the coefficient matrices of these systems are relatively well-conditioned. The estimate of the condition number depends on the value of q - the larger q, the worse the estimate. All systems of equations in (2) are independent of each other, and this is a degree of parallelism of the algorithm. All coefficient matrices in (2) have the same structure of nonzero elements (the same 'portrait'), which makes it possible to use one common initialization stage for all points z_j.

The extension is still in the experimental stage, so two versions have been developed, both based on FEAST:

- UFEAST utilizes Intel® MKL (for BLAS and Lapack) for linear-algebraic calculations with dense matrices of small sizes;
- PyUFEAST is written in Python and instead of Intel® MKL takes linear-algebraic functionality from SciPy.

Both versions use USPARS to solve sparse linear systems of Eqs. (2) that arise in the problem-solving process. Table 1 shows a comparison between PyUFEAST and the scipy.sparse.linalg.eigsh method, which uses multi-threaded ARPACK. Although the optimization work on PyUFEAST is far from complete, it already has certain advantages over ARPACK for large matrices.

Table 1. Comparison of PyUFEAST and ARPACK

Матрица	n	$(\lambda_{min}, \lambda_{max})$	# of λ_j	PyUFEAST, s	ARPACK, s
bcspwr06	1454	(0.9, 1.1)	156	7	5
bcsstk36	23052	(0, 0.0011)	57	55	11
helm2d03	392257	(0, 0.0011)	34	568	130
Ga10As10H30	1.13E + 05	(0, 0.0011)	28	4713	11199
Ge99H100	1.13E + 05	(0, 0.0011)	9	4882	11223

4 Numerical Results

The test matrices used for the results presented in this section were taken from the resource https://sparse.tamu.edu/. This selection includes 24 symmetric and 12 non-symmetric matrices. The characteristics of the matrices (matrix title, order *n*, number of non-zero elements nnz, and condition number cond) are given in Table 2. The selection is quite representative in terms of size ranges (from 14 thousand to 5.5 million) and number of non-zero elements (from 800 thousand to 110 million).

Table 2. Test matrices' characteristics

#	title	n	nnz	cond
1	apache2	7.15E + 05	2.77E + 06	3.05E + 06
2	torso3	2.59E + 05	4.43E + 06	2.27E + 02
3	c-big	3.45E + 05	1.34E + 06	4.05E + 04
4	ldoor	9.52E + 05	2.37E + 07	1.69E + 08
5	F1	3.44E + 05	1.36E + 07	3.52E + 06
6	thermal2	1.23E + 06	4.90E + 06	4.30E + 06
7	G3_circuit	1.59E + 06	4.62E + 06	1.39E + 07
8	H2O	6.70E + 04	1.14E + 06	4.24E + 03
9	sparsine	5.00E + 04	7.99E + 05	2.78E + 06
10	af_shell10	1.51E + 06	2.71E + 07	1.41E + 10
11	boneS10	9.15E + 05	2.82E + 07	1.03E + 08
12	appu	1.40E + 04	1.85E + 06	1.71E + 02
13	PFlow_742	7.43E + 05	1.89E + 07	1.02E + 12
14	memchip	2.71E + 06	1.48E + 07	1.41E + 07
15	dielFilterV3real	1.10E + 06	4.52E + 07	8.67E + 06
16	dielFilterV2real	1.16E + 06	2.48E + 07	8.91E + 06
17	TSOPF_RS_b2383_c1	3.81E + 04	1.62E + 07	2.20E + 08
18	Freescale1	3.43E + 06	1.89E + 07	1.03E + 10
19	StocF-1465	1.47E + 06	1.12E + 07	2.41E + 13
20	Ga10As10H30	1.13E + 05	3.11E + 06	2.90E + 05
21	bone010	9.87E + 05	3.63E + 07	4.42E + 08
22	Ge99H100	1.13E + 05	4.28E + 06	6.40E + 03
23	Flan_1565	1.56E + 06	5.95E + 07	1.21E + 08
24	audikw_1	9.44E + 05	3.93E + 07	1.83E + 10
25	rajat31	4.69E + 06	2.03E + 07	3.33E + 06

(continued)

Table 2. (*continued*)

#	title	n	nnz	cond
26	Ga19As19H42	1.33E + 05	4.51E + 06	3.07E + 06
27	Hook_1498	1.50E + 06	3.12E + 07	3.60E + 06
28	atmosmodl	1.49E + 06	1.03E + 07	1.05E + 03
29	atmosmodd	1.27E + 06	8.81E + 06	4.88E + 03
30	Transport	1.60E + 06	2.35E + 07	1.23E + 06
31	ML_Geer	1.50E + 06	1.11E + 08	6.32E + 08
32	atmosmodj	1.27E + 06	8.81E + 06	6.04E + 03
33	Geo_1438	1.44E + 06	3.23E + 07	1.14E + 13
34	vas_stokes_1M	1.09E + 06	3.48E + 07	1.73E + 07
35	Serena	1.39E + 06	3.30E + 07	1.11E + 14
36	circuit5M	5.56E + 06	5.95E + 07	3.43E + 10

In the tests, it was required to solve the system of linear equations $Ax = f$ with a right-hand side vector obtained by multiplying the coefficient matrix A. by a generated vector of unknowns x_{exact}. . The relative error $\frac{x - x_{\text{exact}}}{x_{\text{exact}}}$ of the computed solution x. , the relative residual $\frac{Ax-f}{f}$, the size of the memory used, and the time taken to obtain the solution were measured. For the characteristics of the computational systems used to obtain the results in this section, see Table 3.

Table 3. Computational systems

Vendor	Characteristics
Intel	2CPU Intel(R) Xeon(R) CPU E5–2680 v3 @ 2.50GHz (12 core, HT disabled), 256 GB RAM, OS Ubuntu 20.04.3 LTS
AMD	2 CPU AMD EPYC 7763 64-Core, 1024 GB RAM, Aramid 3.1 (Red Hat Enterprise Linux 8.3)
Elbrus	4 CPU E8C-SWTX@1.20 GHz (8 cores) (http://ineum.ru/e8c-swtx), 128 GB RAM, OS Elbrus 7.2

The charts presented in Fig. 4 are provided for comparison of USPARS with Intel® MKL PARDISO - it is easy to see that for the matrix sample from Table 2, these two solvers achieve similar results in terms of required memory (see A), relative error (B), and relative residual (C).

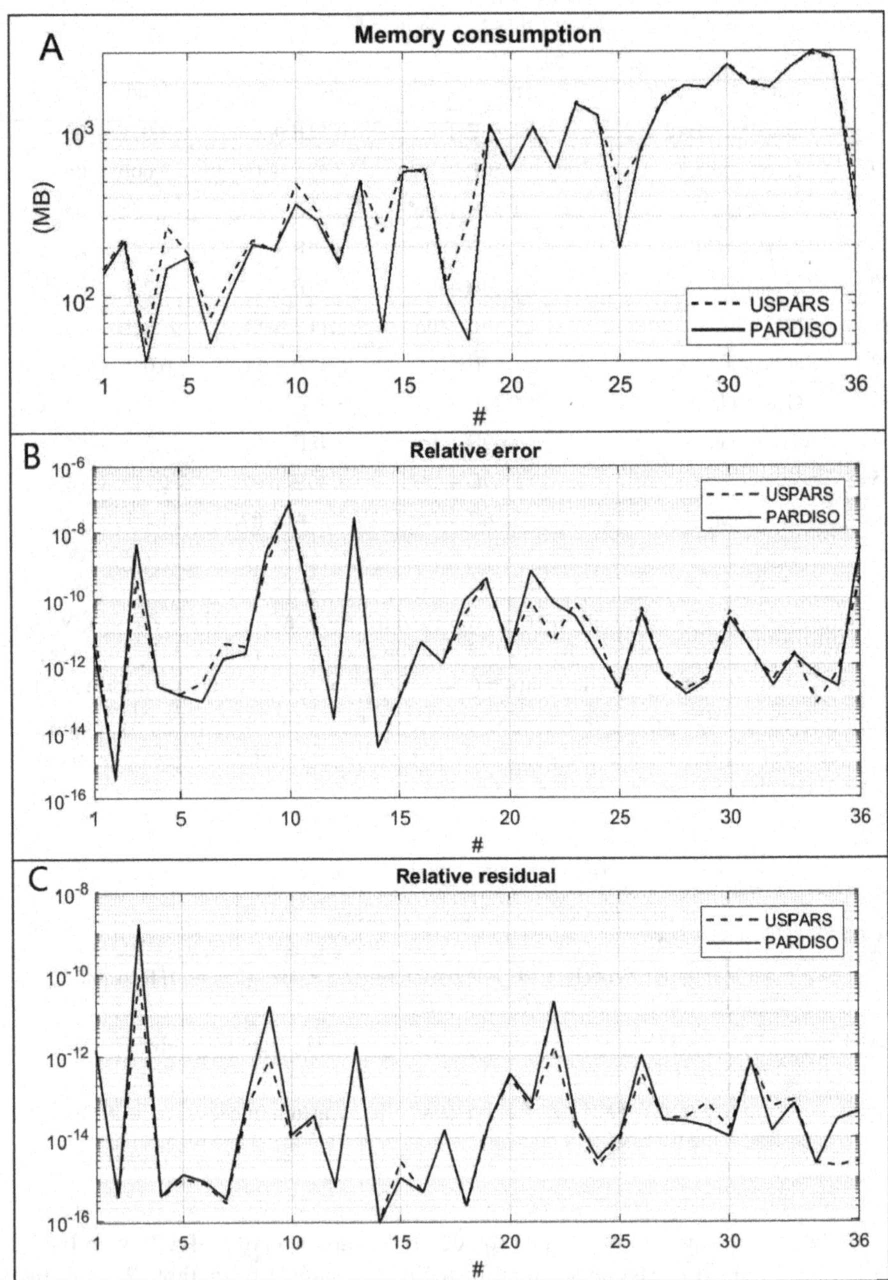

Fig. 4. For USPARS and MKL PARDISO solvers on matrices from Table 2: A – memory consumption, B – the relative error norm, C – the relative residual norm.

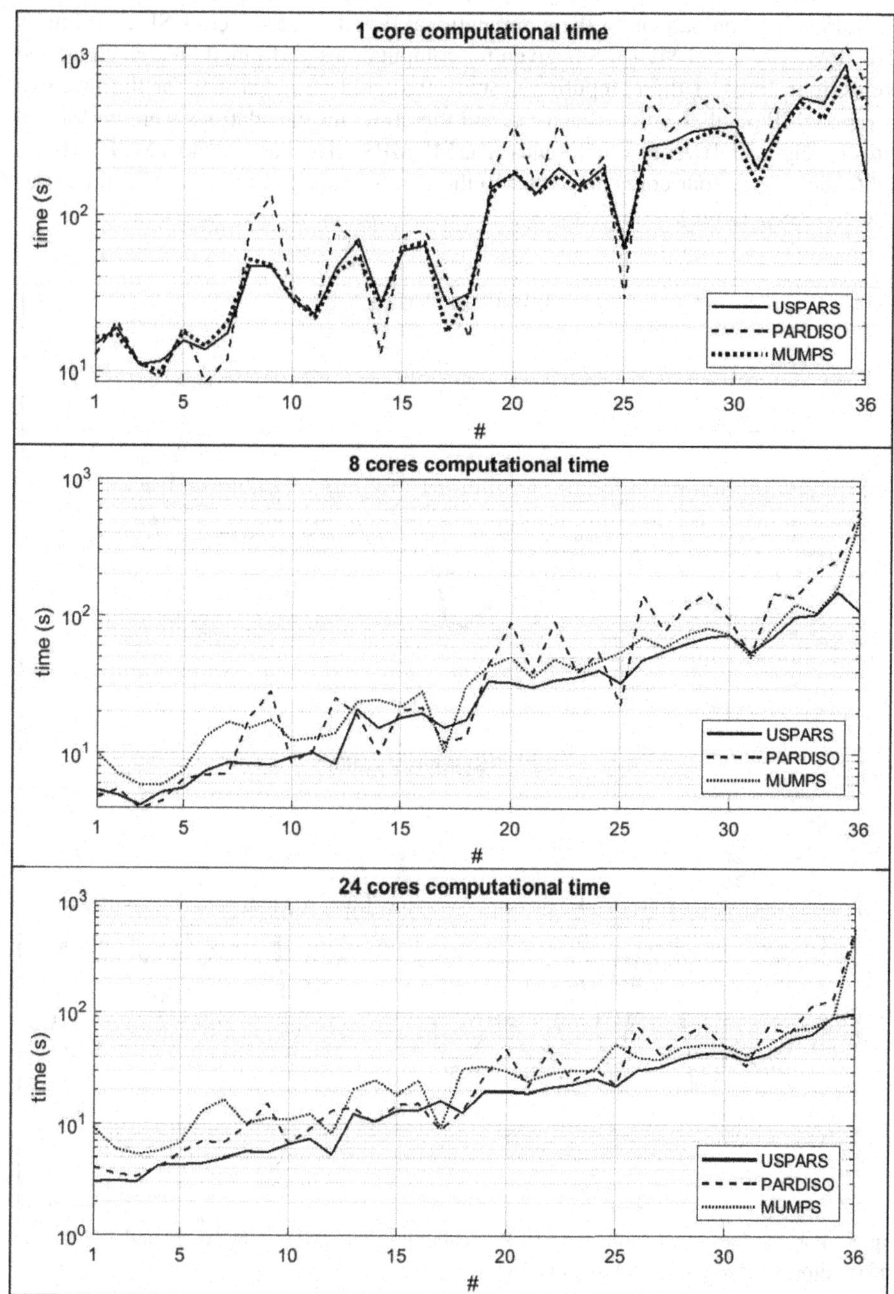

Fig. 5. On matrices from Table 2, comparison in computational time of 3 solvers running on 1, 8 and 24 threads.

In Fig. 5, a comparison of the computational time for the solvers USPARS, Intel® MKL PARDISO, and MUMPS is given for computations performed on one, eight, and twenty-four cores of the computing system. It should be noted that for the first two solvers, OMP parallelization was used, and therefore, the calculations were performed with one, eight, and twenty-four threads. The MUMPS solver has run under MPI, and one, eight, and twenty-four cores here refer to the corresponding number of MPI processes (one process per core).

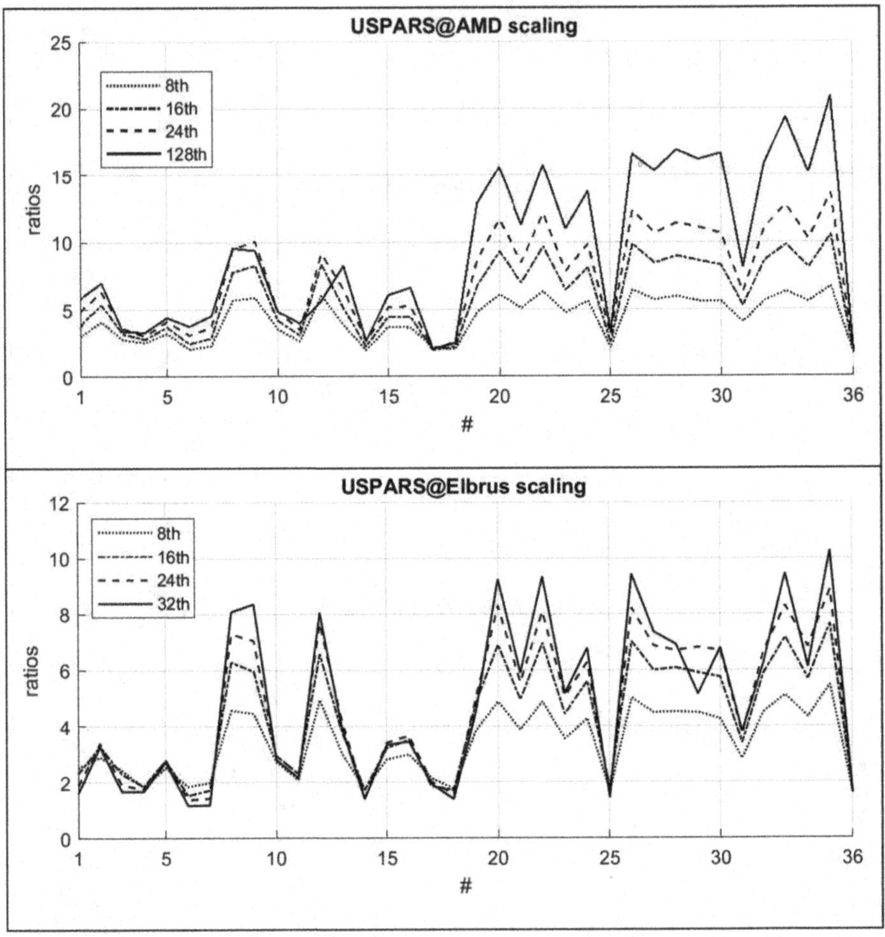

Fig. 6. For matrices from Table 2, USPARS scalability: on AMD for 8, 16, 24 and 128 threads and on Elbrus for 8, 16, 24 and 32 threads.

The scaling factor of the solver on matrix A when using p threads is determined as the ratio of computational times $t(A;1)/t(A;p)$, where $t(A;1)$ is the computational time for solving a system of linear equations with coefficient matrix A using one thread. Similarly, $t(A;p)$. is the computational time for the same task when using p threads. We calculated the geomean of scaling factors for matrices included in Table 2 and obtained respective values $\kappa(p)$, presented in Table 4.

Table 4. USPARS scaling averaged over a sample of matrices Table 2

AMD	p	8	16	24	128
	$\kappa(p)$	3.96	5.19	6.27	7.55
Elbrus	p	8	16	24	32
	$\kappa(p)$	3.18	3.74	3.93	3.86

The values in Table 4 clearly illustrate that the scalability issue on x86 requires attention, and information about "problematic" matrices with minimal scalability can be extracted from the top chart in Fig. 6. Judging by the numbers in the last row of Table 4, the scalability issue is even more significant on Elbrus. Comparing the top and bottom charts in Fig. 6 it is easy to notice that the sets of "problematic matrices" for these two architectures have large intersections.

5 Plans

The project plans to use modern promising areas to expand the functionality and optimize codes. In particular, we can mention the development of regularization methods for solving very ill-conditioned SLAEs [2, 7], the development of a cluster version of the solver, the use of intermediate data compression by using low-rank block approximation [8, 9].

6 Conclusions

The USPARS solver is already successfully competing with popular solvers. At the same time, it has good prospects for development both in terms of expanding functionality and in terms of optimizing performance.

Acknowledgements. Participation of V. Kostin and S. Solovyev in work on this article was partly supported by a grant №22–11-00104 from the Russian Science Foundation, https://rscf.ru/project/22-11-00104.

Authors Contributions. D. Bykov optimized the solution stage, developed the PyUSPARS add-in and the UFEAST/PyUFEAST add-in. As part of the implementation of the grant of the Russian Science Foundation No. 22–11-00104 V. Kostin carried out the general management of the project, developed prototypes for the implementation of the FEAST algorithm, S. Solovyev developed and optimized the main code of the package.

References

1. Karypis, G., Kumar, V.: A fast and high quality multilevel scheme for partitioning irregular graphs. SIAM J. Sci. Comput. **20**(1), 359 (1999)
2. Godunov, S.K., Antonov, A.G., Kiriljuk, O.P., Kostin, V.I. Guaranteed Accuracy in Numerical Linear Algebra, vol. 252. Springer, Heidelberg (1993). https://doi.org/10.1007/978-94-011-1952-8
3. Arioli, M., Demmel, J.W., Duff, I.S.: Solving sparse linear systems with sparse backward error. SIAM J. Matrix Anal. Appl. **10**(2), 165–190 (1989)
4. Higham, N.J.: Accuracy and Stability of Numerical Algorithms. SIAM (2002)
5. Polizzi, E.: Density-matrix-based algorithm for solving eigenvalue problems. Phys. Rev. B **79**(11), 115112 (2009)
6. Tang, P.P.T., Polizzi, E.: FEAST as a subspace iteration eigensolver accelerated by approximate spectral projection. SIAM J. Matrix Anal. Appl. **35**(2), 354–390 (2014)
7. Calvetti, D., Lothar, R.: Tikhonov regularization of large linear problems. BIT Numer. Math. **43**, 263–283 (2003)
8. Ghysels, P., Li, X.S., Rouet, F.H., Williams, S., Napov, A.: An efficient multicore implementation of a novel HSS-structured multifrontal solver using randomized sampling. SIAM J. Sci. Comput. **38**(5), S358–S384 (2016)
9. Amestoy, P., Buttari, A., L'Excellent, J.-Y., Mary, T.: On the complexity of the block low-rank multifrontal factorization. SIAM J. Sci. Comput. **39**(4), A1710–A1740 (2017)

Supercomputer Search for Coagulation Factor XIIa Inhibitors in the Chinese National Compound Library

Danil Kutov[1,2], Alexey Sulimov[1,2], Anna Tashchilova[1,2], Ivan Ilin[2], and Vladimir Sulimov[1,2(✉)]

[1] Dimonta, Ltd., Moscow, Russia
{dk,at}@dimonta.com, vladimir.sulimov@gmail.com
[2] Research Computer Center, Lomonosov Moscow State University, Moscow, Russia

Abstract. A methodology of virtual screening using docking of a large database of organic compounds is presented. The database is the Chinese National Compound Library with over one million low molecular weight organic compounds ready for purchase. In this study, for the first time, new quick parameters of the genetic algorithm were used. Docking is performed in two stages. First, docking of the entire database is performed using the SOL docking program with the quick parameters. Second, the best scored ligands are docked carefully by the same docking program with standard parameters. For the best ligands selected after the second stage, the enthalpy of protein-ligand binding is calculated using the PM7 quantum-chemical semiempirical method with the COSMO solvent model. The target protein is the coagulation factor XIIa. As a result of virtual screening, 18 compounds are selected as candidates for factor XIIa inhibitors. These potential factor XIIa inhibitors are novel and belong to chemotypes not present among reported experimentally confirmed factor XIIa inhibitors. These compounds, having confirmed their inhibitory activity *in vitro* and *in vivo*, can become the basis for the creation of new, safer anticoagulants.

Keywords: Anticoagulants · Factor XIIa · CNCL · Docking · Molecular modeling · High-performance computing · Protein-ligand binding · Quantum chemistry · Inhibitors · Drug discovery

1 Introduction

There is no area of medicine where thrombotic and hemorrhagic complications do not play a significant role in the cause of death and disability. In oncology, hematology, immunology, such situations are especially widespread. Anticoagulants that can prevent pathological conditions without disturbing normal hemostasis are in high demand. To a large extent, the problems of treating of blood coagulation disorders are associated with great difficulties in their regulation. The blood coagulation system is a cascade of enzymatic reactions that is activated by injury and controls the formation of a fibrin clot, a jelly-like substance that clogs the wound. In this cascade, the enzyme obtained as a

V. Voevodin et al. (Eds.): RuSCDays 2023, LNCS 14388, pp. 245–258, 2023.
https://doi.org/10.1007/978-3-031-49432-1_19

result of the previous reaction catalyzes the next one [1]. In this cascade, there are two main ways to initiate blood coagulation: the extrinsic pathway (tissue factor pathway) and the intrinsic (contact) pathway [2]. The position of blood coagulation factor XIIa in the cascade of biochemical reactions connecting the intrinsic and extrinsic pathways makes this factor a promising therapeutic target for the development of a new class of anticoagulants [3–5]. The coagulation factor XIIa inhibitors can become a new class of anticoagulants capable of blocking the internal pathway of blood coagulation activation without interrupting the chain of externally activated hemostasis reactions. It is shown that both of coagulation factors XIa or XIIa are important for thrombosis, while having minor roles in processes that terminate blood loss (hemostasis) [6]. In contrast to factor XIa inhibitors, factor XIIa inhibitors have received little attention for a long time.

Nevertheless, a number of low-molecular weight inhibitors of factor XIIa have been identified to date. Factor XIIa inhibitors of a coumarin-3-carboxamide class with the most active compound having IC_{50} of 4.3 μM were reported in [7]. In ref. [8], one inhibitor of factor XIIa with $K_i = 60$ nM (K_i is an inhibition constant) was identified among substrate-analogue inhibitors of factor Xa. Factor XIIa peptide macrocycle inhibitors with $K_i = 1.2$ μM and $K_i = 22$ nM and high selectivity over related proteases were discovered in [9] and [10], respectively. Several weak 3,6-disubstituted coumarins as factor XIIa inhibitors were identified by Bouckaert et al. [11]. In the study [12], J. Chen and D. Visco used a combination of various methods, including support vector machine, to screen 72 million molecules from the PubChem Compound database, which led to the experimental identification of XIIa inhibitors belonging to several chemotypes, including aminotriazole inhibitors with $IC_{50} = 160$ nM, which however was not selective against thrombin [13]. A good review of factor XIIa inhibitors discovered up to 2020 was presented in [14]. New 3-arylcoumarin inhibitors of factor XIIa have recently been identified [2], the best of which showed an IC_{50} of 7.85 μM and good selectivity for factor Xa and factor XIa. Recently [15], using docking, [1, 2, 4] triazolo [1,5-a] pyrimidine and spirocyclic furo [3,4-*c*] pyrrole hits of factor XIIa inhibitors with micromolar activity were discovered and experimentally confirmed.

Given the importance of the new class of anticoagulants based on factor XIIa inhibitors and the slow progress of existing inhibitors to the late stages of drug development, it is very important to find new chemical classes of factor XIIa inhibitors and thereby increase the chemical diversity of such compounds.

Taking all of the above into account, we conducted a virtual screening of the large database of organic compounds of the Chinese National Compound Library [16] (CNCL) to search for inhibitors of factor XIIa. The CNCL database containing more than 1 million compounds is located in Zhangjiang High-tech Park. The large size of this database made it possible to find candidate compounds for the role of factor XIIa inhibitors belonging to a wide range of diverse chemical classes. Screening was carried out using docking. Docking was carried out in two stages: quick docking of all ligands from the entire CNCL database, followed by standard docking of the best ligands selected in the first stage. As a result, eighteen chemically diverse compounds were selected for further experimental testing of their inhibitory activity against the factor XIIa *in vitro*.

2 Materials and Methods

2.1 Chinese National Compound Library

The CNCL is a specially created and maintained database of 2D structures of molecules of low molecular weight organic compounds in the SDF format. Part of CNCL's mission is to provide compound resources to researchers who are involved in drug discovery or the study of drug mechanisms of action. CNCL consists of a main database and several smaller ones, and all compounds from CNCL are available for order and experimental testing. The main database is available for download, divided into seven parts, one SDF-file for each part, and contains 1 271 139 low molecular weight ligands.

Given the huge size of the database, we first filtered out obviously uninteresting ligands using Open Babel (version 3.1.1) according to the following criteria:

- All ligands with a molecular weight less than 200 Da were filtered out, since such compounds were rarely found among drugs.
- Only ligands with internal rotational degrees of freedom (torsions) of less than 10 were retained, since the docking of very flexible ligands took much longer and often gave dubious result.
- Molecules containing boron atoms were also filtered out, since this element is not parameterized in the MMFF94 force field [17], which is used in the SOL docking program [18, 19].
- Only ligands with the total charge 0 or ± 1 at $pH = 7.4 \pm 0.1$ were retained, since we considered that strongly charged ligands were not perspective as drugs.

After performing this filtering, the database was reduced to 977 240 molecules. The lowest energy 3D ligand conformers and their charge states we obtained using the LigPrep module from Schrodinger Suite 2015. The distribution of ligands in the CNCL database over different numbers of internal rotational degrees of freedom (torsions) is presented in Table 1.

Table 1. The distribution of ligands in the CNCL database over different numbers of torsions.

The number of ligand torsions	The number of ligands
0	501
1	4 415
2	19 778
3	62 203
4	126 093
5	185 339
6	206 442
7	176 276

(*continued*)

Table 1. (*continued*)

The number of ligand torsions	The number of ligands
8	125 786
9	70 407
TOTAL	977 240

2.2 Factor XIIa Model

For the construction of the factor XIIa model, the structure of the complex from Protein Data Bank with PDB ID 6B74 was used. Details of the model preparation and its validation were described in [2, 15, 20], where this model was successfully used to discover new inhibitors of the factor XIIa (see Fig. 1).

The values of the SOL scoring function of ligands shown in Fig. 1 are in the range from −5.11 to −7.03 kcal/mol [2, 15]. Inhibition activity is measured as (1-AI/A), where AI and A are activities of factor XIIa with and without inhibitor, respectively, presented in percent. The numbers in bold correspond to the compound identifier in the database of the Department of Organic Compounds of the Voronezh State University.

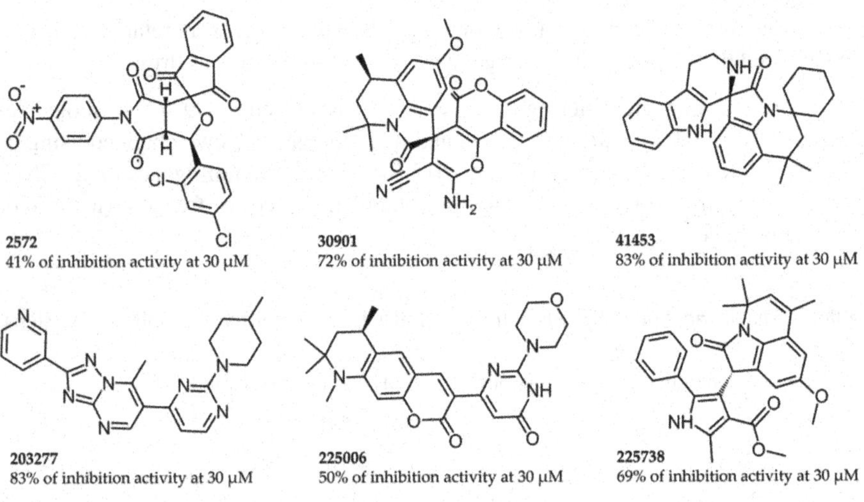

Fig. 1. Factor XIIa inhibitors found using a target protein atomistic model constructed on the base of PDB structure 6B74.

2.3 SOL Program

The main feature of the SOL docking program [18, 19] are as follows. The energy of the protein-ligand system is calculated by the MMFF94 force field, the best position of the ligand in the active site of the target protein corresponds to the global energy minimum, and global energy optimization is performed using the genetic algorithm (GA). GA begins from the initial random generation of the first generation of individuals, which correspond to different positions of the ligand. Then, over a number of generations, the population of a fixed size evolves through several mechanisms, including reproduction, crossover and mutations, when the strongest individuals with the most negative objective energy function survive [18]. The main parameters of GA are: the population size, 30 000 by default, the number of generations, 1000 by default, and the number of independent GA runs, 50 by default; we considered the default GA parameters as the standard GA parameters. Docking of a low molecular weight ligand takes on average 2 to 4 h, depending on the number of ligand torsions.

To speed up the program, the values of the interaction potentials (Coulomb and van der Waals) of the probe ligand atoms with all protein atoms at the nodes of a certain uniform three-dimensional grid covering the active site of the target protein are calculated in advance. The effect of desolvation is approximately taken into account in the form of local characteristics at the grid nodes calculated using a simplified version of the generalized Born model [21]. During docking, the protein is rigid and is represented by the grid of potentials, while the ligand is flexible due to torsion degrees of freedom. The objective energy function is the sum of the energy of the ligand in the protein field and the energy of the internal stresses of the ligand. To increase the reliability of docking, for each ligand, several independent runs of GA are performed. Then, the solutions of the global optimization problem, which are the positions of the ligand corresponding to the most negative values of the objective energy function for various independent runs of the GA, are clustered. Two ligand positions belong to the same cluster if the standard deviation (RMSD) between the coordinates of all their atoms is less than 1 Å. The high population of the 1st cluster containing the positions of the ligand with the most negative objective function is an indicator of the high reliability of docking. Indeed, this means that almost the same ligand positions corresponding to the lowest energy of the protein-ligand complex are found in several independent GA runs. The SOL score estimates the free energy of the protein-ligand binding in kcal/mol using the ligand position corresponding to the global energy value of the objective energy function.

Docking with the standard GA parameters of the entire CNCL database required about 3 000 000 CPU*hours, but there were no such supercomputing resources. Docking of all ligands from such large databases (1 million or more) can be done using some popular docking programs, for example, AutoDock Vina, in which, however, too many simplifications are made for the sake of high speed [22, 23]. In order to use the SOL program to screen the CNCL database, we investigated the reliability of docking using different values of the genetic algorithm parameters. As a result, the so-called quick GA parameters were determined: population size 10 000, number of generations 1000, number of runs 5. On average, SOL performed docking with the quick parameters of GA 30 times faster than with the standard ones.

Therefore, we used a two-stage approach to dock all ligands from the CNCL database. First, all ligands were docked using the SOL program with quick GA parameters. For each ligand, only one of the lowest-energy conformers was docked. After that, to increase the reliability of docking, a significant number of top scored ligands were docked again by the SOL program with the standard GA parameters. At the same time, for the second stage of docking, the selected ligands were re-prepared by the LigPrep module by converting them into their various 3D conformations associated with various configurations of non-aromatic rings and macrocycles.

2.4 Quantum-Chemical Post Processing

The protein-ligand binding enthalpy is calculated using the docked position of the ligand as follows:

$$\Delta H_{bind} = \Delta H_{complex} - \Delta H_{protein} - \Delta H_{ligand}, \quad (1)$$

where $\Delta H_{complex}$ is the enthalpy of formation of the protein–ligand complex, $\Delta H_{protein}$ is the enthalpy of formation of an unbound protein, ΔH_{ligand} is the enthalpy of formation of an unbound ligand. The enthalpy of formation is calculated by the MOPAC [24] program using the PM7 quantum-chemical semiempirical method [25] with the COSMO solvent model [26] implemented in MOPAC. $\Delta H_{protein}$ is calculated for the protein conformation used for docking. $\Delta H_{complex}$ was calculated in two steps: (i) optimizing the energy of the solvent-free protein-ligand complex from the docked position of the ligand by varying the Cartesian coordinates of the ligand atoms, followed by (ii) calculating the enthalpy of formation of the complex for the optimized geometry using the COSMO solvent model. The enthalpy of formation of the unbound ligand was determined by optimizing various initial ligand conformations by the PM7 method with the COSMO solvent model and selecting the conformation with the lowest optimized enthalpy of formation.

3 Results

Docking of 977 240 ligands at the first stage using the SOL program with quick GA parameters required 101 313 CPU*hours on supercomputer Lomonosov-2 [27]. For the second stage of docking, regardless of the population of the 1st cluster, 9 113 best ligands were selected with the SOL score < -5.85 kcal/mol. After the first stage of docking, all selected ligands were converted into their various 3D conformations associated with various configurations of non-aromatic rings and macrocycles. As a result, 22 477 conformers were docked with the standard GA parameters. Docking ligands at the second stage required only 13 288 CPU*hours on supercomputer Lomonosov-2. After the second stage of docking, all ligands were ranked according to the values of the SOL scoring function. For the quantum-chemical post processing stage, 162 best ligands were selected that had a SOL score < -8.5 kcal/mol or had a population of the 1st cluster > 30 and a SOL score < -7.3 kcal/mol. For these selected ligands the enthalpy of protein-ligand binding was calculated by the PM7 method and the COSMO solvent model using the MOPAC program. Calculations of the binding enthalpy of selected 162 ligands required 451 CPU*hours on supercomputer Lomonosov-2.

Selection of the best candidates for experimental validation of their inhibitory activity was made on the base of their most negative values of the SOL scoring function and the protein-ligand binding enthalpy, and also taking into account the number and the energy of hydrogen bonds (H-bonds) between the ligand and the protein. The selection also took into account the results of a visual inspection of the docked position of the ligand in the active site of the protein, as well as the chemical diversity of the ligands. As a result, 18 best ligands were selected for an experimental validation.

For each selected ligand, values of the SOL scoring function are presented in Table 2 after docking with the quick and the standard docking parameters, as well as values of the enthalpy of protein-ligand binding. Ligand name is an ID of the compound in the CNCL database.

Table 2. Calculated values of the SOL scoring function and values of the protein–ligand binding enthalpy ΔH_{bind} for the best 18 ligands selected for experimental testing.

Ligand name	SOL score (QUICK), kcal/mol	SOL score (STD), kcal/mol	Population of 1st cluster (STD)	ΔH_{bind} PM7 + COSMO, kcal/mol
CL00128632	−6.32	−7.71	45	−64.4
CL00827491	−7.36	−7.45	43	−70.2
CL01040342	−7.74	−7.88	35	−48.2
CL01137849	−8.50	−8.54	47	−63.6
CL01813516	−7.73	−7.94	40	−74.4
CL01817525	−7.57	−8.01	37	−72.4
CL01818109	−7.90	−8.09	47	−64.6
CL01833500	−6.54	−7.32	34	−77.9
CL01849634	−7.77	−7.97	30	−53.2
CL01863488	−6.35	−8.19	42	−72.8
CL01874398	−7.86	−8.10	42	−52.8
CL01880829	−7.31	−7.32	50	−65.3
CL01898147	−6.44	−7.95	48	−64.6
CL01912837	−7.42	−7.97	50	−59.0
CL01926532	−6.37	−7.34	40	−70.2
CL01982900	−8.28	−8.58	14	−72.6
CL02011432	−6.61	−8.18	45	−65.2
CL02015860	−7.75	−7.86	50	−65.8

It can be seen that for all ligands in Table 2 values of SOL scoring function with standard docking parameters are more negative than values of SOL scoring function with quick parameters. On the other hand, for most ligands, this difference is small, and only for three ligands it is about 1.5 kcal/mol. This means that, at least for the best ligands, docking with quick parameters has a reliability close to docking with standard parameters.

Hydrogen bonds between the ligand and the protein were determined by the PM7 quantum-chemical semiempirical method using the MOPAC program with the keyword DISP(1.0). The latter meant that all hydrogen bonds with energies greater than 1.0 kcal/mol were displayed. The numbers and sums of energies of the hydrogen bonds for the 18 selected ligands are presented in Table 3.

Table 3. The number of hydrogen bonds (H-bonds) between the protein and the ligand and the total energy of H-bonds obtained by the PM7 quantum-chemical semiempirical method before and after optimization of the ligands in the protein.

Ligand name	Binding before optimization		Binding after optimization	
	Number of H-bonds	Energy of H-bonds, kcal/mol	Number of H-bonds	Energy of H-bonds, kcal/mol
CL00128632	3	−4.0	5	−8.8
CL00827491	4	−6.1	4	−6.6
CL01040342	2	−3.1	2	−4.0
CL01137849	4	−6.8	5	−10.7
CL01813516	3	−5.4	5	−10.8
CL01817525	2	−3.9	5	−8.4
CL01818109	3	−5.7	6	−9.4
CL01833500	3	−5.1	7	−11.6
CL01849634	4	−5.3	3	−6.6
CL01863488	1	−1.4	3	−7.3
CL01874398	2	−3.2	5	−7.9
CL01880829	2	−4.8	5	−10.2
CL01898147	5	−9.2	5	−10.0
CL01912837	2	−2.7	5	−7.8
CL01926532	1	−1.0	3	−7.1
CL01982900	2	−3.1	5	−9.7
CL02011432	3	−5.4	4	−8.9
CL02015860	3	−3.8	7	−12.5

Number of hydrogen bonds and their energies are shown in Table 3 for the two cases: for the docked ligand position and for optimized ligand position, the latter was obtained when calculating the binding enthalpy. Table 3 shows that ligand optimization led to an increase in the number of hydrogen bonds and their energy compared to hydrogen bonds for the initial position of the ligand obtained during docking. Few ligands also had one or two pi-stacking interactions.

4 Discussions

The 2D-structures of the best selected ligands are shown in Fig. 2.

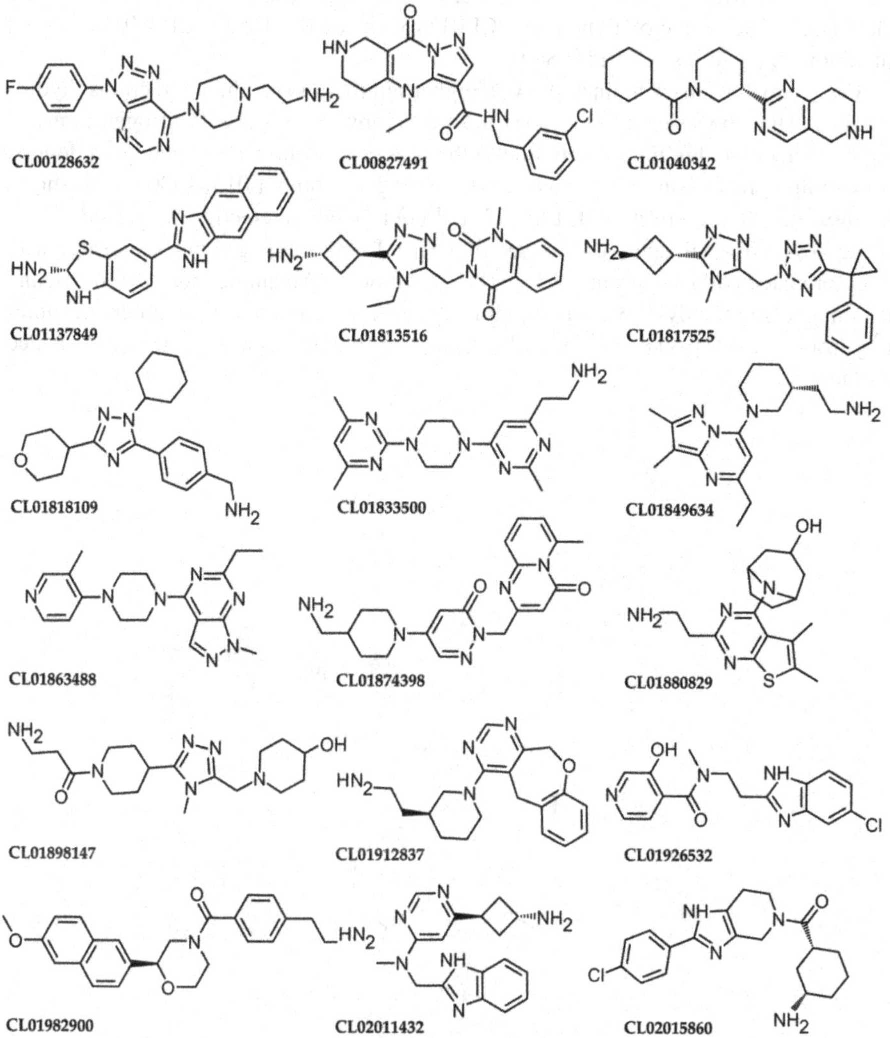

Fig. 2. Structures of the selected best potential inhibitors of factor XIIa presented in Table 2.

All these 18 selected compounds belong to basic entities and contain a nitrogen atom protonated at pH 7.4. In all cases, this positively charged nitrogen atom is predicted in docking to be placed inside S1 pocket and form a salt bridge interaction with a negatively charged side chain of Asp-189. In terms of nature of the basic centre, candidates to inhibit factor XIIa can be classified into three groups: cyclic secondary amines (CL01040342 and CL00827491), 4-aminopyridines (CL01863488 and CL01926532) and primary aliphatic amines (others). Considering nearest basic centre environment, the third class can be further divided into subclasses: acyclic alkylamines (CL01818109, CL01849634, CL01874398, CL01898147, CL01912837, CL01982900, CL00128632, CL01833500, CL01880829 and CL02015860), cyclobutylamines (CL01813516, CL01817525, CL02011432) and diaminomethanethiols (CL01137849).

On average, primary amines shows a higher number of specific interactions (hydrogen bonds) than both secondary amines and 4-aminopyridines since its nitrogen atom can serve as tridentate binding moiety due to the presence of three hydrogen bond donors. For example, possessing a triple protonated nitrogen atom CL01982900 which shows the most negative score in SOL forms 3 hydrogen bonds interacting with a side chain of Asp-189, Gly-219, and Ala-190 (see Fig. 3) and is also engaged in a salt bridge with a deprotonated carboxyl group of Asp-189 (not shown). An amide moiety of the ligand also interacts with Gly-193 via H-bonding. A methoxy-naphthalene fragment occupies a hydrophobic S4 pocket and, visually, seems to interact with Trp-215 via T-shaped pi-stacking.

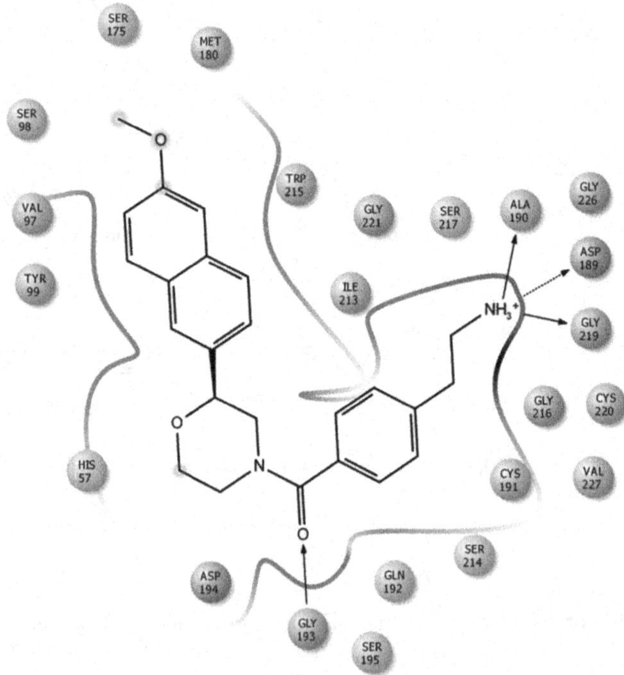

Fig. 3. Interaction diagram of optimized ligand pose of CL01982900 with residues of factor XIIa active site. Arrows indicate hydrogen bonds. The figure is prepared in Maestro [28].

In the contrast, a secondary amine CL01040342 is observed to have H-bonding only to Asp-189 and Ala-190 in its predicted binding mode with the same position of a basic centre as CL01982900 has.

Besides hydrogen bonds and salt bridges, pi-stacking interaction between aromatic rings is quite frequently observed for predicted ligands. For example, CL01813516 in its docked pose has pi-stacking with His-57 (see its interaction profile shown in Fig. 4 where a benzoyleneurea moiety is engaged in pi-stacking with His-57). Also, a protonated basic centre of CL01813516 forms 2 hydrogen bonds with residues of the S1 pocket and a salt bridge with Asp-189. The pi-stacking interaction with His-57 is also found for CL00128632, CL01137849, CL01813516, CL01818109, CL01833500 and CL01912837.

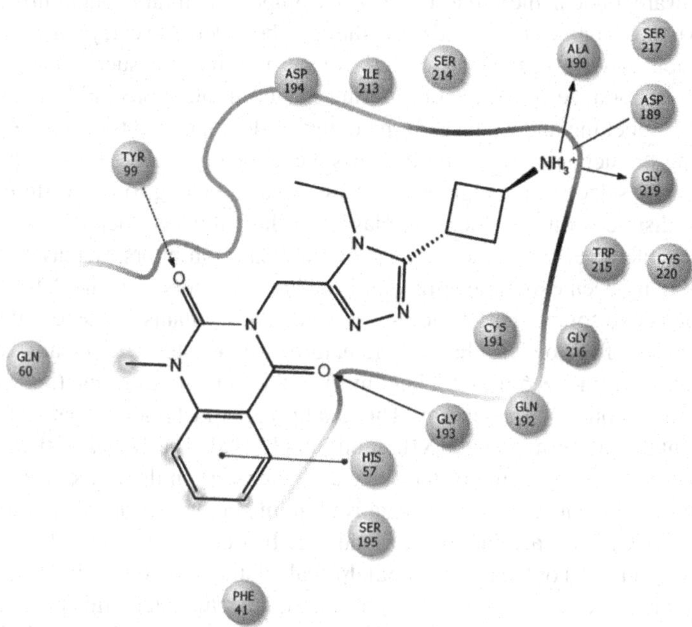

Fig. 4. Interaction diagram of docked pose of CL01813516 with residues of factor XIIa active site. Arrows indicate hydrogen bonds. Line with point endings indicates pi-stacking. The figure is prepared in Maestro [28].

During this study, we found that the number of hydrogen bonds identified by the Maestro graphical interface [28] did not match the number of hydrogen bonds determined using the more reliable PM7 quantum-chemical method implemented in MOPAC. For example, in Fig. 3, Maestro shows four hydrogen bonds for ligand CL01982900, but MOPAC, using a hydrogen bond energy threshold of 1.0 kcal/mol, additionally identifies one more hydrogen bond to GLY-219. In Fig. 4, Maestro shows all five hydrogen bonds for ligand CL01813516 that are identified by MOPAC. We assume that this discrepancy arises from different methods of identifying hydrogen bonds, based only on geometric considerations, as Maestro does, and on the basis of rigorous quantum-chemical calculations, as MOPAC does.

5 Conclusions

In this work, candidate inhibitors of the XIIa coagulation factor are presented. To our knowledge, potential factor XIIa inhibitors identified in this study are novel and belong to chemotypes not present among reported experimentally confirmed factor XIIa inhibitors. Moreover, they differ from predicted and experimentally confirmed inhibitors of factor XIIa we reported recently in [2, 15, 20] (see Fig. 1). For the first time, candidate inhibitors of factor XIIa are found in the Chinese National Compound Library containing more than 1 million existing organic compounds, and they can be ordered to carry out experimental testing of their activity against factor XIIa *in vitro*. Screening such a large database revealed the importance of automatic filtering inappropriate molecules, preparation of the ligands for docking and analysis of the obtained docking results.

Screening of such a large database allows a chemically diverse set of top inhibitor candidates to be selected: the eighteen selected ligands belong to five different chemical classes, distinct from the chemical classes of the published factor XIIa inhibitors. Undoubtedly, the diverse chemical nature of candidate inhibitors increases the likelihood that, having been experimentally confirmed as inhibitors of factor XIIa, they will later become active components of new classes of anticoagulants. All selected here candidate inhibitors of factor XIIa have basic nature. All selected compounds have large negative values (from −8.6 to −7.3 kcal/mol) of the SOL scoring function estimating the protein-ligand binding free energy. These values are much more negative than those of experimentally confirmed factor XIIa inhibitors [2, 15]. The values of the calculated protein-ligand binding enthalpy of the selected ligands are in the range from −77.9 to −48.2 kcal/mol. Too large calculated negative binding enthalpies are a common feature of the PM7 + COSMO calculations [29] and may be due to some imperfections in the COSMO solvent model or the binding enthalpy calculation method itself. Other interesting feature of the selected compounds is presence of specific interactions with the target protein: all these ligands have from 2 to 7 hydrogen bonds with protein. Optimization of the ligand position in the protein by the PM7 method leads to the increase of the number of hydrogen bonds and their energies.

This paper shows that the proposed two-stage docking strategy allows for virtual screening using supercomputer resources of very large databases to search for inhibitor candidates using the SOL docking program.

Acknowledgements. The work was financially supported by the Russian Science Foundation, Agreement no. 21-71-20031. The research is carried out using the equipment of the shared research facilities of HPC computing resources at Lomonosov Moscow State University, including the Lomonosov-2 supercomputer [27].

References

1. Macfarlane, R.G.: An enzyme cascade in theblood clotting mechanism, and its function as a biochemical amplifier. Nature **202**, 498–499 (1964). https://doi.org/10.1038/202498a0
2. Tashchilova, A., et al.: New blood coagulation factor XIIa inhibitors: molecular modeling, synthesis, and experimental confirmation. Molecules **27**(4), 1–18 (2022). https://doi.org/10.3390/molecules27041234
3. Hagedorn, I., et al.: Factor XIIa inhibitor recombinant human albumin infestin-4 abolishes occlusive arterial thrombus formation without affecting bleeding. Circulation **121**(13), 1510–1517 (2010). https://doi.org/10.1161/CIRCULATIONAHA.109.924761
4. Matafonov, A., et al.: Factor XII inhibition reduces thrombus formation in a primate thrombosis model. Blood **123**(11), 1739–1746 (2014). https://doi.org/10.1182/blood-2013-04-499111
5. Larsson, M., et al.: A factor XIIa inhibitory antibody provides thromboprotection in extracorporeal circulation without increasing bleeding risk. Sci. Transl. Med. **6**(222), 222ra17 (2014). https://doi.org/10.1126/scitranslmed.3006804
6. Müller, F., Gailani, D., Renné, T.: Factor XI and XII as antithrombotic targets. Curr. Opin. Hematol. **18**(5) (2011)
7. Robert, S., Bertolla, C., Masereel, B., Dogné, J.-M., Pochet, L.: Novel 3-carboxamide-coumarins as potent and selective FXIIa inhibitors. J. Med. Chem. **51**(11), 3077–3080 (2008). https://doi.org/10.1021/jm8002697
8. Stürzebecher, A., et al.: Highly potent and selective substrate analogue factor Xa inhibitors containing D-homophenylalanine analogues as P3 residue: part 2. ChemMedChem **2**(7), 1043–1053 (2007). https://doi.org/10.1002/cmdc.200700031
9. Baeriswyl, V., Calzavarini, S., Gerschheimer, C., Diderich, P., Angelillo-Scherrer, A., Heinis, C.: Development of a selective peptide macrocycle inhibitor of coagulation factor XII toward the generation of a safe antithrombotic therapy. J. Med. Chem. **56**(9), 3742–3746 (2013). https://doi.org/10.1021/jm400236j
10. Baeriswyl, V., et al.: A synthetic factor XIIa inhibitor blocks selectively intrinsic coagulation initiation. ACS Chem. Biol. **10**(8), 1861–1870 (2015). https://doi.org/10.1021/acschembio.5b00103
11. Bouckaert, C., Zhu, S., Govers-Riemslag, J.W.P., Depoorter, M., Diamond, S.L., Pochet, L.: Discovery and assessment of water soluble coumarins as inhibitors of the coagulation contact pathway. Thromb. Res. **157**, 126–133 (2017). https://doi.org/10.1016/j.thromres.2017.07.015
12. Chen, J.J.F., Visco, D.P.: Identifying novel factor XIIa inhibitors with PCA-GA-SVM developed vHTS models. Eur. J. Med. Chem. **140**, 31–41 (2017). https://doi.org/10.1016/j.ejmech.2017.08.056
13. Korff, M., et al.: Acylated 1H–1,2,4-Triazol-5-amines targeting human coagulation factor XIIa and thrombin: conventional and microscale synthesis, anticoagulant properties, and mechanism of action. J. Med. Chem. **63**(21), 13159–13186 (2020). https://doi.org/10.1021/acs.jmedchem.0c01635
14. Davoine, C., Bouckaert, C., Fillet, M., Pochet, L.: Factor XII/XIIa inhibitors: their discovery, development, and potential indications. Eur. J. Med. Chem. **208**, 112753 (2020). https://doi.org/10.1016/j.ejmech.2020.112753
15. Ilin, I., et al.: Experimentally validated novel factor XIIa inhibitors identified by docking and quantum chemical post-processing. Mol. Inf. **41**, 2200205 (2022). https://doi.org/10.1002/minf.202200205
16. Chinese National Compound Library (CNCL). http://en.cncl.org.cn/
17. Halgren, T.A.: Merck molecular force field. J. Comput. Chem. **17**(5–6), 490–641 (1996)

18. Sulimov, V.B., Ilin, I.S., Kutov, D.C., Sulimov, A.V.: Development of docking programs for Lomonosov supercomputer. J. Turk. Chem. Soc. Sect. A Chem. **7**(1), 259–276 (2020). https://doi.org/10.18596/jotcsa.634130
19. Sulimov, A.V., Kutov, D.C., Oferkin, I.V., Katkova, E.V., Sulimov, V.B.: Application of the docking program SOL for CSAR benchmark. J. Chem. Inf. Model. **53**(8), 1946–1956 (2013). https://doi.org/10.1021/ci400094h
20. Sulimov, A.V., Kutov, D.C., Ilin, I.S., Tashchilova, A.S., Shikhaliev, K.S., Sulimov, V.B.: Supercomputer search for the new inhibitors of the coagulation factor XIIa. Lobachevskii J. Math. **43**(4), 895–903 (2022). https://doi.org/10.1134/S199508022207023X
21. Romanov, A.N., Jabin, S.N., Martynov, Y.B., Sulimov, A.V., Grigoriev, F.V., Sulimov, V.B.: Surface generalized born method: a simple, fast, and precise implicit solvent model beyond the coulomb approximation. J. Phys. Chem. A **108**(43), 9323–9327 (2004). https://doi.org/10.1021/jp046721s
22. Sulimov, V.B., Kutov, D.C., Sulimov, A.V.: Advances in docking. Curr. Med. Chem. **26**(42), 7555–7580 (2019). https://doi.org/10.2174/0929867325666180904115000
23. Sulimov, V.B., Kutov, D.C., Taschilova, A.S., Ilin, I.S., Tyrtyshnikov, E.E., Sulimov, A.V.: Docking paradigm in drug design. Curr. Top. Med. Chem. **21**(6), 507–546 (2021). https://doi.org/10.2174/1568026620666201207095626
24. Stewart, J.J.P.: Stewart Computational Chemistry. MOPAC2016. http://openmopac.net/MOPAC2016.html
25. Stewart, J.J.P.: Optimization of parameters for semiempirical methods VI: more modifications to the NDDO approximations and re-optimization of parameters. J. Mol. Model. **19**(1), 1–32 (2013). https://doi.org/10.1007/s00894-012-1667-x
26. Klamt, A., Schüürmann, G.: COSMO: a new approach to dielectric screening in solvents with explicit expressions for the screening energy and its gradient. J. Chem. Soc. Perkin Trans. **2**(5), 799–805 (1993). https://doi.org/10.1039/P29930000799
27. Voevodin, V.V., et al.: Supercomputer Lomonosov-2: Large scale, deep monitoring and fine analytics for the user community. Supercomput. Front. Innov. **6**(2), 4–11 (2019). https://doi.org/10.14529/jsfi190201
28. Schrödinger, LLC. https://www.schrodinger.com
29. Sulimov, A., Kutov, D., Ilin, I., Sulimov, V.: Quantum-chemical quasi-docking for molecular dynamics calculations. Nanomaterials **12**(2), 1–13 (2022). https://doi.org/10.3390/nano12020274

Supercomputer Technologies for Ultrasound Nondestructive Imaging of Low-Contrast Defects in Solids

Evgeny Bazulin[1], Alexander Goncharsky[2,3], Sergey Romanov[2,3](✉), and Sergey Seryozhnikov[2,3]

[1] ECHO+Scientific Production Association, Moscow, Russia
bazulin@echoplus.ru
[2] Lomonosov Moscow State University, Moscow, Russia
gonchar@srcc.msu.ru, romanov60@gmail.com
[3] Moscow Center of Fundamental and Applied Mathematics, Moscow, Russia

Abstract. This study explores the methods of wave tomography in application to the problem of reconstructing the wave velocity inside flat objects. Numerical simulations were carried out for 2D inverse problems that represent nondestructive tomographic imaging of welded joints in metal samples. Tomographic diagnostic methods employing transducer arrays are proposed for imaging flat objects that are accessible only from a single side. In this case, the waves reflected from the flat bottom of the inspected object can be used for sounding. The thickness of the flat object is assumed to be known. The multistage iterative method made it possible to effectively solve nonlinear inverse problems of ultrasound tomography and to reconstruct the sound speed images of simulated test objects, small cracks and cavities. The gradient method works best if the contrast in sound speed is low. Acoustic and geometric parameters of the simulations correspond to a real experiment. Numerical simulations were performed on supercomputer. Capabilities of CPU and GPU computing platforms for solving inverse problems of ultrasound tomography in non-destructive testing are discussed.

Keywords: Supercomputer simulations · High-performance scientific computing · Inverse problems · Ultrasound tomography · Nondestructive testing

1 Introduction

The paper is aimed at developing tomographic diagnostic methods, effective algorithms and programs in application to non-destructive testing of industrial products. The methods of ultrasound tomography in the wave approximation are applied to the problems of nondestructive testing of industrial products; in particular, simulating in the problem of tomographic imaging of welded joints in metal samples. This task is one of the most important tasks of flaw detection for monitoring high-risk objects, such as pipelines and equipment of nuclear power plants, trunk and field gas pipelines, compressor stations, unique mechanical engineering products [7].

V. Voevodin et al. (Eds.): RuSCDays 2023, LNCS 14388, pp. 259–270, 2023.
https://doi.org/10.1007/978-3-031-49432-1_20

In "full waveform inversion" method, the inverse problem is considered as a nonlinear problem under the wave model, which is solved by iterative algorithms [22, 28]. Synthetic aperture [2, 16, 17, 35] and topological imaging [1, 8, 21, 23, 30] methods are widely used. There are studies on the use of ray models in tomography to determine the wave velocity and absorption factor [20, 37].

Currently, ultrasound tomography is making the first steps in the field of nondestructive testing [3, 10, 27, 29, 36, 38]. Only a few works on tomographic nondestructive testing have been published. Authors' previous works on NDT discussed multi-angle sounding methods [4, 5, 32]. Compared to medical ultrasound tomography [12, 15], the inverse tomographic problems of non-destructive testing are even more difficult because of multiple waves propagating simultaneously in a solid.

In the problem of testing welded joints, sounding is often possible only from a single side of the tested object. Tomographic schemes for ultrasonic nondestructive testing of flat objects with various assumptions for the bottom of the object were discussed in [33, 34]. In this paper, we investigate a tomographic scheme of sounding an object from a single side by antenna array using waves reflected from the bottom of the object. The multistage iterative method is used to solve nonlinear inverse problems of ultrasonic tomography. An important problem in NDT is the presence of structural noise from small crystallites. Even in the presence of structural noise, we reconstruct tomographic images of small cracks and small cavities with a sound speed contrast of up to 40%.

Methods and algorithms of ultrasound tomography for determining the wave velocity structure and identifying defects in objects in application to nondestructive testing of welded joints in metallic samples require large amounts of computation [3, 13, 14]. The developed algorithms have been tested on model problems. The computations have been carried out on "Lomonosov–2" supercomputer.

2 Formulation of the Problem of Ultrasound Tomography of Flat Objects and Its Solution Methods

The presence of multiple wave types (longitudinal, transverse, etc.) in the object is a distinctive feature of inverse problems in NDT. In this publication, inverse problems are studied under a scalar model that describes the propagation of a single wave type. With a certain geometry of the experiment, one can single out the fastest wave. In [5], such a separation of the longitudinal wave from the experimental data was carried out by limiting the signal registration time, based on the fact that the longitudinal wave velocity is almost two times faster than the transverse wave. Thus, a scalar wave model can be used to describe the fastest wave. We consider the scalar wave equation:

$$c(r)u_{tt}(r,t) - \Delta u(r,t) = \delta(r - r_0)g(t), \tag{1}$$

$$u(r, t = 0) = u_t(r, t = 0) = 0. \tag{2}$$

Here, $u(r,t)$ - scalar wave field; $r \in R^2$; $c^{-0.5}(r) = v(r)$ is the velocity of the wave; r_0 is the position of the point source; $g(t)$ describes the sounding pulse from the source.

Experimental setup presented in this study is depicted in Fig. 1. In the experiment a single linear transducer array A is placed on the top surface. Every ninth element of array A emits the sounding pulses in sequence, while all the elements of array A are used as detectors.

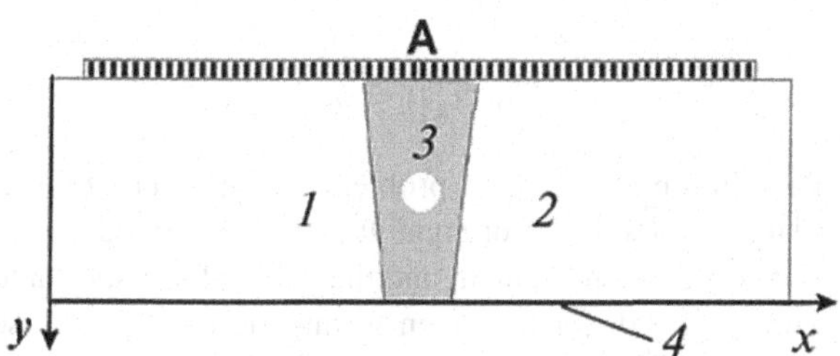

Fig. 1. The scheme of tomographic experiments

Wave propagation velocity $v(r)$ in regions 1 and 2 near the top boundary is a known constant, $v(r) = const = v_0$. Wave propagation velocity $v(r)$ in region 3 and the exact geometry of region 3 are unknown. The position of boundary 4 is assumed to be known. The ultrasound waves are reflected from the bottom surface 4 according to the law

$$\partial_n^k u(r,t) = p(r,t), \tag{3}$$

where $\partial_n^k u(r,t)$ is either a normal derivative to boundary 4 (for $k = 1$), or equal to $u(r,t)$ at boundary 4 (for $k = 0$); $p(r,t)$ is a known function. The parameter k is determined by the reflectivity of the surface. Such boundary conditions can represent, for example, free boundary or fixed boundary. In these cases $p(r,t) = 0$.

In this study, we take into account the waves, which propagate through the object and are possibly reflected once from the boundary 4. We do not take into account the waves reflected multiple times from the surface 4 and the waves traveling from the emitter to the detector along the top surface. These waves can be easily separated by pulse arrival time.

The problem is posed as a coefficient inverse problem, which in this formulation is nonlinear [5, 12, 18, 19, 25, 26]. Consider the residual functional $\Phi(c)$ [5, 12]

$$\Phi(c) = \sum\nolimits_{j=1}^{M} \sum\nolimits_{i=1}^{N} \int_0^T \left(u^{ij}(t;c) - U^{ij}(t)\right)^2 dt.$$

Here, $u^{ij}(t;c)$ are the values of the simulated wave computed via solving the direct problem (1)–(3) with a given $c(r)$. $U^{ij}(t)$ are the data registered by the receiving transducer elements, where j is the index of the emitting element, i is the index of the receiving element (i = 1,….N) (j = 1,….M). The inverse problem is posed as a problem of finding a function $\overline{c}(r)$ that minimizes $\Phi(c)$

$$\overline{c}(r) : \min_{c(r)} \Phi(c) = \Phi(\overline{c}).$$

The found solution $\overline{c}(r)$ is the approximate solution to the inverse problem.

We consider a so-called «conjugate» problem to the main problem (1–3)

$$c(r)w_{tt}(r,t) - \Delta w(r,t) = u(r,t)|_{\Gamma} - U, \tag{4}$$

$$w(r, t = T) = w_t(r, t = T) = 0, \tag{5}$$

$$\partial_n^k w(r,t) = 0, \tag{6}$$

where $u(r, t)$ is the solution of the main problem (1–3); $\partial_n^k w(r,t)$ is either a normal derivative to boundary 4 (for $k = 1$), or equal to $w(r, t)$ at boundary 4 for $k = 0$. The parameter k is known for a given problem and the value of k is the same as in formula (3). By analogy with work [5], for the given formulation of the inverse problem it is possible to derive the gradient of the residual functional $\Phi(c)$:

$$\Phi'_c(c) = \int_0^T w_t(r,t)u_t(r,t)dt.$$

Here, $u(r, t)$ is the solution of the main problem (1–3), and $w(r, t)$ is the solution of the «conjugate» problem (4–6) for a given $c(r)$. We used an explicit finite-difference scheme for the wave Eqs. (1), (4) in the time domain (FDTD) to compute the propagation of the sounding wave over the region not containing sources

$$u_{ij}^{k+1} = \left(2\frac{c_{ij}}{\tau^2}u_{ij}^k - \Delta u_{ij}^k - \frac{c_{ij}}{\tau^2}u_{ij}^{k-1}\right)\left(\frac{c_{ij}}{\tau^2}\right)^{-1}.$$

Here, u_{ij}^k are the values of $u(r, t)$ at the point (i, j) of the imaging plane at the time step k; c_{ij} are the values of $c(r)$ at the point (i, j). A fourth-order approximation on a 5 × 5-point stencil is used for the discrete Laplacian Δu_{ij}^k [24, 31]. Parameters h and τ are related by the Courant stability condition $c^{-0.5}\tau < \frac{h}{\sqrt{2}}$. Homogeneous boundary condition of the first kind (3) was applied at the bottom surface 4. Non-reflecting boundary condition was applied on the rest of the boundaries [9, 11]. A large amount of computation is required to solve the considered nonlinear inverse problem. The number of unknowns reaches 1 million.

A breakthrough result in the field of wave tomography is the multistage method (MSM) [5] as a way to construct an approximate solution to the inverse problem considered. Due to the nonlinearity of this inverse problem, the residual functional $\Phi(c)$ is not convex. This leads to the fact that, for some given values of the parameters, the iterative gradient method may not converge to an exact solution if the sounding pulse wavelength is too small. The iterative process then stops at a local minimum of the residual functional. The multistage method solves the problem of finding the global minimum of the residual functional. At the first stage of the method, low frequencies of the sounding signal are used, which ensures convergence to some low-resolution approximate solution. The second stage is performed using the full spectrum of the available signal and provides high resolution. For the method to work, it is necessary that the sounding signal contains low-frequency components. Thus, in the MSM method, the object is sounded with broadband pulses.

3 Numerical Simulations

Numerical experiments on tomographic reconstruction of the internal structure of objects simulating welded joints of flat metal sheets [6] were carried out. It is assumed that emitters and detectors can only be located above the inspected object, and that the position of the reflective bottom of the object is known. The welded joint contains cavities, cracks and areas with structural noise caused by the accumulation of crystallites. Due to the nonlinearity of the inverse problem, an iterative multi-stage method is employed to obtain an approximate solution. In the problems of nondestructive testing, it is of interest to detect cavities, cracks and holes in the inspected object. The speed of sound in defects can differ significantly from the speed of sound in the material. Therefore, in this study we investigate the possibilities of the MSM method for reconstructing the internal structure of an object with inhomogeneities of various contrasts in speed. Numerical experiments were performed on phantoms with low contrast (20%) and middle contrast (40%).

The first experiment used the low contrast phantom shown in Fig. 3a. The phantom simulates a metal sample (regions 1, 2 in Fig. 1) containing a weld (region 3 in Fig. 1). The speed of sound in a metal sample is 5.9 km/s, the speed of sound in a weld is 5.7 km/s. Several inhomogeneities are included in the phantom: rectangular slots 0.5 × 5 mm and round inclusions 1 mm and 2 mm in diameter. In the low contrast phantom, the speed of sound in inhomogeneities differs from the background by no more than 20%. The minimum speed of sound in inhomogeneities is 4.6 km/s. The material of the welded area and the base metal to the right of the welded area consists of polygonal crystallites with an average size of 0.5 mm. The sound velocity variation in crystallites in the welded area is ±8%, in the area of the base metal on the right the variation is ±4%. The size of the phantom is 70 × 24 mm, the size of the computational grid is 800 × 2400 points with a grid step of 0.04 mm. Model calculations were carried out using 280 transducers located with a step of 0.25 mm. As shown in this study, the number of emitters can be significantly reduced compared to the number of detectors: 32 elements were used as emitters for 2.5 mm or longer wavelength, and 48 emitters were used for 1.2 mm wavelength. The position of the reflective flat bottom is assumed to be known.

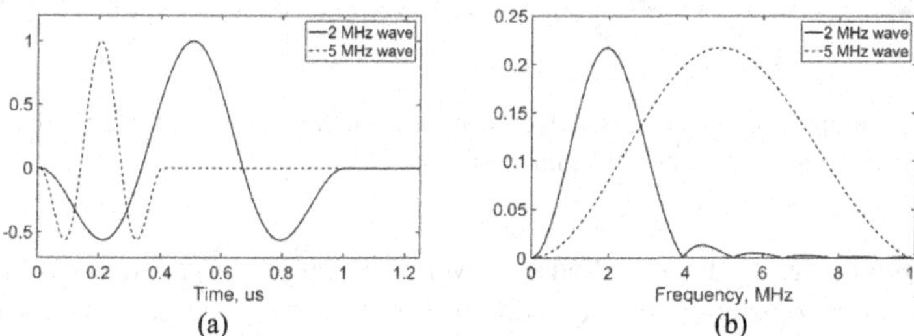

Fig. 2. Waveforms (a) and frequency spectra (b) of sounding pulses with central frequencies of 2 and 5 MHz

The emitters produce broadband short pulses, which are the same for each emitter. At the first stage, only the low-frequency components of the sounding pulse are used.

For example, in a 2 MHz band. The final image is formed using a sounding with a center frequency of 5 MHz. Figure 2 shows the sounding pulse waveforms and frequency spectra.

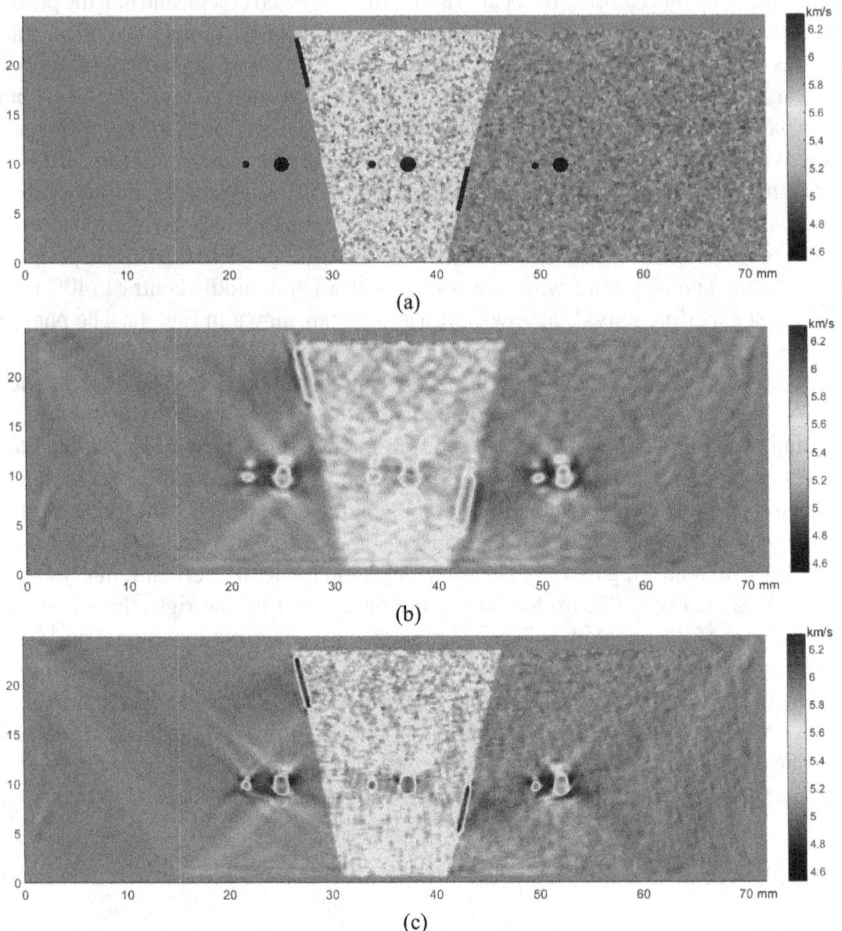

Fig. 3. The phantom with low-contrast defects (a); reconstructed images obtained in the first stage (b) and the second stage (c) of the MSM method

For the multistage gradient method to converge, the phase shift in the wave that passes through the inhomogeneities of the phantom should not exceed half the wavelength. Given the parameters of the phantom, a pulse with a central wavelength of 3 mm (2 MHz band) was used at the first stage of the method. Figure 3b shows an image reconstructed via the gradient method with a central wavelength of 3 mm. The gradient method made it possible to reconstruct the internal structure of the sample with a resolution of about half the wavelength. To increase the resolution, a signal with a wavelength of 1.2 mm is used at the second stage of the multistage gradient method. The image obtained at the first stage is used as the initial approximation for the second stage. Figure 3c shows the image reconstructed at the second stage. It is possible to image rectangular slots 0.5 × 5 mm and round inclusions with a diameter of 1 mm. Note that at the second stage, not only the shape of the defects, but also the wave velocity in the defects is obtained. As shown in Fig. 3, the MSM method allows for a high-quality tomographic image reconstruction with high resolution and high sensitivity to changes in the speed of sound.

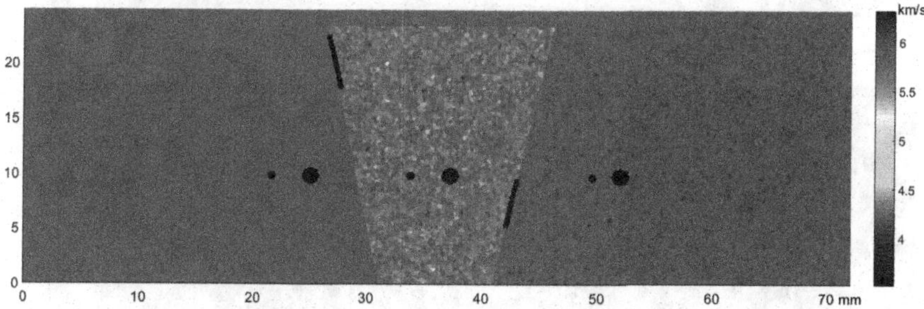

Fig. 4. The phantom with a contrast of 40%

In the second experiment, a middle-contrast phantom was used. Figure 4 shows the middle-contrast phantom. The speed of sound in rectangular slots and round inclusions 1 mm and 2 mm in diameter is 3.6 km/s (the contrast with respect to the background is about 40%). The scheme of the experiment with a reflective bottom is similar to the scheme used in the previous example.

Figure 5a shows the image reconstructed at the first stage of the MSM method with a central wavelength of 5 mm. This wavelength makes it possible to produce an approximate solution given a contrast of 40%. Figure 5b shows the image reconstructed at the second stage with a wavelength of 2.5 mm. Figure 5c shows the image reconstructed at the third stage with a wavelength of 1.2 mm. As an initial approximation for the third stage, the image reconstructed at a wavelength of 2.5 mm obtained at the second stage was used. The multistage gradient method made it possible to reconstruct an image with a contrast of 40% but the reconstruction quality is worse than in Fig. 3.

An attempt to reconstruct a tomographic image at a wavelength of 3 mm from the initial approximation c(x,y) = const turns out to be unsuccessful, as shown in Fig. 6.

This study uses a scalar wave model, which basically describes the propagation of a longitudinal wave. There are software packages that simulate the wave propagation in vector models. The inverse problem in the vector model is extremely difficult, since it reconstructs multiple unknown functions: the components of the elasticity tensor, the density of the medium. Only the first steps are being taken in solving this problem in NDT.

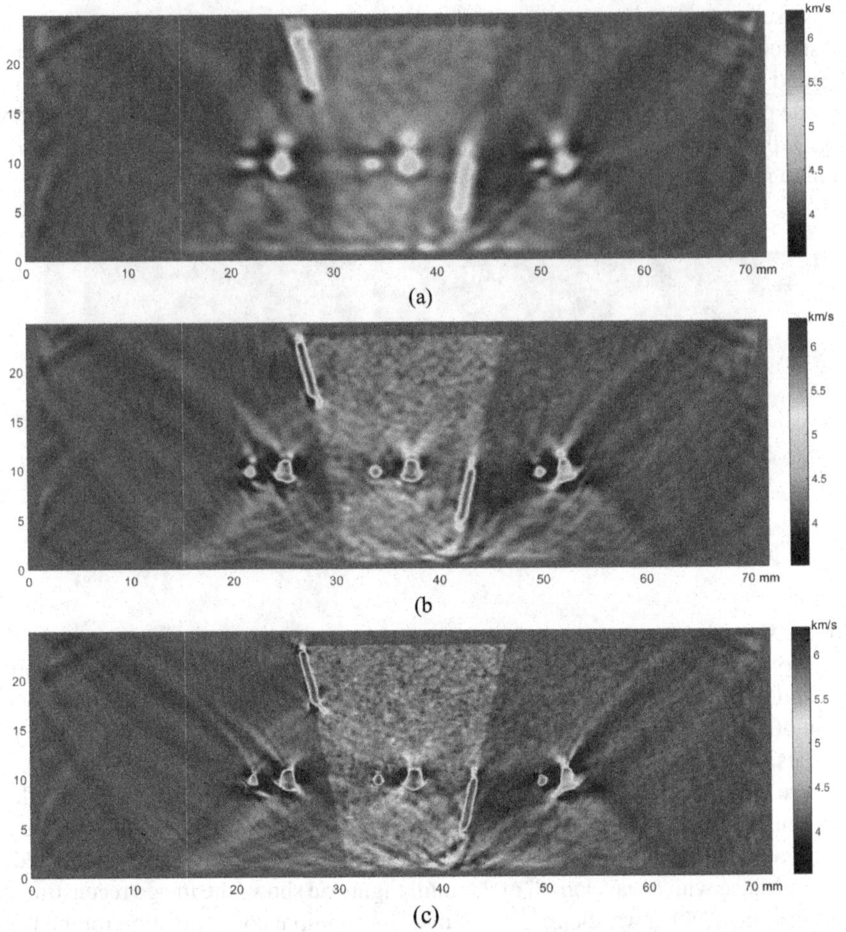

(a)

(b

(c)

Fig. 5. The images reconstructed at the first stage of the MSM method (a), at the second stage (b), at the third stage (c)

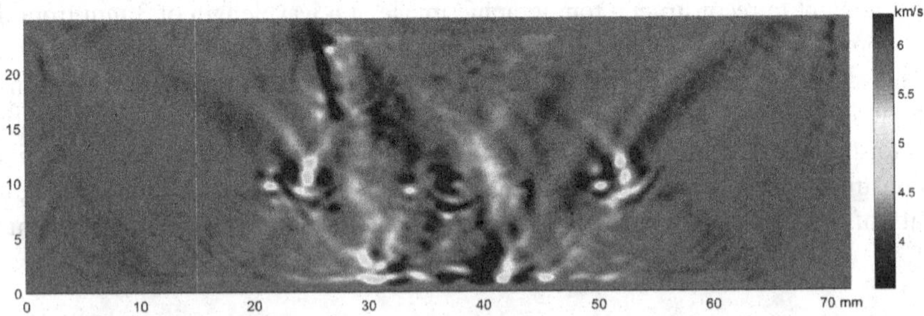

Fig. 6. An attempt to reconstruct the middle-contrast image using a wavelength of 3 mm without the multistage approach

4 Comparison of the Capabilities of CPU and GPU Platforms for Solving Inverse Diagnostic Problems in NDT

The iterative gradient-based methods of solving the inverse problem of wave tomography has been tested on multi-core CPU and GPU computing platforms. The explicit difference scheme makes it possible to use the AVX2 and AVX-512 vector FPUs of modern processors. The Y-marching method is used for computing the difference scheme, while the data for calculating the discrete Laplacian are kept in the FPU registers and are mostly retained when moving to the next line of the data array.

A distinctive feature of the problem considered is a large number of ultrasonic emitters (32 or 48 per imaging plane), for which the calculations of the same type are performed independently. The computational grid size of 800 × 2400 points corresponds to a data volume of approximately 32 MB. This amount corresponds to the size of the cache memory of typical modern multi-core CPUs. The main RAM memory of the computing node is much slower than the CPU cache; thus, for the most efficient execution of the algorithm, one source is allocated to each CPU. The data array is divided equally among the processor cores. 32 or 48 sources in a tomographic scheme allow using the same number of processors in parallel with maximum efficiency. When parallelizing the task, synchronization of data between computing nodes is required only once per iteration in order to sum the gradient. If fewer processors are available, the calculations for each source are carried out by the processor sequentially.

In this study we compare the performance of the parallel wave simulation algorithm employing AVX instructions and without AVX. The parallel algorithm without AVX was parallelized via subdividing the computational domain into 14 equal subdomains, one thread per subdomain. The benchmark was run on Intel Haswell-EP processor (14 cores). The tests were carried out for finite difference grid sizes from 320 × 320 to 4000 × 4000 points. AVX instructions and algorithm optimization resulted in a 3.5- to 4-fold performance gain.

Modern GPUs have enough on-board RAM to accommodate all the data for a typical image reconstruction task. For 48 sources, the volume of data amounts to 1.5 GB. Thus, the computations can be carried out even on a single GPU device. Multi-device parallelization can be used to speed up the computations, or if multiple images are to be reconstructed. To obtain an approximate solution, it is necessary to perform about 100 iterations of gradient descent in total over all stages of the MSM method. At each iteration, 4000 steps of wave propagation simulation in time are performed.

The Table 1 shows the computation time for solving the inverse problem on various multi-core processors and GPUs. The CPU computing platforms tested were Intel Haswell-EP E5-2697v3, 2.6 GHz, 14 cores, and Intel Xeon Gold 6142, 2.6 GHz, 16 cores. The GPU tested platforms were Nvidia Tesla P100 and Nvidia Tesla V100.

Table 1. The computation time for solving the inverse problem on various processors

Platform	Intel Haswell-EP	Intel Xeon Gold	NVidia P100	NVidia V100
Time, CPU*hours	6,4	3.5	1,7	1.1

Thus, the performance of one GPU for this task corresponds to 30–40 AVX512 processor cores (Xeon Gold) or 50–80 AVX2 processor cores (Haswell-EP). The computations were performed on the "Lomonosov–2" supercomputer of Lomonosov Moscow University Supercomputing Center [39].

The multistage method can significantly speed up the image reconstruction due to the fact that at the first stages of the algorithm a much lower grid resolution may be used. Computational time decreases significantly as the grid resolution decreases. The number of operations is proportional to the third power of the number of grid points along one dimension.

5 Conclusion

The article shows that a tomographic imaging scheme with access to the inspected object from a single side in the case of a known position of the reflective bottom allows for high-quality tomographic imaging of the internal structure of the object with high resolution. The multistage gradient method ensures the convergence of the iterative process to the global minimum of the residual functional, which ensures high resolution both in space and in speed of sound.

An important problem in NDT is the presence of structural noise from small crystallites. Using standard ultrasound diagnostic methods, it is not possible to obtain a velocity map of low-contrast inclusions. The proposed method of tomographic diagnostics, in addition to waves reflected from defects, uses waves reflected from the bottom of the object. It is shown that even in the presence of structural noise it is possible to reconstruct tomographic images of small cracks and small cavities with a sound speed contrast of up to 40%. The gradient method works best if the contrast in sound speed is low.

The performance of the algorithm was compared on Intel multi-core SIMD processors and NVidia GPU devices. The task can be efficiently parallelized on dozens of CPU processors employing AVX instructions. Nevertheless, GPUs are better suited for the implementation of algorithms for solving inverse problems of non-destructive testing.

Acknowledgement. The paper was published with the financial support of the Ministry of Education and Science of the Russian Federation as part of the program of the Moscow Center for Fundamental and Applied Mathematics under the agreement № 075-15-2022-284. The research is carried out using the equipment of the shared research facilities of HPC computing resources at Lomonosov Moscow State University.

References

1. Bachmann, E., Jacob, X., Rodriguez, S., Gibiat, V.: Three–dimensional and real–time two–dimensional topological imaging using parallel computing. J. Acoust. Soc. Am. **138**(3), 1796 (2015)
2. Bazulin, E.G.: Comparison of systems for ultrasonic nondestructive testing using antenna arrays or phased antenna arrays. Russ. J. Nondestr. Test. **49**(7), 404–423 (2013). https://doi.org/10.1134/S1061830913070024

3. Bazulin, E.G., Goncharsky, A.V., Romanov, S.Y., Seryozhnikov, S.Y.: Parallel CPU– and GPU–algorithms for inverse problems in nondestructive testing. Lobachevskii J. Math. **39**(4), 486–493 (2018). https://doi.org/10.1134/S1995080218040030
4. Bazulin, E.G., Goncharsky, A.V., Romanov, S., Seryozhnikov, S.: Inverse problems of ultrasonic tomography in nondestructive testing: mathematical methods and experiment. Russ. J. Nondestruct. Test. **55**(6), 453–462 (2019)
5. Bazulin, E., Goncharsky, A., Romanov, S., Seryozhnikov, S.: Ultrasound transmission and reflection tomography for nondestructive testing using experimental data. Ultrasonics **124**, 106765 (2022). https://doi.org/10.1016/j.ultras.2022.106765
6. Bazulin, E.G., Sadykov, M.S.: Determining the speed of longitudinal waves in anisotropic homogeneous welded joint using echo signals measured by two antenna arrays. Russ. J. Nondestruct. Test. **54**(5), 303–315 (2018)
7. Blitz, J., Simpson, G.: Ultrasonic Methods of Non–Destructive Testing. Springer, London (1995)
8. Dominguez, N., Gibiat, V.: Non–destructive imaging using the time domain topological energy. Ultrasonics **50**(3), 367–372 (2010)
9. Engquist, B., Majda, A.: Absorbing boundary conditions for the numerical simulation of waves. Math. Comput. **31**, 629 (1977)
10. Forghani, F., Prasad, M., Behura, J., Fuchs, G.: High resolution acoustic imaging of laboratory rock samples using full waveform inversion. In: SEG International Exposition and 87th Annual Meeting, pp. 3585–3590 (2017)
11. Givoli, D., Keller, J.B.: Non-reflecting boundary conditions for elastic waves. Wave Motion **12**(3), 261–279 (1990)
12. Goncharsky, A.V., Romanov, S.Y., Seryozhnikov, S.Y.: Low–frequency three–dimensional ultrasonic tomography. Doklady Phys. **61**(5), 211–214 (2016). https://doi.org/10.1134/s1028335816050086
13. Goncharsky, A., Romanov, S., Seryozhnikov, S.: Supercomputer technologies in tomographic imaging applications. Supercomput. Front. Innov. **3**, 41–66 (2016)
14. Goncharsky, A.V., Romanov, S., Seryozhnikov, S.: Comparison of the capabilities of GPU clusters and general-purpose supercomputers for solving 3D inverse problems of ultrasound tomography. J. Parallel Distrib. Comput. **133**, 77–92 (2019)
15. Goncharsky, A.V., Romanov, S.Y., Seryozhnikov, S.Y.: Low-frequency ultrasonic tomography: mathematical methods and experimental results. Mosc. Univ. Phys. Bull. **74**(1), 43–51 (2019)
16. Hall, T.E., Doctor, S.R., Reid, L.D., Littlield, R.J., Gilber, R.W.: Implementation of real–time ultrasonic SAFT system for inspection of nuclear reactor components. Acoust. Imaging **15**, 253–266 (1987)
17. Jensen, J.A., Nikolov, S.I., Gammelmark, K.L., Pedersen, M.H.: Synthetic aperture ultrasound imaging. Ultrasonics **44**, 5–15 (2006)
18. Klibanov, M.V., Kolesov, A.E.: Convexification of a 3-D coefficient inverse scattering problem. Comput. Math. Appl. **77**(6), 1681–1702 (2019)
19. Klibanov, M.V., Li, J., Zhang, W.: Convexification for the inversion of a time dependent wave front in a heterogeneous medium. SIAM J. Appl. Math. **79**(5), 1722–1747 (2019)
20. Koshovyy, V.V., Kryvin, E.V., Muraviov, A.M., Romanyshyn, I.M.: Special features of the ultrasonic tomography of thick-sheet products. Russ. J. Nondestr. Testvol. **40**(7), 431–441 (2004)
21. Lubeigt, E., Mensah, S., Rakotonarivo, S., Chaix, J.-F., Baquè, F., Gobillot, G.: Topological imaging in bounded elastic media. Ultrasonics **76**, 145–153 (2017)
22. Marty, P., Boehm, C., Fichtner, A.: Acoustoelastic full-waveform inversion for transcranial ultrasound computed tomography. In: Byram, B.C., Ruiter, N.V. (eds.) Medical Imaging 2021: Ultrasonic Imaging and Tomography, vol. 11602, 1160211. SPIE (2021)

23. Metwally, K., et al.: Weld inspection by focused adjoint method. Ultrasonics **83**, 80–87 (2018)
24. Mu, S.Y., Chang, H.W.: Dispersion and local-error analysis of compact LFE-27 formulas for obtaining sixth-order accurate numerical solutions of 3D Helmholz equation. Pr. Electromagn. Res. S. **143**, 285–314 (2013)
25. Natterer, F.: Incomplete data problems in wave equation imaging. Inverse Probl. Imaging **4**, 685–691 (2010)
26. Natterer, F.: Possibilities and limitations of time domain wave equation imaging. In: AMS: Tomography and Inverse Transport Theory, vol. 559, pp. 151–162. American Mathematical Society (2011). https://doi.org/10.1090/conm/559
27. Nguyen, L.T., Modrak, R.T.: Ultrasonic wavefield inversion and migration in complex heterogeneous structures: 2D numerical imaging and nondestructive testing experiments. Ultrasonics **82**, 357–370 (2018)
28. Pérez-Liva, M., Herraiz, J.L., Udías, J.M., Miller, E., Cox, B.T., Treeby, B.E.: Time domain reconstruction of sound speed and attenuation in ultrasound computed tomography using full wave inversion. J. Acoust. Soc. Am. **141**(3), 1595–1604 (2017)
29. Rao, J., Yang, J., Ratassepp, M., Fan, Z.: Multi-parameter reconstruction of velocity and density using ultrasonic tomography based on full waveform inversion. Ultrasonics **101**, 106004 (2020). https://doi.org/10.1016/j.ultras.2019.106004
30. Rodriguez, S., Deschamps, M., Castaings, M., Ducasse, E.: Guided wave topological imaging of isotropic plates. Ultrasonics **54**, 1880–1890 (2014)
31. Romanov, S.: Optimization of numerical algorithms for solving inverse problems of ultrasonic tomography on a supercomputer. In: Voevodin, V., Sobolev, S. (eds.) Supercomputing. RuSCDays 2017. CCIS, vol. 793, pp. 67–79. Springer, Cham (2017). https://doi.org/10.1007/978-3-319-71255-0_6
32. Romanov, S.Y.: Supercomputer simulations of nondestructive tomographic imaging with rotating transducers. Supercomput. Front. Innov. **5**(3), 98–102 (2018). https://doi.org/10.14529/jsfi180318
33. Romanov, S.Y.: Supercomputer simulations of ultrasound tomography problems of flat objects. Lobachevskii J. Math. **41**(8), 1563–1570 (2020). https://doi.org/10.1134/S199508022008017X
34. Romanov, S.Y.: Simulations in problems of ultrasonic tomographic testing of flat objects on a supercomputer. In: Voevodin V., Sobolev S. (eds). Supercomputing. RuSCDays 2020. CCIS, vol. 1331, pp. 320–331. Springer, Cham (2020). https://doi.org/10.1007/978-3-030-64616-5
35. Schmitz, V., Chakhlov, S., Müller, W.: Experiences with synthetic aperture focusing in the field. Ultrasonics **38**, 731–738 (2000)
36. Seidl, R., Rank, E.: Iterative time reversal based flaw identification. Comput. Math. Appl. **72**, 879–892 (2016)
37. Soldatov, A.A., Sorokin, P.V., Soldatov, A.I., Kostina, M.A., Shul'gina, Yu.V.: Small-angle acoustic tomography under shadow testing with antenna arrays. Russ. J. Nondestr. Test. **54**(7), 463–468 (2018)
38. Tran, K.T., Jalinoos, F., Nguyen, T.D., Agrawal, A.K.: Evaluation of bridge abutment with ultraseismic waveform tomography: field data application. J. Nondestruct Eval. **38** 95 (2019)
39. Voevodin, V.V., et al.: Supercomputer Lomonosov-2: large scale, deep monitoring and fine analytics for the user community. Supercomput. Frontiers Innov. **6**(2), 4–11 (2019). https://doi.org/10.14529/jsfi190201

The Effect of Data Structuring on the Parallel Efficiency of the HydroBox3D Relativistic Code

Igor Chernykh[1(✉)], Vladimir Misilov[2,3], Elena Akimova[2,3], and Igor Kulikov[1]

[1] Institute of Computational Mathematics and Mathematical Geophysics, Siberian Branch of the RAS, Novosibirsk, Russia
{chernykh,kulikov}@ssd.sscc.ru

[2] Krasovskii Institute of Mathematics and Mechanics, Ural Branch of the RAS, Ekaterinburg, Russia
v.e.misilov@urfu.ru

[3] Ural Federal University, Ekaterinburg, Russia

Abstract. The hydrodynamic approach to modeling astrophysics problems has several disadvantages in terms of the implementation of a parallel computing code. One of the main drawbacks is the low arithmetic intensity of the methods that implement the computational problem. This peculiarity produces the performance limitation associated with the performance limitations of the DRAM memory of high-performance computing systems. One of the solutions to this problem is data structuring based on the characteristics of processors and memory of a computer system on which supercomputer simulation is to be carried out. In this work, the authors use the specialized Intel SDLT library, which allows you to organize data in a special way that can help the compiler to vectorize a computational code for Intel server processors. The use of this library made it possible to speed up the computational code by fifty times, and for the first time bring the performance of some code functions to the performance limits of server processors on vector FMA instructions.

Keywords: High Performance Computing · Data Structure Optimization · Massive Parallel System · Performance Optimization

1 Introduction

The problem of structuring data for effective memory usage during computations is still very interesting. At this moment, both CPU chip giants Intel and AMD producing processors with Advanced Vector Extensions (AVX) instructions. AMD company also added AVX-512 for PC chips, and we are waiting for AVX-512 server chips soon. Despite the power of modern compilers, autovectorization without data structuring for most modern scientific codes doesn't show significant performance growth. It means that problems of Single Input

V. Voevodin et al. (Eds.): RuSCDays 2023, LNCS 14388, pp. 271–284, 2023.
https://doi.org/10.1007/978-3-031-49432-1_21

Multiple Data (SIMD) programming are still actual, and we need to try to solve data structuring problems with modern techniques. Last decade, we developed our astrophysical codes based on the hydrodynamic approach [1–3,6,10]. We use Fortran and C/C++ languages in our code development process. In our performance research, we tried to use AVX-512 SIMD instructions by adding corresponding C++ intrinsics to the code, different code optimizations based on the data alignment procedures for different vector registers [4,5,57,58]. The problem of low-level AVX-512 intrinsics usage is the binding of a code to the computing node architecture. You can't use your Intel's AVX-512 intrinsics-based code on AMD systems, even if your chips both support AVX-512 because of the different software interface realization. If we want to save code interoperability and good performance, we need to use, for example, some features based on an array of structures (AoS) to the structure of arrays (SoA) code optimization or code loops simplification, and so on. Array of structures (AoS) to structure of arrays (SoA) optimization complicates the text of the code and is based on the next Listings 1.1, 1.2.

Listing 1.1. AoS loop example

```
struct point3D {
    float x;
    float y;
    float z;
};
struct point3D points[N];
float get_point_x(int i) { return points[i].x; }
```

Listing 1.2. SoA loop example

```
struct pointlist3D {
    float x[N];
    float y[N];
    float z[N];
};
struct pointlist3D points;
float get_point_x(int i) { return points.x[i]; }
```

AoS representation is more intuitive and clear for understanding but for SIMD code is better to use the SoA data representation. In our work, we tried to use Intel's SDLT (SIMD Data Layout Templates) library for our latest C++-based version of astrophysics code HydroBox3d [7]. SIMD Data Layout Templates (SDLT) is a C++11 template library providing containers that represent arrays of "Plain Old Data" objects (a struct whose data members do not have any pointers/references and no virtual functions) using layouts that enable the generation of efficient SIMD (single instruction multiple data) vector code [60]. SDLT uses standard ISO C++11 code.

In the next sections, we will show the mathematical model and numerical method which are used in our astrophysical code, some SDLT optimizations, and performance analysis with or without Intel's templates on Intel Xeon Scalable 2nd generation chips.

2 Mathematical Model and Numerical Method

For our performance tests, we used a relativistic hydrodynamics version of the HydroBox3D code. Here we give a brief description of the mathematical model and numerical method. A more detailed description of astrophysical problems which we solve numerically can be found in [8–56]. First of all, we would like to define the physical variables: density ρ, velocity vector $\boldsymbol{v}$, pressure p, and the speed of light $c \equiv 1$. The Lorentz factor Γ is defined by the following formula:

$$\Gamma = \frac{1}{\sqrt{1-(v/c)^2}} = \frac{1}{\sqrt{1-v^2}}. \tag{1}$$

We use the ideal gas model in our code. The state equation is written as an equation for the special enthalpy h

$$h = 1 + \frac{\gamma}{\gamma-1}\frac{p}{\rho}, \tag{2}$$

where γ is the adiabatic index. In this case, the speed of sound c_s is defined as

$$c_s^2 = \frac{\gamma p}{\rho h}. \tag{3}$$

To write the special relativistic hydrodynamics equations, we introduce conservative variables: $D = \Gamma\rho$ - relativistic density, $M_j = \Gamma^2\rho h v_j$ - the relativistic impulse. The components of the velocity vector $\boldsymbol{v}$ are v_j for $j = x, y, z$, and $E = \Gamma^2\rho h - p$ is the full relativistic energy. The system of equations can be written as follows

$$\frac{\partial}{\partial t}\begin{pmatrix}\Gamma\rho \\ \Gamma^2\rho h v_j \\ \Gamma^2\rho h - p\end{pmatrix} + \sum_{k=1}^{3}\frac{\partial}{\partial x_k}\begin{pmatrix}\rho\Gamma v_k \\ \rho h\Gamma^2 v_j v_k + p\delta_{jk} \\ (\Gamma^2\rho h - p)v_k + p v_k\end{pmatrix} = 0, \tag{4}$$

where δ_{jk} is the Kronecker symbol. The inverse transition requires solving next nonlinear equation

$$f(p) = \Gamma^2\rho h - p - E = 0. \tag{5}$$

We use the iterative Newton method for the solution

$$p_{m+1} = p_m - \frac{f(p_m)}{f'(p_m)}, \tag{6}$$

where derivative of function f has the form

$$f'(p) = \frac{\gamma}{\gamma-1}\Gamma^2 - \frac{M^2\Gamma^3}{(E+p)^3}\left(D + 2\frac{\gamma}{\gamma-1}p\Gamma\right) - 1. \tag{7}$$

We need to stop the iterative process when the required accuracy is reached. In our case, the system of Eqs. (4) can be rewritten in vector form

$$\frac{\partial U}{\partial t} + \sum_{k=1}^{3} \frac{\partial F_k}{\partial x_k} = 0, \tag{8}$$

Then, for the arbitrary cell, the Godunov scheme has the form

$$\frac{U^{n+1}_{i+\frac{1}{2},k+\frac{1}{2},l+\frac{1}{2}} - U^{n}_{i+\frac{1}{2},k+\frac{1}{2},l+\frac{1}{2}}}{\tau} + \frac{F^*_{x,i+1,k+\frac{1}{2},l+\frac{1}{2}} - F^*_{x,i,k+\frac{1}{2},l+\frac{1}{2}}}{h_x} \tag{9}$$
$$+ \frac{F^*_{y,i+\frac{1}{2},k+1,l+\frac{1}{2}} - F^*_{y,i+\frac{1}{2},k,l+\frac{1}{2}}}{h_y} + \frac{F^*_{z,i+\frac{1}{2},k+\frac{1}{2},l+1} - F^*_{z,i+\frac{1}{2},k+\frac{1}{2},l}}{h_z} = 0,$$

where $h_{x,y,z}$ are the steps of the spatial grid and F^* are the fluxes of the corresponding variables through cell boundaries. This values can be obtained from solving the Riemann problem. The numerical solver is based on the piecewise parabolic method on a local stencil (PPML) and is described in detail in works [10,59]. Figure 1 shows the computational scheme of the relativistic hydrodynamics version of HydroBox3D.

3 CPU Efficiency Evaluation

We used compute nodes from the NKS-1P system of the Siberian Supercomputer Center. Each node has two Intel Xeon Scalable 2nd Gen 6248R (24 cores, 3 GHz) CPUs with 192 GB of DRAM4 memory. We also tested on the nodes with two Intel Xeon Scalable 2nd Gen 8268 (24 cores, 2.9 GHz) CPUs with 192 GB of DRAM4 memory. For the comparison between server CPUs and workstations, we did some tests on the PC with an Intel Core i9 10980XE CPU with 64 GB of DRAM4. All of these CPUs support AVX-512 instructions. We installed the same Intel oneAPI base+HPC tools on the NKS-1P system and workstation PC. As we said before, we did many versions of our astrophysical codes such as versions based on Coarray Fortran, C++ with Intel's AVX-512 intrinsics, and versions with manual data alignment for auto-vectorization by Intel's compiler. In this research, we used the C++ 11 version of our HydroBox3D code. We modified our code with Intel's SDLT SIMD templates for the automatic generation of efficient code. The next two listings show the difference between data initializations and modification of loops for the Eulerian stage from Fig. 1. Listing 1.3 shows the original MPI version of HydroBox3D. Listing 1.4 shows the optimized SDLT with the OpenMP version of the code.

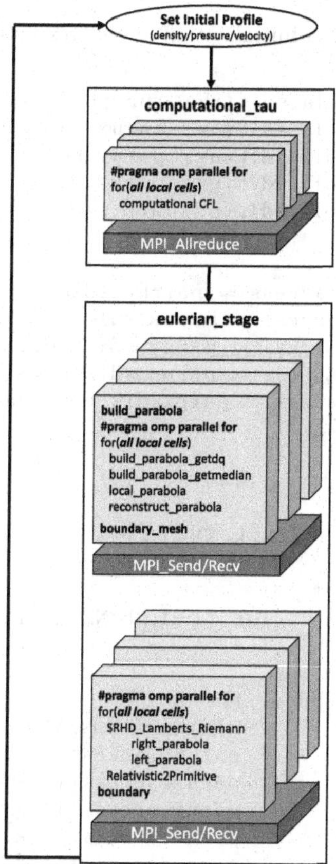

Fig. 1. Numerical method which is realised in HydroBox3D code.

Listing 1.3. Original data initialization in Eulerean stage of HydroBox3D with a part of main loop

```
build_parabola(rho,parrho);
build_parabola(ux,parux);
build_parabola(uy,paruy);
build_parabola(uz,paruz);
build_parabola(p,parp);

for(i=1;i<NX-1;i++)
        for(k=1;k<NY-1;k++)
                for(l=1;l<NZ-1;l++)
                {
                 // Riemann solver
                 SRHD_Lamberts_Riemann(
                 rho[index(i,k,l)],
                 ux[index(i,k,l)],uy[index(i,k,l)],
                 uz[index(i,k,l)],
                 p[index(i,k,l)],...
...
```

Listing 1.4. Modified data initialization in Eulerean stage of HydroBox3D with a part of main loop

```
        build_parabola_sdlt(rho, parrho_sdlt);
        build_parabola_sdlt(ux, parux_sdlt);
        build_parabola_sdlt(uy, paruy_sdlt);
        build_parabola_sdlt(uz, paruz_sdlt);
        build_parabola_sdlt(p, parp_sdlt);


        auto parrho_access = parrho_sdlt.const_access();
        auto parux_access = parux_sdlt.const_access();
        auto paruy_access = paruy_sdlt.const_access();
        auto paruz_access = paruz_sdlt.const_access();
        auto parp_access = parp_sdlt.const_access();

#pragma omp for
        for (i=1; i<NX-1;i++)
        {
                for (k=1; k<NY-1;k++)
                {
#pragma ivdep
                        for (l=1; l<NZ-1; l++)
                        {
//Riemann solver
#pragma forceinline recursive
                         SRHD_Lamberts_Riemann(
                          parrho_access[i][k][l].u(),
                          parux_access[i][k][l].u(),
                          paruy_access[i][k][l].u(),
                          paruz_access[i][k][l].u(),
                          parp_access[i][k][l].u(),...
            ...
```

For the performance evaluation, we used the Intel Advisor tool from oneAPI. Listing 1.5 shows the compiling line and Advisor's command line for the performance data evaluation. The compilation line was created according to Intel's reference guide for the Advisor tool. Unfortunately, due to the recommended disabling of interprocedural optimization between files, the compilation procedure sometimes spent more than two hours with SDLT templates. This recommendation takes an effect on the results of the Intel Advisor tool. In the case of the MPI run of Intel Advisor, we need to start the survey analysis and trip counts separately, despite the recommendations from the manual. The output data from the Intel Advisor tool is the roofline analysis chart [61,62]. This chart shows the performance of each function of the code in comparison with the peak performance of CPU and memory. This is very helpful for developers who want to improve the performance of their codes. NVIDIA and AMD also have similar tools for their chip products.

Listing 1.5. Compilation of HydroBox3D and Advisor's command lines for the performance evaluation

```
mpiicc -o srhd64 main.cpp -std=c++17 -g -debug inline-debug-info
-qopenmp -xcascadelake -axcascadelake -prec-div- -qopt-report=5
-O3 -qopt-zmm-usage=high -fpermissive -no-ipo

mpirun -n 1 advisor --collect=survey --data-limit=0
--trace-mpi --project-dir=./advi_results -- ./srhd64

mpirun -n 1 advisor --collect tripcounts --data-limit=0
  --project-dir ./advi_results --trace-mpi --flop
--no-trip-counts -- ./srhd64
```

For our research, it should be noted some peak performance data for Intel Xeon Scalable 6248R/8268 and Intel Core i9 10980XE CPUs. Compute node with two Intel Xeon 6248R CPUs has Scalar Add Peak - 342 GFLOPS, Dual Precision Vector Add Peak - 1974 GFLOPS, Dual Precision Vector FMA Peak - 3949 GFLOPS, Single Precision Vector FMA Peak - 7899 GFLOPS. Compute node with two Intel Xeon 8268 CPUs has Scalar Add Peak - 333 GFLOPS, Dual Precision Vector FMA Peak - 3948 GFLOPS, Single Precision Vector FMA Peak - 7897 GFLOPS. Workstation PC with one Intel Core i9 10980XE CPU has Scalar Add Peak - 134 GFLOPS, Dual Precision Vector FMA Peak - 875 GFLOPS, Single Precision Vector FMA Peak - 1710 GFLOPS. We can see that the 6248R CPU is similar to the 8268, but the retailer's price of 8268 is two times higher than the 6248R. We used the same physical initial conditions for all of our tests.

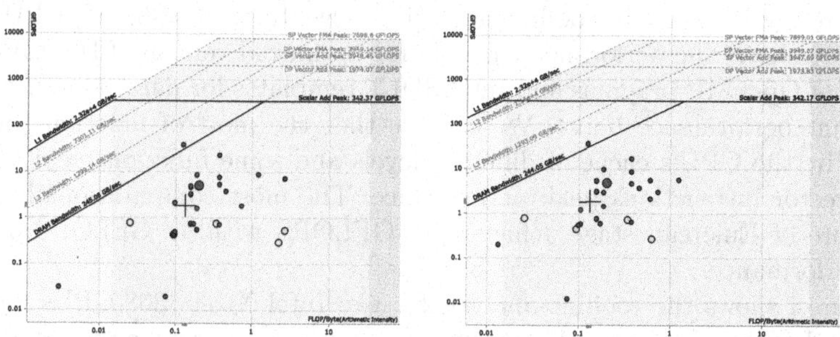

Fig. 2. Roofline analysis results for the original MPI version of HydroBox3D on compute node with two Intel Xeon Scalable 6248R CPUs. The left chart shows performance for the mesh size $256 \times 256 \times 256$. The right picture shows performance for the mesh size $128 \times 128 \times 128$.

Figure 2 shows the roofline analysis results for two Intel Xeon 6248R CPUs. We can see that the mesh size doesn't affect performance, but we need 128^3 mesh to compare the performance results with the workstation PC. Figure 2 shows that most of the functions are limited by DRAM and Scalar Add Peak performance. Only some procedures of parabola buildings are out of these limits. It means that the original MPI version of the HydroBox3D code can't be auto-vectorized without optimizations. Also, we can see a typical picture of the arithmetic intensity for PDE stencil solvers. All functions have an arithmetic intensity of less than 1 FLOPs/Byte. Total program metrics for this version of code show that we have only 1 GFLOPS total performance result with 0.21 GFLOPS of the main loop of the Eulerian stage. Unfortunately, this is typical performance for Magnetohydrodynamics codes.

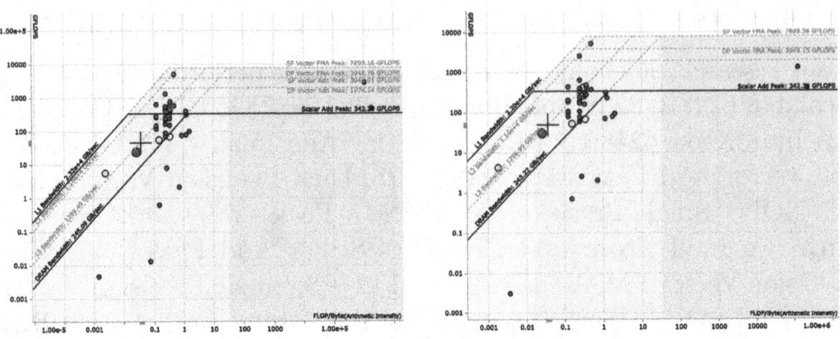

Fig. 3. Roofline analysis results for SDLT+OpenMP version of HydroBox3D on compute node with two Intel Xeon Scalable 6248R CPUs. The left chart shows performance for the mesh size $256 \times 256 \times 256$. The right picture shows performance for the mesh size $128 \times 128 \times 128$.

Figure 3 also shows the roofline analysis for two Intel Xeon 6248R CPUs. But this figure shows the performance results for optimized version of HydroBox3D. Adding of OpenMP pragmas and Intel SDLT templates for data structures gave significant performance boost. We can see that the most of functions became limited by the CPU's cache of different levels and some functions achieved the chip's vector instructions peak performance. The most computationally heavy procedure of Eulerean stage achieved 25 GFLOPS with 47 GFLOPS of total code performance.

Figure 4 shows the roofline analysis for two Intel Xeon 8268 CPUs for optimized code. The results are close to the 6248 CPUs. We provide the results only for 256^3 mesh. As we said before, this CPU is twice more expensive as the 6248R.

Figure 5 shows the roofline analysis for Intel Core i9 10980XE CPU. First of all, we can see that the peak performances are a little bit different between unoptimized and optimized code tests. Unfortunately, we could not cancel all hardware performance optimization in BIOS and Windows OS for this test. We think, that the SDLT+OpenMP version of the code runs with some CPU and memory frequency boost. This is why the peak performance lines for the SDLT+OpenMP version are higher than for the unoptimized code test. As for the server CPU chips, we can see the performance boost of the Eulerian stage from 1 to 22 GFLOPS and the total performance boost from 1 to 16 GFLOPS.

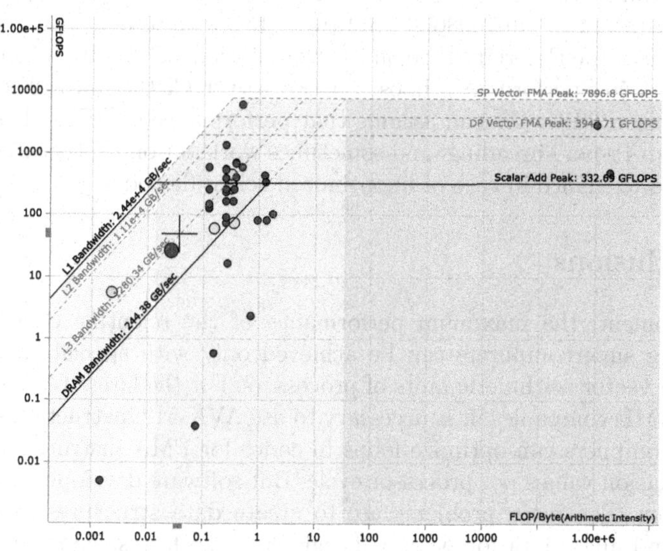

Fig. 4. Roofline analysis results for SDLT+OpenMP version of HydroBox3D on compute node with two Intel Xeon Scalable 8268 CPUs. The mesh size is $256 \times 256 \times 256$.

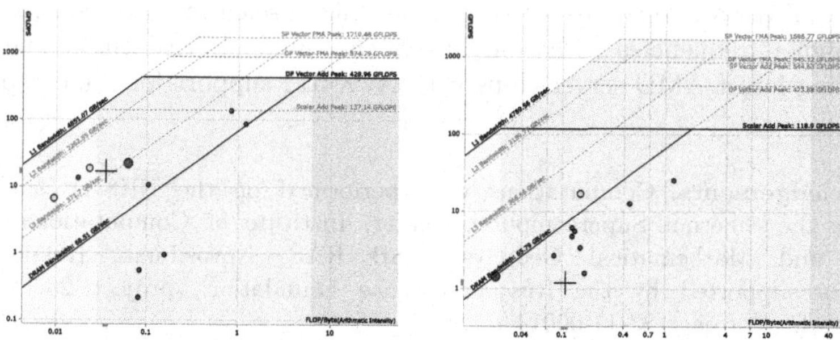

Fig. 5. Roofline analysis results for SDLT+OpenMP (left chart) and original MPI version (right chart) of HydroBox3D on a workstation PC with Intel Core i9 10980XE CPU. The mesh size is $128 \times 128 \times 128$.

All tests on the workstation PC were made with HyperThreading (36 threads). All tests on NKS-1P compute nodes were made on 48 cores (two CPUs) without HyperThreading. We can see that the unoptimized version of the code works similarly on Intel Core i9 10980XE and two Intel Xeon 6248R with better auto-vectorization of the Eulerian stage on the workstation CPU. After optimizations, we can see a 50x performance boost on two server CPUs and a 20x boost on the workstation CPU. We can assume that performance on NKS-1P nodes will increase with HyperThreading, and sometimes workstation CPUs can work with the same performance in case of unoptimized scientific codes.

4 Conclusions

At this moment, the maximum performance of the scientific codes on high-performance supercomputers can be achieved only with special optimizations oriented on vector arithmetic units of processors. For the latest CPU chips from Intel and AMD companies, it is necessary to use AVX-512 instruction sets. Modern C++ compilers can optimize loops in codes for FMA instructions on eight double-precision values per processor cycle. But software developers should help the compiler. The main problems are to create data structures as structures of arrays and align data for AVX-512 registers. The fastest code will be based on assembler-like intrinsics, but this code will be unreadable for future changes and understanding of non-computer science specialists. Intel company developed special C++ 11 templates (Intel SDLT library) for the easy-to-use structure of arrays software design approach. We tested this library on the author's astrophysics HydroBox3D code. We achieved the best performance boost results on compute nodes of high-performance computing systems with Intel Xeon Scalable 2nd generation CPUs. The performance results of the OpenMP+SDLT version of this code are fifty times higher than the simple MPI version of the program. It is worth noting that modern workstation PC systems based on AVX-512 compatible chips also work very fast with fully optimized scientific programs, because of the higher frequencies with comparable core numbers. At this moment, we are waiting latest AMD server chips with AVX-512 support for the comparison tests.

Acknowledgements. Computations were performed on the NKS-1P supercomputer at the Siberian Supercomputer Center, Institute of Computational Mathematics and Mathematical Geophysics SB RAS, Novosibirsk, Russia. This work was supported by the Russian Science Foundation (project 23-11-00014) https://rscf.ru/project/23-11-00014/.

References

1. Kulikov, I.M., Chernykh, I.G., Snytnikov, A.V., Glinskiy, B.M., Tutukov, A.V.: AstroPhi: a code for complex simulation of dynamics of astrophysical objects using hybrid supercomputers. Comput. Phys. Commun. **186**, 71–80 (2015). https://doi.org/10.1016/j.cpc.2014.09.004

2. Kulikov, I., Vorobyov, E.: Using the PPML approach for constructing a low-dissipation, operator-splitting scheme for numerical simulations of hydrodynamic flows. J. Comput. Phys. **317**, 318–346 (2016). https://doi.org/10.1016/j.jcp.2016.04.057
3. Kulikov, I., et al.: A new parallel code based on a simple piecewise parabolic method for numerical modeling of colliding flows in relativistic hydrodynamics. Mathematics **10**(11), 1865 (2022)
4. Kulikov, I.M., Chernykh, I.G., Glinskiy, B.M., Protasov, V.A.: An efficient optimization of HLL method for the second generation of Intel Xeon Phi processor. Lobachevskii J. Math. **39**, 543–550 (2018). https://doi.org/10.1134/S1995080218040091
5. Kulikov, I., Chernykh, I., Tutukov, A.: A new hydrodynamic code with explicit vectorization instructions optimizations that is dedicated to the numerical simulation of astrophysical gas flow. I. numerical method, tests, and model problems. Astrophys. J. Suppl. Ser. **243**, 1–15 (2019). https://doi.org/10.3847/1538-4365/ab2237
6. Kulikov, I.M., Chernykh, I.G., Tutukov, A.V.: A new parallel Intel Xeon Phi hydrodynamics code for massively parallel supercomputers. Lobachevskii J. Math. **39**, 1207–1216 (2018). https://doi.org/10.1134/S1995080218090135
7. Kulikov, I., et al.: Using adaptive nested mesh code HydroBox3D for numerical simulation of type Ia supernovae: merger of carbon-oxygen white dwarf stars, collapse, and non-central explosion. In: Proceedings of the 2018 Ivannikov ISP RAS Open Conference ISPRAS (2018). https://doi.org/10.1109/ISPRAS.2018.00018
8. Popov, M., Ustyugov, S.: Piecewise parabolic method on local stencil for gasdynamic simulations. Comput. Math. Math. Phys. **47**, 1970–1989 (2007). https://doi.org/10.1134/S0965542507120081
9. Popov, M., Ustyugov, S.: Piecewise parabolic method on a local stencil for ideal magnetohydrodynamics. Comput. Math. Math. Phys. **48**, 477–499 (2008). https://doi.org/10.1134/S0965542508030111
10. Kulikov, I.: A new code for the numerical simulation of relativistic flows on supercomputers by means of a low-dissipation scheme. Comput. Phys. Commun. **257**, 107532 (2020). https://doi.org/10.1016/j.cpc.2020.107532
11. Tutukov, A.V., Cherepashchuk, A.M.: Evolution of close binary stars: theory and observations. Phys.-Usp. **63**, 209 (2020)
12. Mezcua, M.: Dwarf galaxies might not be the birth sites of supermassive black holes. Nat. Astron. **3**, 6–7 (2019). https://doi.org/10.1038/s41550-018-0662-2
13. Miceli, M., et al.: Collisionless shock heating of heavy ions in SN 1987A. Nat. Astron. **3**, 236–241 (2019). https://doi.org/10.1038/s41550-018-0677-8
14. Mitchell, N., Vorobyov, E., Hensler, G.: Collisionless stellar hydrodynamics as an efficient alternative to N-body methods. Mon. Not. R. Astron. Soc. **428**, 2674–2687 (2013). https://doi.org/10.1093/mnras/sts228
15. Kulikov, I.: GPUPEGAS: a new GPU-accelerated hydrodynamic code for numerical simulations of interacting galaxies. Astrophys. J. Suppl. Ser. **214**, 1–12 (2014). https://doi.org/10.1088/0067-0049/214/1/12
16. Pabst, C., et al.: Disruption of the Orion molecular core 1 by wind from the massive star θ^1 Orionis C. Nature **565**, 618–621 (2019). https://doi.org/10.1038/s41586-018-0844-1
17. Forbes, J., Krumholz, M., Goldbaum, N., Dekel, A.: Suppression of star formation in dwarf galaxies by photoelectric grain heating feedback. Nature **535**, 523–525 (2016). https://doi.org/10.1038/nature18292

18. Willcox, D., Townsley, D., Calder, A., Denissenkov, P., Herwig, F.: Type Ia supernova explosions from hybrid carbon-oxygen-neon white dwarf progenitors. Astrophys. J. **832**, 13 (2016). https://doi.org/10.3847/0004-637X/832/1/13
19. Spillane, T., et al.: $^{12}C + ^{12}C$ fusion reactions near the Gamow energy. Phys. Rev. Lett. **98**, 122501 (2007)
20. Jiang, J.A., et al.: A hybrid type Ia supernova with an early flash triggered by helium-shell detonation. Nature **550**, 80–83 (2017). https://doi.org/10.1038/nature23908
21. Terreran, G., et al.: Hydrogen-rich supernovae beyond the neutrino-driven core-collapse paradigm. Nat. Astron. **1**, 713–720 (2017). https://doi.org/10.1038/s41550-017-0228-8
22. Mendygral, P.J., et al.: WOMBAT: a scalable and high-performance astrophysical magnetohydrodynamics code. Astrophys. J. Suppl. Ser. **228**, 23 (2017). https://doi.org/10.3847/1538-4365/aa5b9c
23. Schneider, E., Robertson, B.: Cholla: a new massively parallel hydrodynamics code for astrophysical simulation. Astrophys. J. Suppl. Ser. **217**, 24 (2015). https://doi.org/10.1088/0067-0049/217/2/24
24. Schneider, E., Robertson, B.: Introducing CGOLS: the cholla galactic outflow simulation suite. Astrophys. J. **860**, 135 (2018). https://doi.org/10.3847/1538-4357/aac329
25. Schneider, E., Robertson, B., Thompson, T.: Production of cool gas in thermally driven outflows. Astrophys. J. **862**, 56 (2018). https://doi.org/10.3847/1538-4357/aacce1
26. Collela, P.: Multidimensional upwind methods for hyperbolic conservation laws. J. Comput. Phys. **87**, 171–200 (1990). https://doi.org/10.1016/0021-9991(90)90233-Q
27. Gardiner, T., Stone, J.: An unsplit Godunov method for ideal MHD via constrained transport in three dimensions. J. Comput. Phys. **227**, 4123–4141 (2008). https://doi.org/10.1016/j.jcp.2004.11.016
28. Zhang, U., Schive, H., Chiueh, T.: Magnetohydrodynamics with GAMER. Astrophys. J. Suppl. Ser. **236**, 50 (2018). https://doi.org/10.3847/1538-4365/aac49e
29. Benitez-Llambay, P., Masset, F.: FARGO3D: a new GPU-oriented MHD code. Astrophys. J. Suppl. Ser. **223**, 11 (2016). https://doi.org/10.3847/0067-0049/223/1/11
30. Griffiths, M., Fedun, V., Erdelyi, R.: A fast MHD code for gravitationally stratified media using graphical processing units: SMAUG. J. Astrophys. Astron. **36**, 197–223 (2015). https://doi.org/10.1007/s12036-015-9328-y
31. Pandolfi, M., D'Ambrosio, D.: Numerical instabilities in upwind methods: analysis and cures for the "carbuncle" phenomenon. J. Comput. Phys. **166**, 271–301 (2000). https://doi.org/10.1006/jcph.2000.6652
32. Chauvat, Y., Moschetta, J.-M., Gressier, J.: Shock wave numerical structure and the carbuncle phenomenon. Int. J. Numer. Methods Fluids **47**, 903–909 (2005). https://doi.org/10.1002/fld.916
33. Liou, M.S.: Mass flux schemes and connection to shock instability. J. Comput. Phys. **160**, 623–648 (2000). https://doi.org/10.1006/jcph.2000.6478
34. Xu, K., Li, Z.: Dissipative mechanism in Godunov-type schemes. Int. J. Numer. Methods Fluids **37**, 1–22 (2001). https://doi.org/10.1002/fld.160
35. Kim, S.-S., Kim, C., Rho, O.-H., Hong, S.K.: Cures for the shock instability: development of a shock-stable Roe scheme. J. Comput. Phys. **185**, 342–374 (2003). https://doi.org/10.1016/S0021-9991(02)00037-2

36. Dumbser, M., Morschetta, J.-M., Gressier, J.: A matrix stability analysis of the carbuncle phenomenon. J. Comput. Phys. **197**, 647–670 (2004). https://doi.org/10.1016/j.jcp.2003.12.013
37. Davis, S.F.: A rotationally biased upwind difference scheme for the Euler equations. J. Comput. Phys. **56**, 65–92 (1984). https://doi.org/10.1016/0021-9991(84)90084-6
38. Levy, D.W., Powell, K.G., Van Leer, B.: Use of a rotated Riemann solver for the two-dimensional Euler equations. J. Comput. Phys. **106**, 201–214 (1993). https://doi.org/10.1016/S0021-9991(83)71103-4
39. Ren, Y.-X.: A robust shock-capturing scheme based on rotated Riemann solvers. Comput. Fluids **32**, 1379–1403 (2003). https://doi.org/10.1016/S0045-7930(02)00114-7
40. Nishikawa, H., Kitamura, K.: Very simple, carbuncle-free, boundary-layer-resolving, rotated-hybrid Riemann solvers. J. Comput. Phys. **227**, 2560–2581 (2008). https://doi.org/10.1016/j.jcp.2007.11.003
41. Perepelkina, A., Levchenko, V.D.: Functionally arranged data for algorithms with space-time Wavefront. In: Sokolinsky, L., Zymbler, M. (eds.) PCT 2021. CCIS, vol. 1437, pp. 134–148. Springer, Cham (2021). https://doi.org/10.1007/978-3-030-81691-9_10
42. Araudo A., Bosch-Ramon V., Romero G.: Gamma rays from cloud penetration at the base of AGN jets. Astron. Astrophys. **522** (2010)
43. Begelman, M., Blandford, R., Rees, M.: Theory of extragalactic radio sources. Rev. Mod. Phys. **56**, 255–351 (1984)
44. Laing, R.: The sidedness of jets and depolarization in powerful extragalactic radio sources. Nature **331**, 149–151 (1988)
45. Shakura, N., Sunyaev, R.: Black holes in binary systems. Observational appearance. Astron. Astrophys. **24**, 337–355 (1973)
46. Bisnovatyi-Kogan, G., Blinnikov, S.: A hot corona around a black-hole accretion disk as a model for CYG X-1. Sov. Astron. Lett. **2**, 191–193 (1976)
47. Artemova, Y., Bisnovatyi-Kogan, G., Igumenshchev, I., Novikov, I.: Black hole advective accretion disks with optical depth transition. Astroph. J. **637**, 968–977 (2006)
48. Narayan, R., Yi, I.: Advection-dominated accretion: a self-similar solution. Astroph. J. Let. **428**, L13–L16 (1994)
49. Glushak, A.P.: Microquasar jets in the supernova remnant G11.2-0.3. Astron. Rep. **58**, 6–15 (2014)
50. Barkov, M.V., Bisnovatyi-Kogan, G.S.: Interaction of a cosmological gamma-ray burst with a dense molecular cloud and the formation of jets. Astron. Rep. **49**, 24–35 (2005)
51. Istomin, Ya.N., Komberg, B.V.: Gamma-ray bursts as a result of the interaction of a shock from a supernova and a neutron-star companion. Astron. Reps. **46**, 908–917 (2002)
52. Artyukh, V.S.: Phenomenological model for the evolution of radio galaxies such as Cygnus A. Astron. Rep. **59**, 520–524 (2015)
53. Artyukh, V.S.: Effect of aberration on the estimated parameters of relativistic radio jets. Astron. Rep. **62**, 436–439 (2018)
54. Butuzova, M.S.: Search for differences in the velocities and directions of the kiloparsec-scale jets of quasars with and without X-ray emission. Astron. Rep. **60**, 313–321 (2016)
55. Butuzova, M.S.: The blazar OJ 287 jet from parsec to kiloparsec scales. Astron. Rep. **65**, 635–644 (2021)

56. Sotomayor, P., Romero, G.: Nonthermal radiation from the central region of super-accreting active galactic nuclei. Astron. Astrophys. **664**(A178) (2022)
57. Kulikov, I., Chernykh, I., Tutukov, A.: A new hydrodynamic model for numerical simulation of interacting galaxies on Intel Xeon Phi supercomputers. J. Phys: Conf. Ser. **719**, 012006 (2016)
58. Glinsky, B., et al.: The co-design of astrophysical code for massively parallel supercomputers. In: Carretero, J., et al. (eds.) ICA3PP 2016. LNCS, vol. 10049, pp. 342–353. Springer, Cham (2016). https://doi.org/10.1007/978-3-319-49956-7_27
59. Akimova, E.N., Misilov, V.E., Kulikov, I.M., Chernykh, I.G.: OMPEGAS: optimized relativistic code for multicore architecture. Mathematics **10**, 2546 (2022). https://doi.org/10.3390/math10142546
60. relax Intel Corporation. SIMD Data Layout Templates. https://www.intel.com/content/www/us/en/develop/documentation/oneapi-dpcpp-cpp-compiler-dev-guide-and-reference/top/compiler-reference/libraries/introduction-to-the-simd-data-layout-templates.html
61. Intel Corporation. Intel Advisor User Guide. https://www.intel.com/content/www/us/en/develop/documentation/advisor-user-guide/top.html
62. NERSC. Introduction to the Roofline model. https://www.nersc.gov/assets/Uploads/Tutorial-ISC2019-Intro-v2.pdf

The Efficiency Optimization Study of a Geophysical Code on Manycore Computing Architectures

Anna Sapetina(✉) and Boris Glinskiy

Institute of Computational Mathematics and Mathematical Geophysics of SB RAS, Novosibirsk, Russia

afsapetina@gmail.com

Abstract. In this paper, on the example of finite difference solving the problem of seismic wave propagation in elastic 3D media the features of the development and optimization of parallel codes for various multicore architectures (Intel Broadwell, Knights Landing; IBM POWER9; NVIDIA Fermi, Kepler, Pascal) are considered. The effect of various strategies of computations and memory optimization on the final performance is investigated. Specific optimizations for different types of architectures are considered.

Based on the research carried out, rules have been developed for choosing approaches to parallelization and optimization of programs for various computing architectures. The rules are prepared for use in the intelligent support system for solving compute-intensive problems of mathematical physics based on the ontological approach.

Keywords: Elastic Wave · 3D Modeling · Manycore Systems · HPC · Ontology · Intelligent System

1 Introduction

The solution of actual numerical simulation problems requires the development of parallel programs that efficiently use modern computational architectures. There is a possibility of choosing not only various mathematical methods and algorithms for solving a problem but also various computational architectures. Therefore, researchers have to solve the difficult task of determining the optimality of such a choice taking into account the capabilities of computing architectures available to them.

In recent years a global trend in supercomputer architectures is heterogeneous systems with computing accelerators and manycore processors and co-processors. Such systems are included in the lists of the most powerful and energy-efficient systems. For example, such systems are installed in the Siberian Supercomputer Center of the Institute of Computational Mathematics and Mathematical Geophysics of the Siberian Branch of the Russian Academy of Sciences (SSCC ICMMG SB RAS): cluster NKS-30T + GPU with NVIDIA graphics accelerators and cluster NKS-1P with Intel Xeon Phi processors with a total peak performance of 167 TFLOPS. The development of efficient software

V. Voevodin et al. (Eds.): RuSCDays 2023, LNCS 14388, pp. 285–299, 2023.
https://doi.org/10.1007/978-3-031-49432-1_22

codes for such hybrid systems requires additional knowledge and time, but it allows for obtaining a significant performance increase.

The choice of a computing architecture suitable for the problem of numerical modeling and the development of an efficient code for calculations can be simplified by using an intelligent support system for solving compute-intensive problems of mathematical physics developed by the authors based on the ontological approach [1, 2]. This system is based on the methodology of co-design [3, 4], which, in the context of mathematical modeling of physical processes, means the development of a physical and mathematical model of a phenomenon, a numerical method, a parallel algorithm, and its software implementation from the point of view of the efficient parallel computing.

As part of the intelligent support system development for solving compute-intensive problems of mathematical physics, various software optimizations have been studied in terms of the impact on the time of solving the problem and the performance of the final code, using the numerical solution of dynamic elasticity equations on advanced computing architectures as an example. This made it possible to draw up generalized recommendations (rules) for optimizing finite difference solvers for hyperbolic equations for various architectures and to evaluate the efficiency of using the considered architectures for the geophysical code.

There is a significant number of papers on accelerating seismic wave propagation modeling codes on computational accelerators [5, 6], as well as papers on studying approaches to optimizing geophysical codes [7]. This work is distinguished by a large coverage of various manycore architectures, as well as a consistent integrated review of various levels of parallelization.

2 The Intelligent Support System for Solving Compute-Intensive Problems of Mathematical Physics

Let us briefly describe the intelligent support system for solving compute-intensive problems of mathematical physics on supercomputers (ISS), developed by the authors based on ontology [1, 2] (see Fig. 1).

The first main block is a knowledge base that includes an ontology of computational methods and algorithms, an ontology of parallel architectures and technologies, and inference rules. An information-analytical internet resource allows the user to study the objects included in the knowledge base, view the links among them, and also replenish the database with new objects. There is an expert system. The user submits a specification of the problem to be solved to the input of the expert system. Based on this information, the inference engine builds a scheme for solving the problem using ontology objects from the knowledge base and inference rules formulated by experts. Next, a parallel code will be generated using existing modules from a library of software components and taking into account the computational algorithm and an architecture of the selected computing system. The simulation module allows the user to determine the optimal number of computational cores for solving the problem.

To work with ontological models, inference engines are used, which allow checking the consistency of the ontology, operating with the names of classes, properties, and

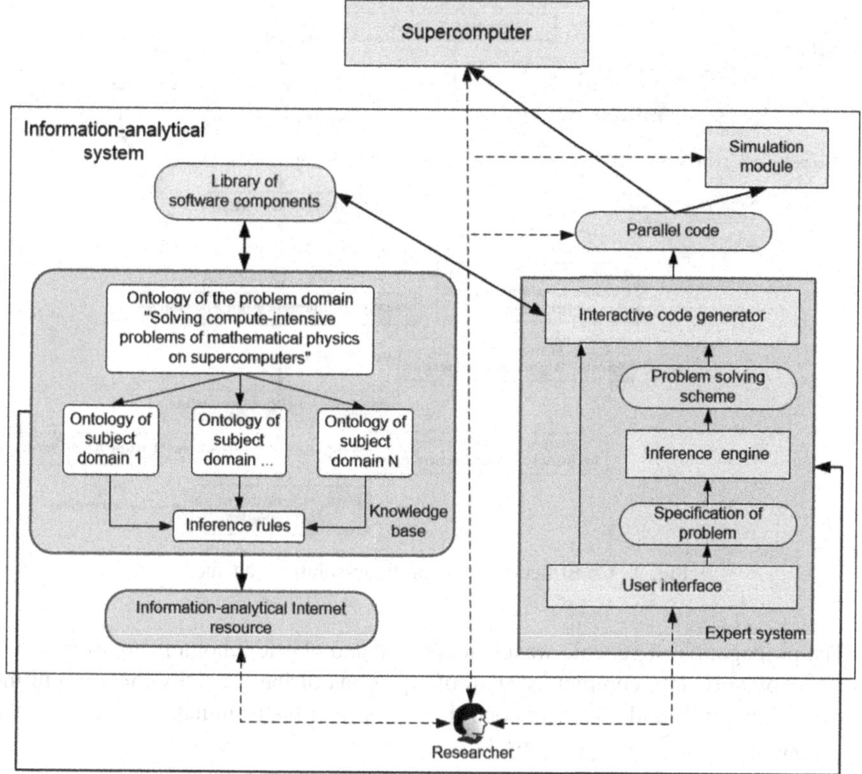

Fig. 1. The intelligent support system for solving compute-intensive problems (IIS).

entities, as well as inferencing based on expert rules information that is not explicitly contained in the ontology.

A conceptual model for constructing a scheme for solving a problem of mathematical physics based on the ISS ontology is shown in Fig. 2 [8]. The main blocks of the problem-solution scheme are given, as well as the groups of rules that must be set for the automatic construction of the solution.

This work is devoted to the formulation of rules for determining the parallel implementation principles and the choice of architectures and technologies for parallel computing on the example of developing and testing a specific code. For each subject area, it is necessary to create a set of such rules that will allow the user to speed up the development of parallel algorithms and programs to solve his problem.

3 Statement of the Problem and the Numerical Method

Modeling the propagation of elastic waves in complicated 3D heterogeneous media is a problem that requires the use of effective methods of parallelizing and scaling algorithms. This class of problems includes the study of seismic waves propagation features in media characteristic of magmatic volcanoes.

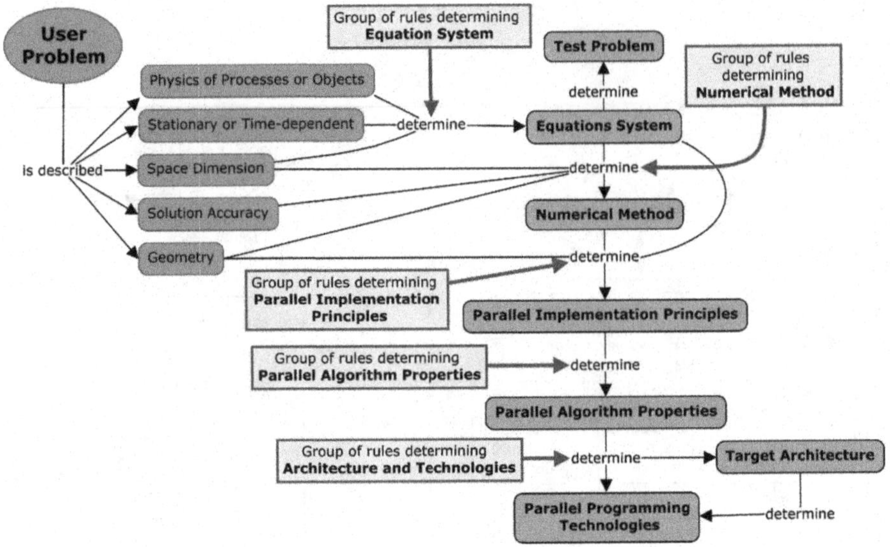

Fig. 2. Construction of the problem-solution scheme.

The propagation of seismic waves in complicated elastic inhomogeneous media is described by solving a complete system of equations of the elasticity theory with the corresponding initial and boundary conditions. Consider the formulation in terms of the displacement vector $\overrightarrow{U} = (U, V, W)^T$:

$$\rho \frac{\partial^2 \vec{U}}{\partial t^2} = \begin{bmatrix} A_1 \\ A_2 \\ A_3 \end{bmatrix} \vec{U} + \vec{F}(t, x, y, z)$$

$$A_1 = \left[(\lambda + 2\mu)\frac{\partial^2}{\partial x^2} + \mu\left(\frac{\partial^2}{\partial y^2} + \frac{\partial^2}{\partial z^2}\right) \; (\lambda + \mu)\frac{\partial^2}{\partial x \partial y} \; (\lambda + \mu)\frac{\partial^2}{\partial x \partial z} \right]$$

$$A_2 = \left[(\lambda + \mu)\frac{\partial^2}{\partial y \partial x} \; (\lambda + 2\mu)\frac{\partial^2}{\partial y^2} + \mu\left(\frac{\partial^2}{\partial x^2} + \frac{\partial^2}{\partial z^2}\right) \; (\lambda + \mu)\frac{\partial^2}{\partial y \partial z} \right]$$

$$A_3 = \left[(\lambda + \mu)\frac{\partial^2}{\partial z \partial x} \; (\lambda + \mu)\frac{\partial^2}{\partial z \partial y} \; (\lambda + 2\mu)\frac{\partial^2}{\partial y^2} + \mu\left(\frac{\partial^2}{\partial x^2} + \frac{\partial^2}{\partial y^2}\right) \right]$$

where t is the time, $\rho(x, y, z)$ is the density, $\lambda(x, y, z)$, $\mu(x, y, z)$ are the Lame coefficients. An isotropic 3D inhomogeneous elastic complicated medium is simulated a parallelepiped domain one of the faces of which is a free surface (the plane $z = 0$). The initial and boundary conditions on the free surface are zero.

In the framework of the co-design, the author has also previously considered the formulation of the velocities of displacement and stress [3, 9]. A comparison of these approaches from the point of view of parallelization has shown the advantages of displacement calculations: it is carried out faster and significantly saved memory, which is very important when solving a full-scale problem.

Despite all the variety of grid methods in the case of the three-dimensional dynamic problems of the elasticity theory, the finite difference method is the most "flexible" and widely used. Including this method, in contrast to the others, allows the use of regular parallelepiped grids without loss of acceptable accuracy. This makes it possible to quite easily parallelize the algorithms obtained based on the method of decomposition of the computational domain with overlapping sub-domains. Let us note that explicit finite difference schemes fit the graphics accelerator architecture quite well, since they imply constructing computational grids that are directly mapped to the GPU architecture, and involve independent computations in each cell of the computational range of values for the next step. Also, this method is suitable for vectorization.

For the numerical solution of the problem, we use the well-known explicit finite difference scheme on staggered grids, described in detail in [10]. The calculation of grid coefficients, which may have a discontinuity, is based on integral conservation laws. The finite-difference scheme used has a second-order approximation for time and space. The calculation of the displacements at each node of the grid requires only the values in the adjacent nodes in the staggered and main grids.

4 Considered Manycore Systems

The considered set of calculating systems is interesting in that it covers manycore, but radically different architectures. On the one hand, various classical processors: Intel processors with vector extensions and different numbers of cores, and an IBM processor with high simultaneous multithreading (SMT). On the other hand, GPUs with hundreds and thousands of lightweight cores and a complex system of fast memory available to the programmer.

The Intel Broadwell and IBM POWER9 architectures have an advantage: they have a rather large cache L3 – 40 MB and 120 MB per chip, respectively. It is much faster than in the case of the MCDRAM KNL. But the KNL permits the use of a maximally large number of cores – 72 cores (versus 16 cores in Intel Broadwell and 12 cores in IBM POWER9). Each core can process 32 DP numbers per tact (versus 16 per core in Broadwell and POWER9). That is why the vectorization of computations with the use of the Intel KNL is supposed to give a gain in productivity by all means.

A brief description of the manycore systems studied in this paper with their main parameters is given in Table 1. The described systems are part of computational clusters of SSCC ICMMG SB RAS and the Computing Center of the Far-Eastern Division of the Russian Academy of Science. Since the test calculations were performed with single precision, the peak performance below is also indicated for single precision.

Test calculations have been carried out on a grid of size 581 × 581 × 581 (total memory used ~11 Gb) for all architectures except the system based on NVIDIA Fermi. A smaller grid has been considered for it: 581 × 581 × 193 (total memory used ~3.6 Gb), to fit the problem into the memory of the accelerator. The calculation of efficiency and performance is based on the execution time.

Table 1. A brief description of the considered manycore systems.

Main architecture	Parameter	Value
Intel Broadwell	Processor	2 × Intel Xeon E5-2697A v4
		2.6 GHz, 16 cores, SMT2
	Memory	128 GB DDR4 RAM
	Peak performance	1331.2 GFLOPS
Intel KNL	Processor	Intel Xeon Phi 7290 KNL
		1.5 GHz, 72 cores, SMT4
	Memory	16 GB MCDRAM, 96 GB DDR4 RAM
	Peak performance	3456 GFLOPS
IBM POWER9	Processor	IBM POWER9 Processor
		3.8 GHz, 2 × 12 core Typical, SMT8
	Memory	32x32 GB DDR4 RAM
	Peak performance	2 918.4 GFLOPS
NVIDIA Fermi	Processor	2 × Intel Xeon X5670
	Memory	96 GB DDR4 RAM
	Accelerator	NVIDIA Tesla M2090
		1300 MHz, 512 cores, 6 GB GDDR5
	GPU peak performance	1331 GFLOPS
NVIDIA Kepler	Processor	2 × Intel Xeon E5-2650 v2
	Memory	64 GB DDR4 RAM
	Accelerator	NVIDIA Tesla K40
		745 MHz, 2880 cores, 12 GB GDDR5
	GPU peak performance	4 291 GFLOPS
NVIDIA Pascal	Processor	IBM POWER8
	Memory	256 GB DDR4 RAM
	Accelerator	NVIDIA Tesla P100
		1480 MHz, 3584 cores, 16 GB HBM2
	GPU peak performance	10 608 GFLOPS

4.1 Optimizations for Intel and IBM Processors

Consider the program implementation for systems equipped with full-fledged manycore processors. Such processors have a relatively small number of cores (several decades) operating at a high clock frequency, independently of each other. A distinctive feature of modern processors is the presence of vector process units that process several floating-point numbers per clock cycle. So KNL supports processing 512 b, Broadwell – 256 b, and POWER9 – 128 b per cycle. Also, all these systems support simultaneous multi-threading (SMT) with 2 (Broadwell), 4 (KNL), and 8 (POWER9) hardware streams per core.

Thus, for parallelization of the 3D modeling algorithm for the seismic wave propagation in an elastic medium, the internal loop of space is vectorized, and the external loop of space is parallelized using OpenMP. For effective access to memory, all main 3D arrays are aligned.

Vectorization and Caching. For Intel processors, two vectorization technics have been compared: auto-vectorization using additional instructions to the compiler for no dependencies between data and a lower-level technic using intrinsic functions. No significant difference in performance has been obtained, which indicates a good initial code auto-vectorization by the Intel compiler. In general, the use of vector operations allows us to speed up the program several times, for example, for KNL, the acceleration reaches 2.75 times (72 OpenMP streams, cache memory mode).

Considered implementation options with different loops sequences, which affect the efficiency of caching and the number of requests in the cache. The influence of the loops sequence on the gain performance is investigated. Figure 3 shows the acceleration in the permutation of cycles relative to the initial order *xyz*. It can be seen that the unsuccessful loops sequence slows down memory access dozens of times. The best option for the sequence of cycles (*zyx*) is the one that coincides with the sequence of storing the components of the 3D array in memory.

The POWER9 and KNL caches are larger and faster than those of Broadwell, so the *yzx* sequence gives a comparable performance gain to the leader (*zyx*): 15.8 and 17.2 times respectively for POWER9. At the same time, consecutive values in memory for KNL give the maximum increase, since this processor processes the vector with the maximum length relative to other architectures once: 19.4 times for the *yzx* sequence and 26.9 times for the *zyx* sequence.

Load Balancing. Since many applications have regions with different computational loads, to reduce the computation time, tasks between threads must be distributed evenly, balancing the computational load. To do this, you can modify the calculation algorithm, as well as configure the OpenMP parallelization parameters. The more manycore a system is, the more important load balancing becomes.

In the tested code the case of the collapse of two external loops in one is considered, while the internal loop is selected in X, which showed the best performance gain in the previous study. Such optimization significantly increases the number of iterations of the outer collapsed loop, while reducing the work size for each iteration. This allows us to get the best load balance and speed up the code compared to the best *zyx* cycle order by 1.48 times for Broadwell on 32 threads, 1.18 times for KNL on 72 threads, and 1.16 times for POWER9 on 192 threads (Fig. 3, case (*zy*)*x*).

We can further improve load balancing by selecting the parameters of the schedule OpenMP directive. The effects of choosing the OpenMP schedule type and chunk size on the load balance for collapsed loops are investigated. Figure 4–6 show the acceleration when changing the type of schedule and chunk size relative to the calculation time with the default schedule parameters (static with chunk size equal to the number of loop iterations divided by the number of threads that are used). For the Broadwell and POWER9 architecture (Fig. 4, 6), the best performance is achieved in the default version. The overhead caused by the dynamic and guided schedulers does not pay off in this case. For KNL (Fig. 5), the guided scheduler gives a small increase of 1.2 times. For the POWER9 architecture (Fig. 6), the type of scheduler does not significantly affect load balancing within the code under test.

Scalability and Multithreading. Figure 7 shows the results of strong scalability (acceleration relative to one thread) for the considered manycore processors with optimal code

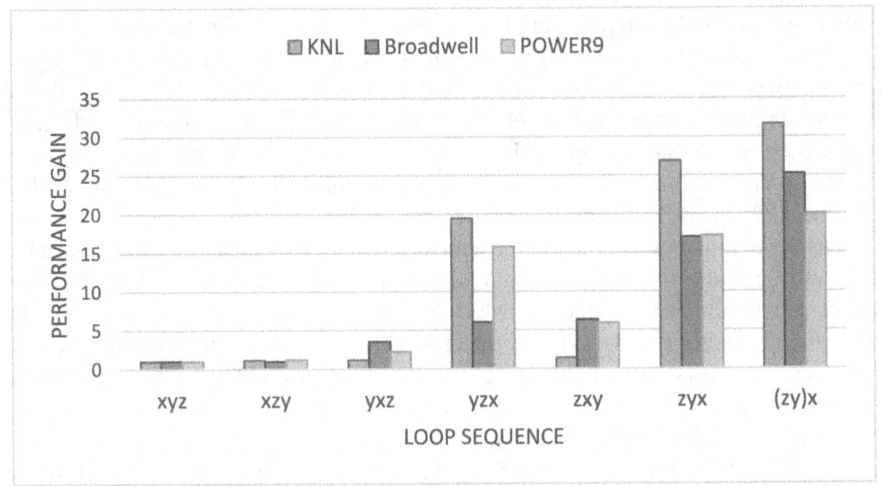

Fig. 3. Depending of the performance gain on the sequence of loops.

settings for each of the architectures. In this case, the number of threads is considered, taking into account SMT. For a Broadwell and KNL system, scalability drops when the number of threads is greater than the number of physical cores, making it inefficient to use hyperthreading. For a Broadwell system, the maximum speed up is 8.8 times on 32 threads (cores), for KNL – 56.6 times on 72 threads (cores). POWER9 maximizes its hyper-threading capabilities, showing a 48x speed up on the tested code on 192 threads with 24 physical cores. One reason for this result is that the smaller the vector code and the smaller the size of the vector registers, the more effect SMT has. At the same time, architectures with a more advanced cache memory system (KNL and POWER9) give the best speed up, since the tested code is memory-bound.

Flat Memory Mode for Intel KNL. Consider additionally the use of Intel KNL. The advantage of KNL is that it is a full-fledged processor, which does not require preprocessing and data copying in the processor memory, unlike its predecessor, the KNC coprocessor. To optimize the work with memory, only fast MCDRAM memory is used, its capacity is 16 GB and can be expanded by using several accelerators. In our case, the use of the flat memory mode instead of the cache mode with the placement of all the main arrays in the MCDRAM memory has accelerated 1.3 times (the hybrid mode does not give any advantages). Let us note that although Intel stopped the further development of the Xeon Phi line, some of the architectural innovations of this line are transferred to new Intel processors.

4.2 Optimizations for NVIDIA Accelerators

A GPU has a large number (hundreds and thousands) of highly simplified computational cores (for example, the absence of predictions, and superscalar execution of commands) operating at a low frequency. At the same time, the GPU is equipped with a complex memory system, part of which is software controlled. To efficiently use the GPU, it is

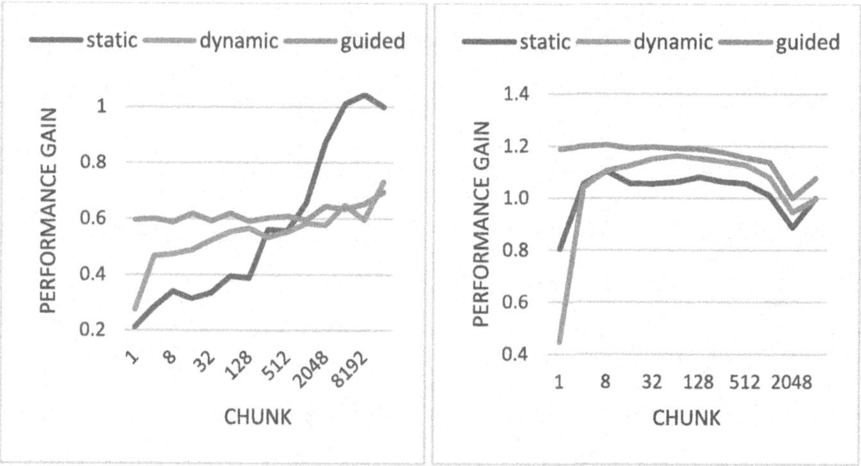

Fig. 4. The performance gain depending on different types of schedules for the Intel Broadwell system (left) and for the Intel KNL system (right).

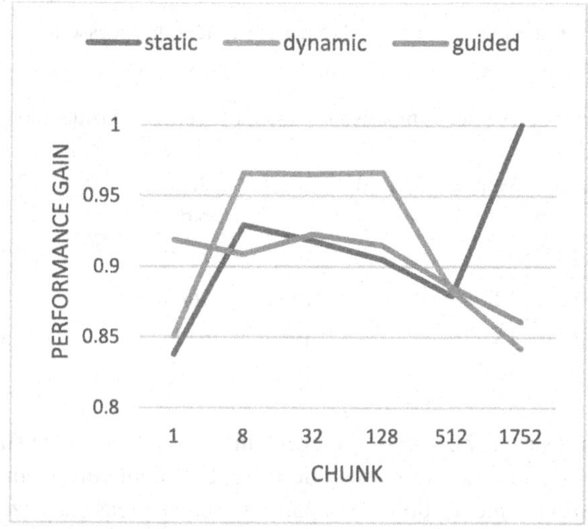

Fig. 5. The performance gain depending on different types of schedules for the IBM POWER9 system.

necessary to use threads many times larger than the number of cores. Table 2 shows a brief comparison of some characteristics of the considered GPUs.

All calculations in the tested code are carried out on the GPU to minimize transfers between the host and the device. First, arrays with the medium coefficients at each point of a difference scheme are formed on the CPU and copied into the accelerator memory. In the course of the calculation, the wave field images in several planes in certain time steps (on average, one image per 500 to 10000 steps is sufficient) are transferred back.

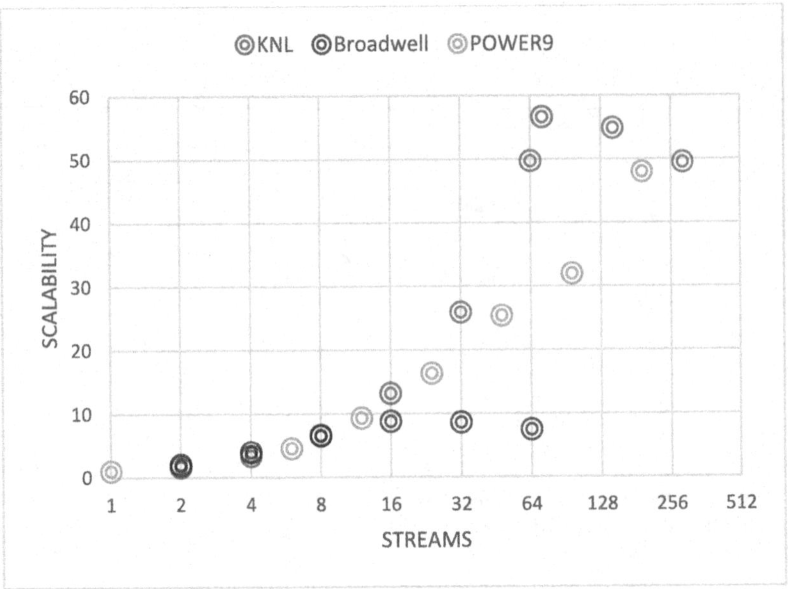

Fig. 6. The strong scalability for different processors.

Table 2. A brief comparison of the GPUs under consideration.

	Cores	Memory size, GB	L2, KB	Shared memory, KB	Memory bandwidth, GB/s
Tesla M2090	512	6	768	16/48	177
Tesla K40	2880	12	1536	16/48	288
Tesla P100	3584	16	4096	64	733

Such an approach restricts the size of the problem to be solved to the size of the device memory but allows one to avoid losses due to repeated copying from the host to the device and back to calculate the domain in parts. We can increase the size of the problem later by using several nodes with graphic accelerators.

Threads Block Size. In the main CUDA-core, each thread calculates the vector components at the current time step in one difference mesh. Increasing the computational load on a thread, for example, calculating several points with one thread or the whole cycle along one of the axes, results in an increase in the kernel execution time. For example, for a problem of size 360^3 on 512 threads of the Tesla M2090 card, the code version with a 3D grid of blocks and threads, where each thread calculates the required components only at one point of the computational grid, is almost 2 times faster than the version with a 2D grid of threads and blocks, where each thread cycles through the z-axis.

For such a distribution of work between threads, the dependence of software performance on the dimension and size of a thread block has been studied for the considered

GPU. As a result, the computational domain at each GPU is split into a three-dimensional grid of blocks, whose size for the component x must be a multiple of the length of the warp. The specific size of a thread block is chosen empirically for each algorithm. Note that the maximum number of threads in a block is limited by the compute capabilities of a particular GPU (512 for M2090 and 1024 for K40 and P100). The results of some measurements are shown in Table 3.

Table 3. The dependence of the performance gain (PGain) on the threads block size (BSize).

Tesla M2090							
BSize 512	PGain	BSize 256	PGain	BSize 128	PGain	BSize 64	PGain
8×8×8	0.52						
16×8×4	1.0	16×4×4	1.05	16×4×2	0.96	16×2×2	0.99
32×4×4	1.47	32×4×2	1.49	32×2×2	1.48	32×2×1	1.26
64×4×2	1.42	64×2×2	**1.65**	64×2×1	1.38	64×1×1	1.35
128×2×2	1.45	128×2×1	1.44	128×1×1	1.41		
256×2×1	1.2	256×1×1	1.41				
512×1×1	0.98						
Tesla K40							
BSize 1024	PGain	BSize 512	PGain	BSize 256	PGain	BSize 128	PGain
16×8×8	1.0	16×8×4	1.11	16×4×4	1.04	16×4×2	1.02
32×8×4	1.53	32×4×4	1.67	32×4×2	1.63	32×2×2	1.55
64×4×4	1.64	64×4×2	1.7	64×2×2	**1.82**	64×2×1	1.72
128×4×2	1.63	128×2×2	1.7	128×2×1	1.78	128×1×1	1.73
256×2×2	1.44	256×2×1	1.58	256×1×1	1.69		
512×2×1	1.13	512×1×1	1.43				
Tesla P100							
BSize 1024	PGain	BSize 512	PGain	BSize 256	PGain	BSize 128	PGain
16×8×8	1.0	16×8×4	1.02	16×4×4	1.02	16×4×2	0.98
32×8×4	1.25	32×4×4	**1.29**	32×4×2	1.23	32×2×2	1.23
4×64×4	0.49	32×8×2	1.23				
4×4×64	0.48	32×16×1	1.12				
64×4×4	1.24	64×4×2	1.26	64×2×2	1.25	64×2×1	1.08
128×4×2	1.25	128×2×2	1.27	128×2×1	1.12	128×1×1	1.08
256×2×2	1.22	256×2×1	1.14	256×1×1	1.13		
512×2×1	1.1	512×1×1	1.14				

The most advantageous have been block sizes equal to 32 (warp size) or 64 (warp size × 2) in the x component and evenly distributed relative to other components. Note that the maximum possible block size is not advantageous, partly because the GPU registers are distributed among the block threads and there may not be enough of them. This optimization, which is not complicated in the context of a code change, makes it possible to speed up the work of the program several times with sufficiently efficient use of the global memory of the graphics accelerator. For new architectures, due to a more perfect memory structure, the efficiency of this optimization is less.

GPU Memory Type Optimization. The program uses three-dimensional arrays that are stored in memory as one connected area. At the same time, it is necessary to distribute calculations in such a way that one warp threads process elements stored side by side. To eliminate the repetition of the same computations at each time step, not the original grid coefficients are stored in the GPU memory, but their modifications.

All the single constants used at each time step (the size of the difference scheme, the pre-calculated values of the source function for each time step), which are included in the device's constant memory, were written there. Although this optimization gives a small performance gain of about 4%.

The efficiency of using global memory on the GPU is provided by the first and second level caches. To reduce the number of cache and global memory accesses, all the arrays were aligned when allocating memory using the CudaMalloc3D function, which automatically expands the array so that the alignment of each row is correct. And an access pattern is organized in such a way that the threads of one warp should access the same cache line whenever possible, thus, the query should combine 32 threads of a warp of 32 consecutive 4-byte elements into one. Since Tesla M2090 and K40 L1 cache and shared memory are located in the same physical medium and can share it in one of two ways, in our case it is better to prefer L1 cache (i.e., 48 KB L1 cache and 16 KB shared memory).

Another step to effectively work with memory is the shared memory usage. A more efficient case has been implemented by copying each block of the corresponding area into shared memory with one additional layer in each direction (wing area) [5]. But, despite the absence of conflicts of banks into which shared memory is divided, during implementation, a small amount of re-use of data loaded into shared memory has led to the fact that the kernel execution time for such a realization was comparable to the implementation without using shared memory for GPU with architectures Fermi and Kepler. And only the more efficient memory system of the Kepler architecture gives an advantage when using shared memory. Performance gain results for different block sizes are listed in Table 4.

4.3 The Performance Comparison on Considerate Manycore Architectures

The elastic wave propagation code has been optimized for different manycore systems with very different architectural characteristics. Figure 7 shows the performance in GFLOPS of the best version for each architecture evaluated (with the best loops sequence, the number of streams, the scheduler type and chunk, the memory mode, the size of threads, etc.).

Against the background of full-fledged processors, KNL stands out – the most many-core and processing the longest vector instructions. Among the GPU leader is Tesla P100 on Pascal architecture. It is more than 3.2 times the real performance of other considered GPUs. At the same time, the P100 is more than 1.6 times ahead of the real KNL performance, although its peak performance is more than 3 times the peak performance of the KNL.

Table 4. The performance gains using shared memory for different GPU architectures

Threads block size	GPU architecture		
	Fermi	**Kepler**	**Pascal**
16×8×8	–	1.2	1.3
16×4×4	1.0	1.2	1.3
32×4×4	0.9	1.0	1.3
64×2×2	0.8	0.6	1.3
64×4×2	0.9	–	1.3
64×4×4	–	0.98	**1.5**
128×2×2	0.9	0.6	1.2

4.4 General Recommendations for Optimization and Parallelization

Summarizing the research on the optimization of a finite difference code for modeling the elastic waves propagation and experience in the development of such codes, we propose the following inference rules for an intelligent support system for solving compute-intensive problems of mathematical physics.

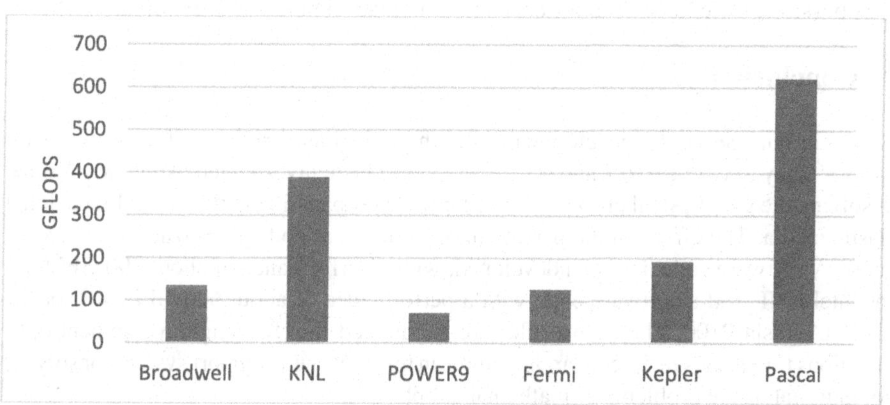

Fig. 7. A real performance on the different architectures for elastic wave propagation problem.

Rules for choosing optimizations for CPU development

1. For 2D and 3D problem codes the inner loop of the algorithm should be vectorized, and the outer loop in space should be parallelized using OpenMP.
2. For memory access efficiency, all central arrays must be aligned in memory, for example, using the `posix_memalign` or `_mm_malloc` functions.
3. It is necessary to mark up the code using vectorization directives or use intrinsic for efficient vectorization to fit the processor's vector registers size.
4. For better caching and load balancing in 3D codes, it is best to choose a nested sequence of (*zy*)*x* loops, where the z and y loops are combined into one.

5. When using OpenMP to parallelize finite difference codes for multicore systems, it is better to use schedule static with a maximum chunk size (default), for manycore systems – schedule guided with a short chunk size.
6. When using SMT for parallelizing finite-difference codes, 1 thread per core is better for Intel processors, and the max thread number per core is better for IBM processors.
7. When using KNL to execute finite difference codes, it is preferable to use flat memory mode instead of cache memory mode with all the main arrays placed in MCDRAM memory.
8. If possible, the choice of manycore computing accelerators is preferable.

Rules for choosing optimizations for GPU development

1. If possible, it is better to load the entire problem into the memory of the GPUs
2. The dimension of the grid of blocks must match the dimension of the problem
3. The block size for 3D finite-difference problems is better to use equal to 32 or 64 for the x component and equal to 4 or 2 for the y and z components. The maximum possible block size is not necessarily better.
4. Use constant memory to store frequently reused constants. The more of them, the more this type of storage is preferable.
5. The use of shared memory for a small data reuse (memory-bound problem) is justified on newer GPUs starting from the Pascal architecture.
6. If possible, the choice of multi-core computing accelerators is preferable

5 Conclusion

The main nuances in the development of high-performance software for clusters with various manycore processors and accelerators have been investigated using the example of solving the geophysical problem of elastic wave propagation in the three-dimensional elastic media. The effect on the performance of different code optimizations is investigated. A software code has been developed, with a performance of about 390 GFLOPS for Intel KNL and a software code with a performance of about 620 GFLOPS for the NVIDIA Tesla P100. The expert rules are formulated for choosing development optimizations for various manycore architectures in the intelligent support system for solving compute-intensive problems of mathematical physics.

Acknowledgments. This research was conducted within the framework of the budget project No. 0251-2022-0005 for ICMMG SB RAS.

References

1. Zagorulko, G., Zagorulko, Y., Glinskiy, B., Sapetina, A.: Ontological approach to providing intelligent support for solving compute-intensive problems on supercomputers. In: Kuznetsov, S., Panov, A. (eds.) RCAI 2019. CCIS, vol. 1093, pp. 363–375. Springer, Cham (2019). https://doi.org/10.1007/978-3-030-30763-9_30
2. Glinskiy, B.M., et al.: Building ontologies for solving compute-intensive problems. JPCS **1715** (2021). Article number 012071

3. Glinskiy, B.M., Kulikov, I.M., Chernykh, I.G., Snytnikov, A.V., Sapetina, A.F., Weins, D.V.: The integrated approach to solving large-size physical problems on supercomputers. In: Voevodin, V., Sobolev, S. (eds.) Supercomputing. RuSCDays 2017. CCIS, vol. 793, pp. 278–289 (2017). https://doi.org/10.1007/978-3-319-71255-0_22
4. Glinskiy, B.M., Kulikov, I.M., Snytnikov, A.V., Chernykh, I.G., Weins, D.: A multilevel approach to algorithm and software design for exaflops supercomputers (in Russian). Vychisl. Metody Programm. **16**, 543–556 (2015)
5. Nakata, N., Tsuji, T., Matsuoka, T.: Acceleration of computation speed for elastic wave simulation using a graphic processing unit. Explor. Geophys. **42**(1), 98–104 (2011)
6. Michéa, D., Komatitsch, D.: Accelerating a three-dimensional finite-difference wave propagation code using GPU graphics cards. Geophys. J. Int. **182**(1), 389–402 (2010)
7. Serpa, M.S., Cruz, E.H.M., Diener, M., et al.: Optimization strategies for geophysics models on manycore systems. IJHPCA **33**(3), 473–486 (2019)
8. Glinskiy, B., Sapetina, A., Snytnikov, A., Zagorulko, Y., Zagorulko, G.: The automated construction of a scheme for solving compute-intensive problems based on the ontological approach and Semantic Web technologies. JPCS **2099** (2021). Article number 012022
9. Glinskiy, B., Sapetina, A., Martynov, V., Weins, D., Chernykh, I.: The hybrid cluster multilevel approach to solving the elastic wave propagation problem. In: Sokolinsky, L., Zymbler, M. (eds.) Parallel Computational Technologies. PCT 2017. CCIS, vol. 753, pp. 261–274 (2017). https://doi.org/10.1007/978-3-319-67035-5_19
10. Bihn, M., Weiland, T.: A stable discretization scheme for the simulation of elastic waves. In: Proceedings of the 15th IMACS World Congress on Scientific Computation, Modelling and Applied Mathematics (IMACS 1997), vol. 2, pp. 75–80 (1997)

Using Parallel Technologies to Calculate Fluid Dynamic Processes in a Fractured-Porous Reservoir Taking into Account Non-isothermality

Ravil M. Uzyanbaev[1,2](✉), Yury A. Poveshchenko[3], Viktoriia O. Podryga[3,4], Sergey V. Polyakov[3], Yuliya O. Bobreneva[1], Parvin I. Rahimly[3], and Irek M. Gubaydullin[1,2]

[1] Institute of Petrochemistry and Catalysis of the Ufa Federal Research Center of the Russian Academy of Sciences, Ufa, Russia
{ravil-11,irekmars}@mail.ru

[2] Ufa State Petroleum Technological University, Ufa, Russia

[3] Keldysh Institute of Applied Mathematics of the Russian Academy of Sciences, Moscow, Russia
hecon@mail.ru, pvictoria@list.ru, polyakov@imamod.ru, pervin@rehimli.info

[4] MADI, Moscow, Russia

Abstract. The work presents a parallel realization of a non-isothermal mathematical model of the process of heat and mass transfer of a two-phase fluid in a fractured-pore medium using a dual porosity model. Based on the algorithm of splitting by physical processes, a time-weighted difference scheme is constructed to ensure correctness and consistency of fluxes between the system of natural fractures and pore part of the reservoir. An implicit finite-difference scheme on a spatial grid is proposed for numerical solution of such a problem. The equation system is linearized by the chord method and solved by the method of matrix sweep. Computing the sweep coefficients for an algebraic problem requires large computational costs. To speed up the calculations, the matrix sweep is parallelized with the coefficients of the equations, which are matrices and vectors.

Keywords: Non-isothermality · Implicit finite-difference schemes · Matrix sweep method · Parallelization based on a matrix sweep · High performance computing

1 Introduction

Hydrocarbon production is becoming more and more difficult every year. Most of the reserves both in Russia and abroad are already referred to as hard-to-recover, characterized by unfavorable geological conditions for extraction. This type may include deposits confined to carbonate sediments [1,2]. Today, the

V. Voevodin et al. (Eds.): RuSCDays 2023, LNCS 14388, pp. 300–315, 2023.
https://doi.org/10.1007/978-3-031-49432-1_23

development of carbonate deposits with a complex and variable structure of the void space is both a complex and promising direction [3]. Carbonate reservoirs are sedimentary formations composed of 50% or more carbonate minerals [4].

A carbonate reservoir is a diverse and broad type of oil-bearing reservoir that contains a high proportion of commonly known oil reserves. Such reservoirs are characterized by improved capacity and filtration properties, but, in turn, development is also complicated by a developed fractured zone. The presence of fractured zones requires a special approach to studying the geological structure of reservoirs, creating geological and hydrodynamic models, selecting effective development systems, controlling and regulating oil production processes [3].

As part of the study of the problem under consideration, a review of domestic and foreign literature in the field of fluid filtration in fractured-porous reservoirs, as well as existing methods for the numerical study of filtration was carried out [5]. The dual porosity models of various authors such as Kazemi [6], Pollard [7], Ode [8], Warren-Root [9] were studied. Approaches and software packages for solving such problems [10–13] were considered. As a result, it was revealed that the development vector of the topic is mainly aimed at building complex hydrodynamic models of the entire field [14]. This approach is not always effective for solving operational production problems within the framework of field monitoring, for example, when conducting hydrodynamic studies at wells [15]. Hydrodynamic studies of wells are activities that are carried out on wells during testing, development and operation of a well. The main purpose of the study is to investigate the properties of the reservoir (productivity, filtration parameters, reservoir boundaries, etc.). However, before conducting a well test, additional questions arise that relate both to the duration of a well shutdown and, in certain situations, the thorough study of flow processes for various filtration parameters of the formation through numerical modeling. Therefore, in order to promptly resolve emerging issues in monitoring the development of a field, a quick calculation tool is needed, which implies a model, an effective algorithm and a software package. The designated goal is pursued by our work.

For traditional single-pore reservoir filtration models, the algorithms have been developed both the direct algorithms to reproduce the filtration process and the methods of data interpretation for identification of model parameters [15]. However, the situation is greatly complicated in the case of applying the models where there are two media - pore reservoir and fractures [4,9]. Consideration of complex heat and mass transfer processes is possible only on the basis of numerical experiment [16,17], since carrying out full-scale experiments entails huge oil losses due to well shutdowns.

Numerical modeling for such process description is fraught with great difficulties associated with a large number of unknowns and using the of small time steps [18,19]. Therefore, studying the peculiarities and regularities of mass and heat transport in the "pore reservoir (matrix) - natural fracture network" system is impossible without an effective, fast and economical algorithm accounting the physical processes occurring in the fractures and the reservoir itself. A solution to this situation would be to develop and implement a parallel numerical algorithm, and then run it on the architecture of large supercomputers. Such a method will allow to considerably reduce the time of solving the problem and, accordingly, to reduce the load on the operating memory.

Previously, in our works [20,21], the isothermal process of mass transfer of a two-phase liquid was considered in a one-dimensional statement. An original implicit scheme on an irregular spatial grid was proposed for the numerical solution of the problem. The final system was solved using a scalar sweep, which was subsequently parallelized. The proposed algorithm and its parallel implementation showed the high efficiency, which was confirmed by calculations. The calculation results are presented in the form for speedup and efficiency depending on the number of processes. The results obtained made it possible to identify the optimal number of processes for the given problem formulation.

In this work, a spatial mathematical model is presented using invariant forms of vector analysis operations (div, grad), which describes the non-isothermal process of heat and mass transfer of fluid in a fractured-pore type reservoir, where there are two different media - a system of natural fractures and a pore part. Each system is characterized by its own filtration and capacitance parameters, the difference between which reaches from one to several orders of magnitude [4]. A discrete version of this model is implemented by the methods of support operators [22,23]. In this work, a spatially one-dimensional formulation of the problem is considered in the calculations. An efficient algorithm is proposed for solving the problem. The software development of the algorithm was implemented using the parallel running method and the MPI standard, taking into account experience in other tasks and the need to run not only on a hybrid computing cluster, but also on personal computers, where CUDA may not be available. Although there are many libraries for the latter (CUSPARSE, cuBLAS) [24,25]. For example, the popular cuSPARSE library from the CUDA Toolkit contains the cusparsegtsv and cusparsegtsv2 functions based on the parallel SPIKE algorithm, as well as the cusparsegtsv_nopivot and cusparsegtsv2_nopivot functions, which use cyclic reduction algorithms. On the basis of the obtained calculations, an analysis of the efficiency of parallelization was carried out and the optimal number of processes necessary to solve the system of equations was determined depending on the size of the grid used.

2 Mathematical Model

In an unrestricted reservoir, a production well is considered, which exploits a carbonate oil-bearing reservoir of a fractured-porous type. After a long period of inactivity, the well is put back into production at constant pressure at the bottom. At the moment the well starts to work, a depression funnel is instantly forms in the formation, which creates an influx of fluid from the reservoir to the bottom of well. Wells of the environment do not create an impact. For the presented problem, a mathematical description of the heat and mass transfer distribution is considered within the framework of a non-isothermal model of a binary medium, based on the law of conservation of the mass of the components, taking into account the interaction of phases. Mathematical description of heat and mass transfer distribution within the framework of non-isothermal dual medium model based on the law of mass conservation of components with regard to phase interaction is considered. Mathematical description of filtration processes is based on classical laws of continuum mechanics and phase equilibrium relations. It is assumed that the fluid flows through the fractures and the matrix is a capacity. So the fluid flow occurs only in one direction, namely, from the matrix to the natural fractures, and is accounted by the introduction of special functions, which were presented in the works of Warren-Root [9]. It is assumed that the formation is homogeneous and the flow in the fracture system is within the justice of Darcy's law, the fluid is considered to be weakly compressible.

$$\frac{\partial(\phi^\alpha \rho_o^\alpha S_o^\alpha)}{\partial t} + \nabla(\rho_o^\alpha \overrightarrow{U_o^\alpha}) + q_o^\alpha = 0, q_o^m = -q_o^f = -\rho_o^m \sigma \lambda_o^m (P^f - P^m), \quad (1)$$

$$\frac{\partial(\phi^\alpha \rho_w^\alpha S_w^\alpha)}{\partial t} + \nabla(\rho_w^\alpha \overrightarrow{U_w^\alpha}) - q_w^\alpha = 0, q_w^m = -q_w^f = -\rho_w^m \sigma \lambda_w^m (P^f - P^m), \quad (2)$$

$$\begin{aligned}\frac{\partial}{\partial t}[(\phi^f \rho_o^f S_o^f \varepsilon_o^f + \phi^m \rho_o^m S_o^m \varepsilon_o^m + \phi^f \rho_w^f S_w^f \varepsilon_w^f + \phi^m \rho_w^m S_w^m \varepsilon_w^m) +\\ (1 - \phi^f - \phi^m)\rho_s \varepsilon_s] + div[\rho_o^f \varepsilon_o^f \overrightarrow{U_o^f} + \rho_w^f \varepsilon_w^f \overrightarrow{U_w^f}] +\\ div[P^f(\overrightarrow{U_o^f} + \overrightarrow{U_w^f})] + div[\overrightarrow{W^f} + \overrightarrow{W^m} + \overrightarrow{W_s}] = 0, \quad (3)\end{aligned}$$

$$\lambda_o^m = \frac{k^m k_{ro}(S_o^m)}{\mu_o}, \lambda_w^m = \frac{k^m k_{rw}(S_w^m)}{\mu_w}.$$

Here $\alpha = f, m$, where f is the system of natural fracture, m is the pore part of the reservoir (matrix), s is the carbonate rock skeleton, $i = o, w$, where o is the oil, w is the water, P^f is the formation pressure in fractures (Pa), P^m is the formation pressure in the pore part of the reservoir (Pa), ϕ^f is the porosity in the fracture system, ϕ^m is the porosity in the pore part of the reservoir, ρ_o^α is the density of oil (g/m^3), ρ_w^α is the density of water (g/m^3), S_i^f is the saturation of oil or water in the fracture system, S_i^m is the saturation of oil or water in the pore part of the reservoir, $\overrightarrow{U_i^\alpha}$ is the flow velocity of oil or water, q_i^α is the coefficient of redistribution of the fluid between the pore part of the reservoir and the natural fractures, σ is the coefficient of fractured rock $(1/m^2)$, ε_i^α is the energy of oil/water, ρ_s, ε_s is density and energy of the skeleton, k^α is the absolute permeability (m^2), k_{rw} and k_{ro} are the relative phase permeabilities of water and oil, μ_o is the viscosity of oil (Pa·s), μ_w is the viscosity of water (Pa·s).

Let's introduce notations:

$$\overrightarrow{W^f} = -(\phi^f[S_w^f\eta_w^f + (1 - S_w^f)\eta_o^f])\nabla T,$$
$$\overrightarrow{W^m} = -(\phi^m[S_w^m\eta_w^m + (1 - S_w^m)\eta_o^m])\nabla T,$$
$$\overrightarrow{W_s} = -[1 - \phi^f - \phi^m]\eta_s\nabla T,$$
$$\overrightarrow{W} = \overrightarrow{W^f} + \overrightarrow{W^m} + \overrightarrow{W_s}. \tag{4}$$

Here T is the temperature (K); $\eta_i^f, \eta_i^m, \eta_s$ are the thermal conductivity coefficients in the system of the fractures, matrix and skeleton.

As functions of the fluid flow between the fractures and the pore reservoir, we use the following functions:

$$q_o^m = -q_o^f = -\frac{\sigma\rho_o^m k^m k_{ro}(S_o^m)}{\mu_o}(P^f - P^m),$$
$$q_w^m = -q_w^f = -\frac{\sigma\rho_w^m k^m k_{rw}(S_w^m)}{\mu_w}(P^f - P^m). \tag{5}$$

A generalised Darcy's law is applied for the velocity of oil and water filtration, according to which the velocities are equal respectively:

$$\overrightarrow{U_o^\alpha} = -\frac{k^\alpha k_{ro}(S_o^\alpha)}{\mu_o} gradP^\alpha, \overrightarrow{U_w^\alpha} = -\frac{k^\alpha k_{rw}(S_w^\alpha)}{\mu_w} gradP^\alpha. \tag{6}$$

Here $\alpha = f, \overrightarrow{U_o^m} = \overrightarrow{U_w^m} = 0$.

The change in density for water and oil is written taking into account pressure:

$$\rho_w^\alpha = \rho_{w0}^\alpha + C_w(P^\alpha - P_0), \rho_o^\alpha = \rho_{o0}^\alpha + C_o(P^\alpha - P_0). \tag{7}$$

where C_w, C_o are the compressibility coefficients, $\rho_{w0}^\alpha, \rho_{o0}^\alpha$ are the densities at atmospheric pressure, P_0 is the atmospheric pressure.

The primary reservoir pressure and temperature in the pore part and natural fractures at the initial moment of time are used as the initial condition. The right boundary condition is set by constant pressure and temperature at the boundary, the left boundary condition is by constant bottomhole pressure and temperature at the bottom of the well, which are different from the initial reservoir ones. It is taken into account that the well is not influenced by other operating wells.

The resulting initial-boundary value problem (1) – (7) with some boundary conditions is a complex quasilinear system of equations of mathematical physics of mixed type. To solve the system, the finite volume method is used [26]. In some cases, the linearized system no longer has the property of self-adjointness, therefore, to solve this problem for the initial equations, the method of splitting by physical processes is used [3,19].

3 Numerical Algorithm

The system of equations and additional conditions (1)–(7) is solved using the method of splitting by physical processes [27] and the grid method of finite volumes [26].

In a split form, system (1)–(7) has the form:

$$\frac{S_w^f}{\rho_w^f}[\phi^f \rho_w^f]_t + \frac{(1-S_w^f)}{\rho_o^f}[\phi^f \rho_o^f]_t + DIG^f = 0,$$
$$DIG^f = \frac{1}{\rho_w^f} div(\rho_w^f \overrightarrow{U_w^f}) + \frac{1}{\rho_o^f} div(\rho_o^f \overrightarrow{U_o^f}) + \frac{q_w^f}{\rho_w^f} + \frac{q_o^f}{\rho_o^f}, \quad (8)$$

$$\frac{S_w^m}{\rho_w^m}[\phi^m \rho_w^m]_t + \frac{(1-S_w^m)}{\rho_o^m}[\phi^m \rho_o^m]_t + DIG^m = 0,$$
$$DIG^m = \frac{q_w^m}{\rho_w^m} + \frac{q_o^m}{\rho_o^m}, \quad (9)$$

$$\phi^f(S_w^f \rho_w^f \frac{\partial \varepsilon_w^f}{\partial t} + (1-S_w^f)\rho_o^f \frac{\partial \varepsilon_o^f}{\partial t} + \phi^m(S_w^m \rho_w^m \frac{\partial \varepsilon_w^m}{\partial t} + (1-S_w^m)\rho_o^m \frac{\partial \varepsilon_o^m}{\partial t} +$$
$$\frac{\partial}{\partial t}(1-\phi^f-\phi^m)\rho_s\varepsilon_s + DIG_\varepsilon^f + DIG_\varepsilon^m + div\overrightarrow{W_s} = 0,$$
$$DIG_\varepsilon^f = [div(\rho_w^f \varepsilon_w^f \overrightarrow{U_w^f}) - \varepsilon_w^f div(\rho_w^f \overrightarrow{U_w^f})] +$$
$$+[div(\rho_o^f \varepsilon_o^f \overrightarrow{U_o^f}) - \varepsilon_o^f div(\rho_o^f \overrightarrow{U_o^f})] + div[P^f(\overrightarrow{U_w^f} + \overrightarrow{U_o^f})] +$$
$$div\overrightarrow{W^f} + (-\varepsilon_w^f q_w^f - \varepsilon_o^f q_o^f), DIG_\varepsilon^m = div\overrightarrow{W^m} + (-\varepsilon_w^m q_w^m - \varepsilon_o^m q_o^m),$$
$$div\overrightarrow{W^f} = -(\phi^f[S_w^f \eta_w^f + (1-S_w^f)\eta_o^f]),$$
$$div\overrightarrow{W^m} = -(\phi^m[S_w^m \eta_w^m + (1-S_w^m)\eta_o^m]). \quad (10)$$

The splitting algorithm by physical processes of mass balances in relation to this problem is as follows. Groups of equations (8) and (9) are distinguished, which represent the piezoconductive evolution of the thermodynamic parameters of the system without saturation transfer for a combination of water and oil mass components in fractures and matrix, respectively (without time derivatives of saturations S_w^f, S_w^m). Also, the piezoconductive evolution (10) of the total energy of the entire system (fractures f, matrix of pores m and heat transfer in the skeleton s) is the time derivatives of the energy combinations of thermodynamic parameters (with saturations S_w^f, S_w^m taken out of the differentiation sign, including determining the transfer of energy in the matrix-pore space).

The split system of equations is approximated on a suitable spatial grid by the finite volume method. In time, an implicit difference approximation with a constant step is used. Figure 1 shows a two-dimensional layer-by-layer discrete partition of the radial layers of the computational domain in (r, z) - geometry (with

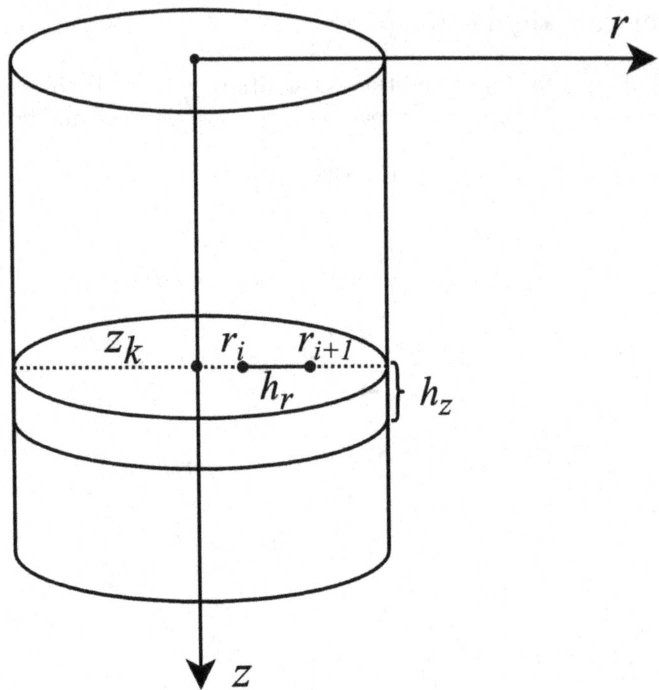

Fig. 1. Two-dimensional layer-by-layer discrete partitioning of the radial layers of the computational domain in (r, z) - geometry (with a radial step h_r and an axial step h_z)

a radial step h_r and an axial step h_z). On this grid partition, a two-dimensional difference approximation of equations (8) - (10) can be made. In the case of one-dimensional geometry, differential equations (8) - (10) are approximated by their well-known grid counterparts [28,29]. Next, the discrete equations are linearized. The resulting linearized system of equations can be reduced to the form:

$$\begin{cases} C_0 y_0 - B_0 y_1 = \Phi_0, k = 0, \\ -A_k y_{k-1} + C_k y_k - B_k y_{k+1} = \Phi_k, 1 \leq k \leq N-1, \\ -A_N y_{N-1} + C_N y_N = \Phi_N, k = 1. \end{cases} \tag{11}$$

where A, B, C are the matrices of dimension 2 by 2 (the first line is responsible for the process of piezoconductivity, the second line - for thermal conductivity); y are the desired pressure δP and temperature δT, Φ are the vectors of dimension 2.

The resulting matrix relations (11) are represented by a system of linear algebraic equations. A matrix sweep is used to solve.

4 Matrix Sweep

The previously obtained system of linear algebraic equations (SLAE) (11) is defined by a block tridiagonal matrix:

$$
\begin{aligned}
A_k &= \begin{pmatrix} A^{11}_{pk} A^{12}_{pk} \\ A^{21}_{\varepsilon k} A^{22}_{\varepsilon k} \end{pmatrix}, \\
B_k &= \begin{pmatrix} B^{11}_{pk} B^{12}_{pk} \\ B^{21}_{\varepsilon k} B^{22}_{\varepsilon k} \end{pmatrix}, \\
C_k &= \begin{pmatrix} C^{11}_{pk} C^{12}_{pk} \\ C^{21}_{\varepsilon k} C^{22}_{\varepsilon k} \end{pmatrix}, \\
\Phi_k &= \begin{pmatrix} \Phi_{pk} \\ \Phi_{\varepsilon k} \end{pmatrix},
\end{aligned} \tag{12}
$$

Here $A^{12}_{pk} = A^{21}_{pk} = 0, B^{12}_{pk} = B^{21}_{pk} = 0$.

For initial testing of the model and obtained matrix coefficients A_k, B_k, C_k, Φ_k, we do a formal check at $\tau- > 0$ (time step) and $h- > 0$ (space step), we obtain $det||C_k|| > 0$. It is also worth noting that, if $A^{21}_{\varepsilon k} = 0, A^{22}_{\varepsilon k} = 0, B^{21}_{\varepsilon k} = 0, B^{22}_{\varepsilon k} = 0, C^{21}_{\varepsilon k} = 0, C^{12}_{\varepsilon k} = 0, C^{22}_{\varepsilon k} = 1, \Phi_{\varepsilon k} = 0$, our model leads to a special case described by us earlier in the work [21].

To solve the system (8)-(10), the matrix sweep method is used, which is similar to the sweep method for scalar three-point equations [21] in the isothermal case. The solution is presented as follows:

The forward move allows one to determine the sweep coefficients:

$$
\begin{aligned}
\alpha_{k+1} &= (C_k - A_k\alpha_k)^{-1}B_k, k = 1, 2, ..., N-1, \alpha_1 = C_0^{-1}B_0, \\
\beta_{k+1} &= (C_k - A_k\alpha_k)^{-1}(F_k + A_k\beta_k), k = 1, 2, ..., N, \beta_1 = C_0^{-1}F_0,
\end{aligned} \tag{13}
$$

Moving backwards finds the solution of the system:

$$
y_k = \alpha_{k+1}y_{k+1} + \beta_{k+1}, k = N-1, N-2, ..., 0, y_N = \beta_{N+1}. \tag{14}
$$

To implement the method, the operations on matrices are required: addition, multiplication, transposition, which are implemented as separate functions. The matrix sweep method itself is moved to a separate function, because during the calculation, it will be accessed on each layer in time (iteration).

The algorithm for parallelizing matrix sweep is based on a well-known algorithm, the implementation of which was described in detail in work [21].

Figure 2 shows the main steps of the program algorithm.

According to the algorithm, first the pressures δP in the fracture system and the temperatures δT are determined, then we find the pressure in the matrix.

The main calculations were performed on the K100 supercomputer at the Center for Collective Usage of the Keldysh Institute of Applied Mathematics of the RAS [30]. The matrix sweep algorithm is implemented in C language using the MPI standard [31]. Multithreading was provided by

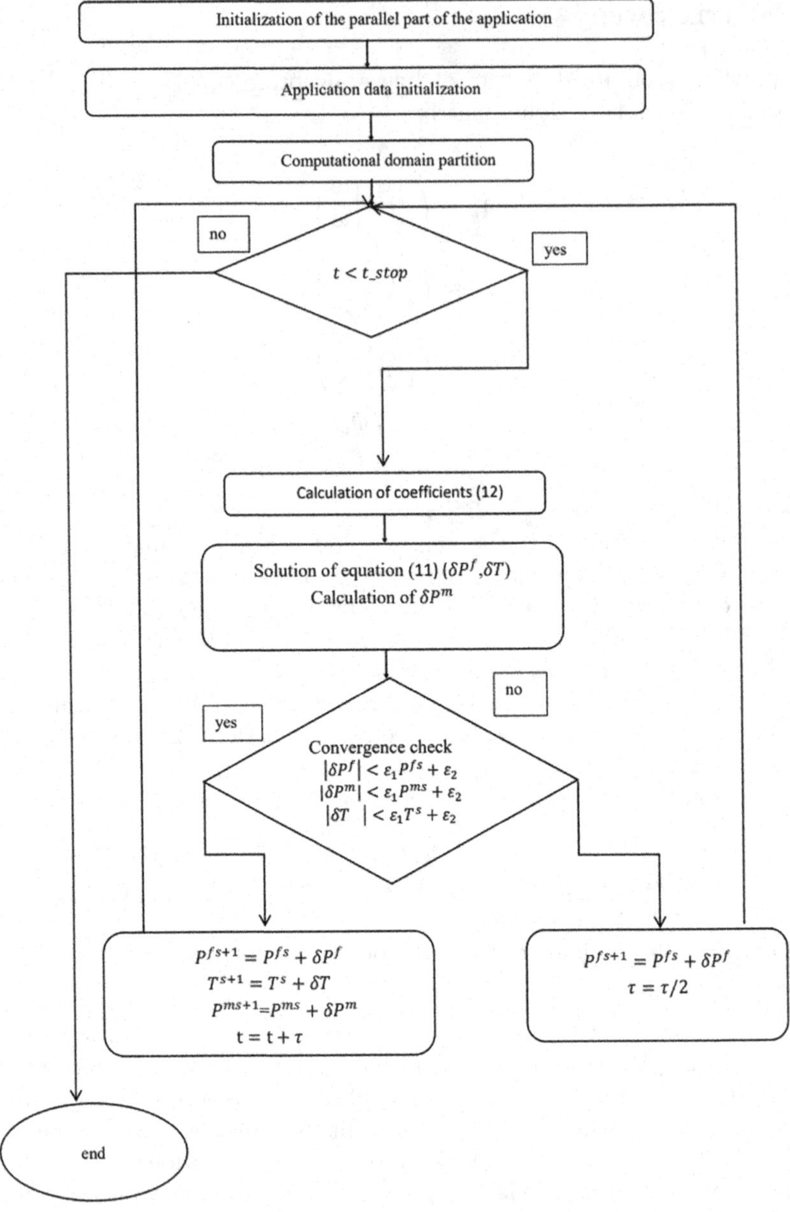

Fig. 2. Basic steps of the program algorithm

placing additional MPI processes inside the computational nodes of the cluster. We used the following MPI functions: MPI_Init, MPI_Comm_size, MPI_Comm_rank, MPI_Get_processor_name, MPI_Bcast (distribution of model parameters), MyRange (computational domain decomposition), MPI_Isend/ MPI_Irecv (data exchange between neighboring processes), MPI_Allreduce.

One important step of matrix sweep parallelization is the solution of a short problem [21]. To solve this problem, all MPI processes carry out a collective exchange of coefficients. Below is a code fragment implementing this algorithm:

```
MPI_Allreduce(dd,ee,14*ncp,MPI_DOUBLE,MPI_SUM,MPI_COMM_WORLD);
for (i=0; i<ncp; i++) {
  j = 14*i;
  aa[i][0][0] = ee[j];
  aa[i][0][1] = ee[j+1];
  aa[i][1][0] = ee[j+2];
  aa[i][1][1] = ee[j+3];
  bb[i][0][0] = ee[j+4];
  bb[i][0][1] = ee[j+5];
  bb[i][1][0] = ee[j+6];
  bb[i][1][1] = ee[j+7];
  cc[i][0][0] = ee[j+8];
  cc[i][0][1] = ee[j+9];
  cc[i][1][0] = ee[j+10];
  cc[i][1][1] = ee[j+11];
  ff[i][0] = ee[j+12];
  ff[i][1] = ee[j+13];
}
```

It is worth paying attention compared to parallel scalar sweep [21], now we have coefficients represented by matrices and vectors. In this regard, it is necessary to allocate more memory for variables that carry out collective interaction between processes, which is reflected in the code fragment above.

5 Calculation Results

The program module has been tested on the example of the following task: after a long downtime, the well is put into production at constant pressure at the bottom. It is assumed that constant pressure is maintained at the reservoir boundary, and the influence of neighboring wells is not observed. Hydrodynamic studies are carried out at small study radii (50–300 m), therefore, the absence of the influence of neighboring wells is important. For a radial reservoir around the well, consisting of a matrix space and a network of fractures, we have the following parameters:

$P^f = 250 \cdot 10^5 (Pa), P^m = 250 \cdot 10^5 (Pa), \phi^f = 0.01, \phi^m = 0.1, \rho_w = 1118 (kg/m^3), \rho_o = 730 (kg/m^3), S_w^\alpha = 0.36, \sigma = 0.12 (1/m^2), k^f = 1 \cdot 10^{-12} (m^2), k^m = 1 \cdot 10^{-16} (m^2), k_{rw} = 7.7 (S_w^\alpha)^4 - 12.07 (S_w^\alpha)^3 + 6.9 (S_w^\alpha)^2 - 1.8 (S_w^\alpha) + 0.2, k_{ro} = (S_w^\alpha)^2 0.03 + 0.002 (S_w^\alpha) + 0.0002, \mu_o = 0.67 \cdot 10^{-3} (Pa \cdot s), \mu_w = 0.3 \cdot 10^{-3} (Pa \cdot s)$.

In the course of calculations, the following results were obtained. Figure 3 shows pressure curves depending on the distance from the well for 3 values of absolute permeability k^f in fractures at the time of production well operation, corresponding to $1 \cdot 10^{-10} m^2, 1 \cdot 10^{-11} m^2, 1 \cdot 10^{-12} m^2$. The graphs show that the higher the permeability in the fractures, the larger the depression funnel around the well and appears faster.

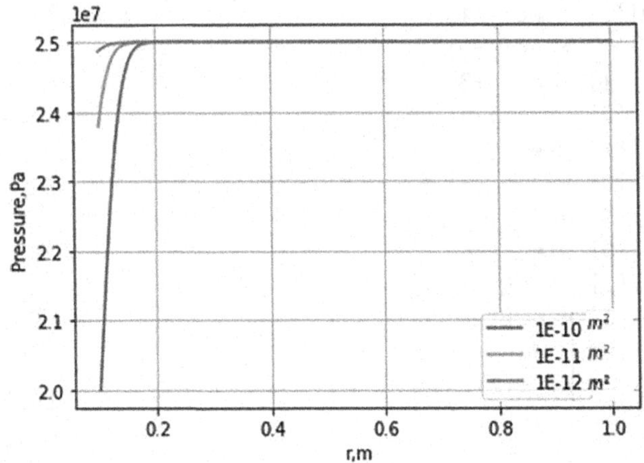

Fig. 3. Pressure curves for different absolute permeabilities in fractures

Figure 4 shows the dynamics of temperature change over time for various values of absolute permeability in fractures. The graphs show that the higher the permeability in the fractures, the faster the temperature drops, which corresponds to the experimentally observed data.

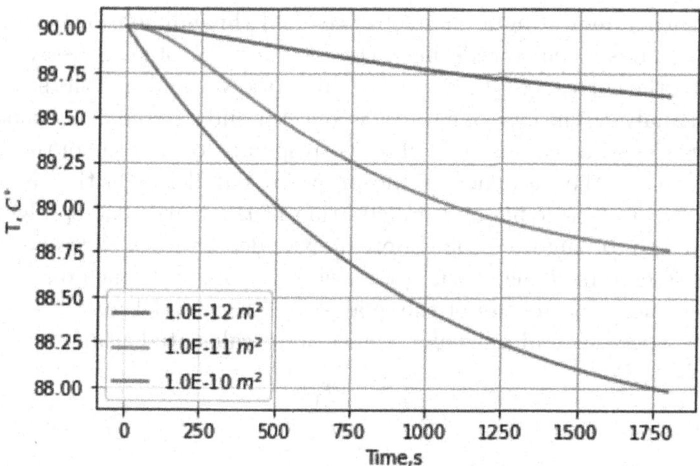

Fig. 4. Temperature curves for different absolute permeabilities in fractures

Figure 5 shows the change in water saturation over space at different time points: 300 s, 600 s for a network of fractures and a matrix. According to the graphs, it is noted that the increase of water saturation in the fractures occurs faster than in the pore part, which is associated with the fluid flow only along the fracture network. Thus, the longer the well is in production, the more water saturation increases, which leads to a decrease in oil production at the well.

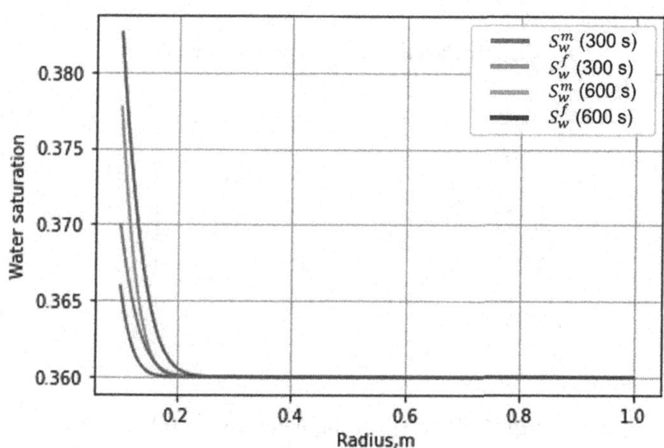

Fig. 5. Variation of water saturation across space at different times

Let us consider in more detail the results of the parallel implementation of the algorithm. Before that, it is important to emphasize that the fundamental necessity of applying the parallelization technique is required in two cases. The first case arises when analyzing a complete two- and three-dimensional model. The second case arises when considering a complex network of pore reservoirs, characterized by the corresponding graph. In this work, we analyzed the second case. For ease of analysis, the case of a solitary collector and a radial dependence of the desired functions was considered, which corresponds to one edge of the network. In this situation, the efficiency of the proposed parallel algorithm is certainly low. However, the principle of parallelization of the matrix sweep algorithm is well adapted to solving the problem on an extended network of reservoirs, when individual reservoirs change their spatial orientation and branch out.

Consider next the results of the analysis of the parallel matrix sweep algorithm. The speedup and efficiency values were calculated using the following standard formulas:

$$S_m = \frac{T_1}{T_m}, \tag{15}$$

$$E_m = \frac{S_m}{m} \cdot 100\%, \tag{16}$$

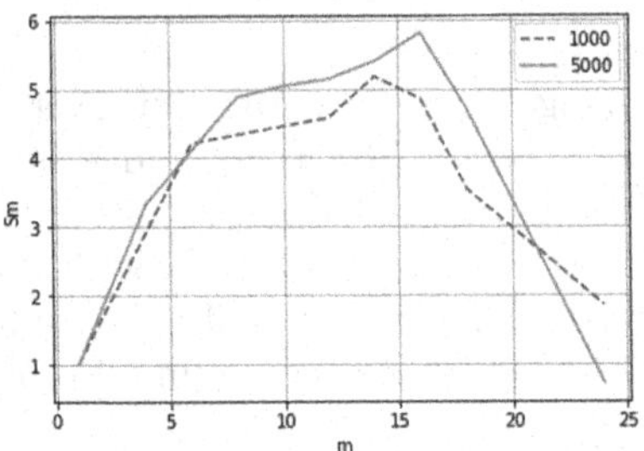

Fig. 6. Parallelization speedup graph

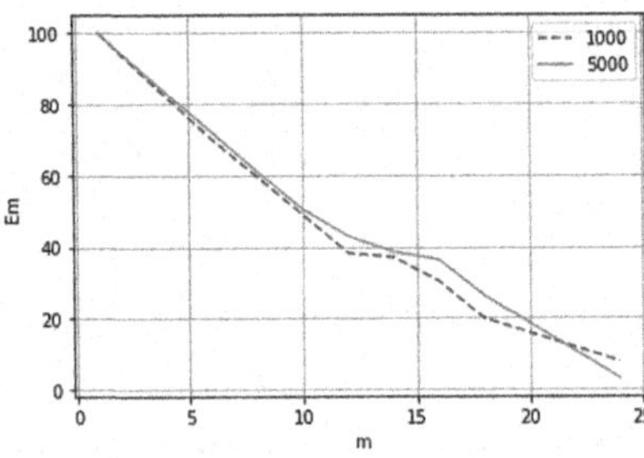

Fig. 7. Parallelization efficiency graph

where S_m is the speedup, E_m is the efficiency, $T_1$is the time to calculate the sequential code, T_m is the time to calculate the parallel code on m processes.

Figures 6, 7 show graphs of speedup (S_m) and efficiency (E_m) of parallelization when dividing the study radius into 1000 and 5000 points. According to the Fig. 6 it can be seen that the values of m = 14 and 16 are the optimal number of parallel processes for 1000 and 5000 calculation points, since then the speedup decreases. It is also clear that with an increase in the number of calculation points, it is necessary to increase the number of parallel processes. In specific calculations, the effect of limited maximum speedup also manifests itself; more details about this effect for scalar sweep are described in the article [21]. The consequence of the indicated fact is that there is a number of nodes that is optimal for a specific computational grid for a fixed number of grid nodes. Returning to the network of collectors, it should be noted that in this situation the efficiency of parallelization will depend on the total number of branches and the minimum length of the edges of the network graph. The first parameter will actually determine the required number of parallel processes. The second parameter will affect the final efficiency. The longer or wider individual collectors are, the more points of the computational grid will be required for their numerical analysis, and the more noticeable will be the final effect of parallelism.

6 Conclusion

The work presents a one-dimensional formulation of a mathematical non - isothermal model of the process of heat and mass transfer in a fractured-porous reservoir based on a dual porosity model. Using the splitting algorithm by physical processes, a difference scheme with time weights was constructed, which ensured the correctness and consistency of fluxes between the system of natural fractures and the pore part of the reservoir. The resulting system of equations was solved using a matrix sweep, which is parallelized. To test the considered approach, computational experiments were carried out. The obtained calculations confirmed the effectiveness of the proposed numerical algorithm, including its parallel implementation. Graphs of speedup and efficiency of parallel algorithms depending on the number of processes are given. The optimal number of processes was obtained for the considered formulation of the problem, which was equal to 14 and 16. Curves of pressure, temperature and saturation were plotted, which showed the behavior of these parameters around an operating production well and allowed adjustments to be made to the modes and settings of the well operation.

Acknowledgments. The work was funded by the Russian Science Foundation (project № 21-71-20047). URL to information about the project: https://rscf.ru/en/project/21-71-20047/. Numerical experiments were performed on the hybrid supercomputer K100 installed in the Supercomputer Centre of Collective Usage of KIAM RAS.

References

1. Cholovsky, I.P.: Handbook: Oil and Gas Geologist's Companion. Nedra, Moscow (1989)
2. Denk, S.O.: Problems of Fractured Productive Objects. Electronic Publishing, Perm (2004)

3. Aziz, H., Settari, E.: Mathematical Modeling of Reservoir Systems. Institute for Computer Research, Moscow-Izhevsk (2004). (in Russian)
4. Aguilera, R.: Naturally Fractured Reservoirs. T. Pennwell Corp, Tulsa, Oklahoma (1980)
5. Rao, X., et al.: Numerical simulation of two-phase heat and mass transfer in fractured reservoirs based on projection-based embedded discrete fracture model (pEDFM). J. Petroleum Sci. Eng. 208(part A), 109323 (2022). https://doi.org/10.1016/j.petrol.2021.109323
6. Kazemi, H., Seth, M.S., Thomas, G.V.: The interpretation of interference tests in naturally fractured reservoirs with uniform fracture distribution. SPE J. **9**(04), 463–471 (1969)
7. Pollard, P.: Evaluation of acid treatments from pressure build-up analysis. Trans. AIME. **216**(01), 38–43 (1959). https://doi.org/10.2118/981-G
8. Odeh, A.S.: Unsteady-state behaviour of naturally fractured reservoirs. J. Soc. Petrol. Eng. **5**(1), 60–66 (1965). https://doi.org/10.2118/966-PA
9. Warren, J.E., Root, P.J.: The behavior of naturally fractured reservoirs. J. Soc. Petrol. Eng. **3**(03), 245–255 (1963). https://doi.org/10.2118/426-PA
10. Kotlyar, L.A.: Mathematical modeling and interpretation of non-stationary thermohydrodynamic processes in the well-reservoir system: Ph.D. dis. ... cand. Phys.-Math. Sciences: 25.00.10. Moscow (2013). (in Russian)
11. Kuchuk, F., Biryukov, D., Fitzpatrick, T.: Fractured-reservoir modeling and interpretation. SPE J. **20**(05), 983–1004 (2015)
12. Grigoriev, A.V.: Numerical modeling of filtration in fractured-porous media based on the dual porosity model: Ph.D. dis. ... cand. Phys.-Math. Sciences: 05.13.18. Yakutsk (2013). (in Russian)
13. Vasiliev, V.I., Vasil'eva, M.V.; Grigoriev, A.V.; Prokopiev G.A.: Mathematical modeling of the problem of two-phase filtration in inhomogeneous fractured porous media using the dual porosity model and the finite element method. Uchenye zapiski Kazanskogo universiteta. Series of Physical and Mathematical Sciences **160**(1), pp. 165–182 (2018). (in Russian)
14. Sukhodanova, S.S.: Creation of a 3D model of a reservoir with carbonate fractured reservoirs based on the integration of hydrodynamic, geophysical, seismic and field data (on the example of the Lower Permian deposits of the Varandeyskoye field): author. dis. ... cand. tech. Sciences: 25.00.17. Moscow (2016). (in Russian)
15. Deeva, T.A., Kamartdinov, M.R., Kulagina, T.E., Mangazeev, P.V.: Gidrodinamicheskie issledovaniya skvazhin: analiz i interpretaciya dannyh. TPU, Tomsk (2009). (in Russian)
16. Paskonov, V.M., Polezhaev, V.I., Chudov, L.A.: Numerical Modeling of Heat and Mass Transfer Processes. Nauka, Moscow (1984). (in Russian)
17. Chekalyuk, E.B.: Thermodynamics of Oil Reservoir. Nedra, Moscow (1965). (in Russian)
18. Bobreneva, Y.O., Gubaidullin, I.M.: Mathematical simulation of a pressure field exemplified by dual porosity reservoir. J. Phys.: Conf. Ser. **1368**, 042067 (2019)
19. Bobreneva, Y.O.: Modeling the piezoconductivity process of a two-phase fluid system in a fractured-porous reservoir. Math. Models Comput. Simul. **4**(14), 645–653 (2022)

20. Uzyanbaev, R., Bobreneva, Y., Poveshchenko, Y., Podryga, V., Polyakov, S.: Modeling of two-phase fluid flow processes in a fractured-porous type reservoir using parallel computations. In: Sokolinsky, L., Zymbler, M., (eds) Parallel Computational Technologies. PCT 2022. Communications in Computer and Information Science, vol. 1618, pp. 276–292. Springer, Cham (2022). https://doi.org/10.1007/978-3-031-11623-0_19
21. Uzyanbaev, R.M., Poveshchenko, Y.A., Podryga, V.O., Polyakov, S.V., Bobreneva, Y.O., Gubaydullin, I.M.: Analysis of parallel algorithm efficiency for numerical solution of mass transfer problem in fractured-porous reservoir. In: Lecture Notes in Computer Science 2022, LNCS, vol. 13708, pp. 33–47 (2022)
22. Samarskiy, A.A., Koldoba, A.V., Poveshchenko, Y.A., Tishkin, V.F., Favorskiy, A.P.: Raznostnyye skhemy na neregulyarnykh setkakh. ZAO "Kriterii", Minsk (1996)
23. Koldoba, A.V., Poveshchenko, Y.A., Samarskaia, E.A., Tishkin, V.F.: Metody matematicheskogo modelirovaniia okruzhaiushchei sredy. Nauka, Moscow (2000). (in Russian)
24. cuSPARSE Library. https://docs.nvidia.com/cuda/cusparse/(04.06.2023)
25. CUDA 12 Features. https://developer.nvidia.com/blog/cuda-toolkit-12-0-released-for-general-availability/(04.06.2023)
26. Eymard, R., Gallouet, T. R., Herbin, R.: The finite volume method. In: Handbook of Numerical Analysis (Editors: Ciarlet, P.G., Lions, J.L.), vol. 7, pp. 713–1020 (2022)
27. Marchuk, G.I.: Splitting Methods. Nauka, Moscow (1988). (in Russian)
28. Tikhonov, A.N., Samarskii, A.A.: Equations of Mathematical Physics. Nauka, Moscow (1972). (in Russian)
29. Samarskii, A.A., Gulin, A.V.: Numerical Methods. Nauka, Moscow (1989). (in Russian)
30. Center for Collective Usage of the Keldysh Institute of Applied Mathematics of RAS. http://ckp.kiam.ru
31. MPI: A Message-Passing Interface Standard. http://www.mpi-forum.org/docs/(04.06.2023)

Author Index

V. Voevodin et al. (Eds.): RuSCDays 2023, LNCS 14388, pp. 317–318, 2023.
https://doi.org/10.1007/978-3-031-49432-1

Printed in the United States
by Baker & Taylor Publisher Services